GRADE
6

Printed in the U.S.A.

ISBN 978-0-358-41639-5

2 3 4 5 6 7 8 9 10   0029   29 28 27 26 25 24 23 22 21

4500824448

r11.20

Program Consultants:

Kylene Beers

Martha Hougen

Tyrone C. Howard

Elena Izquierdo

Carol Jago

Weston Kieschnick

Erik Palmer

Robert E. Probst

GRADE
6

Program Consultants

Kylene Beers

Nationally known lecturer and author on reading and literacy; coauthor with Robert Probst of *Disrupting Thinking, Notice & Note: Strategies for Close Reading,* and *Reading Nonfiction;* former president of the National Council of Teachers of English. Dr. Beers is the author of *When Kids Can't Read: What Teachers Can Do* and coeditor of *Adolescent Literacy: Turning Promise into Practice,* as well as articles in the *Journal of Adolescent and Adult Literacy.* Former editor of *Voices from the Middle,* she is the 2001 recipient of NCTE's Richard W. Halle Award, given for outstanding contributions to middle school literacy.

Martha Hougen

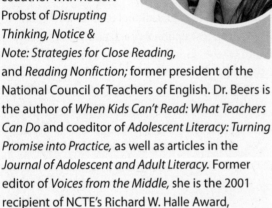

National consultant, presenter, researcher, and author. Areas of expertise include differentiating instruction for students with learning difficulties, including those with learning disabilities and dyslexia; and teacher and leader preparation improvement. Dr. Hougen has taught at the middle school through graduate levels. Dr. Hougen has supported Educator Preparation Program reforms while working at the Meadows Center for Preventing Educational Risk at The University of Texas at Austin and at the CEEDAR Center, University of Florida.

Tyrone C. Howard

Veteran teacher, author, and professor in the Graduate School of Education and Information Studies at UCLA. Dr. Howard is the inaugural director of the UCLA Pritzker Center for Strengthening Children and Families, a campus-wide consortium examining academic, mental health, and social and emotional experiences and challenges for the most vulnerable youth populations. Dr. Howard has published over 75 peer-reviewed journal articles and several bestselling books, including, *Why Race & Culture Matters in Schools* and *Black Male(d): Peril and Promise in the Education of African American Males.* He is considered one of the premier experts on educational equity and access in the country.

Elena Izquierdo

Nationally recognized teacher educator and advocate for English language learners. Dr. Izquierdo is a linguist by training, with a Ph.D. in Applied Linguistics and Bilingual Education from Georgetown University. She has served on various state and national boards working to close the achievement gaps for bilingual students and English language learners. Dr. Izquierdo is a member of the Hispanic Leadership Council, which supports Hispanic students and educators at both the state and federal levels.

Carol Jago

Teacher of English with 32 years of experience at Santa Monica High School in California; author and nationally known lecturer; former president of the National Council of Teachers of English. Ms. Jago currently serves as Associate Director of the California Reading and Literature Project at UCLA. With expertise in standards' assessment and secondary education, Ms. Jago is the author of numerous books on education, including *With Rigor for All* and *Papers, Papers, Papers*; and she is active with the California Association of Teachers of English, editing its scholarly journal *California English* since 1996. Ms. Jago also served on the planning committee for the 2009 NAEP Reading Framework and the 2011 NAEP Writing Framework.

Weston Kieschnick

Author, award-winning teacher, principal, instructional development coordinator, and dean of education. Mr. Kieschnick has driven change and improved student learning in multiple capacities over his educational career. Now, as an experienced instructional coach and Senior Fellow with the International Center for Leadership in Education (ICLE), Mr. Kieschnick shares his expertise with teachers to transform learning through online and blended models. He is the author of *Bold School: Old School Wisdom + New School Innovation = Blended Learning That Works* and coauthor of *The Learning Transformation: A Guide to Blended Learning for Administrators*.

Erik Palmer

Veteran teacher and education consultant based in Denver, Colorado. Author of *Well Spoken: Teaching Speaking to All Students* and *Digitally Speaking: How to Improve Student Presentations*. His areas of focus include improving oral communication, promoting technology in classroom presentations, and updating instruction through the use of digital tools. He holds a bachelor's degree from Oberlin College and a master's degree in curriculum and instruction from the University of Colorado.

Robert E. Probst

Nationally respected authority on the teaching of literature; Professor Emeritus of English Education at Georgia State University. Dr. Probst's publications include numerous articles in *English Journal* and *Voices from the Middle,* as well as professional texts including (as coeditor) *Adolescent Literacy: Turning Promise into Practice* and (as coauthor with Kylene Beers) *Disrupting Thinking, Notice & Note: Strategies for Close Reading,* and *Reading Nonfiction.* He has served NCTE in various leadership roles, including the Conference on English Leadership Board of Directors, the Commission on Reading, and column editor of the NCTE journal *Voices from the Middle.*

Discovering Your Voice

Page 1

ESSENTIAL QUESTION:
What are the ways you can make yourself heard?

KEY LEARNING OBJECTIVES

- Analyze text structure and purpose
- Analyze memoir
- Analyze print and graphic features
- Analyze author's use of language
- Determine author's purpose and point of view
- Analyze figurative language
- Trace and evaluate arguments

READER'S CHOICE

SHORT READS

I Was a Skinny Tomboy Kid
Poem **by Alma Luz Villanueva**

Words are Birds
Poem **by Francisco X. Alarcón**

Eleven
Short Story **by Sandra Cisneros**

On Dragonwings
Short Story **by Lucy D. Ford**

Carved on the Walls
Informational Text **by Judy Yung**

Available
online

🙂*Ed*

LONG READS

Recommendations

The Giver
Novel
by Lois Lowry

Beethoven in Paradise
Novel
by Barbara O'Connor

Brown Girl Dreaming
Memoir in Verse
by Jacqueline Woodson

UNIT 1 TASKS

WRITING

🙂*Ed*

Go online for
Unit and Selection Videos
Interactive Annotation and Text Analysis
Selection Audio Recordings
Collaborative Writing

Never Give Up

Page 92

Page 92

ESSENTIAL QUESTION:

? **What keeps people from giving up?**

KEY LEARNING OBJECTIVES

- Analyze features of informational texts
- Generate questions
- Analyze poetic forms
- Make inferences about theme
- Analyze plot and character
- Analyze setting
- Compare time periods

READER'S CHOICE

SHORT READS

Paul Revere's Ride
Poem **by Henry Wadsworth Longfellow**

The Road Not Taken
Poem **by Robert Frost**

Available
online

Damon and Pythias
Dramatized **by Fan Kissen**

Education First _from_ **Malala's Speech
to the United Nations**
Speech **by Malala Yousafzai**

LONG READS

Recommendations

New Kid
Graphic Novel
by Jerry Craft
Color
by Jim Callahan

**I am Malala,
Young Reader's
Edition**
Memoir
by Malala Yousafzai

Esperanza Rising
Novel
by Pam Muñoz Ryan

UNIT 2 TASKS

WRITING

SPEAKING & LISTENING

Go online for
Unit and Selection Videos
Interactive Annotation and Text Analysis
Selection Audio Recordings
Collaborative Writing　　Writable

UNIT 3

Finding Courage

Page 174

ESSENTIAL QUESTION:

? *How do you find courage in the face of fear?*

KEY LEARNING OBJECTIVES

- Analyze character and plot
- Analyze character and setting
- Analyze structure
- Analyze media
- Compare across genres
- Determine central idea
- Compare presentations

READER'S CHOICE

SHORT READS

Horrors
Poem **by Lewis Carroll**

Vanquishing the Hungry Chinese Zombie
Short Story **by Claudine Gueh**

Running into Danger on an Alaskan Trail
Narrative Nonfiction **by Cinthia Ritchie**

Face Your Fears: Choking Under Pressure Is Every Athlete's Worst Nightmare
Informational Text **by Dana Hudepohl**

Available online

☺️*Ed*

LONG READS

Recommendations

Dragonwings
Novel
by Laurence Yep

The Parker Inheritance
Novel
by Varian Johnson

The Breadwinner
Novel
by Deborah Ellis

UNIT 3 TASKS

☺️*Ed*

Go online for
Unit and Selection Videos
Interactive Annotation and Text Analysis
Selection Audio Recordings
Collaborative Writing　　Ｗritable

UNIT 4

Through an Animal's Eyes

Page 302

 ESSENTIAL QUESTION:
What can you learn from seeing the world through an animal's eyes?

KEY LEARNING OBJECTIVES

- Analyze point of view
- Analyze word choice
- Infer theme
- Analyze text structure
- Analyze central ideas
- Analyze personification and imagery
- Analyze and evaluate arguments

© Houghton Mifflin Harcourt Publishing Company

READER'S CHOICE

SHORT READS

The Caterpillar
Poem **by Robert Graves**

The Pod
Short Story **by Maureen Crane Wartski**

The Flying Cat
Poem **by Naomi Shihab Nye**

Available online

☺**Ed**

Tribute to the Dog
Speech **by George Graham Vest**

Views on Zoos
Arguments

LONG READS

Recommendations

Julie of the Wolves
Novel
by Jean Craighead George

Primates: The Fearless Science of Jane Goodall, Dian Fossey, and Biruté Galdikas
Graphic Nonfiction
by Jim Ottaviani and Maris Wicks

Pax
Novel
by Sara Pennypacker

UNIT 4 TASKS

☺**Ed**

Go online for
Unit and Selection Videos
Interactive Annotation and Text Analysis
Selection Audio Recordings
Collaborative Writing

Surviving the Unthinkable

Page 386

ESSENTIAL QUESTION:

? **What does it take to be a survivor?**

KEY LEARNING OBJECTIVES

- Analyze setting and character
- Analyze structure
- Integrate information from media
- Determine author's purpose and point of view
- Analyze free verse
- Analyze figurative language
- Analyze setting

COMPARE
ACROSS
GENRES

READER'S CHOICE

SHORT READS

Watcher: After Katrina, 2005
Poem **by Natasha D. Trethewey**

The Day I Didn't Go to the Pool
Short Story **by Leslie J. Wyatt**

Tuesday of the Other June
Short Story **by Norma Fox Mazer**

In Event of Moon Disaster
Speech **by Bill Safire**

Ready: Preparing Your Pets for Emergencies Makes Sense
Informational Text **by Ready.gov**

Available
online

😊**Ed**

LONG READS

Recommendations

Hatchet
Novel
by Gary Paulsen

A Long Walk to Water
Novel
by Linda Sue Park

Ninth Ward
Novel
by Jewell Parker Rhodes

UNIT 5 TASKS

😊**Ed**

Go online for
Unit and Selection Videos
Interactive Annotation and Text Analysis
Selection Audio Recordings
Collaborative Writing   _Writable_

UNIT 6

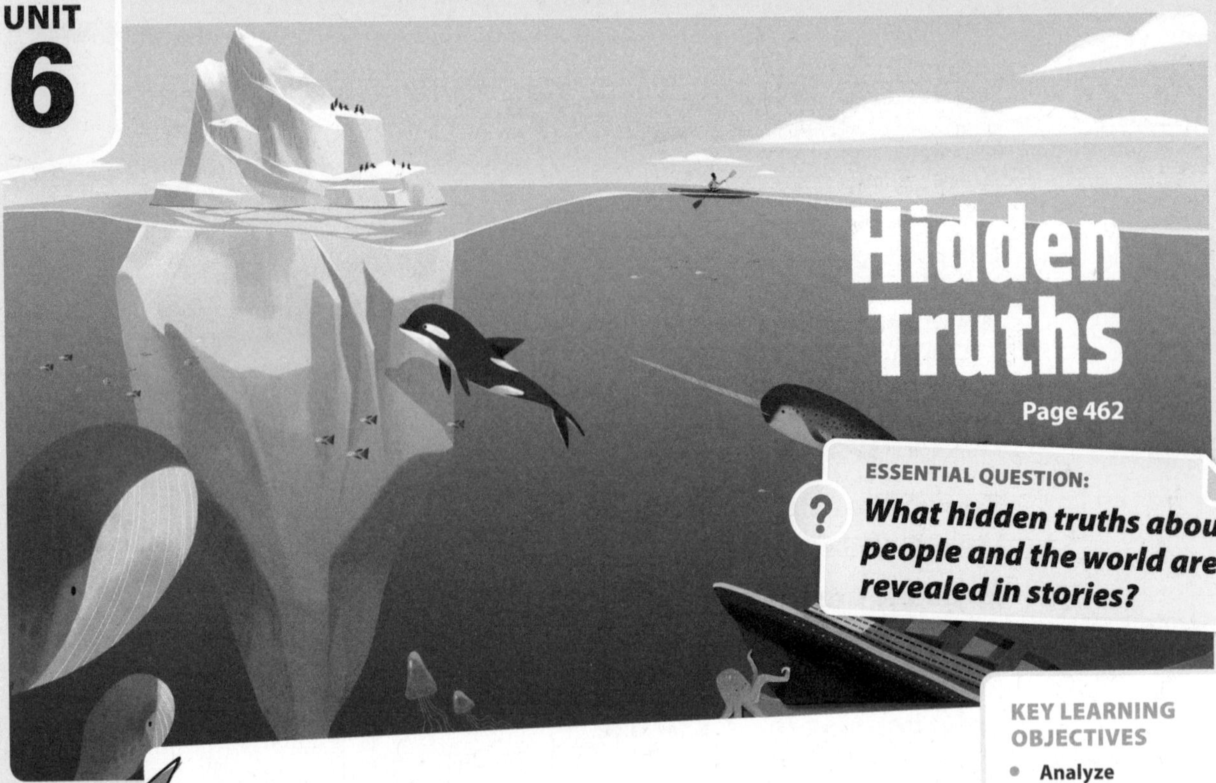

Hidden Truths

Page 462

ESSENTIAL QUESTION:

What hidden truths about people and the world are revealed in stories?

KEY LEARNING OBJECTIVES

- Analyze informational texts
- Analyze central ideas
- Analyze elements of drama
- Analyze theme
- Analyze plot
- Explain narrator and point of view
- Analyze purpose and text structure

ⓔ**Ed**

Go online for
Unit and Selection Videos
Interactive Annotation and Text Analysis
Selection Audio Recordings
Collaborative Writing   **Writable**

SELECTIONS BY GENRE

© Houghton Mifflin Harcourt Publishing Company

HMH | (into) **Literature™** Online

 **Experience the Power of**
HMH Into Literature

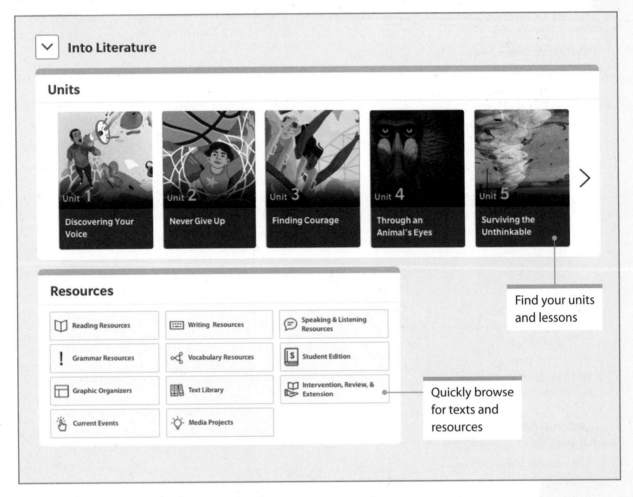

Find your units and lessons

Quickly browse for texts and resources

Tools for Today—All in One Place

Whether you're working alone or collaborating with others, it takes effort to analyze the complex texts and competing ideas that bombard us in this fast-paced world. What will help you succeed? Staying engaged and organized. The digital tools in this program will help you take charge of your learning.

Engage!

Spark Your Learning

These activities kick-start the unit and help get you thinking about the unit theme.

Engage Your Brain

Before you read, take some time to do a fun activity designed to rev up your brain and connect to the text.

Interact with the Texts

- As you read, highlight and take notes to mark the text in your own customized way.
- Use interactive graphic organizers to process, summarize, and track your thinking as you read.
- Play the audio to listen to the text read aloud. You can also turn on read-along highlighting.

Choices

Choose from engaging activities, such as writing an advice column, creating a podcast, or participating in a debate, to demonstrate what you've learned.

Stay Involved!

Collaborate with and Learn from Your Peers

- Watch brief **Peer Coach Videos** to learn more about a particular skill.
- Flex your creative muscles by digging into **Media Projects** tied to each unit theme.
- Bring your writing online with **Writable,** where you can share your work and give and receive valuable feedback.

Read On!

Find helpful **Reader's Choice** suggestions with each unit, and access hundreds of texts online.

No Wi-Fi? No Problem!

With HMH *Into Literature,* you always have access; download when you're online and access what you need when you're offline.

AN ABSOLUTELY, POSITIVELY, MUST-READ ESSAY ABOUT READING

Your Teacher Agrees!

by two people you have never heard of

Dr. Kylene Beers

I've been a teacher all my adult life. I've worked with students at all grades, and now I spend most of my time working with teachers—maybe even your teacher! I live in Texas and when I'm not on an airplane flying off to work in a school, I'm on my ranch, plowing a field. I like to read, cook, read, garden, read, spend time with my family and friends, and (did I mention?) read!

Dr. Robert E. Probst

I've also been a teacher all my adult life. When I first started teaching, I taught kids in middle school and high school, and then I spent most of my career teaching people how to be teachers. For many years now, Dr. Beers and I have written books together—books that are about teaching kids how to be better readers. I live in Florida, and when I'm not in schools working with teachers and kids, I enjoy watching my grandkids play soccer and baseball, and I love being out on the ocean. And, like Dr. Beers, I love reading a great book, too.

So, we're teachers. And we're writers. Specifically, we write books for teachers—books teachers read so that they can help their students become better readers. And we're going to try to help you become a better reader this year. We think that's important, because we both believe TWO things.

© Houghton Mifflin Harcourt Publishing Company • Image Credits: (t) ©Lester Laminack; (b) ©Heinemann; (bg) ©Luria/

First, we've never met a kid who didn't want to get better at reading. Reading is important for almost everything you do, so doing it well is important.

Yes, true!

Second, we believe that reading opens doors. Reading something can open up your mind, your thinking, your ideas, your understanding of the world and all the people in it, so that you might choose to change yourself.

Become a Better You

Too often it's easy to forget why reading is important. You can come to believe that you need to read better just so your grades will go up, or you need to read better so that you do well on a big test. Those things are important—you bet—but they aren't as important as reading better so that you can become better.

Can reading really make me a better person?

How would that happen—how can reading help you change yourself? Sometimes it is obvious. You read something about the importance of exercise and you start walking a little more.

Or, you read something about energy and the environment and you decide to always turn off the lights when you leave any room.

Other times, it might be less obvious. You might read *Wonder* and begin to think about what it means to be a good friend. Maybe you walk over to that person sitting alone in the cafeteria and sit with him or her. Perhaps you'll read *Stella by Starlight* and that book helps you take a stand against racism. Or maybe it happens as you read *Mexican Whiteboy* and discover that who you are on the inside is more important than what anyone sees on the outside. And when you realize that, perhaps it will give you the courage you need to be truer to yourself.

Reading gives us moments to think, and as we think we just might discover something about ourselves that we want to change. And that's why we say reading can help us change ourselves.

Find Important Messages

It would be easy to find important messages in the things we read if the authors would just label them and then maybe send us a text.

But that would mean that every reader is supposed to find the same message. Not true! While the author has a message he or she wants to share, the reader—that's you!—has at least three jobs to do:

My Job

First, enjoy what you are reading.

Second, figure out the message the author wanted to share. This year we'll be showing you some ways to really focus in on that.

Third, you need to decide what matters most to **YOU**. (Yes, we saved the best for last!!!) Sometimes the author's message and what matters most to you will be the same; sometimes not. For instance, it's obvious that J.K. Rowling wrote the Harry Potter series to show us all the sustaining power of love.

> **From Dr. Beers:**
>
> But when I read these books, what really touched my heart was the importance of standing up to our fears.

> **From Dr. Probst:**
>
> And what mattered most to me was the idea that one person, one small person, can make a huge difference in the world. I think that's a critically important point.

Understanding the author's message requires you to do some work while you read—work that requires you to read the text closely. No, you don't need a magnifying glass. But you do need to learn how to notice some things in the text we call **SIGNPOSTS**.

So as I read, I have to think about something called signposts?

A signpost is simply something the author says in the text that helps you understand how characters are changing, how conflicts are being resolved, and, ultimately, what theme—or lesson—the author is trying to convey.

You can also use signposts to help you figure out the author's purpose when you are reading nonfiction. If you can identify the author's purpose—why she or he wrote that particular piece of nonfiction—then you'll be better able to decide whether or not you agree, and whether you need more information.

Where Literature Comes In

English Language Arts classes can provide some of the best opportunities to develop these skills. That's because reading literature allows you to imagine yourself in different worlds and to understand what it's like to be in a wide range of situations. You can think through your own feelings and values as you read about various characters, conflicts, historical figures, and ideas, and you can become more aware of why others might act and feel as they do.

Throughout this book, you will find opportunities for Social and Emotional Learning in the Choices section of many lessons. But you don't need to wait for a special activity to practice and learn. Reading widely and discussing thoughtfully is a natural way to gain empathy and self-knowledge. The chart below shows the five main areas of Social and Emotional Learning and tells how reading can help you strengthen them.

Areas of Social and Emotional Learning	How Reading Can Help
If you have **self-awareness,** you're conscious of your own emotions, thoughts, and values, and you understand how they affect your behavior.	Understanding why characters act the way they do can increase your understanding of your own responses and motivations.
If you're good at **self-management,** you are able to control your emotions, thoughts, and behaviors in different situations.	Paying attention to why characters explode in tumultuous ways or how they keep calm under pressure can help you recognize what to do and not to do when faced with stressful situations in your own life.
If you have **social awareness,** you can empathize with others, including people who are different from you.	Reading about people with different life experiences can help you understand the perspectives of others.
If you have well-developed **relationship skills,** you can get along with different kinds of people and function well in groups.	Reflecting on the conflicts between characters can help you gain insight into what causes the conflicts in your life and how to reach mutual satisfaction.
If you are good at **responsible decision-making,** you make good choices that keep you and others safe and keep you moving toward your goals.	Evaluating the choices characters make and thinking about what you would do in their place can help you understand the consequences of your decisions.

Having the Hard Conversations

The more widely and deeply you read, the more you'll strengthen your social and emotional skills, and the more likely you are to encounter ideas that are different from your own. Some texts might bring up strong reactions from you, and you'll need to take a step back to understand how you're feeling. Or, your classmates might have responses that are dramatically different from yours, and you'll need to take a breath and decide how to engage with them. Remember: it's okay to disagree with a text or with a peer. In fact, discussing a difference of opinion can be one of the most powerful ways to learn.

Tips for Talking About Controversial Issues

> The reason I think so is because I've noticed that I . . .

> So what I hear you saying is . . . Did I get that right?

Communicate clearly.
Speak honestly and carefully, rather than for dramatic effect. Notice if the person listening seems confused and give them room to ask questions.

Listen actively.
Try your best to understand what the other person is saying, and why they might think or feel that way. If you don't understand, ask questions or rephrase what you thought you heard and ask them if you're getting it right.

> When you use that word I have a negative reaction because it sounds like you are saying you think that person isn't smart.

> I'm sorry. That's not what I meant.

Take a stand against name-calling, belittling, stereotyping, and bias.
Always try exploring ideas further rather than making personal attacks. If someone feels hurt by something you said, listen to them with an open mind. Perhaps you expressed bias without realizing it. Apologize sincerely if that happens. And if you are hurt by a comment or hear something that could be interpreted as hurtful, calmly let the person who said it know why you feel that way.

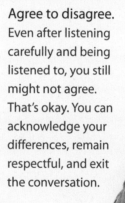

> *I need to take a break from this conversation now.*

Pay attention to your feelings.
Recognize the topics or situations that make it hard for you to stay calm. Try to separate your strong feelings from what the person is saying. If you need to, excuse yourself from the conversation and find a place where you can help yourself relax.

> *We see this really differently, so let's move on for now.*

Consider the relationship.
It's likely that the people you're in class with are people you will be seeing regularly for years. You don't have to be friends with them or agree with their point of view, but you do have to get an education alongside each other. Speaking respectfully even if you're on opposite sides of an issue will make it easier to work together if you ever have to collaborate. Try to assume the best about them rather than the worst. Acknowledge that our experiences affect our points of view.

Agree to disagree.
Even after listening carefully and being listened to, you still might not agree. That's okay. You can acknowledge your differences, remain respectful, and exit the conversation.

> *I don't agree with you, but I understand why it looks that way from your perspective.*

Learning, growing, and working with others isn't always easy. If you read widely and deeply and try your best to speak honestly, you're likely to gain the understanding and compassion that can help you manage the stresses, challenges, and opportunities that life brings your way.

Discovering Your Voice

*"When I speak,
the words come pouring out of me."*
—Jacqueline Woodson

Analyze the Image

What does the image suggest about ways that we express ourselves?

Spark Your Learning

Here's a chance to spark your learning about ideas in **Unit 1: Discovering Your Voice.**

As you read, you can use the **Response Log** (page R1) to track your thinking about the Essential Question.

?

Make the Connection

When was the last time you had to make yourself heard? Maybe you were talking with friends or were drawing something important. Take a few moments to freewrite about a time you needed someone to hear you.

Think About the Essential Question

What are the ways you can make yourself heard? People express themselves in many ways. What's your favorite way to make yourself heard? Why?

✔

Prove It!

Turn to a partner and use one of the words in a sentence about making your voice heard.

Sound Like an Expert

You can use these Academic Vocabulary words to write and talk about the topics and themes in the unit. How many of these words do you already feel comfortable using when speaking or writing?

	I can use it!	I understand it.	I'll look it up.
appropriate	☐	☐	☐
authority	☐	☐	☐
consequence	☐	☐	☐
element	☐	☐	☐
justify	☐	☐	☐

Preview the Texts

Look over the images, titles, and descriptions of the texts in the unit. Mark the title of the text that interests you most.

from **Brown Girl Dreaming**

Memoir in Verse by **Jacqueline Woodson**

How did the author find her voice when she was growing up?

from **Selfie: The Changing Face of Self-Portraits**

Informational Text by **Susie Brooks**

Selfies have been around a lot longer than you have!

What's So Funny, Mr. Scieszka?

Humor by **Jon Scieszka**

The author remembers getting called out for laughing in elementary school.

A Voice

Poem by **Pat Mora**

This poem explores the importance of speaking up.

Words Like Freedom

Poem by **Langston Hughes**

The poet expresses his desire for freedom.

Better Than Words: Say It with a Selfie

Argument by **Gloria Chang**

Why are selfies so popular?

OMG, Not *Another* Selfie!

Argument by **Shermakaye Bass**

Do you think selfies are bad for you? This author does.

I Wonder . . .

Why is it important to discover your own voice and make yourself heard? What feelings do you have that might get in the way? Write or sketch your answer.

from

Brown Girl Dreaming

Memoir in Verse by **Jacqueline Woodson**

Engage Your Brain

Choose one or more of these activities to start connecting with the memoir you are about to read.

(You) Dreaming

Think about the title of this selection. What dreams do you have for your own life? Write or sketch a response. Give your answer a title describing you.

Kiddie Book Club

Pick a children's book that you remember well. Then, with a group—

- share what the book is about
- discuss its importance to you

"When I Grow Up . . ."

Adults sometimes can make children feel that their dreams about life are silly. What would you say to someone who feels that a child's dream is unrealistic? Share your ideas.

© Houghton Mifflin Harcourt Publishing Company

Analyze Text Structure and Purpose

Poems, rather than chapters, create the **structure** for *Brown Girl Dreaming*, Jacqueline Woodson's memoir in verse.

Memoirs are written from the first-person point of view, detailing a writer's observations about significant events and people in the writer's life. Most memoirs are written in prose; however, Jacqueline Woodson relies on a series of poems that include all of the elements of a conventional memoir.

Why might Woodson have used this particular style and approach? As you read the excerpt from *Brown Girl Dreaming*, note instances in which Woodson uses the elements of memoir, and consider how they connect to the **author's purpose**—her main reason for writing the text.

Focus on Genre
↳ **Memoir in Verse**

- is a personal narrative told from first-person point of view
- includes the writer's own experiences and observations of significant events or people
- has an informal or even intimate tone
- presents insights into the impact of historical events on people's lives, particularly the writer's
- tells the story through verse

ELEMENTS OF A MEMOIR	AUTHOR'S PURPOSE

Analyze Memoir

As you read, use a web diagram like this one to analyze how the ideas of *Brown Girl Dreaming* connect to your own experiences and ideas, as well as to other texts.

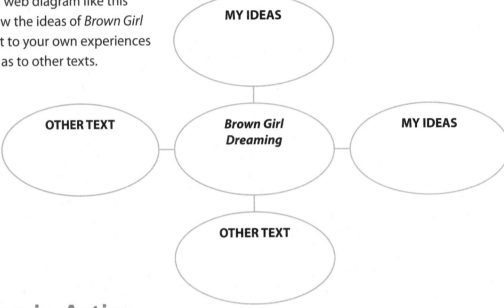

Annotation in Action

This model shows how one reader made notes about a possible author's purpose for *Brown Girl Dreaming*. As you read, note details that help reveal other possible purposes.

> It's easier to make up stories
> than it is to write them down. When I speak,
> the words come pouring out of me. The story
> wakes up and walks all over the room. Sits in a chair,
> crosses one leg over the other, says,
> *Let me introduce myself.* Then just starts going on and on.

When she tells a story, it's as if she's meeting a new friend.

Background

Jacqueline Woodson (b. 1963) had difficulty reading when she was young, but she has now written more than 30 books. She wrote *Brown Girl Dreaming* to learn about her family and to discover what led her to become a writer. She says her memoir is a series of poems "because memories come to people in small bursts." *Brown Girl Dreaming* won the National Book Award in 2014, and Woodson was named National Ambassador for Young People's Literature for 2018–2019.

from
Brown Girl Dreaming

Memoir in Verse
by **Jacqueline Woodson**

How did the author find her voice when she was growing up?

writing #1

It's easier to make up stories
than it is to write them down. When I speak,
the words come pouring out of me. The story
wakes up and walks all over the room. Sits in a chair,
5 crosses one leg over the other, says,
Let me introduce myself. Then just starts going on and on.
But as I bend over my composition notebook,
only my name
comes quickly. Each letter, neatly printed
10 between the pale blue lines. Then white
space and air and me wondering, *How do I
spell introduce?* Trying again and again
until there is nothing but pink
bits of eraser and a hole now.
15 where a story should be.

ANALYZE TEXT STRUCTURE AND PURPOSE

Annotate: Mark the result of the author not being able to spell *introduce*.

Infer: What might this reveal about the author's purpose?

late autumn

NOTICE & NOTE
MEMORY MOMENT

When you notice the speaker or narrator bringing up something from the past, you've found a **Memory Moment** signpost.

Notice & Note: What does the author remember writing on the board? Mark what she writes, and then mark why she writes it.

Analyze: Why might this memory be important to the author?

Ms. Moskowitz calls us one by one and says,
Come up to the board and write your name.
When it's my turn, I walk down the aisle from
my seat in the back, write *Jacqueline Woodson*—

20   the way I've done a hundred times, turn back
toward my seat, proud as anything
of my name in white letters on the dusty blackboard.
But Ms. Moskowitz stops me, says,
In cursive too, please. But the *q* in Jacqueline is too hard

25   so I write *Jackie Woodson* for the first time. Struggle
only a *little* bit with the *k*.

Is that what you want us to call you?

I want to say, *No, my name is Jacqueline*
but I am scared of that cursive *q*, know

30   I may never be able to connect it to *c* and *u*
so I nod even though
I am lying.

the other woodson

Don't forget to
Notice & Note as you
read the text.
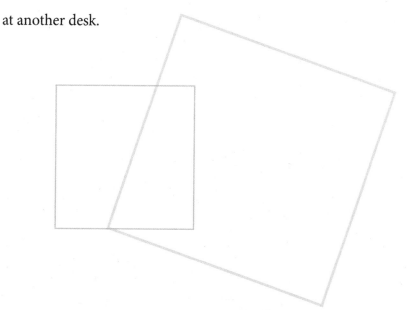

Even though so many people think my sister and I
are twins,

35 I am the other Woodson, following behind her each year
into the same classroom she had the year before. Each
teacher smiles when they call my name. *Woodson*, they
say. *You must be Odella's sister.* Then they nod
slowly, over and over again, call me Odella. Say,

40 *I'm sorry! You look so much like her and she is SO brilliant!*
then wait for my brilliance to light up
the classroom. Wait for my arm to fly into
the air with every answer. Wait for my pencil
to move quickly through the too-easy math problems

45 on the mimeographed sheet.[1] Wait for me to stand
before class, easily reading words even high school
students stumble over. And they keep waiting.
And waiting
and waiting

50 and waiting

until one day, they walk into the classroom,
almost call me Odel—then stop

remember that I am the other Woodson

and begin searching for brilliance

55 at another desk.

© Houghton Mifflin Harcourt Publishing Company

---

[1] **mimeographed sheet** (mĭm′ē-ə-grăft′ shēt): a page from a duplicating machine,
which makes copies of written, drawn, or typed material by pressing ink through a
stencil onto paper.

ANALYZE MEMOIR

Annotate: Mark comparisons
other people make about the
author and her sister.

Connect: Have you ever been
compared to someone else?
According to Woodson, what
is one effect of comparing one
person to another?

reading

I am not my sister.
Words from the books curl around each other
make little sense
until
60 I read them again
and again, the story
settling into memory. *Too slow*
the teacher says.
Read faster.
65 *Too babyish*, the teacher says.
Read older.
But I don't want to read faster or older or
any way else that might
make the story disappear too quickly from where it's settling
70 inside my brain,
slowly becoming
a part of me.
A story I will remember
long after I've read it for the second, third,
75 tenth, hundredth time.

© Houghton Mifflin Harcourt Publishing Company • Image Credits: ©Skynesher/E+/Getty Images

stevie and me

Don't forget to
Notice & Note as you
read the text.

Every Monday, my mother takes us
to the library around the corner. We are allowed
to take out seven books each. On those days,
no one complains
80 that all I want are picture books.

Those days, no one tells me to read faster
to read harder books
to read like Dell.

No one is there to say, *Not that book,*
85 when I stop in front of the small paperback
with a brown boy on the cover.
Stevie.

I read:
One day my momma told me,
90 *"You know you're gonna have*
a little friend come stay with you."
And I said, "Who is it?"

If someone had been fussing with me
to read like my sister, I might have missed
95 the picture book filled with brown people, more
brown people than I'd ever seen
in a book before.

The little boy's name was Steven but
his mother kept calling him Stevie.
100 *My name is Robert but my momma don't*
call me Robertie.

If someone had taken
that book out of my hand
said, *You're too old for this*
105 maybe
I'd never have believed
that someone who looked like me
could be in the pages of the book
that someone who looked like me
110 had a story.

**ANALYZE TEXT STRUCTURE
AND PURPOSE**

Annotate: Mark the type of
library books the author likes.

Analyze: How might the books
relate to the author's purpose for
writing about this memory?

when i tell my family

When I tell my family
I want to be a writer, they smile and say,
We see you in the backyard with your writing.
They say,
115 *We hear you making up all those stories.*
And,
We used to write poems.
And,
It's a good hobby, we see how quiet it keeps you.
120 They say,
But maybe you should be a teacher,
a lawyer,
do hair . . .

I'll think about it, I say.

125 And maybe all of us know

this is just another one of my stories.

ANALYZE MEMOIR

Annotate: Mark the italicized phrases.

Connect: How do these messages compare to ones you have heard from adults in your life?

?

ESSENTIAL QUESTION:

What are the ways you can make yourself heard?

Review your notes and add your thoughts to your Response Log.

TURN AND TALK

Get together with a partner and discuss the excerpt from the memoir in verse you just read. What do these poems tell you about what Woodson's life was like when she was a child?

Assessment Practice

Answer these questions before moving on to the **Analyze the Text** section.

1. Which **two** excerpts from the text show that the author struggled with reading as a child?

   Ⓐ "When I speak, / the words come pouring out of me." (lines 2–3)

   Ⓑ "I am not my sister." (line 56)

   Ⓒ *Too slow* / the teacher says." (lines 62–63)

   Ⓓ "We are allowed / to take out seven books each." (lines 77–78)

   Ⓔ "Those days, no one tells me to read faster / to read harder books / to read like Dell." (lines 81–83)

2. Why is the book *Stevie* important to the author?

   Ⓐ It has people of color in it.

   Ⓑ It has a character in it who is a writer.

   Ⓒ It is the first book the author can read.

   Ⓓ It is the first library book she checks out.

3. Which words best describe the author's sister?

   Ⓐ helpful and kind

   Ⓑ intelligent and studious

   Ⓒ protective and watchful

   Ⓓ competitive and ambitious

4. How does the author's family react to her desire to become a writer?

   Ⓐ They offer encouragement.

   Ⓑ They suggest more realistic goals.

   Ⓒ They reveal how much they enjoy her stories.

   Ⓓ They point out how often hobbies become careers.

Test-Taking Strategies

Analyze the Text

Support your responses with evidence from the text.

(1) SYNTHESIZE How do the last three lines of the memoir capture its central idea?

(2) DRAW CONCLUSIONS Review the titles and subjects of the verses in this excerpt. What do the titles and subjects have in common? How do you think the titles relate to the author's overall purpose in writing the memoir?

NOTICE & NOTE

Review what you **noticed and noted** as you read the text. Your annotations can help you answer these questions.

TITLES	SUBJECTS	AUTHOR'S OVERALL PURPOSE

(3) ANALYZE Review the italicized words throughout the selection. Why do you think the author italicized these words? Cite evidence in your answer.

(4) SUMMARIZE Review and summarize the first poem, "writing #1." How do the first two lines provide structure and meaning?

(5) ANALYZE Review lines 56–75. Why does the author reread books? How might this **Memory Moment** reveal something important about the development of the author's writing?

Choices

Here are some other ways to demonstrate your understanding of the ideas in this lesson.

Social & Emotional Learning
↳ **Describe a Connection**

Write a brief, formal letter or email to Jacqueline Woodson that describes a meaningful connection you found between your life and an idea or event in her memoir.

1. Include the date and the name and address of the person you're writing to.

2. Use the body of your letter to describe the connection.

3. What ideas or events in the memoir are meaningful to you? Provide details that will help Woodson understand the connection.

4. Revise and edit your letter to ensure that you've used a formal style. Eliminate slang, spell out any contractions, abbreviations, or "text speak" you may have used, and check your grammar and spelling.

5. Remember to sign your letter.

As you write and discuss, be sure to use the **Academic Vocabulary** words.

| **appropriate** |
| **authority** |
| **consequence** |
| **element** |
| **justify** |

Speaking & Listening
↳ **Compose and Present a Biographical Poem**

Choose an event that affected your life, and write a poem, your own memoir in verse, about it.

● Choose an event, and select a poetic form that best conveys your experience, either free verse or formal. Write your poem.

● Practice reading your poem aloud, and present it to a small group or to the class.

● Make eye contact with your audience, and use pacing, tone, and voice to convey your meaning.

● Answer questions about your work, and ask questions about the poems of other students.

Research
↳ **Who's Jacqueline Woodson?**

Use multiple sources to answer the following questions about Jacqueline Woodson.

● What helped Woodson most as she learned to write?

● How did "lying" influence her writing?

● What did her teachers think of her writing?

● What are some fun facts about Woodson?

Selfie: The Changing Face of Self-Portraits

Informational Text by **Susie Brooks**

ESSENTIAL QUESTION:
What are the ways you can make yourself heard?

Engage Your Brain

Choose one or more of these activities to start connecting with the informational text you are about to read.

Your Selfie Here

Draw your own selfie, capturing parts of your personality that you want your viewer to understand. If you don't want to draw, note details of your personality that you'd express in a selfie.

What Makes a Good Selfie?

What do you think makes a good selfie? Get together with a partner and make a list of things that make a selfie great. Then, share your list with the rest of the class.

Gallery Walk

Skim through the selection, examining each of the self-portraits. Pick one that you find interesting and study it—*without* reading a word. What do you think the artist may have been trying to "say" in the portrait?

Analyze Informational Texts

The informational selection you are about to read conveys ideas through text and visual details. To find the text's key ideas—

- Identify the specific topic of each paragraph or section.

- Examine all the details the author provides, including details found in the text, illustrations, images, and graphic features.

- Reread the text after studying the artwork, integrating information from both.

Analyze Print and Graphic Features

Print features are elements of text design, such as boldface type, headings, captions, and fonts.

Graphic features are visual elements such as charts, diagrams, graphs, photographs, maps, and art.

You can skim—quickly read or view—these features before a close reading to help you get a sense of the author's purpose and the text's main ideas. These features can also help you quickly locate topics or ideas after reading.

PRINT FEATURES	GRAPHIC FEATURES
A **heading** or **subheading** indicates the beginning of a new topic or section. New sections may begin with a **drop cap,** or a large capital letter at the beginning of a paragraph.	**Color effects,** such as highlighted text, doodles, and colored backgrounds, can organize and call attention to information.
A **caption** contains information about an image or illustration.	A box, speech balloon, or other shape may be used to display information about an image or to call attention to additional information.

Annotation in Action

Here is an example of notes a student made about a paragraph from *Selfie*. As you read, highlight words that help you understand key details in the text.

But next time you smile/hug a celebrity and post the pic, spare a thought for Rembrandt van Rijn and Vincent van Gogh, among others. They never saw a smartphone, or the Internet, and most of them couldn't even tell you what a camera was. But they did all know about selfies!

What did these guys know about selfies?

Expand Your Vocabulary

Put a check mark next to the vocabulary words that you feel comfortable using when speaking or writing.

reflection	☐
haughty	☐
span	☐
prim	☐

Turn to a partner and talk about the vocabulary words you already know. Then, use as many words as you can in a paragraph about taking selfies. As you read *Selfie,* use the definitions in the side column to learn the vocabulary words you don't already know.

Background

Does it surprise you to learn that selfies actually have a long history in art? Children's author and art historian **Susie Brooks** explains how even before the invention of photography, the Internet, and the smartphone, people throughout history have longed to put their best face forward and share their images with the world.

from

Selfie:
The Changing Face of Self-Portraits

Informational Text by **Susie Brooks**

Selfies have been around a lot longer than you have!

NOTICE & NOTE
As you read, use the side margins to make notes about the text.

All By Your Selfie

1 You can probably do it with your eyes closed: point your phone camera at your face; press the shutter button and bingo—a selfie! But next time you smile/hug a celebrity and post the pic, spare a thought for Rembrandt van Rijn and Vincent van Gogh, among others. They never saw a smartphone, or the Internet, and most of them couldn't even tell you what a camera was. But they did all know about selfies!

2 Back in the old days, selfies were more commonly known as self-portraits. Before photography was invented, people who wanted pictures of themselves (and could afford it) commissioned artists to paint their portraits. If you were an artist it was even easier—you just looked in the mirror and painted what you saw!

3   Self-portraits can often tell us about the clothing of a particular time, about art material and styles, and how old or rich or handsome the artist was or is—but most of all they let us look right inside the minds of the brilliant (and sometimes a bit bonkers) people who created them.

4   Take Vincent van Gogh, who cut off a piece of his ear, but still thought it would make a nice picture. Rembrandt drew, painted and etched his own **reflection** so many times we can see almost every stage of his life!

Albrecht Dürer

5   Dürer looks **haughty** and confident, with a stiff but elegant pose. His clothing is expensive, extravagant and Italian in style.

6   We all want to look good in a selfie—and 500 years ago it was the same. Albrecht Dürer dressed up in fancy clothes for this self-portrait, announcing to the world that he was rich and grand.

7   Dürer was 26 when he painted this and already a leading artist, best known for his woodcut prints. On a trip to Italy, he noticed that great artists had a higher social status than they did at home in Germany. Dürer wanted to be treated like that too! After Dürer's death, admirers cut locks of his hair to remember him by. You can still see some at the Academy of Fine Arts in Vienna, Austria.

reflection
(rĭ-flĕk´shən) *n.* A *reflection* is an image shown back, as from a mirror.

haughty
(hô´tē) *adj.* A *haughty* person is scornfully proud.

ANALYZE PRINT AND GRAPHIC FEATURES

Annotate: Mark the subheading for this section, along with information included in the caption for the Dürer painting.

Compare: How can you distinguish the caption from other features, such as headings? What is the purpose of the caption?

Born: 1471 in Germany
Died: 1528, aged 56
Self-Portrait, c. 1500

Born: 1606 in the Netherlands
Died: 1669, aged 63
Self-Portrait as a Young Man,
1634

Self-Portrait with Saskia, 1636

Don't forget to
Notice & Note as you
read the text.

**ANALYZE PRINT AND
GRAPHIC FEATURES**

Annotate: Mark the print and
graphic features on this page,
such as headings, captions, and
images.

Analyze: How does each feature
help organize and present the
information in an effective way?

Rembrandt van Rijn

8   Rembrandt was the biggest selfie maker of his time, creating
nearly 100 self-portraits that **spanned** 40 years of his life.
They track his changing appearance, as well as his developing
painting style.

9   Rembrandt pictured himself in all sorts of poses, outfits
and moods. As a young man, he often appeared in fine
clothing, perhaps in the style of the rich people whose
portraits he painted. Sometimes his scenes were theatrical,
like the one he painted at the age of 29 with his wife Saskia
sitting on his knee.

span
(spăn) *v.* To *span* is to extend over
a period of time.

NOTICE & NOTE
CONTRASTS AND CONTRADICTIONS

When you notice a sharp contrast or a difference between two or more elements in the text, you've found a **Contrasts and Contradictions** signpost.

Notice & Note: What are the differences between Rembrandt's final self-portrait and his earlier self-portraits? Mark the painting's description and study the image.

Connect: How does Rembrandt's final "selfie" surprise you? Why do you think he redid his original painting?

Self-Portrait at the Age of 63, 1669

10   By the end of his life, Rembrandt was an expert at capturing character. He stripped away all the fancy dress and showed us simply Rembrandt the person. In his last self-portrait aged 63, he seems sad yet calm and dignified. We see him inside and out, with every lump, sag and wrinkle on display.

11   When experts examined his painting under X-ray, they discovered that the artist had made some changes. Originally his hat was much bigger and all white, and his hands had held a paintbrush. Rembrandt painted over this detail, bringing all our attention back to his face.

Elizabeth Vigée Le Brun

Don't forget to **Notice & Note** as you read the text.

12 This lady looks pretty in her straw hat and pink dress. She has a gentle smile and a friendly and welcoming gaze. Vigée Le Brun wanted people to like her in this selfie—and they did.

13 In the 18th century, female artists had to work hard to be taken seriously. Traditionally, painting was something that women did mostly as a hobby. Vigée Le Brun was extremely talented and she also sold her skills well. Self-portraits like this one were a way to attract attention and win people's hearts.

14 Elizabeth looks natural and relaxed in the painting. She seems comfortable with her palette and brushes, but they aren't the focus of the scene.

ANALYZE INFORMATIONAL TEXTS

Annotate: In paragraphs 12–14, mark the descriptions of the painting.

Summarize: Use details in the text to explain how Vigée Le Brun used her self-portraits to help promote her work.

Born: 1755 in France
Died: 1842, aged 86
Self-Portrait in a Straw Hat, 1782

Joseph Ducreux

prim
(prĭm) *adj.* A *prim* person is
excessively proper and prudish.

15 These days, funny faces in selfies are nothing unusual, but in
the 1700s people tended to be more straight-faced.[1] Most
self-portraits avoided any strong feeling of being happy, cross or
tired. It was different for the artists on these pages, though!

16 Joseph Ducreux found traditional portraiture[2] too **prim** and
proper. Instead, he tried to capture the personalities of everyone
he painted. In this self-portrait, he caught himself in the middle
of a yawn. There's nothing shy or self-conscious about it—he
pushes out his belly and opens his mouth wide, in a way that
makes us want to yawn too.

Born: 1735 in France
Died: 1802, aged 67
Self-Portrait, Yawning, 1783

---

[1] **straight-faced:** showing no sign of emotion.
[2] **portraiture** (pôr´trĭ-chŏŏr´): the practice of creating portraits.

Born: 1853 in Netherlands
Died: 1890, aged 37
Self-Portrait with Bandaged Ear, 1889

Don't forget to
Notice & Note as you
read the text.

Vincent van Gogh

17 You might take a selfie when something unusual happens to you. Van Gogh made this one after he cut a piece from his ear following an argument with his friend and fellow artist, Gauguin.

18 Can you see the bandage on the side of van Gogh's head? The unlucky ear was actually the left one, but he was looking in a mirror when he painted this. Rather than hiding his injury, he made it the focus of the picture. His face looks as if he's lost in thought.

19 Notice how van Gogh used big, thick brushstrokes. They bring out the different textures of his clothes, fur cap, bandage and bony face. Sometimes he squeezed paint straight from the tube onto the canvas, and it would take weeks and weeks to dry! Behind the artist we can see a Japanese print. Van Gogh was fascinated by Japanese art. He loved its bold outlines, flat colours and shapes, and did his best to use them in his own work.

20 When he painted this selfie, van Gogh was mentally ill. After cutting the chunk off his ear, he gave it to a woman as a "gift." He was taken into a hospital and a few months later checked into an asylum.

ANALYZE PRINT AND GRAPHIC FEATURES

Annotate: Mark the print and graphic features used with the Vincent van Gogh painting and section.

Summarize: What effect do the features have on the presentation of the author's ideas?

Annotate: Mark the sentence in paragraph 21 that suggests a key idea for this section of the text. Then, mark supporting details in paragraph 22.

Evaluate: How do the supporting details help explain the key idea? What additional details might the author have included as support?

Selfies Today

21 Selfies today are everywhere! With digital cameras and smartphones, anyone can snap themselves in an instant and share the picture with their friends or the world. Celebrities are doing it. Politicians are doing it. Will the selfie craze ever end?

22 2013 was the year that "#selfie" took off. More than 17 million people were posting a selfie on social media every week. In 2014, the word "selfie" made it into the Oxford Dictionary and was approved for the board game Scrabble! Technologies such as front-facing cameras, selfie sticks and hand-gesture sensors have made selfie-snapping easier than ever before.

23 In 2013, Pope Francis went viral in the first "Papal selfie," taken with young fans at the Vatican.

24 When you post a selfie, you're displaying a view of yourself that you want other people to see. When artists make self-portraits, it's the same! So next time you pose, remember you have something in common with every famous face in this book!

Selfie with Pope Francis

? **ESSENTIAL QUESTION:**

What are the ways you can make yourself heard?

Review your notes and add your thoughts to your Response Log.

TURN AND TALK

Get together with a partner and discuss what you now know about "selfies" from the past. Will what you learned change the way you take selfies in the future? Why or why not?

Assessment Practice

Answer these questions before moving on to the **Analyze the Text** section.

1. Which sentence states the central idea of the text?

   (A) Selfies tell us about the artists who painted them.

   (B) Selfie poses have become more relaxed over time.

   (C) Selfies show a view of yourself that you want others to see.

   (D) Selfies are part of the centuries-old tradition of self-portraits.

2. This question has two parts. First, answer **Part A**. Then, answer **Part B**.

   Part A

   Why does the author claim that 2013 was an important year for selfies?

   (A) It's the year that van Gogh's portrait was considered a selfie.

   (B) It's the year that selfies became more playful and funny.

   (C) It's the year that taking selfies became really popular.

   (D) It's the year smartphones were invented.

   Part B

   Select **two** excerpts that support the answer to Part A.

   (A) "Back in the old days, selfies were more commonly known as self-portraits." (paragraph 2)

   (B) "We all want to look good in a selfie—and 500 years ago it was the same." (paragraph 6)

   (C) "His face looks as if he's lost in thought." (paragraph 18)

   (D) "More than 17 million people were posting a selfie on social media every week." (paragraph 22)

   (E) "In 2013, Pope Francis went viral in the first 'Papal selfie'. . . ." (paragraph 23)

   ☺**Ed**
   Test-Taking Strategies

Analyze the Text

Support your responses with evidence from the text.

NOTICE & NOTE

Review what you **noticed and noted** as you read the text. Your annotations can help you answer these questions.

1 **ANALYZE** Why do you think the author chose to include Rembrandt in the text? How does the author illustrate his significance as a self-portrait artist?

DETAILS ABOUT REMBRANDT	WHY REMBRANDT IS SIGNIFICANT

2 **ANALYZE** In the section about Vincent van Gogh, how does the author use writing and visual modes of communication to express key ideas?

3 **DRAW CONCLUSIONS** Review the section "Selfies Today," and note the selfie of Pope Francis. How does this selfie support the author's ideas about selfies and self-portraits?

4 **INFER** What is the author's purpose in writing this text? How is the purpose conveyed?

5 **INFER** Review the sections on Elizabeth Vigée Le Brun and Joseph Ducreux. Why does the author reveal a **Contrasts and Contradictions** signpost about how the two artists approached their work?

Choices

Here are some other ways to demonstrate your understanding of the ideas in this lesson.

Writing

So What Did It Mean?

Write a summary of the key ideas in the selection. Your summary should:

- Clearly state the key ideas presented in the selection.

- Support the ideas with evidence from the text, including print and graphic features.

- Exclude personal opinions or judgments.

- Include a variety of sentence types, using commas correctly.

Speaking & Listening
Post Those "Selfies"

In a small group, imagine that you're going to post images from this selection to a social media site, along with your own comments.

- Select several paintings from the selection that others might like to see.

- Then, discuss comments that might accompany each painting; take notes about the group's ideas.

- Finally, share your comments with the class.

Research
Learn More About the Artist

With a partner, research one of the artists mentioned in the text. Use more than one source, and guide your research with *who, what, where, when, how,* and *why* questions, like those below.

- Who was the artist, and when did the artist live?

- What was the artist's medium and style?

- Where did the artist work?

- How was the artist's work viewed during the artist's lifetime?

- Why is the artist remembered today?

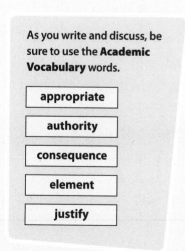

As you write and discuss, be sure to use the **Academic Vocabulary** words.

| appropriate |
| authority |
| consequence |
| element |
| justify |

Expand Your Vocabulary

PRACTICE AND APPLY

Complete each sentence to show the vocabulary word's meaning.

1. The **reflection** in the car's rearview mirror showed

   _____

2. A **haughty** salesperson is less likely to make a sale because

   _____

3. The **span** of one year is equal to

   _____

4. The other children ran and shrieked, but the **prim** little girl

   _____

Vocabulary Strategy

↳ Connotations and Denotations

**Interactive Vocabulary
Lesson: Denotation
and Connotation**

The **denotation** of a word is its definition. Words can have multiple denotations. *Feeling*, for example, has multiple meanings:

> **He lost the feeling in his left toe.** (sense of touch)
> **She likes the feeling of the cool breeze.** (a sensation)
> **The poem gave her a feeling of peace.** (an emotion)

The **connotation** of a word, however, is the emotional response or set of associations it evokes. Consider this sentence:

> **Dürer looks haughty and confident. . . .**

The denotation of *haughty* is "proud." However, its connotation can be negative. A thesaurus reveals that synonyms include *snobbish, stuck-up,* and *conceited.*

PRACTICE AND APPLY

Working with a partner, discuss the denotations and connotations of the word *elegant*. First, check the definition in a dictionary. Then, use a thesaurus to identify three synonyms that help you understand the word's connotations.

Watch Your Language!

Commas and Sentence Variety

Sentence variety is one way authors make their work clear and interesting to read. To vary sentence structure and add clarity, you can begin some sentences with **introductory elements,** such as phrases and dependent clauses. A **phrase** is a group of related words that does not contain a subject and a predicate but functions in a sentence as a single part of speech. A **dependent clause** is a group of words that contains a subject and a predicate but cannot stand alone as a sentence. Commas are used after introductory elements to make sentences easier to understand.

Interactive Grammar Lessons: Punctuation I

In *Selfie: The Changing Face of Self-Portraits,* the author uses commas to—

- set off an introductory word

  Instead, he tried to capture the personalities of everyone he painted. (paragraph 16)

- set off an introductory phrase

  On a trip to Italy, he noticed that great artists had a higher social status than they did at home in Germany. (paragraph 7)

- set off a dependent clause used as an introductory element

  When he painted this selfie, van Gogh was mentally ill. (paragraph 20)

"I have trouble with punctuation. I just don't have any comma sense."

PRACTICE AND APPLY

Write a paragraph that expresses an opinion about a self-portrait in the selection or describes your own experience with selfies. Include sentences that use an introductory word, phrase, or dependent clause set off with a comma. When you are finished, share your work with a partner and compare your use of commas.

What's So Funny, Mr. Scieszka?

Humor by **Jon Scieszka**

Engage Your Brain

Choose one or both activities to start connecting with the story you're about to read.

On-the-Spot

Have you ever had to make an on-the-spot choice that could change your life forever? Think of a big choice you made and how it has changed your life. Write your thoughts about what changed and why.

Uh-oh. *Now* You've Done It.

Think about a time that you or someone you know did something and immediately felt sorry for having done it. Describe or sketch what happened in the space below.

Analyze Author's Use of Language

Writers use descriptive words, imagery, and figurative language to create a feeling, or **mood.** A mood might be tense, peaceful, or humorous, for example. Writers also use language to create **voice,** or the distinct personality readers hear as they read a text.

- To analyze how the author uses language to create mood, mark figurative language, imagery, and word choices, noting their effects.

- To determine voice, mark significant words and phrases that capture personality.

Determine Author's Purpose and Point of View

An **author's purpose** is the main reason for writing the text. The purpose may be to inform, to entertain, to persuade, or to express thoughts and feelings. Most writers do not state a text's purpose directly, but suggest it through the information they present and the text's tone and structure.

An author's **point of view,** or how the author presents information on a topic, is connected to his or her purpose. An **objective point of view** focuses on factual information and leaves out personal opinions. A **subjective point of view** includes the author's personal opinions, feelings, and beliefs.

Here is an inference, citing evidence about point of view and tone, on the purpose of "What's So Funny, Mr. Scieszka?"

EVIDENCE FROM THE TEXT	INFERENCE ABOUT THE PURPOSE
The author includes personal opinions, so he's using a subjective point of view. He tells a story about a day that he told a silly joke in class, but he includes serious language about the event's meaning: "That day I reached a life-choice fork in the road."	The purpose, although the author is being funny, may be to express a serious opinion about choices in life.

Annotation in Action

Here are one reader's notes about how the author uses language to create mood in "What's So Funny, Mr. Scieszka?" As you read, note other instances of how the author uses language to create the story's mood.

> The voice flew across the room and nailed me to the back of my seat.
>
> "What's so funny, Mr. Scieszka?"
>
> The voice belonged to Sister Margaret Mary. And it had just flown across our fifth-grade religion class at St. Luke's Elementary School to find me in what I had thought was the safety of the back row.

Her voice "flew" and "nailed" him to his seat? That's a pretty tense and frightening sort of mood.

Expand Your Vocabulary

Put a check mark next to the vocabulary words that you feel comfortable using when speaking or writing.

apology	☐
history	☐
terror	☐

Turn to a partner and talk about the vocabulary words you already know. Then, write a few sentences about a funny incident you've heard about. As you read "What's So Funny, Mr. Scieszka?", use the definitions in the side column to learn the vocabulary words you don't already know.

Background

Jon Scieszka (b. 1954) grew up in Flint, Michigan, with five brothers who provided plenty of material for writing funny stories. Scieszka's *The Stinky Cheese Man and Other Fairly Stupid Tales* won a Caldecott Honor medal. In 2008, the Library of Congress appointed Scieszka the first Ambassador for Young People's Literature. "What's So Funny, Mr. Scieszka?" is from *Knucklehead*, a humorous memoir about his rambunctious childhood.

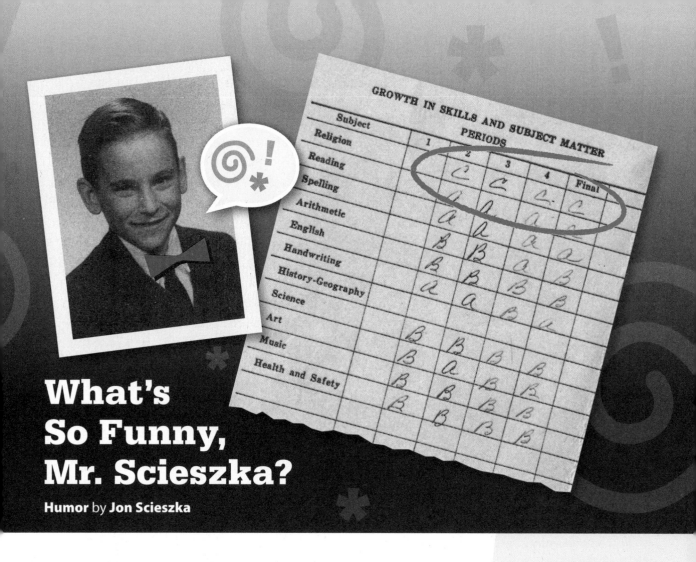

What's So Funny, Mr. Scieszka?

Humor by **Jon Scieszka**

The author remembers getting called out for laughing in elementary school.

1   The voice flew across the room and nailed me to the back of my seat.

2   "What's so funny, Mr. Scieszka?"

3   The voice belonged to Sister Margaret Mary.[1] And it had just flown across our fifth-grade religion class at St. Luke's Elementary School to find me in what I had thought was the safety of the back row.

4   "What's so funny?" I repeated, trying desperately to stop laughing.

5   I knew the correct answer to this question was, "Nothing, Sister."

6   "I'm sorry, Sister," was also a very good reply.

> **NOTICE & NOTE**
> As you read, use the side margins to make notes about the text.

ANALYZE AUTHOR'S USE OF LANGUAGE

Annotate: Reread paragraphs 1–3. Mark examples of descriptive words and imagery.

Infer: How does this language create the mood and voice of the story?

---

[1] **Sister Margaret Mary:** the nun teaching religion class; *Sister* is the form of address for a nun.

7   And nine times out of ten, ninety-nine times out of a hundred, I would have used one of those answers. But that day in fifth-grade religion class, something happened. That day I reached a life-choice fork in the road.[2]

8   My friend and back-row pal, Tim K. had just told me the funniest joke I had ever heard. The fact that he had told it while Sister Margaret Mary was droning on about our future place in heaven or hell only made it funnier.

9   Now I was called out.

10 I saw two life paths laid out clearly before me. Down the one path of the quick **apology** lay a good grade for religion class, a spot in heaven, maybe even sainthood if things worked out later in life. Down the other path lay the chance of a very big laugh . . . though mixed with punishment, maybe a note to my parents, quite possibly one mad God and forever in hell.

11 A good grade in religion class is always a good thing in Catholic school. I knew that. But I also knew this was a really funny joke. I was torn between going for the A and heaven, and going for the laugh with a chance of hell. Both were right in front of me.

---

apology

(ə-pŏl´ə-jē) *n*. An *apology* is an expression of regret or a request for forgiveness.

NOTICE & NOTE
EXTREME OR ABSOLUTE LANGUAGE

When you notice language that seems to exaggerate or overstate a case, you've found an **Extreme or Absolute Language** signpost.

Notice & Note: Read paragraphs 7–10. Mark instances of extreme language or exaggeration.

Infer: Why do you think the author uses extreme language and exaggeration?

---

[2] **fork in the road:** a metaphor referring to a moment in life when you have to make a big choice.

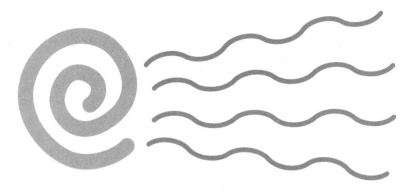

Don't forget to
Notice & Note as you
read the text.

12   So when Sister Margaret Mary asked her next question, "Would you like to share it with the rest of the class?" I chose my life's path.

13   "Well, there's this guy who wants to be a bell ringer,"[3] I begin. "But he doesn't have any arms."

14   Sister Margaret Mary's eyes pop open wider than I have ever seen them. The whole class turns to look at me and the train wreck about to happen. Even my pal Tim K. is shaking his head. Nobody in the **history** of St. Luke's Elementary School has ever chosen to "share it with the rest of the class." But I feel it. I have to do it. It is my path.

15   "The priest who is looking for a good bell ringer says, 'You can't ring the bells. You don't have any arms.' "

16   The faces of my fellow fifth-graders are looking a bit wavy and blurry. " 'I don't need arms,' says the bell-ringing guy. 'Watch this.' And he runs up the bell tower and starts bouncing his face off the bells and making beautiful music."

17   Half of the class laughs. I'm not sure if it's out of nervousness or pity. But it's a lot of laughs.

18   Sister Margaret Mary's eyes open impossibly wider.

19   Light floods the classroom. I can't really see anybody now. I can only feel the punch line building. I head toward the light.

20   "So the bell-ringing guy goes to finish his song with one last smack of his face, but this time he misses the bell and falls right out of the tower. He lands on the ground and is knocked out. A whole crowd gathers around him."

21   The whole fifth-grade religion class has gathered around me. It is a feeling of unbelievable power mixed with **terror** for a low-profile[4] fifth-grader like myself.

22   " 'Who is this guy?' the villagers ask."

23   I feel the whole world pause for just a single beat, like it always does before a good punch line.

24   " 'I don't know his name,' says the priest. 'But his face rings a bell.' "

history
(hĭs´tə-rē) *n. History* is a chronological record of events.

ANALYZE AUTHOR'S USE OF LANGUAGE

Annotate: Reread paragraphs 14–21. Mark descriptive words and imagery that create mood.

Infer: What do you think Scieszka is feeling as he tells the joke? What do you think Sister Margaret Mary and the class are feeling?

terror
(tĕr´ər) *n. Terror* is extreme fear of something.

---

[3] **bell ringer:** a person who rings the bells of a church or tower, usually by pulling on a rope.

[4] **low profile:** subdued or modest behavior to avoid attracting attention.

DETERMINE AUTHOR'S PURPOSE AND POINT OF VIEW

Annotate: Reread the last paragraph. Mark words or phrases that help identify the author's point of view.

Infer: What is the author's purpose in this story?

I don't remember the grade I got in fifth-grade religion class. But I do remember the laugh I got. It was huge. It was the whole class (except Sister Margaret Mary). It was out-of-control hysterical. It was glorious. And it set me on my lifelong path of answering that classic question, "What's so funny, Mr. Scieszka?"

?

ESSENTIAL QUESTION:

What are the ways you can make yourself heard?

Review your notes and add your thoughts to your Response Log.

TURN AND TALK

Get together with a partner and talk about the ending of the story. Did you find it funny? Why or why not?

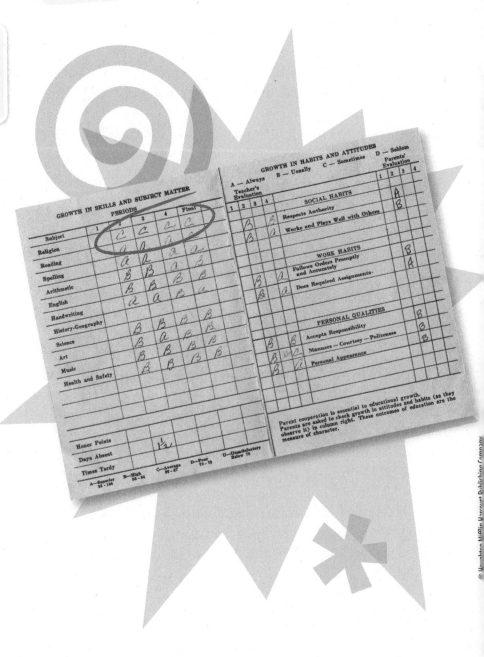

Assessment Practice

Answer these questions before moving on to the **Analyze the Text** section.

1. This question has two parts. First, answer **Part A**. Then, answer **Part B**.

   Part A

   What is the author's main purpose in writing this humorous narrative?

   Ⓐ to convince people to tell jokes

   Ⓑ to describe a life-changing moment in his life

   Ⓒ to describe what it's like to go to Catholic school

   Ⓓ to explain why he didn't get a good grade in religion class

   Part B

   Select the sentence that supports the answer in Part A.

   Ⓐ "That day I reached a life-choice fork in the road." (paragraph 7)

   Ⓑ "The whole class turns to look at me and the train wreck about to happen." (paragraph 14)

   Ⓒ "I can only feel the punch line building." (paragraph 19)

   Ⓓ "I don't remember the grade I got in fifth-grade religion class." (paragraph 25)

2. What can the reader infer about Mr. Scieszka's ability to tell jokes as a child?

   Ⓐ He was shy, and jokes helped him gain confidence.

   Ⓑ He enjoyed telling jokes, but he often messed up the punch line.

   Ⓒ Even as a child, he already knew how to get an audience laughing.

   Ⓓ Even as a child, he knew how to make humorous connections with adults, like Sister Margaret Mary.

   ☺Ed
   Test-Taking Strategies

Analyze the Text

Support your responses with evidence from the text.

(1) **IDENTIFY** Review paragraphs 10–24. How would you describe the author's style? What techniques does the author use to capture a reader's interest?

(2) **ANALYZE** One of the author's purposes in "What's So Funny, Mr. Scieszka?" is to entertain readers. What other possible purposes might the author have had? Support your ideas with evidence from the text.

(3) **INTERPRET** What does the figure of speech *train wreck* mean in paragraph 14? How do you know?

(4) **DRAW CONCLUSIONS** Is the author usually someone who seeks attention or who likes to perform? Cite evidence from the text to support your answer.

(5) **EXPLAIN** Find examples of **Extreme or Absolute Language** in "What's So Funny, Mr. Scieszka?" Explain how this language contributes to the mood and voice of the story.

EXAMPLES OF EXTREME OR ABSOLUTE LANGUAGE	CONTRIBUTION TO MOOD AND VOICE
$\longrightarrow$	
$\longrightarrow$	
$\longrightarrow$	

Choices

Here are some other ways to demonstrate your understanding of the ideas in this lesson.

Writing
↳ Analyze Author's Purpose and Point of View

Review your notes and annotations from the reading. Then, write a three- to four-paragraph analysis of Scieszka's purpose. What is his point of view? Why does he tell this story? Follow these steps:

- Include a clear central idea or thesis about the author's purpose.

- Use a logical structure and provide text evidence to support your ideas.

- Make sure that your pronouns clearly agree with their antecedents.

As you write and discuss, be sure to use the **Academic Vocabulary** words.

| appropriate |
| authority |
| consequence |
| element |
| justify |

Speaking & Listening
↳ Explain the Steps for Telling a Joke

In a small group, discuss how to deliver a silly joke to someone much younger than you.

- Select a joke that is appropriate for a younger audience.

- Outline the steps for telling the joke. Note what facial expressions and gestures to use, tone of voice, when to pause, and how often to make eye contact.

- Deliver your joke to the class, following the steps in your outline. After you tell the joke, explain the steps in your outline.

Social & Emotional Learning
↳ Watch That Mouth, Friend!

Sometimes, even if you've got your own Sister Margaret Mary glaring down at you, it can be terribly difficult *not* to say something. Get with a small group and discuss your ideas about when it's best to keep your mouth closed.

- First, list times that it's best to let your voice be heard, no matter what.

- Next, list times that it might be best to stay silent, and explain why.

- Then, discuss why it can be so hard to know when to speak up and when to stay silent.

- Finally, work together to create a poster summarizing your group's thoughts.

Expand Your Vocabulary

PRACTICE AND APPLY

Answer the questions to show your understanding of the vocabulary words. With a partner, discuss and write down an answer to each question. Then, work together to write a sentence for each vocabulary word.

| apology | history | terror |

1. Which vocabulary word goes with *fright?* Why?

2. Which vocabulary word goes with *the past?* Why?

3. Which vocabulary word goes with *regret?* Why?

Vocabulary Strategy
↳ **Word Origins**

A **root** is a word part that contains the core meaning of the word. For example, *tech* comes from a Greek root that can mean "art," "skill," or "craft." You can use the root to figure out that *technician* refers to someone who has a specific skill.

☺**Ed**

Interactive Vocabulary Lesson: Word Origins

PRACTICE AND APPLY

Using dictionaries and online resources, determine the origin and source of meaning for each vocabulary word. Then build related words, emphasizing the role of the Greek or Latin root.

WORD	ORIGIN/MEANING	ROOT	RELATED WORDS FROM SAME ROOT
apology	a thoughtful reply or response (as a defending speech in court)	from *apologiā* *apo-* (from) + *logos* (speech)	apologist apologize apologetic
history			
terror			

Watch Your Language!

Pronouns

A **pronoun** is a word used in place of a noun or another pronoun. The word or group of words that the pronoun refers to is its **antecedent**.

☺Ed

Interactive Grammar Lesson: Pronouns

There are different types of pronouns. **Personal pronouns** may replace nouns representing people or things. **Indefinite pronouns** refer to one or more persons or things not specifically mentioned, and they usually have no antecedents. **Intensive pronouns** place emphasis on a noun or another pronoun, and they often appear right after the noun or pronoun they are modifying.

PERSONAL	INDEFINITE	INTENSIVE
I, you, she, he, it, we, they, me, her, him, them, *etc.*	another, anybody, both, all, none, most, no one, *etc.*	myself, himself, herself, themselves, yourself, yourselves, *etc.*
Maria is tall; she is taller than I am.	No one is taking the bus today.	It took me all summer, but I painted the house myself.

Pronoun-Antecedent Agreement To make sure a pronoun agrees with its antecedent, ask yourself: Which noun or pronoun is this pronoun replacing? Decide which of the following sentences is correct.

> **The little girl fed the cat; she was kind to animals.**

> **The little girl fed the cat; they were kind to animals.**

The first sentence is correct. The noun being replaced—the antecedent—is *girl*. It is singular and feminine. The personal pronoun *she* agrees with the antecedent *girl* because it is singular and feminine.

PRACTICE AND APPLY

Write two humorous sentences using each type of pronoun listed above—personal, indefinite, and intensive. Don't use the same pronoun twice.

Collaborate & Compare

Compare Poems

You're about to read two poems describing the power of words and speech. As you read, notice the use of figurative language, and identify details that help you understand each poem's speaker and tone.

A

A Voice

Poem by **Pat Mora**
pages 48–51

B

Words Like Freedom

Poem by **Langston Hughes**
pages 52–53

After you have read both poems, you'll get a chance to compare and contrast your reading experience with listening to a performance. You'll follow these steps:

- Perform Live Readings

- Take Detailed Notes

- Compare and Contrast Experiences

- Share What You've Learned

A Voice

Poem by **Pat Mora**

Words Like Freedom

Poem by **Langston Hughes**

Engage Your Brain

Choose one or both activities to start connecting with the poems you are about to read.

A Voice

In the poem you are about to read, the speaker compares her aunt's voice to a peacock. How would you describe the voice of someone you know really well? Sketch an image or describe that person's voice.

The Power of Words

What do you think about when you hear the words *freedom* and *liberty*? Make a list of the connections you make with these words. How meaningful are they to you and the people you know? Share your list and thoughts with the class.

Analyze Figurative Language

Poets use **figurative language,** including similes, metaphors, and personification to express ideas in an imaginative way.

A **simile** compares two unlike things by using the word *like* or *as.* A **metaphor** compares two unlike things that have some qualities in common, but a metaphor does not use *like* or *as.*

The poem "A Voice" opens with a simile:

> **Even the <u>lights on the stage</u> unrelenting / as <u>the desert sun</u> couldn't hide the other / students . . .**

The simile compares the stage lights to a desert sun, emphasizing how unforgiving and severe the lights seem.

Personification is a type of figurative language in which an object, animal, or idea is given human qualities.

The poem "Words Like Freedom" contains personification:

> **On my heartstrings <u>freedom</u> <u>sings</u>**

Here, the poet gives the abstract idea of freedom the human ability to sing.

As you read "A Voice" and "Words Like Freedom," use a chart like the following to analyze each poet's use of figurative language.

Focus on Genre
↳**Poetry**

- uses sound devices, imagery, and figurative language, such as simile, metaphor, and personification, to express ideas and emotions

- includes rhyme or rhythm to emphasize the musical quality of language

- arranges words and lines in different ways to produce an effect

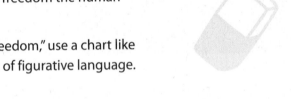

EXAMPLE	TYPE OF FIGURATIVE LANGUAGE	WHAT IS THE POET TELLING ME?
Their eyes were pinpricks	metaphor	Their stares were painful.

Make Inferences About Tone and Speaker

To make an **inference** about a literary work, use evidence from the text and your own knowledge to make a logical guess.

The **tone** of a work expresses the writer's attitude toward a subject, which influences a work's **mood.** Words such as *angry*, *playful*, or *mocking* describe different tones. In a poem, tone and mood are reflected by the **speaker,** the voice that "talks" to the reader.

To make inferences about speaker and tone, try the following:

- Identify the poem's topic.

- Note qualities of the poem's images, descriptions, and comparisons. Are they serious, silly, happy, or sad?

- Consider the speaker's feelings about the topic. Does the speaker seem happy, sad, proud, or angry about it?

Annotation in Action

In the model, you can see one reader's notes about the poet's use of figurative language in "A Voice." As you read, pause often to note and explain instances of figurative language.

> Even the lights on the stage unrelenting
> as the desert sun couldn't hide the other
> students, their eyes also unrelenting,

Interesting! The speaker compares stage lights to the desert sun. Why?

Background

Pat Mora (b. 1942) was born in El Paso, Texas, to a Mexican American family, and today she writes in English and in Spanish. In 1996, she founded a holiday called "El día de los niños / El día de los libros," or "Children's Day / Book Day."

Langston Hughes (1902–1967) gained fame after he met a famous poet in a restaurant where Hughes worked. Hughes left several poems at the poet's table, and the poet was impressed, introducing Hughes to a wider audience. Hughes became one of the most important voices of the Harlem Renaissance.

A Voice

Poem by **Pat Mora**

This poem explores the importance of speaking up.

MAKE INFERENCES ABOUT TONE AND SPEAKER

Annotate: In lines 1–8, mark the differences between the students who spoke English and the person in the poem referred to as "you."

Compare: What does this comparison tell you about the speaker of the poem and her subject, "you"?

1   Even the lights on the stage unrelenting[1]
    as the desert sun couldn't hide the other
    students, their eyes also unrelenting,
    students who spoke English every night

5   as they ate their meat, potatoes, gravy.
    Not you. In your house that smelled like
    rose powder, you spoke Spanish formal
    as your father, the judge without a courtroom

    in the country he floated to in the dark
10 on a flatbed truck. He walked slow
    as a hot river down the narrow hall
    of your house. You never dared to race past him,

---

[1] **unrelenting** (ŭn´rĭ-lĕn´tĭng): steady and persistent; continuing without stopping.

© Houghton Mifflin Harcourt Publishing Company • Image Credits: ©buildun/DigitalVision Vectors/Getty Images

to say, "Please move," in the language
you learned effortlessly, as you learned to run,
15 the language forbidden at home, though your mother
said you learned it to fight with the neighbors.

You liked winning with words. You liked
writing speeches about patriotism and democracy.
You liked all the faces looking at you, all those eyes.
20 "How did I do it?" you ask me now. "How did I do it

when my parents didn't understand?"
The family story says your voice is the voice
of an aunt in Mexico, spunky[2] as a peacock.
Family stories sing of what lives in the blood.

> **Ed**
> **Text in Focus Video**
> Learn more about the figurative language used in this poem.

---

[2] **spunky** (spŭng´kē): spirited, plucky; having energy and courage.

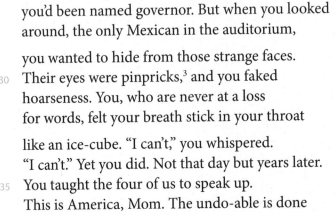

© Houghton Mifflin Harcourt Publishing Company • Image Credits: ©buildup/DigitalVision Vectors/Getty Images

 NOTICE & NOTE
MEMORY MOMENT

When you notice a speaker bringing up something from the past, you've found a **Memory Moment** signpost.

Notice & Note: In lines 25–29, mark the speaker's memory.

Infer: What does this memory help explain?

ANALYZE FIGURATIVE LANGUAGE

Annotate: Mark the figurative language in lines 30–34.

Interpret: What emotions are expressed by these comparisons?

25　You told me only once about the time you went
　　to the state capitol, your family proud as if
　　you'd been named governor. But when you looked
　　around, the only Mexican in the auditorium,

　　you wanted to hide from those strange faces.
30　Their eyes were pinpricks,[3] and you faked
　　hoarseness. You, who are never at a loss
　　for words, felt your breath stick in your throat

　　like an ice-cube. "I can't," you whispered.
　　"I can't." Yet you did. Not that day but years later.
35　You taught the four of us to speak up.
　　This is America, Mom. The undo-able is done

　　in the next generation.[4] Your breath moves
　　through the family like the wind
　　moves through the trees.

? ESSENTIAL QUESTION:
What are the ways you can make yourself heard?

Review your notes and add your thoughts to your Response Log.

TURN AND TALK

Get together with a partner and discuss this poem. How would you describe how the speaker feels about her mother?

---

[3] **pinpricks** (pǐn´prǐkz´): small wounds or punctures made by, or as if by, a pin.
[4] **generation** (jĕn´ə-rā´shən): people at the same stage of descent from a common ancestor; grandparents, parents, and children represent three different generations.

Assessment Practice

Answer these questions before moving on to the next poem.

1. Read the excerpt from the poem. Then, answer the question.

> But when you looked / around, the only Mexican in the auditorium, / you wanted to hide from those strange faces. / Their eyes were pinpricks, and you faked / hoarseness. (lines 27–31)

Based on this excerpt, what inference can you make about the speaker's mother?

(A) She did not like speaking in public.

(B) It was exciting for her to be in front of an audience.

(C) It was painful and frightening for her to feel different.

(D) She liked to speak Spanish only when talking to large groups.

2. This question has two parts. First, answer **Part A**. Then, answer **Part B**.

Part A

What is a theme or central idea of the poem?

(A) Learning a new language is difficult.

(B) People should memorize family stories.

(C) Family stories communicate a family's history.

(D) Family stories should be spoken only in native languages.

Part B

Select **two** excerpts from the poem that most clearly support the answer to Part A.

(A) "In your house that smelled like / rose powder, you spoke Spanish formal" (lines 6-7)

(B) "You liked winning with words." (line 17)

(C) "Family stories sing of what lives in the blood." (line 24)

(D) "The undo-able is done / in the next generation." (lines 36–37)

(E) "Your breath moves / through the family like the wind / moves through the trees." (lines 37–39)

☺️ **Ed**
Test-Taking Strategies

B

Words Like Freedom

Poem by **Langston Hughes**

There are words like *Freedom*
Sweet and wonderful to say.
On my heartstrings freedom sings
All day everyday.

5   There are words like *Liberty*
That almost make me cry.
If you had known what I know
You would know why.

?

ESSENTIAL QUESTION

What are the ways you can make yourself heard?

Review your notes and add your thoughts to your Response Log.

TURN AND TALK

Get together with a partner after you've read this poem. What do you think the speaker refers to when he says "If you had known what I know"?

Assessment Practice

Answer these questions before moving on to the **Analyze the Texts** section.

1. This question has two parts. First, answer **Part A**. Then, answer **Part B**.

   Part A

   What two words best describe the tone of the poem?

   (A) courageous and curious

   (B) angry and frustrated

   (C) happy and proud

   (D) joyful and sad

   Part B

   Select **two** lines that best support the answer in Part A.

   (A) "There are words like *Freedom*" (line 1)

   (B) "On my heartstrings freedom sings" (line 3)

   (C) "All day everyday." (line 4)

   (D) "That almost make me cry." (line 6)

   (E) "If you had known what I know" (line 7)

2. What perspective is shared by the speaker of "Words Like Freedom" and the speaker of "A Voice"?

   (A) Everyone shares similar experiences in life.

   (B) People long to be free and to feel accepted.

   (C) Once you have freedom, everything becomes easier.

   (D) It is important to write about what it is like to grow up in America.

Test-Taking Strategies

Analyze the Texts

Support your responses with evidence from the texts.

1. **INFER** Reread lines 7–14 of "A Voice," in which the speaker describes her grandfather. What is the simile in these lines? How can you use the meaning of the simile to make inferences about the relationship between the speaker's mother and her father?

NOTICE & NOTE
Review what you **noticed and noted** as you read the texts. Your annotations can help you answer these questions.

2. **INTERPRET** Reread lines 17–18 of "A Voice." What do the lines tell you about the speaker's view of her mother? What word would you use to describe the mood?

3. **ANALYZE** Identify the figurative language in line 3 of "Words Like Freedom." What effect do the words *freedom* and *liberty* have on the speaker? Why might they have this effect?

4. **ANALYZE** Describe how and why the tone changes through "Words Like Freedom."

5. **CONNECT** Reread lines 20–24 of "A Voice." How does the speaker's **Memory Moment** about the family story connect to lines 35–39?

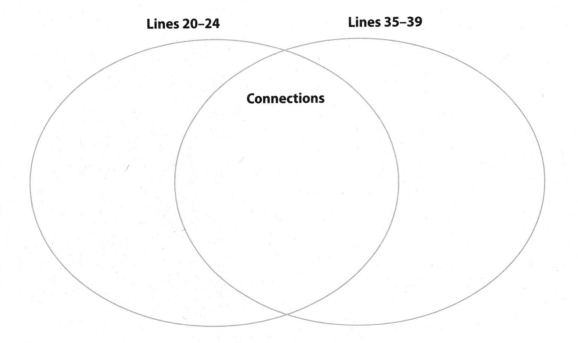

Lines 20–24   **Lines 35–39**

Connections

Choices

Here are some other ways to demonstrate your understanding of the ideas in this lesson.

Writing
↳Characterize the Speaker

Write a brief informative essay describing the speaker of one or both poems. Cite evidence to support your description.

- Review what you've learned about tone and speaker.

- Develop a clear central or controlling idea, or thesis statement.

- Make inferences about the speaker(s) based on textual evidence and your own experiences.

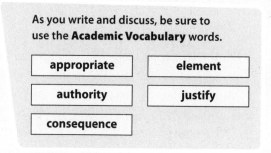

As you write and discuss, be sure to use the **Academic Vocabulary** words.

appropriate	element
authority	justify
consequence	

Research
↳Investigate the Harlem Renaissance

The Harlem Renaissance was a movement in the 1920s and 1930s centered in Harlem. African American poets, writers, artists, and musicians gathered there to create art and to press for civil rights.

Research three artists of the Harlem Renaissance. Write descriptions of the art they created, and explain each artist's message or messages.

Speaking & Listening
↳Discuss and Analyze Figurative Language

With a group, analyze figurative language in the poems.

- Review and share your notes and annotations on each poem.

- Identify each use of figurative language in "A Voice" and "Words Like Freedom."

- Identify what is being compared or given human characteristics, and analyze the effects.

- Explain what the figurative language suggests about each poem's speaker and ideas.

Compare Poems

When you watch a performance of, listen to a recording of, and read aloud the same poem, you may arrive at a new, deeper understanding of the work.

For the following task, you will experience different versions of "A Voice" and "Words Like Freedom"—and then compare and contrast your experiences. First, silently reread "A Voice" and "Words Like Freedom." Then, with your group, complete the chart for each poem.

ANALYZE YOUR READING EXPERIENCE				
	"I SEE . . ."	**"I HEAR . . ."**	**"I FEEL . . ."**	**IDEAS/ MESSAGES**
A Voice				
Words Like Freedom				

Analyze the Texts

Discuss these questions in your group.

1 **ANALYZE** Reread lines 1–5 of "A Voice." How does the image of the desert sun suggest meaning and tone?

2 **EVALUATE** Describe the importance of the human voice in "Words Like Freedom." Cite evidence from the text in your response.

3 **COMPARE** Read "Words Like Freedom" aloud, and compare the experience of reading the poem aloud with silently reading it.

4 **INFER** What themes, or messages, are conveyed by each poem? Cite evidence from the text and your analysis in your discussion.

Collaborate and Present

Poetry Reading

Now that you have analyzed the reading experience, it's time to examine the experience of a live presentation. Select members of your group to read each poem aloud. Follow these steps.

(1) PERFORM LIVE READINGS If you are one of the performers, imagine you are the poem's speaker. Take care not to rush through the performance. Instead, take cues from the poem's rhythms and wording to guide pacing. Use your voice, facial expressions, and relevant gestures to convey ideas and emotions.

(2) TAKE DETAILED NOTES If you are a non-performer, listen carefully and take detailed notes about the experience of each performance. What do you see, hear, feel, and understand about the poem as you observe the performance? How does it affect your understanding of the poem?

(3) COMPARE AND CONTRAST EXPERIENCES As a group, work together to complete the chart below. As you work, refer to the Analyze Your Reading Experience chart you completed earlier, as well as to your watching and listening notes.

READING EXPERIENCE	WATCHING/LISTENING EXPERIENCE	SIMILARITIES/ DIFFERENCES

(4) SHARE WHAT YOU'VE LEARNED When you have finished, share your group's observations with the class.

Collaborate & Compare

Compare and Evaluate Arguments

You're about to read two arguments about our love of selfies. As you read, focus on the reasons and evidence used by each author, and think about which points seem convincing and which do not.

MENTOR TEXT

A

Better Than Words:
Say It with a Selfie

Argument by Gloria Chang
pages 62–67

B

OMG, Not Another Selfie!

Argument by Shermakaye Bass
pages 68–73

After you've read both arguments, you'll learn more about cell phones and present what you've learned. You'll follow these steps:

- Develop Questions
- Gather Information
- Share What You Learn
- Prepare Your Presentation
- Practice and Share Your Presentation

Better Than Words: Say It with a Selfie

Argument by **Gloria Chang**

OMG, Not *Another* Selfie!

Argument by **Shermakaye Bass**

Engage Your Brain

Choose one or both activities to start connecting with the arguments you are about to read.

Pros and Cons

Think about why people take selfies. Write down two good reasons for taking a selfie; then, write down two bad reasons.

Selfie Swap!

Draw your own selfie. Then, gather with a group, and mix up your sketches so that no one knows who drew what. Finally, have a member of the group hold up the sketches one at a time, and work together to see whether you can identify who's who.

Trace and Evaluate an Argument

In arguments, writers establish a **claim,** an opinion or position about a topic, and then support that claim. To **trace and evaluate** an argument, analyze the reasoning and evidence.

Look for clear reasoning—reasoning that connects evidence to the claim, showing how the evidence supports it:

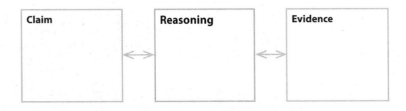

Claim ⟷ Reasoning ⟷ Evidence

In your analysis, note **rhetorical devices,** persuasive techniques used to convince readers. A few of these devices include:

- **parallelism**—repetition of similar grammatical structures
- **hyperbole**—exaggerations of the truth for effect
- **repetition**—repetition of words, phrases, or lines

Your analysis will help you draw conclusions about the writer's reliability, credibility, and bias, as well as help you determine an argument's strength.

Determine an Author's Purpose

How a writer presents and supports an argument depends on the intended audience. For example, some audiences may be persuaded by statistics, while others may respond more strongly to evidence that focuses on personal experience.

Recognizing how an author appeals to a specific audience can help you determine that author's **purpose,** or reason for writing, as well as **point of view,** or perspective.

To determine the author's purpose, ask: *Why does the author want to persuade this audience? What does this reveal about the author's purpose, the author's reason for writing?*

> **Focus on Genre**
> ↳ **Argument**
>
> - states a position or makes a claim about a topic
> - includes evidence— facts, statistics, quotations, examples, or personal experience—for support
> - appeals to logic *(logos)*, credibility *(ethos)*, and emotions *(pathos)*, using a variety of rhetorical devices to persuade readers

A **B** **Get Ready**

Annotation in Action

In the model, you can see one reader's notes about the author's use of hyperbole in "Better Than Words: Say It with a Selfie." As you read, note other ways that the writer tries to persuade readers.

> Everyone everywhere owns and uses a smart phone, and, with at least a million different social media platforms available, you'd have to live in a cave not to take part in and appreciate this form of communication.

"Everyone everywhere" and "at least a million"?

That's a LOT of exaggeration.

Expand Your Vocabulary

Put a check mark next to the vocabulary words that you feel comfortable using when speaking or writing.

saturated	☐
indulgent	☐
narcissist	☐
intimacy	☐
eternity	☐

Turn to a partner and talk about the vocabulary words you already know. Then, answer this question: *Are selfies good for you?* Use as many vocabulary words as you can in your answer. As you read the following arguments, use the definitions in the side column to learn the vocabulary words you don't already know.

Background

Though the word *selfie* entered our vocabulary as recently as the early 2000s, people of all ages now post pictures of meals, sporting events, vacations, outfits, and pets to social media.

With the rise in the popularity of selfies, people, including these two authors, Gloria Chang (top) and Shermakaye Bass (bottom), have developed strong opinions about them. As you read, consider your own opinions.

Better Than Words: Say It with a Selfie

Argument by **Gloria Chang**

Why are selfies so popular?

NOTICE & NOTE
As you read, use the side margins to make notes about the text.

TRACE AND EVALUATE AN ARGUMENT

Annotate: Mark the author's claim in paragraph 1.

Connect: What is the effect of the repetition in the claim?

---

narcissist
(när´sĭ-sĭst´) *n.* A self-obsessed person is a *narcissist*.

1 In our digital age, the selfie is the best way to express oneself, empower oneself, and even surround oneself with friends. Everyone everywhere owns and uses a smart phone, and, with at least a million different social media platforms available, you'd have to live in a cave not to take part in and appreciate this form of communication. Sure, there are critics who say that selfies are taken only by **narcissists** craving attention, but those critics really do live in caves—and they certainly have no friends.

Don't forget to **Notice & Note** as you read the text.

Selfies are about art and about life.

2 In a society **saturated,** stuffed to the brim, with social media, selfies are an artistic form of self-expression. Humans, since the beginning of time, have used self-portraits to express themselves. From ancient Egypt to the early Greeks to famous painters such as Rembrandt and van Gogh,[1] people have expressed themselves artistically through self-portraits.

3 The only difference between the artists of old and modern selfie-takers is that technology now allows anyone and everyone to be an artist, and a "self-portrait" is now called a "selfie." It's easy to create a "self-portrait" with a smart phone and its filters. You don't need to know how to draw or paint when you have a cell phone!

Selfies are about self discovery.

4 Selfies allow people to show different parts of themselves. Maybe it's their artistic side, maybe it's their silly side, or maybe it's to show an interest or passion, such as a love of certain foods. Whatever that side may be, by showing the selfie-taker's interests, selfies become more real than any boring photographer's work. Photographers don't care if they show who you truly are in those boring photos; they're interested only in making sure you are in focus. They don't know what you are like. How can they? None of us even know ourselves until we experiment with different views, explore different interests, and discover the things that influence us.

5 In this way, selfies—unlike past self-portraits that weren't taken on handy mobile devices—allow us an easier and better way to find out who we are. Just like trying on different clothes to find what works best for our personalities, taking selfies is an excellent way to test how we look and feel in certain outfits, poses, and places. Our own reactions to these pictures, along with the reactions of friends and strangers, help us figure out what works for us as unique individuals.

---

saturated

(săch´ə-rāt´əd) *adj.* Something that is *saturated* is filled until it is unable to hold or contain more.

NOTICE & NOTE
EXTREME OR ABSOLUTE LANGUAGE

When you notice language that exaggerates or overstates a case, you've found an **Extreme or Absolute Language** signpost.

Notice & Note: Mark extreme or absolute language used in paragraph 4.

Analyze: Why does the author use this language? Do you think it shows a bias? Explain.

---

[1] **Rembrandt and van Gogh:** Rembrandt van Rijn (rĕm´ brănt´ văn rīn´) (1606–1669) and Vincent van Gogh (văn gō´) (1853–1890) were Dutch painters known for their self-portraits.

Selfies are about self-expression.

6   Taking a selfie is like saying to the world, "this is me, right now, right here!" And a selfie does a better job of communicating this who, when, and where than spoken or written words can. After all, the human brain, as science shows, is hard-wired to recognize faces. In other words, we naturally recognize things and people visually. The effect is more immediate. The objects, people, and background in a selfie can show what a selfie-taker likes, hates, admires, or aspires to.[2] The taker's attitude will naturally affect his or her facial expressions. As they say, a picture is worth a thousand words.

7   Even museums and art galleries know that selfies can be an artistic means of self-expression. They encourage visitors to take selfies with works of art to share as art. One gallery in London even held an international selfie competition for people to submit the most artistic selfies.

8   But don't just trust the artists and everyone who takes selfies. Trust science. One scientist who studied the motivation for taking selfies found that we take selfies as a form of self-expression, not to be narcissistic. So don't assume that you're a narcissist; don't assume that it's all about you.

DETERMINE AN AUTHOR'S PURPOSE

Annotate: Mark evidence in paragraph 8 used to support the claim.

Draw Conclusions: Who do you think the writer's audience might be? What purpose is suggested by appealing to this audience?

---

[2] **aspires to:** strives toward, wants to be like.

Selfies are about self-confidence.

Don't forget to **Notice & Note** as you read the text.

9   Selfies empower us because they fulfill our need for validation from friends, family, and the rest of the world. If you don't believe it, try it. Science has shown, once again, that taking selfies makes you more confident, especially kids. We all know it. Some people are not allowed to say positive things about themselves because other people will say that they are full of themselves. But a selfie is a photo, so it's acceptable for those people to show what they're proud of.

10   Sure, people may get fixated on selfies being about physical things, but that doesn't mean the selfie has to be about how someone looks. Everything in a selfie can tell you about a person. For example, a selfie can show that someone may be the next celebrity chef because that person always posts selfies of himself or herself cooking and eating at different places in the world.

11   Selfies also empower us because they make us happy. In two studies, researchers discovered that people who took selfies and people who didn't both thought pictures taken by themselves (those are selfies!) made them more attractive and likable. If you like photos of yourself, taking them boosts your confidence. In another study, scientists had college students take selfies and share them. This made them more confident and comfortable with their smiling faces. It may not even be possible to take too many selfies.

12   In short, taking and sharing selfies boosts both self-confidence and self-esteem. People who say otherwise are like cavemen. They're probably people who've never taken selfies, so they probably don't have any self-confidence whatsoever. They probably hate people who do have self-confidence.

Selfies are about making connections.

13   The best part of taking selfies is that they're a great way to connect with friends or even make new friends. Since we all have smart phones and social media is everywhere and here to stay, we stay in touch with friends by taking selfies. It's like sending a letter in past times. But selfies are faster and are sent with a phone instead of a horse. By taking and sharing a selfie, you can share what you are thinking, feeling, or doing with your friends. Social media is made for others to give feedback so friends can tell you what they are thinking, feeling, or doing.

TRACE AND EVALUATE AN ARGUMENT

Annotate: Mark examples of name-calling and stereotyping (an oversimplification based on biased views) in paragraph 12.

Draw Conclusions: Are these examples of clear reasoning? Explain. How do these examples affect the writer's credibility and the argument's strength?

Annotate: Mark evidence the
writer uses to support her claim
in paragraph 14.

Analyze: To whom might
this type of evidence appeal?
How does the evidence and its
intended audience reveal the
author's purpose?

NOTICE & NOTE
WORD GAPS

When you notice vocabulary that
is unfamiliar—for example, a rare
or technical word—you've found
a **Word Gaps** signpost.

Notice & Note: Mark the words
in quotation marks and their
explanations in paragraph 16.

Draw Conclusions: Why would
the writer include these words?

They can do this by sending their favorite emoticons[3] or posting
comments or sending a selfie of themselves back to you.

14 Selfies are all about online social networks, and social
networks lead to better relationships. Teens especially say they
have more positive experiences than negative ones when using
social media. Selfies may have been around for only about a
dozen years, but they're today's way to connect with other people.

Selfies are about making memories.

15 Selfies also help us create special memories. By posing with
friends or at special events or places, we create snapshots that
we can look back on with fond feelings. Obviously, taking selfies
helps create memories because people naturally take selfies
when something is happening right there close to them. They
also take selfies when visiting places they like or think are funny
or strange or interesting.

16 There are even "relfies," where couples take photos of
themselves. Did you know that couples who take and show
more relfies are more satisfied with and committed to their
relationships than people who don't? And there are "groupies,"
selfies that include the selfie-taker and friends or family or even
celebrities. They make the best memories since they include
people we want to remember.

Selfies really are better than words.

17 Whether by ourselves, or with our favorite things, places, or
people, selfies obviously say it better than words.

18 They express who we are and what matters most to us.

?

ESSENTIAL QUESTION:
*What are the ways
you can make yourself
heard?*

Review your notes and
add your thoughts to your
Response Log.

TURN AND TALK

Partner up and discuss this argument. Do you agree with the
author's claim? Why or why not?

---

[3] **emoticons:** emojis, or icons used to express an emotion in text messages or online.

Assessment Practice

Answer these questions before moving on to the next selection.

1. Which of the following statements is the writer's primary claim?

    (A) People who take selfies are more confident than those who don't.

    (B) You don't need to be a good photographer to take good selfies.

    (C) Selfies are the most effective tool for expressing ourselves.

    (D) Everyone needs a cell phone to survive.

2. Select **two** quotations that illustrate the author's belief that selfies are effective ways for us to express ourselves.

    (A) "From ancient Egypt to the early Greeks to famous painters such as Rembrandt and van Gogh, people have expressed themselves artistically through self-portraits." (paragraph 2)

    (B) "Photographers don't care if they show who you truly are in those boring photos; they're interested only in making sure you are in focus." (paragraph 4)

    (C) "By taking and sharing a selfie, you can share what you are thinking, feeling, or doing with your friends." (paragraph 13)

    (D) "Selfies are all about online social networks, and social networks lead to better relationships." (paragraph 14)

    (E) "Teens especially say they have more positive experiences than negative ones when using social media." (paragraph 14)

☺ Ed
Test-Taking Strategies

NOTICE & NOTE
As you read, use the side margins to make notes about the text.

indulgent
(ĭn-dŭl´jənt) *adj.* *Indulgent* means excessively permissive. *Self-indulgent* is when one is overly permissive with oneself. The pun *selfie-indulgent* means that a person indulges in taking many selfies.

OMG, Not *Another* Selfie!

Argument by **Shermakaye Bass**

Do you think selfies are bad for you? This author does.

1   "Hey, guys—look! Look at me! Here I am on summer vacation at the beach. Oh, and here I am with my bestie at the soccer game! And check this out: Me doing duck face. And, oh, here I am with this morning's . . . pancakes."

2   Those lines might have been spoken by any one of us who's caught up in the selfie craze these days. Social media sites are filled with the selfie-**indulgent,** people who've given in to the desire to be seen. But do people really want to see what you had for breakfast? And do you really want to see how much "fun" other people are having? Especially if their lives seem so much cooler than yours?

3   The answer is probably "no," yet most of us do look at our friends' selfies, and most of us do post selfies ourselves. In fact, one search engine giant has found that almost 24 billion selfies were uploaded through its online photo application in 2015. That number doesn't even include those uploaded to popular social media sites.

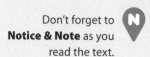

Don't forget to
Notice & Note as you
read the text.

4   We take selfies without even thinking. We strike a favorite pose. We click. We tap a couple of times. We share. This allows the rest of the world to see us as we'd like to be seen; however, it's not as we usually look in person.

5   One problem with this selfie mania is that once you've posted a picture of yourself you can't take it back, even if you decide that it's not quite your best shot. It's out there. For as many years as there are stars in the sky or grains of sand in the Sahara.[1] For all of **eternity.**

6   The only cure for a bad selfie is to take another one and post *it,* but you know what happens next: this reposting and re-snapping and reposting and re-snapping and reposting can go on and on and on, creating a cycle of frustration and wounded confidence! That cycle, inspired by the desire to control and "improve" our own images can lead to some serious psychological trouble, especially for young people. Selfies can be downright bad for us—bad for our self-esteem and body image, bad for our productivity and our schoolwork, even bad for our friendships. If we're too selfie obsessed, we start to look as foolishly self-centered and shallow as poor old Narcissus[2] as he sat there falling madly in love with his own reflection. And no one wants to sit in the school cafeteria with a known narcissist, anyway, right? After all, selfie takers are *so* in love with themselves!

7   The truth is that taking selfies may seem harmless and fun, but more and more research shows that this fad can confuse a person's sense of identity, and it may even fiddle with his or her sense of reality. We might start to think that we look better than we actually do. That wouldn't be so terrible. But we also might start comparing ourselves to others too often. We might start believing negative things like, "I'll never be as cute as my best friend," or "I'll never be as popular as the new kid," or "I'll never have that much fun. Ever."

8   On the other hand, we may continue to think that "if I can just make myself look good enough and cool enough, I'll get more 'likes,' which means I'll get more friends. Then people will like me for real. Then, one day I'll become a real celebrity." However, selfies can put distance between us and the people we care about; they can sometimes create jealousy and competition. That's certainly no way to become a star.

Close Read Screencast

Listen to a modeled close read of this text.

eternity
(ĭ-tûr´nĭ-tē) *n.* Eternity refers to infinite time; forever.

TRACE AND EVALUATE AN ARGUMENT

Annotate: Mark an overgeneralization or an exaggeration in paragraph 6 about people who take selfies.

Evaluate: How does the writer's use of this device affect her credibility? Explain.

---

[1] **grains of sand in the Sahara:** the Sahara is a desert in Africa that covers an area the size of the United States.
[2] **Narcissus** (när-sĭs´əs): in Greek mythology, Narcissus was a young man who fell in love with his own reflection in a pool of water.

9   Selfies can even have the opposite effect of what we'd hoped. Recent studies show that the selfie process not only has become oddly addictive and dangerous, but it can even set up the selfie-taker for ridicule. Some people will spend hours taking photos of themselves, trying for that perfect shot, and still wind up disappointed. Their thinking is that if they can just find the right "capture," they'll be popular, pretty—a somebody.

10   Of course, this is not true. Therefore, when we take certain actions (posting selfie after selfie) expecting certain results (fame and friendship) and then don't get those results, we get hurt feelings instead. We feel rejected, as if we don't matter. And that's a sure-fire formula for low self-esteem: "I posted this picture of myself and nobody has liked it," we think, "so I must be a nobody."

N NOTICE & NOTE
QUOTED WORDS

When you notice the author citing other people to provide support for a point, you've found a **Quoted Words** signpost.

Notice & Note: In paragraph 11, mark the quotation used to support a point.

Evaluate: Why was this person quoted and what did this add to the argument?

11   "One of the reasons kids take selfies is to post those pictures online. And the purpose of posting online often is to get 'likes,'" affirms author and former teacher Katie Schumacher, who launched the "Don't Press Send Campaign" in 2013. "If you post something and get a lot of 'likes,' it reinforces the feeling of importance and the sense of approval from others," Mrs. Schumacher says in a 2016 *ParentCo* story, "The Dangers of the Selfie and How You Can Help Your Kids."

Don't forget to **Notice & Note** as you read the text.

12   "The 'like' is the reward. But if you don't get enough 'likes,' you will keep trying to get a better picture from a different angle or with someone more popular," Mrs. Schumacher says.

13   On top of hunting for "likes," young people often take selfies hoping to impress or catch the attention of someone in particular. Maybe it's someone they have a crush on or someone who's bullied them. Maybe they want that person to have a better opinion of them. If that someone doesn't notice the post or makes a negative comment, then the selfie-taker can feel worse than if he or she had never posted at all!

14   Dr. Allison Chase, a psychologist and behavior specialist in Austin, Texas, also has weighed in. "This is particularly challenging for kids and teens, as they are trying to figure out who they are and what their identity is." In that 2016 *ParentCo* article, Dr. Chase warns about getting caught in the trap of worrying too much about appearances and approval.

15   She warns against believing that posting and sharing and liking creates actual friendship and **intimacy**. As Dr. Chase says, we "create the illusion of feeling more connected and more 'liked' in a way that is controllable and oftentimes, staged. The end result is a competitive environment with increased self-focus, less true connection and, more often than not, increased self-criticism."

16   That, as you now know, can lead to more selfie sessions and even deeper disappointment. We begin to think that if we could only catch that perfect angle, or frame the picture to disguise our braces or acne or big nose, we'd be more popular. But, seeing all these selfies of cool kids in cool places with cool parents and friends, we wonder, "How can I possibly compete?"

17   Still, all dangers aside, the selfie has grown to be as much a part of our culture as the Declaration of Independence or our Constitution.[3] And the person who invented the selfie stick—Wayne Fromm, who patented a version in 2005—is probably pretty rich by now. But believe it or not, the term "selfie" wasn't even used until 2002, when the word first entered our vocabulary, according to Merriam-Webster's Dictionary. Now, more than 15 years later, we've turned it into a verb ("I'm going to selfie on my new kick-scooter!"). And in 2013, a national news agency reported that the Oxford Dictionaries had chosen "selfie" as its Word of the Year, claiming that the use of the word had grown by 17,000 percent between 2012 and 2013!

DETERMINE AN AUTHOR'S PURPOSE

Annotate: Mark the quoted words and source in paragraph 14.

Draw Conclusions: How does this information help you determine the author's purpose?

intimacy
(ĭn′tə-mə-sē) *n. Intimacy* means close friendship and familiarity.

---

[3] **Declaration of Independence or our Constitution:** foundational documents of the United States.

Annotate: In paragraph 19, mark the repeated phrases.

Respond: What effect does the writer achieve by repeating these phrases?

18 Wow.

19 Don't let all the hoopla fool you, though. The reality—the "real" reality—is that spending too much time taking our own pictures or focusing on how we look or spending too much time on other people's selfies can be more harmful than helpful to our tender egos. Selfies are carefully posed and selected images that present us at our best (we think). They're images that literally put our best face forward (we think!). But that's not actually so.

20 Selfies don't represent reality, and they certainly don't represent who we truly are.

?

ESSENTIAL QUESTION

What are the ways you can make yourself heard?

Review your notes and add your thoughts to your Response Log.

TURN AND TALK

Get together with a partner and discuss the argument you just read. What do you think? Are selfies really bad for you? Why or why not?

Assessment Practice

Answer these questions before moving on to the **Analyze the Texts** section.

1. Read the excerpt from the argument. Then, answer the question.

> Therefore, when we take certain actions (posting selfie after selfie) expecting certain results (fame and friendship) and then don't get those results, we get hurt feelings instead. (paragraph 10)

Which of the following statements reflects the writer's position in the excerpt?

(A) Taking and sharing selfies can help develop friendships.

(B) If you take selfies, you won't think about your self-esteem.

(C) Taking too many selfies can be bad for a person's self-esteem.

(D) People who take many selfies become skilled photographers.

2. This question has two parts. First, answer **Part A**. Then, answer **Part B**.

Part A

What perspective is shared by the author of "Better Than Words: Say It with a Selfie" and the author of "OMG, Not *Another* Selfie!"?

(A) Selfies make the best use of cell phones.

(B) Adults who take selfies have high self-esteem.

(C) Taking and sharing selfies is a significant social activity.

(D) Too many people take selfies and share them on social media.

Part B

Choose a quotation from "OMG, Not *Another* Selfie!" that supports the answer in Part A.

(A) "We take selfies without even thinking." (paragraph 4)

(B) "Maybe they want that person to have a better opinion of them." (paragraph 13)

(C) "Don't let all the hoopla fool you, though." (paragraph 19)

(D) "... the selfie has grown to be as much a part of our culture as the Declaration of Independence or our Constitution." (paragraph 17)

Test-Taking Strategies

Analyze the Texts

Support your responses with evidence from the texts.

1. **EVALUATE** Find an instance of overgeneralization, a generalization that is too broad, in either argument and evaluate its impact. Does the use of an overgeneralization make the argument stronger? Explain.

2. **CRITIQUE** In "OMG, Not *Another* Selfie!," review paragraphs 1–2. What is the writer's attitude toward the group of people she is describing? How does the writer's perspective affect her credibility in this instance?

TYPE OF PEOPLE BEING DESCRIBED	WRITER'S ATTITUDE TOWARD THEM

3. **COMPARE** Reread paragraph 11 in "Better Than Words: Say It with a Selfie" and paragraph 15 in "OMG, Not *Another* Selfie!" Both writers use experts to back up their claims. What **Quoted Words** does each writer use to support her argument? Explain which writer's evidence you think is more persuasive and credible and why.

4. **EVALUATE** Review paragraph 13 in "Better Than Words: Say It with a Selfie." What is the writer's claim? Is the reasoning clear? Explain. Cite evidence from the text to support your answer.

5. **ANALYZE** Find and then list an example of **Extreme or Absolute Language** in either argument. Why do you think the writer chose these words?

6. **IDENTIFY** What, if any, **Word Gaps** did you fill that helped you better understand and evaluate either of the authors' arguments?

Choices

Here are some other ways to demonstrate your understanding of the ideas in this lesson.

Writing
↳ Compose an Argument

Take a position—pro or con—about whether the use of cell phones should be permitted in movie theaters or at the dinner table, and write a three- to four-paragraph argument.

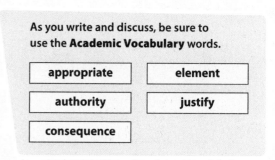

As you write and discuss, be sure to use the **Academic Vocabulary** words.

appropriate	element
authority	justify
consequence	

- Use a formal style and vocabulary appropriate to your audience.

- Provide evidence, use sound reasoning, and identify and address at least one objection to your claim.

- State a conclusion that follows from your argument.

- Check to ensure that you have correctly used commonly confused words.

Media
↳ Put That Phone Away, Please!

With a partner, produce a video Public Service Announcement or poster to help people who feel that they're spending too much time on their phones. Discuss ways to encourage a change in behavior. Then, create your PSA or poster. Include—

- a creative title that hints at your purpose and attracts your audience

- a clear statement that describes why the issue is of concern

- visuals and text or audio to support your ideas

Speaking and Listening
↳ Create and Present "The Perfect Selfie"

In a small group, discuss how to explain the "perfect selfie" to someone who has never taken one and doesn't want to. Identify the qualities that make a perfect selfie. Then, write a short speech explaining the perfect selfie.

- Anticipate your audience's opposing viewpoints and identify evidence to help overcome your audience's objections.

- Listen closely and respectfully to gain information from all speakers in your group.

Expand Your Vocabulary

PRACTICE AND APPLY

To show your understanding of the vocabulary words, choose the better answer to each question.

1. Which of the following is an example of **indulgent?**

   a. eating three desserts   **b.** eating one dessert

2. Which of these is more likely to be **saturated?**

   a. a sponge   **b.** a waterproof jacket

3. Which of the following is the better example of **intimacy?**

   a. a close friendship   **b.** a new acquaintance

4. Which of the following is an example of a **narcissist?**

   a. someone who loves himself   **b.** someone who loves only flowers

5. Which of the following is most similar to **eternity?**

   a. the future   **b.** forever

Vocabulary Strategy
↳ Context Clues

Interactive Vocabulary Lesson: Context Clues

One way to figure out an unfamiliar word's meaning is to use **context clues,** or hints found in the surrounding text. Here is an example:

> **There are critics who say that selfies are taken only by narcissists craving attention.**

To figure out the meaning of *narcissists,* note the words *craving attention* that appear after the unfamiliar word. These words hint that narcissists are people who crave attention.

PRACTICE AND APPLY

Find an unfamiliar word in each of the texts. Use clues to help you determine each word's meaning.

Watch Your Language!

Spell Commonly Confused Words Correctly

Many common English words, such as *its* and *it's,* are spelled similarly but have different meanings. Remember that *it's* is the contraction of "it is" or "it has," and the word *its* is the possessive form of the pronoun *it.* Other commonly confused words include *affect/effect,* and *there/their/they're.* Study how these words are used correctly in the selections.

☺**Ed**

**Interactive Grammar
Lesson: A Glossary of Usage**

> **The effect is more immediate.** (noun)
>
> **The taker's attitude will naturally affect his or her facial expressions.** (verb)
>
> **People naturally take selfies when something is happening right there close to them.** (adverb describing location)
>
> **This made them more confident and comfortable with their smiling faces.** (adjective, possessive form of *they*)
>
> **They're probably people who've never taken selfies.** (contraction of "they are")

PRACTICE AND APPLY

Choose the word that correctly completes each sentence.

1. My mom comes in to say goodnight when (its/it's) bedtime.

2. Jerome decided not to use the black-and-white (affect/effect) on his photograph.

3. (There/Their/They're) all obsessed with playing the latest computer game.

4. What time will you be (there/their/they're)?

5. How much you study may (affect/effect) your grade on the test.

Compare and Evaluate Arguments

To **compare and evaluate** arguments on the same topic, **trace and evaluate** each argument, analyzing how effective it is. Determine each argument's claim. Then, examine the strength of the evidence. Does it effectively support the claim? Finally, identify any instances of flawed reasoning. How sound is the argument's logic?

As a group, complete a chart like the one below. Ask questions to clarify group members' positions, and notice points on which you agree and disagree. Then, reach agreement about which text presents its argument more effectively.

	BETTER THAN WORDS: SAY IT WITH A SELFIE	**OMG, NOT *ANOTHER* SELFIE!**
Claim		
Evidence and Support		
Sources		
Flaws in the Argument		

Analyze the Texts

Discuss these questions in your group.

1. **COMPARE** Do you think the two writers are addressing the same audience or share the same perspective? How do you know?

2. **COMPARE** Compare the way the authors conclude their arguments. How are their approaches similar or different?

3. **EVALUATE** How does each writer introduce the topic and state her argument's primary claim? How effective is each approach?

4. **CRITIQUE** Which argument provides the strongest evidence to support its claim?

Collaborate and Research

How have cell phones changed since they were first invented? With your group, briefly discuss how cell phones have changed since you—or your parents or grandparents—first began using them. Then, research developments and advances in cell phone technology.

(1) DEVELOP QUESTIONS What would you like to know about the history of cell phones? As a group, brainstorm questions you would like to research. Then, decide who in your group is going to research which questions.

(2) GATHER INFORMATION As you research, make sure your sources are reliable and credible. Take notes from two or more sources, paraphrasing and summarizing key information to avoid plagiarism (the unauthorized use of someone else's words), and keep track of your sources. Cite those sources, following the format your teacher prefers.

(3) SHARE WHAT YOU LEARN As a group, discuss your research. Listen closely to what others say, ask questions to request and clarify information, and build on the ideas of others as you examine the history of cell phones. Use your research notes to back up your ideas with text evidence.

(4) PREPARE YOUR PRESENTATION Use the information you gathered with your group to create an informational presentation that describes major events in the history of the cell phone. Consider using a sequence chart like the one below to help organize important events in the development of the cell phone.

History of the Cell Phone

(5) PRACTICE AND SHARE YOUR PRESENTATION Decide who in your group will be responsible for sharing the different parts of your presentation with the class. Make sure all members participate. Practice your presentation and identify areas that need improvement. Finally, deliver your presentation to the class. As you present, make sure to make eye contact with the class, speak at a comfortable rate, enunciate clearly, and use natural gestures.

Reader's Choice

Continue your exploration of the Essential Question by doing some independent reading on discovering your voice. Read the titles and descriptions shown. Then mark the texts that interest you.

ESSENTIAL QUESTION:
What are the ways you can make yourself heard?

Short Reads Available on Ed

These texts are available in your ebook. Choose one to read and rate. Then defend your rating to the class.

I Was a Skinny Tomboy Kid
Poem by **Alma Luz Villanueva**

As a tomboy grows up, her self-perception shifts.

Rate It

Words are Birds
Poem by **Francisco X. Alarcón**

A poet imagines that words have the qualities and characteristics of birds.

Rate It

Eleven
Short Story by **Sandra Cisneros**

Can you be eleven but still feel ten, eight, or even two years old?

Rate It

On Dragonwings
Short Story by **Lucy D. Ford**

If you saw dragons in the night sky, would your life change?

Rate It

Carved on the Walls
Informational Text by **Judy Yung**

A discovery on the walls of an immigration detainment center reveals a painful history.

Rate It

Long Reads

Here are three recommended books that connect to this unit topic. For additional options, ask your teacher, school librarian, or peers. Which titles spark your interest?

The Giver

Novel by **Lois Lowry**

Jonas must decide whether he should comply with his community's rules, no matter how horrible they may be, or undertake a plan to break those rules and change everything.

Beethoven in Paradise

Novel by **Barbara O'Connor**

Martin is a musical genius, but his father doesn't support him. Will Martin abandon his talents to please his father? Or will he finally stand up for himself?

Brown Girl Dreaming

Memoir in Verse by **Jacqueline Woodson**

A child searches for her place—and her own voice—in the world as she grows up in the 1960s and 1970s.

Extension
↳Connect & Create

MEDIA TROLL? Create a series of social media posts to convince followers either to read or to skip one of the Reader's Choice texts. First, list what you like and dislike about the text. Then, decide if you would recommend it to others. Finally, craft posts to support your opinion. State at least one specific piece of evidence to support the idea expressed in each post.

IN-DEPTH INTERVIEW Work with a partner to draft questions that a reporter might ask to learn more about someone. Then, select a person or character from one of the texts, and write answers that this character or person would be likely to give.

- Create revealing and difficult questions, such as "What were your greatest struggles? Why did you decide to . . . ?"

- Base answers on your detailed knowledge of the traits, attitudes, and behaviors of the character or person.

 NOTICE & NOTE

- Pick one of the texts and annotate the Notice & Note signposts you find.

- Then, use the **Notice & Note Writing Frames** to help you write about the significance of the signposts.

- Compare your findings with those of other students who read the same text.

 Ed

Notice & Note Writing Frames

Write an Argument

Writing Prompt

Your local library is hosting an essay contest about the ways people express themselves. Community members will judge the essays. Write an argumentative essay in which you select your favorite mode of self-expression (such as music or comedy) and argue why that medium is effective. Include graphics or images to support your ideas.

Manage your time carefully so that you can

- review the texts in the unit;
- plan your essay;
- write your essay; and
- revise and edit your essay.

Be sure to

- clearly state the claim of your argument in the introduction;
- use logical reasoning and provide relevant evidence;
- use a formal style;
- use and cite evidence from multiple credible sources; and
- conclude by effectively summarizing your claim.

> ### Review the
> ### Mentor Text
>
> For an example of a strong argument you can use as a mentor text and source for your essay, review:
>
> - **"OMG, Not _Another_ Selfie!"** (pages 68–73)
>
> Review your notes and annotations about this text carefully. Think about the techniques the author uses to make the argument convincing.

Consider Your Sources

Review the list of texts in the unit and choose at least three that you may want to use as support for your argument.

As you review potential sources, consult the notes you made on your **Response Log** and make additional notes about any ideas that might be useful as you write. Include titles and page numbers so that you can easily find information later.

UNIT 1 SOURCES

- [ ] from **Brown Girl Dreaming**
- [ ] from **Selfie**
- [ ] **What's So Funny, Mr. Scieszka?**
- [ ] **A Voice**
- [ ] **Words Like Freedom**
- [ ] **Better Than Words: Say It with a Selfie**
- [ ] **OMG, Not _Another_ Selfie!**

Analyze the Prompt

Analyze the prompt to make sure you understand what you are required to do.

Mark the part of the sentence in the prompt that identifies the topic of your argument. Rephrase the topic in your own words.

Next, look for words that indicate the purpose and audience for your essay, and write a sentence describing each.

Find a Purpose

Three common purposes of an argument are

- to **persuade** others to see the validity of your position
- to **defend** or **explain** your position
- to **convince** your audience to agree with your position

What is my topic?

What is my purpose?

Who is my audience?

Review the Rubric

Your argument will be scored using a rubric. As you write, focus on the characteristics described in the chart. You will learn more about these characteristics as you work through the lesson.

PURPOSE, FOCUS, AND ORGANIZATION	EVIDENCE AND ELABORATION	CONVENTIONS OF STANDARD ENGLISH
The response includes: • A strongly maintained claim • Effective responses to opposing claims • A variety of transitions to connect ideas • Logical progression of ideas • Appropriate style and tone	The response includes: • Relevant evidence • Precise references to sources • Effective use of elaboration • Clear and effective expression of ideas • Appropriate use of academic and domain-specific vocabulary • Varied sentence structure	The response may include the following: • Some minor errors in usage but no patterns of errors • Correct use of punctuation, capitalization, sentence formation, and spelling • Command of basic conventions

1 PLAN YOUR ARGUMENT

Develop a Claim

In an argument, the **claim** is the writer's position on an issue. Determine your favorite mode of self-expression and think about why it's effective. Then, write a claim that states why the mode you have identified is effective.

State Your Claim

A **strong claim** has a single, clearly stated focus. Be specific and direct.

My favorite mode of self-expression:	
My claim:	

Identify Support

To build a strong argument, provide solid support for your claim. Support includes reasons plus evidence and elaboration.

- **Reasons** explain why you hold a particular position.

- **Evidence** and **elaboration,** such as facts, examples, statistics, or expert opinions, support your reasons.

Use the chart below to outline your support. Refer to notes you took as you read. Record page numbers for information you're citing.

Reason:	Evidence:	Source:
Reason:	Evidence:	Source:
Reason:	Evidence:	Source:

Incorporate Graphics and Images

Look for ways to use text features, such as **headings,** as well as **images** and **graphics,** to strengthen your argument. Make sure anything you use relates directly to your argument without distraction. In the chart below, identify graphics or images you might use.

😊 **Ed**

Help with Planning

Consult **Interactive Writing Lesson: Writing Arguments**

Graphic/Image and Source:	Notes:
Graphic/Image and Source:	Notes:
Graphic/Image and Source:	Notes:

Organize Ideas

Organize your material in a way that will help you draft your argument. Keep in mind that a well-written argument demonstrates **coherence.** Coherent writing has a logical progression of ideas. Transitional words and phrases help readers understand how ideas relate to one another.

Organize for Impact

Organize ideas logically to persuade readers to agree with you.

- Use a variety of transitions between ideas to make your argument flow smoothly for readers.
- Order your reasons from strongest to least strong or from least strong to strongest.

INTRODUCTION	• Clearly state your claim. • Grab readers' attention with an interesting question, quotation, image, or graphic.
BODY PARAGRAPHS	• Present reasons and evidence to support your claim, devoting a paragraph to each main idea. • Make clear why you have included each image or graphic.
CONCLUSION	• Restate your claim and its significance. • Leave readers with something to think about.

2 DEVELOP A DRAFT

Now it is time to draft your essay. Seeing how the experts do it is one way to develop your own writing skills. Read about the techniques that a professional writer uses to craft an argument.

Ed

Drafting Online

Check your assignment list for a writing task from your teacher.

Use a Formal Style

EXAMINE THE MENTOR TEXT

Notice how the author of "OMG, Not *Another* Selfie!" uses a formal style as she makes her argument.

OMG, Not *Another* Selfie!

The author's **reference** to a Greek myth illustrates a point.

> If we're too selfie obsessed, we start to look as foolishly self-centered and shallow as poor old Narcissus as he sat there falling madly in love with his own reflection.
>
> ***
>
> Therefore, when we take certain actions (posting selfie after selfie) expecting certain results (fame and friendship) and then don't get those results, we get hurt feelings instead.

Therefore is a **formal transition.** The author then makes her point with the help of parenthetical expressions.

APPLY TO YOUR DRAFT

Complete these sentence frames to practice using a formal style. Then, apply this technique to other parts of your draft argument.

Among the numerous forms of self-expression, the most effective one is _____

_____

While all forms of self-expression are valid, _____ is the most

_____

Try This Suggestion

Ask yourself these questions:

- How would I state my claim if I were talking to a friend?

- How would I state my claim if I were talking to the principal?

To write using a formal style, write as if you are talking to the principal.

Provide Clear Reasons

EXAMINE THE MENTOR TEXT

In "OMG, Not *Another* Selfie!" the author explains why the selfie trend can be problematic.

The author uses **clear and direct language** to provide a reason to support her claim.

> One problem with this selfie mania is that once you've posted a picture of yourself you can't take it back, even if you decide that it's not quite your best shot.

She **emphasizes** and **elaborates** on the problem.

Try These Suggestions

Here are some different ways to state a reason clearly and provide support.

- It is an ideal form of expression because . . .
- Another reason that I value this form of self-expression is . . .

APPLY TO YOUR DRAFT

Look back at the reasons and evidence you jotted down earlier. Practice writing sentences that clearly state each reason you have chosen to support your claim.

CLEAR REASON #1 — Practice Sentence:

CLEAR REASON #2 — Practice Sentence:

CLEAR REASON #3 — Practice Sentence:

CLEAR REASON #4 — Practice Sentence:

3 REVISE YOUR ARGUMENT

Even experienced writers recognize the importance of revision. Review your argument and consider how you can improve it. Use the guide below to help you revise your essay.

Help with Revision

Find a **Peer Review Guide** and **Student Models** online.

REVISION GUIDE		
ASK YOURSELF	**PROVE IT**	**REVISE IT**
Claim Does my introduction contain a clear claim?	**Underline** your claim.	**Add** or **revise** your claim to clarify or strengthen the statement of your position.
Organization Are your reasons organized in a logical order that helps you drive your point home?	**Highlight** each of your reasons. Then number them in order of importance.	**Rearrange** paragraphs to strengthen the impact of your message.
Style Do I use a formal style throughout the essay?	**Underline** formal language. **Circle** informal language, such as slang.	**Replace** any informal language.
Support Are the graphics or images I included directly related to my reasons and evidence?	**Underline** sentences or phrases that explain the graphics or images.	**Strengthen** connections between graphics and images and the text that explains them.
Sources Do I effectively use multiple texts in my support?	**Put a check mark** (✓) next to each source reference.	**Add** source references and/or **clarify** how your sources support your claim.
Conclusion Does my conclusion follow from and support my argument?	**Highlight** the parts of the conclusion that directly reflect your claim and reasons.	**Add** or **revise** the conclusion to make sure it flows logically from your argument.

APPLY TO YOUR DRAFT

Consider the following as you look for opportunities to improve your writing.

- Make sure that your claim is clear and direct.
- Make sure that each reason is logical and that you support it adequately.
- Read your draft aloud to make sure the style sounds formal throughout.

Peer Review in Action

Once you have finished revising your argument, you will exchange papers with a partner in a peer review. During a peer review, you will give suggestions to improve your partner's draft.

Read the first few sentences from a student's draft and examine the comments made by his peer reviewer.

First Draft

Discovering Identity
by LaShon Walker, Riverside Middle School

Painting a portrait is the most effective means of self-expression. This lets the artist include a variety of interests, which can tell us a lot about him or her.

> Do you mean a self-portrait? Or just anybody's portrait? Can you be more specific?

> The word "this" is vague. What does it refer to? Also, can you replace the word "us" with formal language?

Now read the revised sentences below. Notice how the writer has improved the draft by making revisions based on the peer reviewer's comments.

Revision

A self-portrait—a traditional form of art—is the most effective means of self-expression. In a self-portrait, an artist can incorporate objects, colors, scenery, or just about anything that expresses his or her identity. These details give the viewer an intimate insight into who the artist happens to be.

> What an improvement! You've clarified your position.

> You removed the vague pronoun and included specific examples of the "interests." The language is formal, but not stiff. Nice work!

APPLY TO YOUR DRAFT

During your peer review, give each other specific suggestions for how you could make your arguments more effective. Use your revision guide to help.

When receiving feedback from your partner, listen attentively and ask questions to make sure you fully understand the revision suggestions.

4 EDIT YOUR ARGUMENT

Edit your final draft to to correct any misspellings, errors in usage, or grammatical errors.

Ed

Interactive Grammar Lesson: Pronouns

Watch Your Language!

USE PRONOUNS

A **pronoun** replaces a noun or another pronoun. The word that a pronoun refers to is its **antecedent.** Pronouns should always agree in number with their antecedents. In the example, the pronoun *they* replaces the noun *selfies*.

> Since selfies are so popular, they are the topic of much discussion.

Avoid using **vague** pronouns, or pronouns with unclear antecedents. Notice the vague pronoun in the second sentence of this example.

> The invention of the selfie stick has increased the selfies on social media. It causes people to waste time.

Here, the second sentence has been rewritten for clarity:

> This invention causes people to waste time.

APPLY TO YOUR DRAFT

Apply what you've learned to your own work.

1. **Read your paper** and circle pronouns, checking to ensure that their antecedents are clear.

2. **Exchange drafts** with a peer and review for pronouns.

Types of Pronouns

Personal pronouns express gender and number: *I, you, he, she, it, we, they, them.*

Indefinite pronouns refer to one or more people or things and usually have no antecedents: *no one, anybody, some, most, none.*

Intensive pronouns include -*self* or -*selves*, and they refer to the immediately preceding noun or pronoun: *myself, yourself, himself, ourselves.*

Ways to Share

- **Create a multimedia presentation** to share your ideas.

- **Publish a blog** for your classmates. Invite readers to weigh in on the topic.

- **Make a poster** that conveys your position.

- **Collaborate** with classmates and **record a podcast.**

5 PUBLISH YOUR ARGUMENT

Share It!

The prompt asks you to provide your argument in the format of an essay for entry in a contest. You may also use your essay as inspiration for other projects.

Reflect & Extend

Here are some other ways to show your understanding of the ideas in Unit 1.

Reflect on the Essential Question

(?)

What are the ways you can make yourself heard?

Has your answer to the question changed after reading the texts in the unit? Discuss your ideas.

You can use these sentences to help you reflect on your learning.

- **I think differently now because . . .**
- **I want to learn more about . . .**
- **I still don't understand . . .**

© Houghton Mifflin Harcourt Publishing Company

Project-Based Learning
↳ Create a Photo Collage

You've read about ways that people express themselves and make themselves heard. Now, create a photo collage of original photographs that reveal who you are and what you care about.

Here are some questions to ask yourself as you get started.

- What are my favorite hobbies or interests?
- What objects, people, or places mean the most to me?
- How can I show my personality in a photo?
- If I could share only *one* selfie, what would it communicate?

> **☺ Ed**
>
> **Media Projects**
>
> To find help with this task online, access **Create a Photo Collage.**

Writing
↳ Write a Memoir

Think about the moment you discovered your favorite form of self-expression. Then, write a brief memoir describing that moment. Use the chart to develop details you might include in your memoir.

ASK YOURSELF	MY NOTES
What **event** led me to first use this form of self-expression?	
What **motivated** me to try it? What **conflicts** did I experience?	
What was the event's **setting?** Where was I? What did I see, hear, feel, smell, or taste?	
What makes this form of expression so important to me?	

Ed

Get hooked by the unit topic.

Stream to Start Video

ESSENTIAL QUESTION:

What keeps people from giving up?

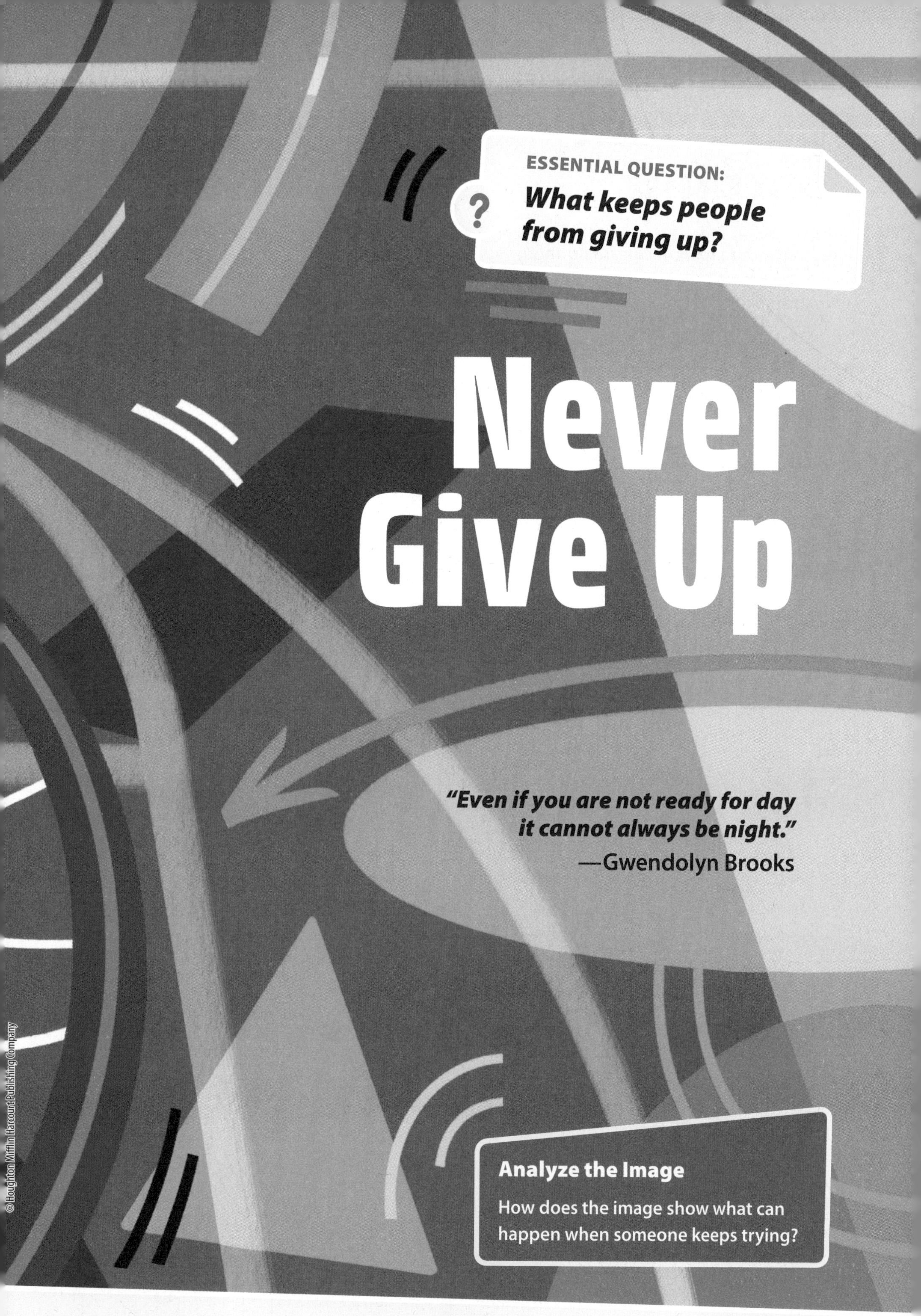

Never Give Up

"Even if you are not ready for day it cannot always be night."

—Gwendolyn Brooks

Analyze the Image

How does the image show what can happen when someone keeps trying?

Spark Your Learning

Here's a chance to spark your learning about ideas in **Unit 2: Never Give Up.**

As you read, you can use the **Response Log** (page R2) to track your thinking about the Essential Question.

Make the Connection

What was the last challenge you faced? Maybe you were trying to convince yourself to study for a test. Maybe you were struggling to change an attitude. Think about what you faced and what kept you from giving up. Then, list your ideas in the box below.

Think About the Essential Question

What keeps people from giving up?
People face challenges every single day, some of which are small, some of which are spectacular, and some of which are terrifying. What keeps them from giving up? Explain your ideas.

Prove It!

Turn to a partner and use one of the words in a sentence about not giving up.

Sound Like an Expert

You can use these Academic Vocabulary words to write and talk about the topics and themes in the unit. How many of these words do you already feel comfortable using when speaking or writing?

	I can use it!	I understand it.	I'll look it up.
achieve	☐	☐	☐
individual	☐	☐	☐
instance	☐	☐	☐
outcome	☐	☐	☐
principle	☐	☐	☐

Preview the Texts

Look over the images, titles, and descriptions of the texts in the unit. Mark the title of the text that interests you most.

A Schoolgirl's Diary
from **I Am Malala**

Memoir by **Malala Yousafzai** with **Patricia McCormick**

Along with every other girl who lives nearby, Malala's been told that she can't go to school. Still, she insists on going—and on telling the rest of the world about what's happening.

Speech to the Young: Speech to the Progress-Toward

Poem by **Gwendolyn Brooks**

How do we keep hope alive, especially when so many people seem to be trying to take it away?

The First Day of School

Short Story by **R. V. Cassill**

It's the morning of the first day of school, but this day isn't like any other. What was it like for those first brave students to integrate our schools?

from **New Kid**

Graphic Novel by **Jerry Craft**
Color by **Jim Callahan**

Jordan's the "new kid" at a fancy school, where he discovers that the kids sometimes don't get along— for reasons he doesn't understand.

I Wonder . . .

Why is it so important for people to learn to face challenges without giving up? Write or sketch your answer.

MENTOR TEXT

A Schoolgirl's Diary

from **I Am Malala**

Memoir by **Malala Yousafzai** with **Patricia McCormick**

? ESSENTIAL QUESTION:
What keeps people from giving up?

Engage Your Brain

Choose one or more of these activities to start connecting with the memoir you are about to read.

School's Out!

Imagine that you've heard that you won't be allowed to go to school—*ever* again. What would you miss? Write or sketch how you'd react to the announcement.

Radio Diary

Think about a student's average day. Then, for a radio broadcast, write a fictional diary entry about an event in that day. What sights and sounds would you describe? Create your entry.

Speech to the United Nations

As a teenager, the author of the memoir you're about to read presented ideas about changing the world to the United Nations. List the ideas you might present, if you were offered a similar chance. Then, share one with a partner.

Analyze Features of Informational Texts

The following selection is an excerpt from *I Am Malala*, which is a **memoir,** a form of autobiography in which a writer shares personal experiences and observations. As you read, note characteristics and features that this memoir shares with other informational texts—

- A **prologue,** or preface, that provides background information about the text.

- A **map,** or graphic feature illustrating where events take place, that clarifies the text's context.

- A **central idea,** or main point, conveyed through details, descriptions, quotations, and examples. In a memoir, the central idea may be tied to the author's purpose for writing the work.

Focus on Genre
↳ **Memoir**

- told in the first-person point of view, describing events from the writer's perspective

- includes descriptions of people and events that have influenced the writer

- expresses the writer's personal thoughts and feelings, often using an informal or intimate tone

Generate Questions

Readers improve their understanding of a text when they ask questions before, during, and after they read. Ask *who, what, when, where, why,* and *how* questions to help you analyze how ideas, events, and people are introduced and elaborated upon.

GENERATE QUESTIONS	TRY THIS
Set a purpose **before** reading. Ask yourself what you expect to learn from the text.	Preview the text by scanning headings, maps, etc. **Ask:** What do I know about the subject already? What am I going to learn?
Monitor comprehension **during** reading. Ask questions as you read, pause to reread, and confirm your understanding.	Reread as needed to clarify understanding. **Ask:** Why did the author add this detail? What idea is the author sharing?
Identify or confirm the central idea **after** reading. The questions you ask yourself will help you understand the work as a whole.	Take time to think about what you just read. Review the key ideas. **Ask:** Did I learn what I thought I would? What was the author's purpose in writing?

Annotation in Action

Here is an example of how one reader generated questions during reading. As you read, mark questions you might have.

It was the most ordinary of days. I was fifteen, in grade nine, and I'd stayed up far too late the night before, studying for an exam.

I'd already heard the rooster crow at dawn but had fallen back to sleep. I'd heard the morning call to prayer from the mosque nearby but managed to hide under my quilt. And I'd pretended not to hear my father come to wake me.

This sounds like mornings I know, except the rooster and "call to prayer." Where does she live?

Expand Your Vocabulary

Put a check mark next to the vocabulary words that you feel comfortable using when speaking or writing.

debate	☐
edict	☐
defy	☐
pseudonym	☐
anonymous	☐

Turn to a partner and talk about the vocabulary words you already know. Then, use as many words as you can in a paragraph about challenges faced by young people. As you read "A Schoolgirl's Diary," use the definitions in the side column to learn the vocabulary words you don't already know.

Background

In 2007, a militant group took control of the area of Pakistan where **Malala Yousafzai's** family lived, banning girls from attending school. Yousafzai (b. 1997) publicly supported girls' education, and in 2012 she was attacked and wounded by gunmen. Her family moved to England, where she continued to advocate for girls' rights. In 2014 she became the youngest recipient of the Nobel Peace Prize. This excerpt is from the Young Reader's Edition of her memoir, *I Am Malala*.

A Schoolgirl's Diary
from I am Malala

Memoir by **Malala Yousafzai** with **Patricia McCormick**

Along with every other girl who lives nearby, Malala has been told that she can't go to school. Still, she insists on going—and on telling the rest of the world about what's happening.

NOTICE & NOTE
As you read, use the side margins to make notes about the text.

Dedication

1 To those children all over the world who have no access to education, to those teachers who bravely continue teaching, and to anyone who has fought for their basic human rights and education.

Prologue

2 It was the most ordinary of days. I was fifteen, in grade nine, and I'd stayed up far too late the night before, studying for an exam.

3 I'd already heard the rooster crow at dawn but had fallen back to sleep. I'd heard the morning call to prayer from the mosque nearby but managed to hide under my quilt. And I'd pretended not to hear my father come to wake me.

ANALYZE FEATURES OF INFORMATIONAL TEXTS

Annotate: Mark details in paragraphs 2–3 that help set the scene of the prologue.

Identify: What does this background information reveal about the author?

Annotate: What can you tell about the author from her interaction with her mother? Mark the quoted words in paragraph 4.

Draw Conclusions: What do these words suggest about Malala's relationship to her mother?

4   Then my mother came and gently shook my shoulder. "Wake up, *pisho*," she said, calling me *kitten* in Pashto, the language of the Pashtun people. "It's seven thirty and you're late for school!"

5   I had an exam on Pakistani studies. So I said a quick prayer to God. *If it is your will, may I please come in first?* I whispered. *Oh, and thank you for all my success so far!*

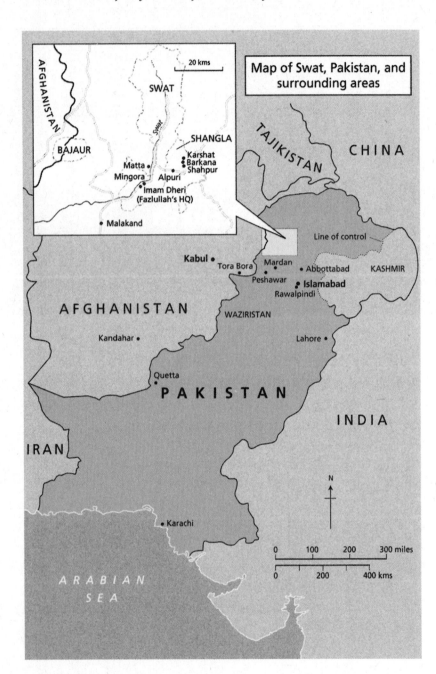

Map of Swat, Pakistan, and surrounding areas

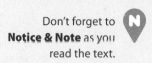

6   I gulped down a bit of fried egg and chapati[1] with my tea. My youngest brother, Atal, was in an especially cheeky mood that morning. He was complaining about all the attention I'd received for speaking out about girls getting the same education as boys, and my father teased him a little at the breakfast table.

7   "When Malala is prime minister[2] someday, you can be her secretary," he said.

8   Atal, the little clown in the family, pretended to be cross. "No!" he cried. "She will be *my* secretary!"

9   All this banter nearly made me late, and I raced out the door, my half-eaten breakfast still on the table. I ran down the lane just in time to see the school bus crammed with other girls on their way to school. I jumped in that Tuesday morning and never looked back at my home.

GENERATE QUESTIONS

Annotate: In paragraph 9, mark details that lead you to pause and ask questions.

Draw Conclusions: What questions do you have at this point in the text? Look for the answers as you continue to read.

10   The ride to school was quick, just five minutes up the road and along the river. I arrived on time, and exam day passed as it always did. The chaos of Mingora city surrounded us with its honking horns and factory noises while we worked silently, bent over our papers in hushed concentration. By day's end I was tired but happy; I knew I'd done well on my test.

11   "Let's stay on for the second trip," said Moniba, my best friend. "That way we can chat a little longer." We always liked to stay on for the late pickup.

12   When our bus was called, we ran down the steps. As usual, Moniba and the other girls covered their heads and faces before we stepped outside the gate and got into the waiting *dyna*,[3] the white truck that was our Khushal School "bus." And, as usual, our driver was ready with a magic trick to amuse us. That day, he made a pebble disappear. No matter how hard we tried, we couldn't figure out his secret.

13   We piled inside, twenty girls and two teachers crammed into the three rows of benches stretching down the length of the *dyna*. It was hot and sticky, and there were no windows, just a yellowed plastic sheet that flapped against the side as we bounced along Mingora's crowded rush-hour streets.

---

[1] **chapati** (chə-päʹtē): a flat, circular bread common in Pakistan and northern India.
[2] **prime minister:** in Pakistan, the prime minister is the head of government.
[3] **dyna** (dĭnʹə): a small, bus-like truck with a roof, sides, an open back, and benches for seats.

When you read informational texts, you should take a **Questioning Stance,** which means you don't automatically accept everything the author says.

Notice & Note: Mark any details in paragraph 14 that you find interesting.

Analyze: What challenged, changed, or confirmed what you already knew?

14   Haji Baba Road was a jumble of brightly colored rickshaws,[4] women in flowing robes, men on scooters, honking and zigzagging through the traffic. We passed a shopkeeper butchering chickens. A boy selling ice-cream cones. A billboard for Dr. Humayun's Hair Transplant Institute. Moniba and I were deep in conversation. I had many friends, but she was the friend of my heart, the one with whom I shared everything. That day, when we were talking about who would get the highest marks[5] this term, one of the other girls started a song, and the rest of us joined in.

15   Just after we passed the Little Giants snack factory and the bend in the road not more than three minutes from my house, the van slowed to a halt. It was oddly quiet outside.

16   "It's so calm today," I said to Moniba. "Where are all the people?"

17   I don't remember anything after that, but here's the story that's been told to me:

18   Two young men in white robes stepped in front of our truck.

19   "Is this the Khushal School bus?" one of them asked.

20   The driver laughed. The name of the school was painted in black letters on the side.

21   The other young man jumped onto the tailboard and leaned into the back, where we were all sitting.

22   "Who is Malala?" he asked.

23   No one said a word, but a few girls looked in my direction. He raised his arm and pointed at me. Some of the girls screamed, and I squeezed Moniba's hand.

24   Who is Malala? I am Malala, and this is my story.

---

[4] **rickshaws** (rĭk´shôz): in Pakistan, small motorized vehicles that carry passengers.
[5] **marks:** school grades.

My friends keep a chair in class for me (far right) at the Khushal School.

A Schoolgirl's Diary

25 "After the fifteenth of January, no girl, whether big or little, shall go to school. Otherwise, you know what we can do. And the parents and the school principal will be responsible."

26   That was the news that came over Radio Mullah[6] in late December 2008. At first, I thought it was just one of his crazy pronouncements. It was the twenty-first century! How could one man stop more than fifty thousand girls from going to school?

27   I am a hopeful person—my friends may say too hopeful, maybe even a little crazy. But I simply did not believe that this man could stop us. School was our right.

28   We **debated** his **edict** in class. "Who will stop him?" the other girls said. "The Taliban[7] have already blown up hundreds of schools, and no one has done anything."

29   "We will," I said. "We will call on our government to come and end this madness."

30   "The government?" one girl said. "The government can't even shut down Fazlullah's radio station!"[8]

debate
(dĭ-bāt´) v. To *debate* is to discuss opposing points or ideas.

edict
(ē´dĭkt´) n. An *edict* is a command or pronouncement enforced as law.

---

[6] **Radio Mullah:** the on-air name for radio broadcaster Maulana Fazlullah, who spread his radical beliefs that girls should not go to school and encouraged violence.
[7] **Taliban** (tăl´ə-băn´): a group of militant Islamic fundamentalists. The name comes from *Talib,* which means "religious student."
[8] **Fazlullah's radio station:** Maulana Fazlullah, the voice of Radio Mullah (see footnote 6). Fazlullah became head of the Taliban in Pakistan.

31 The debate went round and round. I didn't give in. But even to me, my argument sounded a bit thin.

32 One by one, girls stopped coming to school. Their fathers forbade them. Their brothers forbade them.

33 Within days we had gone from twenty-seven girls in our grade to ten.

34 I was sad and frustrated—but I also understood. In our culture, girls do not **defy** the males in their families. And I realized that the fathers and brothers and uncles who made my friends stay home were doing so out of concern for their safety. It was hard not to feel a bit depressed sometimes, not to feel as though the families who kept their girls at home were simply surrendering to Fazlullah. But whenever I'd catch myself giving in to a feeling of defeat, I'd have one of my talks with God. *Help us appreciate the school days that are left to us, God, and give us the courage to fight even harder for more.*

35 School had been due to end the first week of January for our usual winter break, so my father decided to postpone the holiday. We would remain in classes through 14 January. That way we could squeeze in every minute left to us. And the ten remaining girls in my class lingered in the courtyard every day after school in case these were our last chances to be together.

36 At home in the evenings I wondered what I would do with my life if I couldn't go to school. One of the girls at school had gotten married off before Fazlullah's edict. She was twelve. I knew my parents wouldn't do that to me, but I wondered, what *would* I do? Spend the rest of my life indoors, out of sight, with no TV to watch and no books to read? How would I complete my studies and become a doctor, which was my greatest hope at the time? I played with my shoebox dolls and thought: *The Taliban want to turn the girls of Pakistan into identical, lifeless dolls.*

37 While we girls savored the days until January 15, Fazlullah struck again and again. The previous year had been hard, but the days of January 2009 were among the darkest of our lives. Every morning, someone arrived at school with a story about another killing, sometimes two, sometimes three a night. Fazlullah's men killed a woman in Mingora because they said she was "doing *fahashi*," or being indecent, because she was a dancer. And they killed a man in the valley because he refused to wear his pants short the way the Taliban did. And now, we would be forbidden from going to school.

© Houghton Mifflin Harcourt Publishing Company

defy

(dĭ-fīʹ) *v.* To *defy* someone is to oppose or refuse to cooperate with that person.

ANALYZE FEATURES OF INFORMATIONAL TEXTS

Annotate: Why does Malala include numbers and dates in paragraphs 33 and 35? Mark where numbers are used.

Infer: What is the importance of understanding these details?

Don't forget to
Notice & Note as you
read the text.
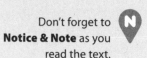

38   One afternoon I heard my father on the phone. "All the teachers have refused," he said. "They are too afraid. But I will see what I can do." He hung up and rushed out of the house.

39   A friend who worked at the BBC, the powerful British Broadcasting Corporation network, had asked him to find someone from the school to write a diary about life under the Taliban for its Urdu[9] website—a teacher or an older student. All the teachers had said no, but Maryam's younger sister Ayesha, one of the older girls, had agreed.

40   The next day, we had a visitor: Ayesha's father. He would not allow his daughter to tell her story. "It's too risky," he said.

41   My father didn't argue with him. The Taliban were cruel; but even *they* wouldn't hurt a child, he wanted to say. But he respected Ayesha's father's decision and prepared to call the BBC with the bad news.

42   I was only eleven, but I said, "Why not me?" I knew he'd wanted someone older, not a child.

43   I looked at my father's hopeful—nervous—face. He had been so brave for speaking out. It was one thing to talk to national and local media, but this diary might be read by people outside Pakistan. It was the BBC, after all. My father had always stood by me. Could I stand by him? I knew without even thinking that I could. I would do anything to be able to continue going to school. But first we went to my mother.

44   If she was afraid, I wouldn't do it. Because if I didn't have her support, it would be like speaking with only half my heart.

45   But my mother agreed. She gave us her answer with a verse from the Holy Quran.[10] "Falsehood has to die," she said. "And truth has to come forward." God would protect me, she said, because my mission was a good one.

46   Many people in Swat[11] saw danger everywhere they looked. But our family didn't look at life that way. We saw possibility. And we felt a responsibility to stand up for our homeland. My father and I are the starry-eyed ones. "Things have to get better," we always say. My mother is our rock. While our heads are in the sky, her feet are on the ground. But we all believed in hope. "Speaking up is the only way things will get better," she said.

ANALYZE FEATURES OF INFORMATIONAL TEXTS

Annotate: In paragraph 45, mark the term that is footnoted.

Analyze: How does the footnote help you understand the reason that Malala's mother agrees to the decision?

[9] **Urdu** (ûr´dōō): Pakistan's national language.
[10] **Quran** (kə-rän´): the sacred book of the religion of Islam, also spelled Koran.
[11] **Swat:** the Swat Valley of northwest Pakistan and the town of Mingora is where the memoir's narrative takes place.

Students outside during a science fair at the Khushal School.

pseudonym
(sōōd´n-ĭm´) *n.* A *pseudonym* is
a fictitious name, particularly a
pen name.

47   I had never written a diary before and didn't know how to begin, so the BBC correspondent said he would help me. He had to call me on my mother's phone because, even though we had a computer, there were frequent power cuts and few places in Mingora with Internet access. The first time he called, he told me he was using his wife's phone because his own phone had been bugged[12] by the intelligence services.

48   He suggested that I use a fake name so the Taliban wouldn't know who was writing the diary. I didn't want to change my name, but he was worried about my safety. That is why he chose a **pseudonym** for me: Gul Makai, which means "cornflower" and is the name of a heroine in a Pashtun folk story.

49   My first diary entry appeared on 3 January 2009, about two weeks before Fazlullah's deadline. The title was "I Am Afraid." I wrote about how hard it was to study or to sleep at night with the constant sounds of fighting in the hills outside town. And I described how I walked to school each morning, looking over my shoulder for fear I'd see a Talib following me.

50   I was writing from the privacy of my bedroom, using a secret identity, but thanks to the Internet, the story of what was happening in Swat was there for the whole world to see. It was as if God had at long last granted my wish for that magic pencil.

---

[12] **bugged:** equipped with a concealed listening device to overhear private conversations.

51   In my next entry, I wrote about how school was the center of my life and about how proud I was to walk the streets of Mingora in my school uniform.

52   As exciting as it was to be Gul Makai, it was hard not to tell anyone—especially at school. The diary of this **anonymous** Pakistani schoolgirl was all anyone talked about. One girl even printed it out and showed it to my father.

53   "It's very good," he said with a knowing smile.

———— ❀ ————

54   With the threat of school closing quickly becoming a reality, I appreciated going even more. In the days leading up to the last one, it was decided that wearing our uniforms was too dangerous, so we were told to dress in our everyday clothes. I decided I wasn't going to cower in fear of Fazlullah's wrath. I would obey the instruction about the uniform, but that day I chose my brightest pink *shalwar kamiz*.[13]

55   As soon as I left the house, I thought for a second about turning back. We'd heard stories of people throwing acid in the faces of girls in Afghanistan. It hadn't happened here yet, but with everything that *had* happened, it didn't seem impossible. But somehow my feet carried me forward, all the way to school.

56   What a peculiar place Mingora had become. Gunfire and cannons as background noise. Hardly any people in the streets. (And if you did see anyone, you couldn't help but think, *This person could be a terrorist.*) And a girl in a pink *shalwar kamiz* sneaking off to school.

———— ❀ ————

57   The BBC correspondent asked for more news from Swat for the next diary post. I didn't know what to tell him. He asked me to write about the killings. It seemed so obvious to him that this was news. But to me, what you experience every day is no longer news.

Don't forget to **Notice & Note** as you read the text.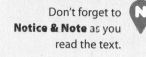

anonymous
(ə-nŏn´ə-məs) *adj.* Someone who is *anonymous* has an undisclosed or unknown name.

ANALYZE FEATURES OF INFORMATIONAL TEXTS

Annotate: Mark words in paragraph 54 that convey facts. Then, mark words that convey thoughts and feelings.

Synthesize: How does the author use facts, thoughts, and feelings to convey an idea in the paragraph? What is that idea?

---

[13] **shalwar kamiz** (shäl´vär kə-mēz´): a type of long, loose shirt and pants, worn by both men and women.

© Houghton Mifflin Harcourt Publishing Company

58   It was as if I had become immune to fear. Until one day, on my way home from school, I heard a man behind me say, "I will kill you." My heart stopped, but somehow my feet kept going. I quickened my pace until I was far ahead of him. I ran home, shut the door, and, after a few seconds, peeked out at him. There he was, oblivious to me, shouting at someone on his phone.

59   I laughed a bit at myself. "Malala," I told myself, "there are real things to be afraid of. You don't need to imagine danger where there is none."

60   The real worry, it seemed to me, was being found out. And, of course, it was Moniba who was first to guess the identity of Gul Makai. "I read a diary in the newspaper," she told me one day at recess, "and the story sounded like our story, what happens in our school. It's you, isn't it?" she said.

61   I could not lie, not to Moniba. But when I confessed, she became more angry than ever. "How can you say you're my best friend when you're keeping such an important secret from me?" She turned on her heel and left. And yet I knew, as angry as she was, she wouldn't reveal my secret.

62   It was my father who did that. By accident, of course. He was telling a reporter how terrifying it was for children just to walk to and from school. His own daughter, he said, thought a man on his phone had threatened to kill her. Just about everyone recognized the story from the diary, and by April, my days as Gul Makai, the secret diarist, would be over.

63   But the diary had done its job. Now a number of reporters were following the story of Fazlullah's attempt to shut down the girls' schools of Pakistan, including a man from the *New York Times*.

GENERATE QUESTIONS

Annotate: Mark any words in paragraphs 62 and 63 that lead you to ask questions.

Predict: What questions do you have at the end of the excerpt? What do you predict will happen?

?

ESSENTIAL QUESTION:
What keeps people from giving up?

Review your notes and add your thoughts to your Response Log.

TURN AND TALK

With a partner, discuss the excerpt from the memoir you just read. What does the memoir reveal about the power of "fortitude," the courage to stand up to a challenge?

© Houghton Mifflin Harcourt Publishing Company

Assessment Practice

Answer these questions before moving on to the **Analyze the Text** section.

1. Select **two** sentences that show Malala's beliefs about the importance of education.

   A. "I'd already heard the rooster crow at dawn but had fallen back to sleep." (paragraph 3)

   B. "'After the fifteenth of January, no girl, whether big or little, shall go to school.'" (paragraph 25)

   C. "How would I complete my studies and become a doctor, which was my greatest hope at the time?" (paragraph 36)

   D. "I wrote about how hard it was to study or to sleep at night with the constant sounds of fighting in the hills outside town." (paragraph 49)

   E. "In my next entry, I wrote about how school was the center of my life and about how proud I was to walk the streets of Mingora in my school uniform." (paragraph 51)

2. This question has two parts. First answer **Part A**, then **Part B**.

   Part A

   What inference can you make about Malala's parents?

   A. They want Malala to become famous.

   B. They want Malala to follow the Taliban's rules.

   C. They want Malala to be brave and to speak out against injustice.

   D. They are afraid of the Taliban and want to silence Malala so that she will not get hurt.

   Part B

   Select the excerpt that best supports the answer to Part A.

   A. "In our culture, girls do not defy the males in their families." (paragraph 34)

   B. "School had been due to end the first week of January for our usual winter break, so my father decided to postpone the holiday." (paragraph 35)

   C. "My father didn't argue with him. The Taliban were cruel; but even *they* wouldn't hurt a child, he wanted to say." (paragraph 41)

   D. " 'Speaking up is the only way things will get better,' [my mother] said." (paragraph 46)

Test-Taking Strategies

Analyze the Text

Support your responses with evidence from the text.

NOTICE & NOTE

Review what you **noticed and noted** as you read the text. Your annotations can help you answer these questions.

(1) **ANALYZE** Review paragraph 2 and paragraphs 10–11. What question about Malala's life is answered in paragraphs 10–11? Why do you think the author includes these details? What is her purpose?

(2) **EVALUATE** Review the memoir's title and paragraphs 22–24. How has the author used the statement "I am Malala" to communicate an idea? Is it an effective way to communicate her idea?

(3) **CITE EVIDENCE** Review paragraphs 61–63. How does the author use characteristics common to a memoir to convey a central idea?

(4) **ANALYZE** What quoted words does the author use in paragraphs 58–59? How do these quotations help you understand Malala's character and the central idea of the text?

(5) **DESCRIBE** Consider **Big Questions** and review paragraphs 54–56. What challenged, changed, or confirmed what you knew about teenagers' attitudes toward school?

My Attitudes Toward School

Malala's Attitude Toward School

Choices

Here are some other ways to demonstrate your understanding of the ideas in this lesson.

Writing
↳ Let Them Know What You Think

Should a news organization, such as the British Broadcasting Corporation, ever ask a student to provide reports under dangerous conditions?

Compose a formal email or letter addressed to a news organization that reflects your opinion on the topic. Include these features:

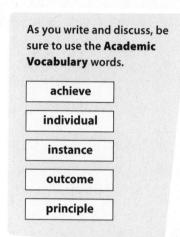

As you write and discuss, be sure to use the **Academic Vocabulary** words.

- achieve
- individual
- instance
- outcome
- principle

- **Subject Line** or **Heading:** An email's subject line specifies its purpose; a letter's heading includes names, addresses, and the date.

- **Salutation:** Include a greeting such as *To Whom It May Concern* or, if you have a specific person's name, *Dear Mr./Ms.* _____. End the greeting with a colon.

- **Body:** Include an introduction, your point, and a concluding sentence or two. Be brief, polite, and clear. Capitalize proper nouns.

- **Closing and Signature:** Use *Sincerely,* or *Respectfully,* and your full name.

- **Formal Style:** Edit to ensure that you have used a formal style. Eliminate slang and contractions, and make sure that your tone is serious and dignified.

Social & Emotional Learning
↳ School's Out!

Freewrite in response to this question: What would you do with your time if you couldn't go to school? Share your response with a small group. Then, discuss what the long-term consequences would be. What would Malala tell someone who felt like skipping school?

Research
↳ What Happens Next?

Use the Young Reader's Edition of *I Am Malala* or other sources to find out what happens next to Malala, her family, and her friends.

EVENT	SOURCE

Expand Your Vocabulary

PRACTICE AND APPLY

Answer the questions to show your understanding of the vocabulary words.

1. How would you know that an article was written by an **anonymous** author?

   _____

2. Do you like to **debate?** Why or why not?

   _____

3. What kind of **edict** might you **defy?** Why?

   _____

4. If you wanted to use a **pseudonym,** what would you choose? Why?

   _____

Vocabulary Strategy
↳ Greek and Latin Roots

Many English words contain Greek or Latin **roots,** word parts that contain the core meaning of a word. Knowing the meaning of roots and affixes can help you better understand unfamiliar words.

A **prefix** is an affix that appears at the beginning of a word, and a **suffix** is an affix that appears at the end of a word. For example, the word *pseudonym* contains the Greek prefix *pseudo-*, meaning "false," and *nym*, which comes from a Greek root meaning "name."

> **☺Ed**
>
> **Interactive Vocabulary Lesson: Analyzing Word Structure**

PRACTICE AND APPLY

Work in small groups to determine the origin and meaning of the word parts in *anonymous, debate, defy,* and *edict*. Use a print or online dictionary to look up entire words.

1. anonymous: _____

2. debate: _____

3. defy: _____

4. edict: _____

Watch Your Language!

Capitalization

Writers capitalize proper nouns to distinguish them from common nouns. A **proper noun** names a particular person, place, thing, or idea; a **common noun** is a general name for a person, place, thing, or idea. In the selection, proper nouns are capitalized in the following ways:

Ed

Interactive Grammar Lesson: Capital Letters

CATEGORY OF PROPER NOUN	EXAMPLE
Names of schools	the Khushal School
Titles used before a name, names of people, and names of businesses	Dr. Humayun's Hair Transplant Institute
Organizations	British Broadcasting Corporation BBC
Countries	Pakistan
Ethnicities	Pashtun
Languages	Urdu, Pashto
Titles of books, chapters, published works, and newspapers	Quran "A Schoolgirl's Diary" "I Am Afraid" *New York Times*
Days of the week, months of the year	Tuesday October

PRACTICE AND APPLY

Write your own sentences with proper nouns, using the examples from "A Schoolgirl's Diary" as models. Your sentences can be about Malala Yousafzai or your own experiences with challenges and persistence. When you have finished, share your sentences with a partner and compare your work.

Speech to the Young: Speech to the Progress-Toward

Poem by **Gwendolyn Brooks**

ESSENTIAL QUESTION:
What keeps people from giving up?

Engage Your Brain

Choose one or both activities to start connecting with the poem you are about to read.

Where Would You Like to Go?

Think about the title of this poem. What would you like to make progress toward? Draw a timeline that starts today and ends with where you'd like to wind up one day. Then, add the steps you'll take to get there.

A Bit of Advice

What advice would you give to others about keeping their hopes and dreams alive, even if no one else believes in them? List your ideas and share them with a partner.

Analyze Poetic Forms

"Speech to the Young: Speech to the Progress-Toward" is a **free verse poem,** which means that it does not follow a specific rhyming pattern or metrical form. However, it does use other elements of poetry to convey meaning and ideas, including:

- **Line breaks** and lengths that create effects and emphasis

- **Repetition** of sounds, words, phrases, or lines that reinforce meaning and create rhythm, emphasis, and a sense of unity

- **Rhythm,** a pattern of stressed and unstressed syllables that adds a musical quality, creates mood, and emphasizes ideas

- **Alliteration,** a repetition of consonant sounds at the beginning of words that creates rhythm and emphasis

As you read, complete a chart like this to help you analyze what the poetic elements reveal about tone and meaning.

Focus on Genre
 Poetry

- may include rhyme, rhythm, and meter

- features line breaks and the use of white space for effects and meaning

- may use repetition and rhyme to create a melodic quality

- often contains figurative language and literary devices such as alliteration, consonance, and assonance

POETIC ELEMENT	EXAMPLE IN POEM	EFFECT
Line break		
Repetition		
Rhythm		
Alliteration		

Make Inferences About Theme

A work's **theme** is its message about life or human nature. Some themes are **universal;** their messages apply across cultures to anyone, anywhere, any time.

Authors may state themes directly, but most themes are implied, which means that a reader must **infer,** or form a logical opinion about what the message may be. To make an inference, draw upon evidence from the text and upon your own knowledge. Remember to note tone, as well as structural or metrical elements that might help reveal a poem's theme.

Evidence from the Work:
My Own Knowledge:
Possible Theme:

Annotation In Action

This model shows one reader's notes for making an inference about a list in "Speech to the Young." As you read, make inferences that help you determine a possible theme and purpose for the poem.

> Say to them,
> say to the down-keepers,
> the sun-slappers,
> the self-soilers,
> the harmony-hushers,
> "Even if you are not ready for day
> it cannot always be night."

These are people who put people down. Are they trying to keep people from feeling hope?

Background

Gwendolyn Brooks (1917–2000) published more than twenty books of poetry and several books of prose. Her writing portrays the daily lives of African Americans, and in 1950, for her book of poetry *Annie Allen,* she became the first African American to win a Pulitzer Prize. The longtime Chicago resident became Poet Laureate of Illinois in 1968, and in 1985, she was named Poet Laureate Consultant in Poetry to the Library of Congress.

Speech to the Young: Speech to the Progress-Toward

Poem by **Gwendolyn Brooks**

How do we keep hope alive, especially when so many people seem to be trying to take it away?

NOTICE & NOTE
As you read, use the side margins to make notes about the text.

Say to them,
say to the down-keepers,
the sun-slappers,
the self-soilers,
5 the harmony-hushers,
"Even if you are not ready for day
it cannot always be night."

MAKE INFERENCES ABOUT THEME

Annotate: Mark the quotation in the poem.

Infer: Why do you think these lines are in quotes, and what is the meaning of these lines?

Annotate: Mark lines in the poem that give direct advice.

Analyze: How do these lines contribute to the poem's rhythm and meaning?

You will be right.
For that is the hard home-run.

10   Live not for battles won.
Live not for the-end-of-the-song.
Live in the along.

?

ESSENTIAL QUESTION:

What keeps people from giving up?

Review your notes and add your thoughts to your Response Log.

TURN AND TALK

Get together with a partner and discuss the "speech" you just read. What does the poem tell you about maintaining hope? What does it tell you to avoid?

Assessment Practice

Answer these questions before moving on to the **Analyze the Text** section.

1. How does the repetition of the word "live" in lines 10–12 contribute to the speaker's message?

- (A) by suggesting that life is repetitive
- (B) by praising creative self-expression
- (C) by telling the reader to live life in the present
- (D) by encouraging the reader to be a competitor

2. Read the excerpt from the poem. Then, answer the question.

> "Even if you are not ready for day
> it cannot always be night."
> You will be right.
> For that is the hard home-run. (lines 6–9)

What does the phrase "hard home-run" suggest in this excerpt?

- (A) that standing up for what is right is a big achievement
- (B) that people who are critical lack confidence
- (C) that sports boost one's confidence
- (D) that the loudest voices usually win

3. Whom is the speaker addressing in the poem?

- (A) her family
- (B) her critics
- (C) other poets
- (D) young people

Test-Taking Strategies

Analyze the Text

Support your responses with evidence from the text.

1 **INFER** What conclusions can you draw about the meaning of the phrase "self-soilers" in line 4?

2 **ANALYZE** Identify the instances of alliteration in lines 3–9. What is the effect of the alliteration? How might this use of alliteration support the speaker's message?

NOTICE & NOTE

Review what you **noticed and noted** as you read the text. Your annotations can help you answer these questions.

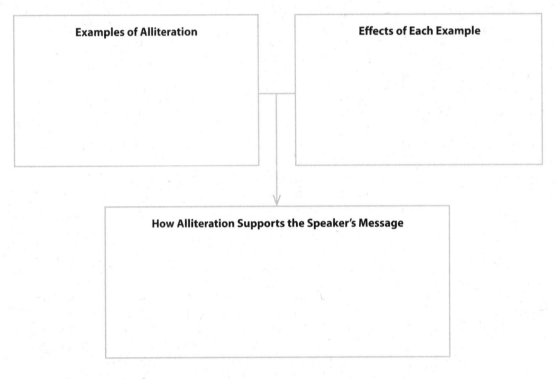

Examples of Alliteration	Effects of Each Example

How Alliteration Supports the Speaker's Message

3 **CITE EVIDENCE** What is the theme, or central idea, of the poem? How does the poet convey this theme? Cite evidence to support your inference. You can refer to the chart you used as you read.

4 **SYNTHESIZE** Explain the author's purpose in using the word "speech" twice in the long title, yet making the poem itself very brief.

5 **SUMMARIZE** Summarize the speaker's words of the wiser—that is, what advice is the speaker giving the audience? What can you infer about the speaker's experiences from reading the poem?

Choices

Here are some other ways to demonstrate your understanding of the ideas in this lesson.

Social & Emotional Learning
↳ A "Speech" for Someone Who Needs It

Write a short, inspirational poem in the spirit of "Speech to the Young." Think of a challenge faced by someone younger than you. Then, write your poem, offering advice about how to face that challenge.

- Include points about how your audience might manage difficult thoughts, emotions, and behaviors.

- Include poetic elements, such as alliteration, repetition, rhythm, rhyme, and thoughtful use of line breaks.

As you write and discuss, be sure to use the **Academic Vocabulary** words.

| achieve |
| individual |
| instance |
| outcome |
| principle |

Media
↳ Video Interpretation

Work with a group to create a short video interpretation of Brooks's poem.

- First, decide who'll read the poem aloud and discuss how it should be read; determine where to pause, how quickly to read lines, and where to place emphasis.

- Next, analyze the poem to identify image possibilities; find or create images to capture each of the poem's ideas.

- Finally, create your video; combine images with your audio recording of the poem.

When you've finished, discuss how viewing your interpretation differs from the experience of reading the poem itself.

Research
↳ "You Will Be Right"

Explore the life and career of poet Gwendolyn Brooks. Use the organizer to guide your exploration.

KEY LIFE EVENTS	
KEY CAREER EVENTS	
IMPORTANCE OF HER POETRY	

Collaborate & Compare

Compare Time Periods

You're about to read a short story and an excerpt from a graphic novel about students who struggle to fit in at school. As you read, focus on how the time period in which each selection is set affects how its topic and theme are treated.

A

The First Day of School

Short Story by R.V. Cassill
pages 126–133

B

from New Kid

Graphic Novel by **Jerry Craft**
with color by **Jim Callahan**
pages 141–155

After you have read the selections, you'll get a chance to present your ideas. You'll follow these steps:

- Gather Information
- Organize
- Draft Your Essay
- Review and Revise
- Present

The First Day of School

Short Story by **R.V. Cassill**

Engage Your Brain

Choose one or more of these activities to start connecting with the story you are about to read.

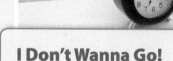

Your Very First Day

Once upon a time, it was your very first day at your school. Describe your experiences on that day. Write or sketch your response.

I Don't Wanna Go!

Think about reasons why students might decide that they *really* don't want to go to school. In a small group, list possible reasons. Then, vote on which ones are good and which ones are bad.

Way Back When

With a group, list what you've heard about schools sixty years ago—way back when today's seventy-year-olds were children. Then, share your list with the class.

Analyze Plot and Character

The sequence of events in a story form its **plot.**

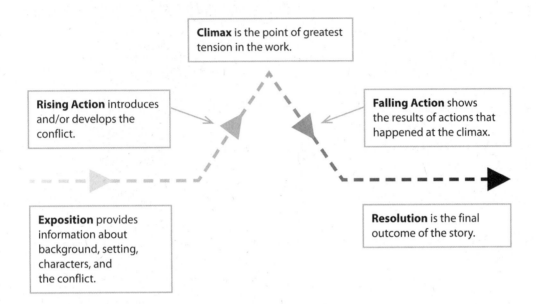

Climax is the point of greatest tension in the work.

Rising Action introduces and/or develops the conflict.

Falling Action shows the results of actions that happened at the climax.

Exposition provides information about background, setting, characters, and the conflict.

Resolution is the final outcome of the story.

Plots usually center on a character's **conflict,** or struggle against opposing forces. **External conflicts** are struggles against outside forces, while **internal conflicts** are conflicts within a character.

Some stories include **nonlinear plot elements,** such as flashbacks, which interrupt a plot's forward action by revealing events in the past, to provide a better understanding of characters and actions.

Analyze Setting

The characters in "The First Day of School" are fictional, but the historical events described in the story are not. As you read, note aspects of the story's **time period,** its historical and cultural setting.

Read the background information and look for clues about the time and place of the story as you read. Ask yourself, how does the setting help create and reveal the conflicts of the plot?

Focus on Genre
↳**Short Story**

- is a work of short fiction that centers on a single idea and can be read in one sitting

- usually includes one main conflict that involves the characters and keeps the story moving

- includes the basic elements of fiction—plot, character, setting, and theme

- may be based on real people and historical events

Annotation in Action

In the model, you can see one reader's notes on setting in "The First Day of School." As you read, note details about the setting's impact.

> He heard the tap of heels on the stairs, and his sister came down into the kitchen. She looked fresh and cool in her white dress. Her lids looked heavy. She must have slept all right—and for this John felt both envy and a faint resentment. He had not really slept since midnight. The heavy traffic in town, the long wail of horns as somebody raced in on the U.S. highway holding the horn button down, and the restless murmur, like the sound of a celebration down in the courthouse square, had kept him awake after that.

John didn't sleep well because it was so noisy from car horns and people.

The whole town was noisy all night long.

Expand Your Vocabulary

Put a check mark next to the vocabulary words that you feel comfortable using when speaking or writing.

resentment	☐
lament	☐
stealthily	☐
linger	☐
serene	☐
poised	☐

Turn to a partner and talk about the vocabulary words you already know. Then, use as many words as you can in a paragraph about how schools have changed in your own lifetime. As you read "The First Day of School," use the definitions in the side column to learn the vocabulary words you don't already know.

Background

In 1954, the United States Supreme Court ruled that segregation in public schools (the practice of having "separate but equal" schools for White people and Black people) was unconstitutional. Schools began integrating students at all levels. Schoolchildren sometimes faced the anger, hatred, and violence of those who opposed this policy. In 1958, in the midst of this difficult time, **R. V. Cassill** (1919–2002) wrote this story.

The First Day of School

Short Story by **R. V. Cassill**

It's the morning of the first day of school, but this day isn't like any other. What was it like for those first brave students to integrate our schools?

NOTICE & NOTE
As you read, use the side margins to make notes about the text.

1   Thirteen bubbles floated in the milk. Their pearl transparent hemispheres[1] gleamed like souvenirs of the summer days just past, rich with blue reflections of the sky and of shadowy greens. John Hawkins jabbed the bubble closest to him with his spoon, and it disappeared without a ripple. On the white surface there was no mark of where it had been.

ANALYZE SETTING

Annotate: In paragraph 2, mark details of setting.

Analyze: What does the setting reveal about this stage of the plot?

2   "Stop tooling[2] that oatmeal and eat it," his mother said. She glanced meaningfully at the clock on the varnished cupboard. She nodded a heavy, emphatic affirmation[3] that now the clock was boss. Summer was over, when the gracious oncoming of morning light and the stir of early breezes promised that time was a luxury.

---

[1] **hemispheres** (hĕm´ ĭ-sfîrz´): halves of a sphere, which is a three-dimensional circular, or ball, shape.
[2] **tooling** (tōō´lĭng): working with something, as with a tool such as a spoon.
[3] **affirmation** (ăf´ər-mā´shən): positive, strong support of the truth of something.

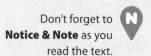
3   "Audrey's not even down yet," he said.

4   "Audrey'll be down."

5   "You think she's taking longer to dress because she wants to look nice today?"

6   "She likes to look *neat*."

7   "What I was thinking," he said slowly, "was that maybe she didn't feel like going today. Didn't feel *exactly* like it."

8   "Of course she'll go."

9   "I meant she might not want to go until tomorrow, maybe. Until we see what happens."

10   "Nothing's going to happen," his mother said.

11   "I know there isn't. But what if it did?" Again John swirled the tip of his spoon in the milk. It was like writing on a surface that would keep no mark.

12   "Eat and be quiet. Audrey's coming, so let's stop this here kind of talk."

13   He heard the tap of heels on the stairs, and his sister came down into the kitchen. She looked fresh and cool in her white dress. Her lids looked heavy. She must have slept all right—and for this John felt both envy and a faint **resentment**. He had not really slept since midnight. The heavy traffic in town, the long wail of horns as somebody raced in on the U.S. highway holding the horn button down, and the restless murmur, like the sound of a celebration down in the courthouse square, had kept him awake after that. Each time a car had passed their house his breath had gone tight and sluggish. It was better to stay awake and ready, he had told himself, than to be caught asleep.

14   "Daddy gone?" Audrey asked softly as she took her place across the table from her brother.

15   "He's been gone an hour," their mother answered. "*You* know what time he has to be at the mine."

16   "She means, did he go to work today?" John said. His voice had risen impatiently. He met his mother's stout[4] gaze in a staring contest, trying to make her admit by at least some flicker of expression that today was different from any other day. "I thought he might be down at Reverend Specker's," John said. "Cal's father and Vonnie's and some of the others are going to be there to wait and see."

17   Maybe his mother smiled then. If so, the smile was so faint that he could not be sure. "You know your father isn't much of a hand for waiting," she said. "Eat. It's a quarter past eight."

ANALYZE PLOT AND CHARACTER

Annotate: In paragraphs 3–12, mark the details that show you John is worried and upset about something.

Analyze: What conflict is introduced here? What stage of the plot is this?

resentment
(rĭ-zĕnt´mənt) *n.* If you feel *resentment*, you feel anger or irritation.

VOCABULARY

Thesaurus: A thesaurus reveals that synonyms for *wail* include *cry, screech, howl,* and *lament.* Knowing a word's synonyms can help you better understand the word.

Analyze: Based on its synonyms, what does the use of the word *wail* suggest about John's feelings about the horns he hears?

---

4 stout (stout): bold, brave, determined.

lament

(lə-mĕnt´) *v.* If you *lament*, you are wailing or crying as a way of expressing grief.

ANALYZE SETTING

Annotate: Mark details in paragraphs 21–23 that help you better understand the setting of the story.

Analyze: How does the time period, the story's cultural and historical setting, affect John and create conflict?

stealthily

(stĕl´thə-lē) *adv.* To do something *stealthily* is to do it quietly and secretly.

18   As he spooned the warm oatmeal into his mouth he heard the rain crow calling again from the trees beyond the railroad embankment. He had heard it since the first light came before dawn, and he had thought, Maybe the bird knows it's going to rain, after all. He hoped it would. *They won't come out in the rain,* he had thought. Not so many of them, at least. He could wear a raincoat. A raincoat might help him feel more protected on the walk to school. It would be a sort of disguise, at least.

19   But since dawn the sun had lain across the green Kentucky trees and the roofs of town like a clean, hard fire. The sky was as clear as fresh-washed window glass. The rain crow was wrong about the weather. And still, John thought, its **lamenting,** repeated call must mean something.

20   His mother and Audrey were talking about the groceries she was to bring when she came home from school at lunch time. A five-pound bag of sugar, a fresh pineapple, a pound of butter . . .

21   "Listen!" John said. Downtown the sound of a siren had begun. A volley of automobile horns broke around it as if they meant to drown it out. "*Listen* to them."

22   "It's only the National Guard, I expect," his mother said calmly. "They came in early this morning before light. And it may be some foolish kids honking at them, the way they would. Audrey, if Henry doesn't have a good-looking roast, why then let it go, and I'll walk out to Weaver's this afternoon and get one there. I wanted to have something a little bit special for our dinner tonight."

23   So . . . John thought . . . she wasn't asleep last night either. Someone had come **stealthily** to the house to bring his parents word about the National Guard. That meant they knew about the others who had come into town, too. Maybe all through the night there had been a swift passage of messengers through the neighborhood and a whispering of information that his mother meant to keep from him. Your folks told you, he reflected bitterly, that nothing is better than knowing. Knowing whatever there is in this world to be known. That was why you had to be one of the half dozen kids out of some nine hundred colored[5] of school age who were going today to start classes at Joseph P. Gilmore High instead of Webster. Knowing and learning the truth were worth so much they said—and then left it to the hooting rain crow to tell you that things were worse than everybody had hoped.

---

[5] **colored:** at the time in which the story is set, a term commonly used to describe Black people. The term is now considered derogatory. Previously, Black children had been required to attend their own separate schools.

© Houghton Mifflin Harcourt Publishing Company • Image Credits: ©Bettmann/Getty Images

Don't forget to **Notice & Note** as you read the text.

24   Something had gone wrong, bad enough wrong so the National Guard had to be called out.

25   "It's eight twenty-five," his mother said. "Did you get that snap sewed on right, Audrey?" As her experienced fingers examined the shoulder of Audrey's dress they **lingered** a moment in an involuntary, sheltering caress. "It's all arranged," she told her children, "how you'll walk down to the Baptist Church and meet the others there. You know there'll be Reverend Chader, Reverend Smith, and Mr. Hall to go with you. It may be that the white ministers will go with you, or they may be waiting at school. We don't know. But now you be sure, don't you go farther than the Baptist Church alone." Carefully she lifted her hand clear of Audrey's shoulder. John thought, Why doesn't she hug her if that's what she wants to do?

26   He pushed away from the table and went out on the front porch. The dazzling sunlight lay shadowless on the street that swept down toward the Baptist Church at the edge of the colored section. The street seemed awfully long this morning, the way it had looked when he was little. A chicken was clucking contentedly behind their neighbor's house, feeling the warmth, settling itself into the sun-warmed dust. Lucky chicken.

linger

(lĭng′gər) v. To *linger* means to leave slowly and reluctantly, not wanting to go.

ANALYZE SETTING

Annotate: In paragraph 25, mark details about who will walk to school with John and his sister.

Draw Conclusions: Why is it necessary that the children are walked to school by adults?

Annotate: In paragraph 27,
mark words that show that a
flashback—the description of an
event that happened before the
story begins—has started. Then,
mark the words that signal the
flashback has ended.

Analyze: How does the flashback
help you understand John's
character?

27   He blinked at the sun's glare on the concrete steps leading
down from the porch. He remembered something else from
the time he was little. Once he had kicked Audrey's doll buggy
down these same steps. He had done it out of meanness—for
some silly reason he had been mad at her. But as soon as the
buggy had started to bump down, he had understood how
terrible it was not to be able to run after it and stop it. It had
gathered speed at each step and when it hit the sidewalk it
had spilled over. Audrey's doll had smashed into sharp little
pieces on the sidewalk below. His mother had come out of the
house to find him crying harder than Audrey. "Now you know
that when something gets out of your hands it is in the Devil's
hands," his mother had explained to him. Did she expect him
to forget—now—that that was always the way things went to
smash when they got out of hand? Again he heard the siren and
the hooting, mocking horns from the center of town. Didn't his
mother think *they* could get out of hand?

28   He closed his eyes and seemed to see something like a doll
buggy bump down long steps like those at Joseph P. Gilmore
High, and it seemed to him that it was not a doll that was riding
down to be smashed.

29   He made up his mind then. He would go today, because
he had said he would. Therefore he had to. But he wouldn't go
unless Audrey stayed home. That was going to be his condition.
His bargaining looked perfect. He would trade them one for
one.

30   His mother and Audrey came together onto the porch. His
mother said, "My stars, I forgot to give you the money for the
groceries." She let the screen door bang as she went swiftly back
into the house.

31   As soon as they were alone, he took Audrey's bare arm
in his hand and pinched hard. "You gotta stay home," he
whispered. "Don't you know there's thousands of people down
there? Didn't you hear them coming in all night long? You slept,
didn't you? All right. You can hear them now. Tell her you're
sick. She won't expect you to go if you're sick. I'll knock you
down, I'll smash you if you don't tell her that." He bared his
teeth and twisted his nails into the skin of her arm. "Hear them
horns," he hissed.

32 He forced her halfway to her knees with the strength of his fear and rage. They swayed there, locked for a minute. Her knee dropped to the porch floor. She lowered her eyes. He thought he had won.

33 But she was saying something and in spite of himself he listened to her almost whispered refusal. "Don't you know anything? Don't you know it's harder for them than us? Don't you know Daddy didn't go to the mine this morning? They laid him off on account of us. They told him not to come if we went to school."

34 Uncertainly he relaxed his grip. "How do you know all that?"

35 "I listen," she said. Her eyes lit with a sudden spark that seemed to come from their absolute brown depths. "But I don't let on all I know the way you do. I'm not a . . ." Her last word sunk so low that he could not exactly hear it. But if his ear missed it, his understanding caught it. He knew she had said "coward."

36 He let her get up then. She was standing beside him, **serene** and prim when their mother came out on the porch again.

37 "Here, child," their mother said to Audrey, counting the dollar bills into her hand. "There's six, and I guess it will be all right if you have some left if you and Brother get yourselves a cone to lick on the way home."

38 John was not looking at his sister then. He was already turning to face the shadowless street, but he heard the unmistakable **poised** amusement of her voice when she said, "Ma, don't you know we're a little too old for that?"

39 "Yes, you are," their mother said. "Seems I had forgotten that."

40 They were too old to take each other's hand, either, as they went down the steps of their home and into the street. As they turned to the right, facing the sun, they heard the chattering of a tank's tread on the pavement by the school. A voice too distant to be understood bawled a military command. There were horns again and a crescendo[6] of boos.

41 Behind them they heard their mother call something. It was lost in the general racket.

42 "What?" John called back to her. "What?"

---

[6] **crescendo** (krə-shĕn′dō): a slow, gradual increase in volume, intensity, or force.

NOTICE & NOTE
AHA MOMENT

When you notice a sudden realization that shifts a character's actions or understandings, you've found an **Aha Moment** signpost.

Notice & Note: Mark new information in paragraph 33.

Analyze: How might this change things?

_____

_____

_____

_____

serene
(sə-rēn′) *adj.* If you are *serene*, you are calm and unflustered.

poised
(poizd) *adj.* To be *poised* means to be calm and assured.

ANALYZE PLOT AND CHARACTER

Annotate: Mark details in paragraphs 40–44 that contribute to the resolution of the story.

Summarize: What is the resolution, or final outcome, of the story?

_____

_____

_____

She had followed them out as far as the sidewalk, but not past the gate. As they hesitated to listen, she put her hands to either side of her mouth and called to them the words she had so often used when she let them go away from home.

"Behave yourselves," she said.

TURN AND TALK

With a partner, discuss your ideas about what convinces John to go to school, despite his fears of what may happen. What gives him the strength to stand up to this challenge?

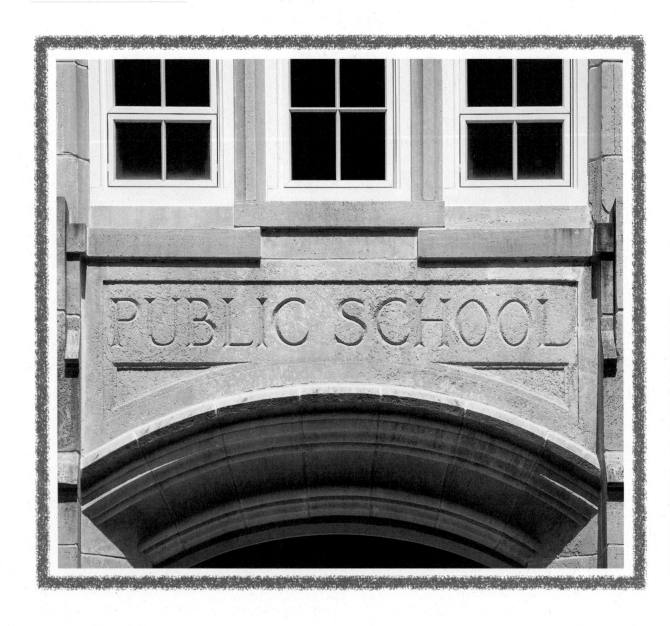

© Houghton Mifflin Harcourt Publishing Company • Image Credits: ©BanksPhotos/iStock/Getty Images

Assessment Practice

Answer these questions before moving on to the **Analyze the Text** section.

1. Why does the author include details about the National Guard?

   (A) to show how John's character develops

   (B) to distract the reader from the real story

   (C) to describe the National Guard's role in events

   (D) to add information that increases tension in the plot

2. This question has two parts. First answer **Part A**, then **Part B**.

   Part A

   What word best describes John's feelings toward his sister?

   (A) envious

   (B) annoyed

   (C) resentful

   (D) protective

   Part B

   What excerpt from the story best supports the answer to Part A?

   (A) "She looked fresh and cool in her white dress." (paragraph 13)

   (B) "Once he had kicked Audrey's doll buggy down these same steps." (paragraph 27)

   (C) "But he wouldn't go unless Audrey stayed home." (paragraph 29)

   (D) "As soon as they were alone, he took Audrey's bare arm in his hand and pinched hard." (paragraph 31)

3. Which detail reveals information about the story's time period, it's historical setting?

   (A) There are parents who work at mines.

   (B) Audrey and John are expected to walk to school.

   (C) Summer is over, so it's time for the school year to begin.

   (D) Angry protestors have gathered because schools are being integrated.

Test-Taking Strategies

Analyze the Text

Support your responses with evidence from the text.

1 **IDENTIFY** What are three details in the story that help you understand the text's time period, its historical and cultural setting?

NOTICE & NOTE

Review what you **noticed and noted** as you read the text. Your annotations can help you answer these questions.

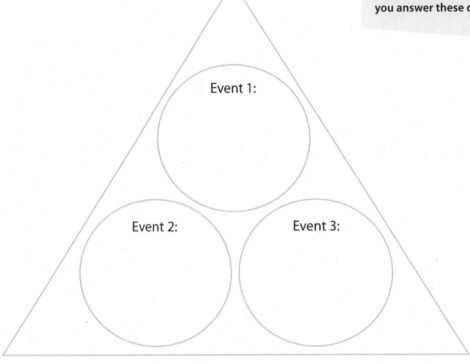

Event 1:

Event 2:

Event 3:

Time Period

2 **INFER** Reread paragraphs 18–19. How does the setting reveal, contribute to, and create conflict in the story?

3 **ANALYZE** Reread paragraphs 27–29. What is the connection between what John remembers and what is happening in the story? Describe what you learn about John in this episode and how the flashback moves the plot toward a resolution.

4 **INTERPRET** What is the climax of the story? Explain.

5 **ANALYZE** Review paragraphs 33–36, considering John's **Aha Moment.** Explain what he realizes about other members of his family. How does this episode help John resolve his own internal conflict?

Choices

Here are some other ways to demonstrate your understanding of the ideas in this lesson.

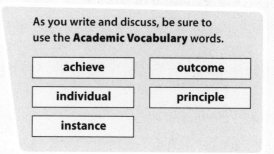

As you write and discuss, be sure to use the **Academic Vocabulary** words.

achieve	outcome
individual	principle
instance	

Writing
↳ There's Something About John

Write a brief essay analyzing John's feelings and actions. What conflicts does he experience? How is he affected by the story's setting?

- Introduce a central idea about John. Consider what you know about the setting, John's perspective, his internal conflicts, and how he changes.

- Provide evidence from the story to support your ideas.

- Use transitions to connect ideas, include a variety of sentence structures, and punctuate your sentences correctly.

Social & Emotional Learning
↳ Compare and Contrast Experiences

Discuss John and Audrey's experiences on the first day of school. Share ideas about the story's events, conflicts, and setting. Then, compare and contrast the characters' experiences with your own.

- Encourage everyone to participate.

- Take notes, ask questions, and listen respectfully, considering other viewpoints.

Research
↳ How Have Schools Changed?

"The First Day of School" is based on events following a 1954 Supreme Court ruling known as *Brown v. Board of Education* and on the actions of a group of students known as the Little Rock Nine. Investigate what happened and how schools have changed since then.

WHAT HAPPENED?	HOW SCHOOLS HAVE CHANGED

Expand Your Vocabulary

PRACTICE AND APPLY

Answer the questions to show your understanding of the vocabulary words.

1. Does a **serene** sky indicate stormy or sunny weather? Explain.

2. Why are you likely to **linger** after your team wins a game?

3. Does a **poised** person appear calm or appear nervous? Explain.

4. How can you tell if a teammate is **lamenting** the score?

5. Describe what **resentment** feels like.

6. Describe the behavior of an animal that moves **stealthily.**

Vocabulary Strategy
↳Thesaurus

A **thesaurus** is a reference book of **synonyms,** or words that have nearly the same meaning, and **antonyms,** or words with opposite meanings. You can use a print or online thesaurus to clarify a word's precise meaning or to find just the right word to use.

 Ed

Interactive Vocabulary Lesson: Using Reference Sources

PRACTICE AND APPLY

Use a thesaurus to select a synonym for each vocabulary word. Then, use the synonym in a sentence that shows its meaning.

WORD	SYNONYM	SENTENCE
resentment	animosity	Our opponents scowled after we won; I could sense their animosity.
lament		
stealthily		
linger		

Watch Your Language!

Sentence Patterns

Authors use a variety of sentence patterns to make their writing clear, meaningful, and interesting to read. Review the sentence patterns in the chart.

☺Ed

Interactive Grammar Lesson: Simple Sentences and Compound Sentences

PATTERN	DESCRIPTION AND EXAMPLE
Simple	an independent clause **She looked fresh and cool in her white dress.**
Compound	independent clauses joined with a coordinating conjunction **He heard the tap of heels on the stairs, and his sister came down into the kitchen.**
Complex	an independent clause and one or more subordinate clauses **Summer was over, when the gracious oncoming of morning light and the stir of early breezes promised that time was a luxury.**
Compound-Complex	independent clauses and one or more subordinate clauses **As the traffic increased, the highway's noise kept him awake, yet his sister slept soundly.**

PRACTICE AND APPLY

Change the sentence type for each sentence or group of sentences. Identify both the original pattern and the pattern you used.

1. John hadn't slept very well the night before because the sounds of car horns and loud voices kept him awake.

2. Audrey came down the stairs. She acted prim. The dress she had chosen looked fresh and cool.

3. Their mother came onto the porch. She called to them. She followed them down the street.

from
New Kid

Graphic Novel by **Jerry Craft**
Color by **Jim Callahan**

Engage Your Brain

Choose one or both activities to start connecting with the excerpt from a graphic novel you are about to read.

Out of Many, One

Work together to list different groups at your school. You can include social groups, sports groups, or even groups that like certain movies. Then, gather a pile of interlocking bricks and label each one with the name of a group. Finally, take the bricks and build something out of all of those different groups.

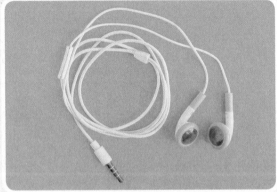

Everybody's Playlist

Get together with a small group, and come up with a list of songs you think would help different groups of kids get along. What songs are about things that everyone might agree on? What songs might bond groups to each other? Create your playlist below.

Analyze Plot and Character

A fictional **character** is any person, animal, or imaginary creature that takes part in the **plot**, or the series of events, in a work of literature.

- The behavior of characters—how they interact with each other and respond to events—helps reveal conflict and develop the plot.

- Characters' responses to events can be external (actions and words), or they can be internal (thoughts and feelings).

- In graphic novels, clues to conflict can be found in speech balloons or thought bubbles, as well as in images and other visual cues.

As you read *New Kid*, use a chart similar to this one to analyze how the speech and actions of characters help reveal conflict.

Focus on Genre

↳ **Graphic Novel**

- uses both text and images to tell a full-length story

- includes illustrated panels, frames, speech balloons, and thought bubbles, as well as other comic-strip elements

- includes the basic elements of stories, including plot, characters, and setting

CHARACTER	TEXT OR VISUAL DETAIL	WHAT IT REVEALS ABOUT CONFLICT
Jordan		
Gran'pa		

Analyze Setting and Theme

The **setting,** or place and time period in which the action occurs, can influence both the plot and the story's **theme,** its message about life or human nature.

- Characters in stories set in different time periods may encounter similar conflicts but in different ways.

- Themes in stories with very different settings, including different time periods, may be similar, perhaps even "universal"; they may apply to anyone at any time or place.

- Settings in graphic novels are usually established through images and captions, and their themes are developed through both text and images.

Annotation in Action

Here are one student's notes about a conflict revealed in the dialogue between two characters in *New Kid*. As you read, note how and when the text reveals conflicts in the story.

Gran'pa: So tell me about this new school of yours.

Jordan: It's way bigger than St. Harwell's, and trees *everywhere!* It's like having class in Central Park.

Gran'pa: Wow! And what are the kids like?

Jordan: Some are **really** rich. You should see the cars that pick them up.

Jordan seems surprised by the size of his new school and how wealthy his schoolmates are.

Is he intimidated? How will he fit in?

Background

Jerry Craft (b. 1963) was born in Harlem, New York, and grew up in the nearby Washington Heights neighborhood. After working as an advertising writer, Craft got a job as a comic book cartoonist, and he is now an award-winning comic-strip artist, author, and illustrator. He is the creator of the popular *Mama's Boyz* comic strip, and, in 2020, *New Kid* won the prestigious John Newbery Medal for the year's best children's book, as well as the Coretta Scott King Award for outstanding work by an African American author.

from **New Kid**

Graphic Novel by **Jerry Craft; Color** by **Jim Callahan**

Jordan's the "new kid" at a fancy school, where he discovers that the kids sometimes don't get along—for reasons he doesn't understand.

NOTICE & NOTE
As you read, use the side margins to make notes about the text.

INTRODUCTION

The main character in New Kid, *Jordan Banks, is a seventh-grader living in an apartment in the Washington Heights neighborhood of New York City. He is a talented artist who draws cartoons about daily life, and he wants to go to art school. His parents, however, have different plans. They send him to a prestigious private school, Riverdale Academy, instead.*

Jordan is one of Riverdale's few Black students, and he is able to attend only because he receives financial aid. In his first few weeks as the "new kid," Jordan experiences both subtle and not-so-subtle forms of discrimination. He discovers just how divided students and teachers can be today—socially, racially, and economically.

Now Jordan has to learn how to get along at a new school where he often feels like an outsider. How can he start making connections and help his friends get along?

© Houghton Mifflin Harcourt Publishing Company • Image Credits: (t) ©littlenySTOCK/Shutterstock

ANALYZE PLOT AND CHARACTER

Annotate: Mark words and image details that help reveal the nature of the relationship between the characters.

Analyze: Where does Gran'pa seem to be? Why does this seem to bother Jordan? How do elements in the illustration help reveal this?

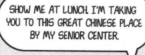

ANALYZE PLOT AND CHARACTER

Annotate: Mark details in the text and illustrations that reveal a conflict.

Analyze: How does the author use humor to establish what is bothering Jordan about Gran'pa?

ANALYZE SETTING AND THEME

Annotate: Mark details in the text and illustrations that help reveal the time period.

Analyze: How do these details of setting hint at a theme about adjusting to new situations?

---

[1] **Yonkers:** a city northeast of New York City on the Hudson River, about a twenty- to forty-minute car ride from Washington Heights.

[2] **Chuck:** Jordan's father; Gran'pa's son.

³ **ground him:** a form of punishment in which a person is prevented from leaving the house to socialize or see friends.

⁴ **handshake force:** a reference to an earlier part of the story in which Jordan's father teaches him the importance of an overly firm handshake.

Don't forget to
Notice & Note as you
read the text.

ANALYZE SETTING AND THEME

Annotate: Mark clues in Gran'pa's speech that suggest a theme about fitting in.

Analyze: How are both characters dealing with a similar problem in their lives? Why might the author have set this scene in this particular restaurant?

---

[5] **St. Harwell's:** Before he switched to Riverdale Academy, Jordan had attended Saint Harwell's.

[6] **The Lion King on Broadway:** *The Lion King* is a popular musical theater production; Broadway is a section of New York City famous for its many theaters.

Annotate: Mark details in the text and illustrations that reveal a conflict with which Jordan is struggling.

Analyze: Why might the author have changed the outline of the speech bubble in the third panel? What does this reveal about a challenge Jordan is facing?

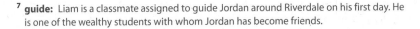

[7] **guide:** Liam is a classmate assigned to guide Jordan around Riverdale on his first day. He is one of the wealthy students with whom Jordan has become friends.

ANALYZE PLOT AND CHARACTER

Annotate: Mark details in the text and illustrations that clarify the conflict with which Jordan is struggling.

Analyze: Is Jordan's conflict internal or external? How do the speech and images work together to reveal this?

---

8 **The Three Musketeers:** This is an allusion to the main characters of a famous French adventure novel, *The Three Musketeers*, written in 1844 by Alexandre Dumas.

WORDS OF THE WISER

When you notice an older, wiser character giving advice, you've found a **Words of the Wiser** signpost.

Notice & Note: Mark the advice Jordan receives.

Infer: What is the life lesson for Jordan? How might it affect him?

9–11 Strimp Lo Mein, Pepper Steak, General Tso's Chicken: three dishes often found on menus of Chinese restaurants in the United States; "strimp" is how Jordan pronounced "shrimp" when he was younger.

In this section, the author interrupts the plot by including pages from Jordan's sketchbook. Mark places in the sketchbook that indicate the time period.

Infer: How does the setting help reveal a possible theme?

Taking Photos with My Mom
A Tale of Terror!

First, my mom can NEVER find her camera. It could be anywhere!

behind potato salad

Plus, it's really old! It used to be her dad's so she refuses to get a new one or use her phone. It still uses something called film! Google it!

Then she makes us take a *jillion* shots in hopes that a few of them might *actually* turn out good.

But they almost never do!

Furman Fooser

12 **photos developed:** A way to create photographs taken with film cameras rather than digital cameras. Photos taken on film must be developed, or processed, into pictures.

ANALYZE PLOT AND CHARACTER

Annotate: Mark the text and parts of the image that hint at a possible resolution to the main conflict in the story.

Analyze: What does Jordan mean about a metaphor? How has the character of Jordan changed by this point in the story?

ANALYZE SETTING AND THEME

Annotate: Mark the details in the text and illustrations that help reveal the setting.

Analyze: How does the setting establish the time period and help develop themes about diversity and fitting in?

13–14 Jaquavious and Darius: Drew and Jordan are mocking students and teachers who have repeatedly called them by the wrong names.

© Houghton Mifflin Harcourt Publishing Company

© Houghton Mifflin Harcourt Publishing Company

TURN AND TALK

Meet with a partner and discuss what finally brings Jordan and his friends together, despite their differences. What else might have helped bring them together?

Assessment Practice

Answer these questions before moving on to the **Analyze the Text** section.

1. What is the challenge that both Jordan and Gran'pa are dealing with?
   - (A) using new technology
   - (B) fitting in to a new place
   - (C) maintaining old friendships
   - (D) living up to Chuck's expectations

2. This question has two parts. First answer **Part A**, then **Part B**.

   Part A

   How does Jordan resolve the main conflict by the end of the story?
   - (A) He has dinner with Gran'pa at a restaurant.
   - (B) He decides to go to an art school in ninth grade.
   - (C) He follows Gran'pa's advice about making choices.
   - (D) He uses his art skills to draw a solution to his trouble.

   Part B

   Select the excerpt that best supports the correct resolution in Part A.
   - (A) "I played soccer. It was okay. Even scored a goal. But it was freezing!" (page 146)
   - (B) "No, it's usually just me and Liam, or me and Drew." (page 147)
   - (C) "But luckily, the High School of Art, Music, and Mime doesn't start till ninth grade." (page 149)
   - (D) "So I decided to see if General Tso's Chicken could get along with Pepper Steak." (page 152)

   ☺Ed
   Test-Taking Strategies

Analyze the Text

Support your responses with evidence from the graphic novel.

(1) SYNTHESIZE Review the organizer you completed as you were reading. How does the author use the relationship between Jordan and Gran'pa to reveal the main conflict in the graphic novel?

NOTICE & NOTE

Review what you **noticed and noted** as you read the graphic novel. Your annotations can help you answer these questions.

(2) IDENTIFY What are four details in the story that help establish the time period in which the story is set?

DETAIL	WHAT IT REVEALS ABOUT TIME PERIOD

(3) INFER In the scene in the Chinese restaurant, Jordan and Gran'pa are talking about Jordan's new friend Liam. Jordan says, "That's the thing, he's just like you or me. He's cool." What does that detail reveal about an important theme in the story?

(4) INTERPRET Explain the metaphor that Jordan is referring to in this sentence from the end of the story: "It took me a few days to realize that Gran'pa's story was a metaphor. . . . So I decided to see if General Tso's Chicken could get along with Pepper Steak." How do Gran'pa's **Words of the Wiser** help Jordan resolve both an internal and an external conflict?

(5) SYNTHESIZE How does the author use elements unique to graphic novels to help establish Jordan's relationship to Gran'pa and to each of his parents? What do these details reveal about Jordan's family?

© Houghton Mifflin Harcourt Publishing Company

Choices

Here are some other ways to demonstrate your understanding of the ideas in this lesson.

Writing
↳ Analyze the Characters

Write an essay that analyzes the relationship between Jordan and Gran'pa. Make sure to—

- Include a claim, support it logically with reasons and evidence, and end with a conclusion that follows from your claim.

- Explore how the relationship between the characters impacts the plot.

- Use precise and domain-specific language, such as *character*, *conflict*, and *dialogue*.

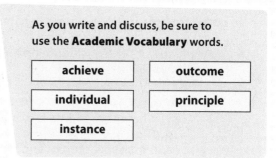

As you write and discuss, be sure to use the **Academic Vocabulary** words.

achieve	outcome
individual	principle
instance	

Research
↳ A Vlog for the New Kids

Every student who transfers to a new school has to deal with a new, unfamiliar environment. With a small group, investigate what students have said about their experiences as "new kids." Then, using what you've learned, create a vlog (video blog) offering "how to" advice to other new kids.

- Credit your sources of information.

- Include photos, cartoons, videos, or other forms of visual information.

- Share your vlog by posting it on a secure school website or social media page.

Social & Emotional Learning
↳ Roundtable

In *New Kid,* Jordan struggles with feeling welcome at Riverdale. With a group, hold a roundtable discussion about how your school could be more welcoming to newcomers. Explore how your school might help newcomers overcome obstacles such as differences in language, background, or culture.

When you've finished your discussion, present your group's suggestions about how to make your school more welcoming.

Compare Time Periods

To **compare time periods** across texts, take these steps:

- Identify the settings, including time periods, of each text.

- Determine how time period affects other elements in each text, such as characters, plot, and theme.

- Compare how texts written and set in different time periods address similar topics and themes.

As you review "The First Day of School" and *New Kid*, think about similarities and differences in the conflicts faced by the characters. How does each text explore themes concerning diversity and discrimination? How does Jordan's experience differ from the experiences of students who first integrated American schools?

In a small group, complete a Venn diagram with details from the two texts. Focus on details related to historical setting and its impact.

The First Day of School   **Both**   *New Kid*

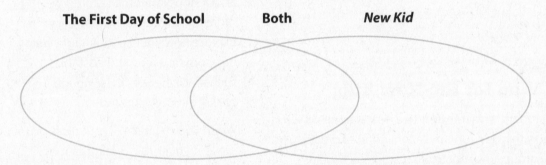

Analyze the Texts

Discuss these questions in your group.

1. **SUMMARIZE** What topics and issues do both authors explore?

2. **COMPARE** What do conversations in the texts reveal about the conflicts? How are their conflicts similar? How do they differ?

3. **CONNECT** Cite evidence in each text that reveals information about its historical setting.

4. **EVALUATE** How effectively do the authors show how discrimination affects the characters and plot?

Collaborate and Present

Now you can continue reflecting on the topics, themes, and historical time periods of these texts. Write a compare and contrast essay to answer the following question: *How do the two authors, writing in two different time periods, view the struggle to overcome discrimination?* Follow these steps:

(1)   **GATHER INFORMATION**   Review each story's historical setting, conflicts and resolutions, and possible themes. If necessary, research the time period at which "The First Day of School" is set. Draw from your own experiences and insights into the setting and conflicts revealed in *New Kid*.

(2)   **ORGANIZE**   Organize your notes and ideas using a graphic organizer.

AUTHORS' VIEWS ABOUT OVERCOMING DISCRIMINATION	
Author in Late 1950s	**Author Today**

(3)   **DRAFT YOUR ESSAY**   Write a draft of your essay comparing the views of the two authors. Use precise language that signals comparisons and contrasts, such as *unlike*, *similar to*, *in the same way*, and *on the other hand*.

(4)   **REVIEW AND REVISE**   Review your draft with a partner, offering each other constructive feedback about making clear comparisons and contrasts.

(5)   **PRESENT**   Read your essay aloud to a group. When everyone has presented, discuss the unique insights each writer brings to the topic. Summarize your group's findings.

Reader's Choice

Continue your exploration of the Essential Question by doing some independent reading on refusing to give up. Read the titles and descriptions shown. Then mark the texts that interest you.

? ESSENTIAL QUESTION:
What keeps people from giving up?

Short Reads Available on Ed

These texts are available in your ebook. Choose one to read and rate. Then defend your rating to the class.

Paul Revere's Ride
Poem by **Henry Wadsworth Longfellow**

Paul Revere gallops through villages all night, alerting settlers of the coming attack by the British.

Rate It

The Road Not Taken
Poem by **Robert Frost**

How do you choose which way to go in life, when you don't know anything about what might happen along the way?

Rate It

Damon and Pythias
Dramatized by **Fan Kissen**

In prison, Damon waits for his best friend to return to face the consequences.

Rate It

Education First
from Malala's Speech to the United Nations
Speech by **Malala Yousafzai**

A near fatal gunshot wound makes Malala even more committed to speaking up for change.

Rate It

Long Reads

Here are three recommended books that connect to this unit topic. For additional options, ask your teacher, school librarian, or peers. Which titles spark your interest?

New Kid

Graphic Novel by **Jerry Craft, Color** by **Jim Callahan**

Jordan's parents enroll him in a private school for the wealthy and gifted, although he wants to study art. When he gets there, he discovers just how divided a school can be, and he can't seem to find a way to fit in.

I Am Malala, Young Reader's Edition

Memoir by **Malala Yousafzai**

The Taliban announces that girls will no longer attend school. Malala resists, and she's nearly killed for her beliefs. The youngest winner of a Nobel Prize, Malala Yousafzai continues to speak for those without voices, and this is her story.

Esperanza Rising

Novel by **Pam Muñoz Ryan**

Esperanza's life of privilege ends when her family flees from Mexico to California. She isn't at all ready for the hard work, financial struggles, and danger she now faces.

Extension
↳ Connect & Create

GO FISH The Reader's Choice texts reveal a lot about facing challenges. On each of five index cards, write down one idea about facing a challenge, along with an explanation about how a text supports that idea. Then, gather in a small group, and read a card aloud. See if anyone else in your group has written a similar idea. If so, take their card. How many cards will you each collect?

ILLUSTRATE IT The characters and people who appear in the Reader's Choice texts face difficult challenges. Pick one of these challenges and list reasons that the character or person either overcame or failed to overcome the challenge. When you've finished, create an illustration, using digital tools if they're available, showing what went right or what went wrong for your character or person. Then, share and explain your illustration.

NOTICE & NOTE

- Pick one of the texts and annotate the Notice & Note signposts you find.

- Then, use the **Notice & Note Writing Frames** to help you write about the significance of the signposts.

- Compare your findings with those of other students who read the same text.

Notice & Note Writing Frames

Write a Nonfiction Narrative

Writing Prompt

This unit focuses on what makes people keep trying. A local magazine is seeking submissions of inspirational, real-life stories for a special publication about local heroes. Write a nonfiction narrative about a time that you or someone you know faced a challenge but refused to give up.

Manage your time carefully so that you can

- review the texts in this unit;
- plan your nonfiction narrative;
- write your narrative; and
- revise and edit your narrative.

Be sure to

- maintain an appropriate point of view, and establish and develop a situation involving real people, places, and events;
- organize an event sequence that unfolds logically and naturally;
- convey your central or controlling idea effectively, using precise words and sensory and figurative language;
- maintain a consistent style, tone, and mood; and
- provide a conclusion that follows from and reflects on events.

> ### Review the
> ### Mentor Text
>
> For an example of a well-written narrative that you can use as mentor text, review the memoir:
>
> - **"A Schoolgirl's Diary"** (pages 99–109)
>
> Review your notes and annotations about this text carefully. Think about how the author makes her memoir both interesting and meaningful.

Consider Your Sources

Review the list of texts in the unit and choose at least two that you may want to use as inspiration for ideas or as models for effective use of narrative elements.

As you review potential sources, consult the notes you made on your **Response Log** and make additional notes about ideas that might be useful as you write your narrative.

UNIT 2 SOURCES

- [ ] **A Schoolgirl's Diary**
- [ ] **Speech to the Young: Speech to the Progress-Toward**
- [ ] **The First Day of School**
- [ ] *from* **New Kid**

Analyze the Prompt

Analyze the prompt to make sure you understand the assignment.

Mark the phrase in the prompt that identifies the topic of your nonfiction narrative. Rephrase the topic in your own words.

Then, look for words that indicate the purpose and audience for your narrative. Write a sentence describing each.

What is my topic? What is my writing task?

What is my purpose?

Who is my audience?

Consider Your Audience

Ask yourself:

- Who will read my narrative?
- What do I want readers to "get" from my narrative? What message will it communicate?
- What mood and tone will engage my audience?

Review the Rubric

Your narrative will be scored using a rubric. As you write, focus on the characteristics described in the chart. You will learn more about these characteristics as you work through the lesson.

PURPOSE, FOCUS, AND ORGANIZATION	DEVELOPMENT OF IDEAS	CONVENTIONS OF STANDARD ENGLISH
The response includes: • An introduction that identifies the subject and grabs readers' attention • A clear and logical sequence of events supported by the effective use of transitions • Precise words and phrases, and effective use of sensory and figurative language • A conclusion that reflects on the significance of the event or experience, providing new insights for readers	The response includes: • Background information that helps explain events • Descriptions that effectively establish setting and mood • Use of dialogue, conflict, and description to create a strong sense of character • A central point about refusing to give up	The response may include the following: • Some minor errors in usage but no patterns of errors • Correct use of punctuation, capitalization, sentence formation, and spelling • Command of basic conventions

1 PLAN YOUR NONFICTION NARRATIVE

Choose an Experience or Event

Help with Planning

Consult **Interactive Writing Lesson: Writing Narratives**

First, decide on an experience or event.

- Remember that your narrative will need a structure—a beginning, a middle, and an ending.

- It should also center on a **conflict,** a problem faced by your narrative's subject, and it should convey a clear message.

EXPERIENCE OR EVENT	THE CONFLICT
THE MESSAGE I INTEND TO CONVEY	

Plan Characters, Setting, and Point of View

Your narrative will include **characters** and a **setting,** people, and the time and location of events. It should also be told from a consistent **point of view,** a vantage point from which events are described. Make some initial notes in the chart.

Plan Story Elements

Ask yourself:

- **What do readers need to know about my characters?**

- **What details of the setting are most important?**

CHARACTER(S)	SETTING
Who is this narrative about?	Where did events take place?
What other people will I include? Why?	What is important about the setting?
MY NARRATIVE'S POINT OF VIEW	

Identify Details

Your nonfiction narrative will include details about events, people, and setting. Using **sensory language**, language that appeals to the senses, will help bring those details to life. Record some important and vivid details below.

DETAILS ABOUT . . .	
EVENTS	
PEOPLE	
SETTING	

Organize Sequence of Events

Order your ideas in a way that will help readers understand what happened and why it matters. In a nonfiction narrative, events are often told in **chronological order,** the sequence in which they took place. Use the sequence chart to organize your narrative's events.

Develop Your Narrative

Remember that in a narrative—

- The **beginning** provides vital background information and introduces the conflict.

- The **middle** tells about events, develops the conflict, and resolves it.

- The **ending** wraps up events and closes with thoughts that convey your reflections and message.

Events in My Narrative

Beginning

Middle

Ending

2 DEVELOP A DRAFT

Now it is time to draft your nonfiction narrative. Examining what other, experienced writers have done can help you develop your own writing skills. Consider the techniques that another writer uses in her memoir.

Use Precise Words and Phrases

EXAMINE THE MENTOR TEXT

Notice how the author of "A Schoolgirl's Diary" (pages 99–109) uses precise words and phrases as she tells her story.

A Schoolgirl's Diary
from **I am Malala**
Memoir by Malala Yousafzai with Patricia McCormick

> Rather than simply calling the ride "quick," the author describes precisely how long it lasts—"five minutes."

The ride to school was quick, just five minutes up the road and along the river. I arrived on time, and exam day passed as it always did. The chaos of Mingora city surrounded us with its honking horns and factory noises while we worked silently, bent over our papers in hushed concentration.

> Sensory details create tension by contrasting the busy city with the "hushed" silence of the students.

Try These Suggestions

The words you choose will create the **tone** and **mood** of your narrative. Consider the **connotations** of descriptive words. For example:

- Is a bright room "stark" or is it "cheerful"?
- Is a windy day "refreshing" or is it "threatening"?

APPLY TO YOUR DRAFT

Complete these sentence frames to practice using precise words and phrases. Then, apply the technique to other parts of your draft narrative.

Precise words that describe how someone in my narrative looks include

_____

_____

Precise words that describe my setting include

_____

_____

_____

Use Sensory Details

EXAMINE THE MENTOR TEXT

Using words that appeal to senses helps readers imagine how things look, sound, smell, taste, and feel. Notice how Malala Yousafzai uses sensory details.

Drafting Online

Check your assignment list for a writing task from your teacher.

Words that appeal to the sense of **touch** tell readers how it feels.

Other words help readers **hear** and **feel** what it is like to be on the bus.

> We piled inside, twenty girls and two teachers crammed into the three rows of benches stretching down the length of the *dyna*. It was hot and sticky, and there were no windows, just a yellowed plastic sheet that flapped against the side as we bounced along Mingora's crowded rush-hour streets.

Words that appeal to the sense of **sight** help readers picture what the author sees.

Try This Suggestion

Sensory details help bring events and settings to life. As you draft your narrative, pause often to consider how you might describe sights, sounds, smells, and sensations so that readers better understand and imagine them.

APPLY TO YOUR DRAFT

As you write, keep readers interested by using sensory details. Try to appeal to a range of your readers' senses. List some sensory words or phrases related to your narrative below.

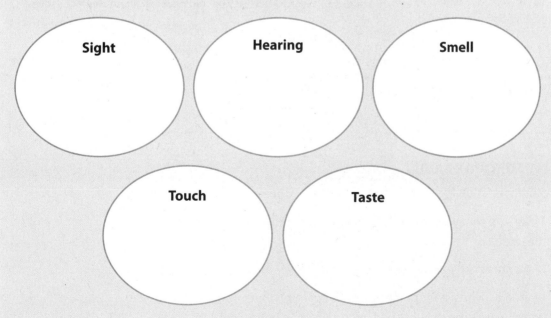

REVISE YOUR NONFICTION NARRATIVE

Help with Revision

Find a **Peer Review Guide** and **Student Models** online.

Experienced writers revise their work—often more than once—to make sure their audiences understand their ideas. Use the guide below to help you revise your narrative.

ASK YOURSELF	PROVE IT	REVISE IT
Introduction Do I orient readers by introducing people, the setting, and the conflict?	**Label** details about people with **P,** details about setting with **S,** and details about conflict with **C.**	**Add** details to help orient readers so that they can easily follow the rest of your narrative.
Point of View Do I maintain a consistent point of view?	**Make a check mark** (✔) next to each pronoun.	Evaluate pronouns to confirm that you're using a consistent point of view. **Change** them if they indicate a shift in point of view.
Sequence Do I tell events in chronological order?	<u>Underline</u> words that indicate time order.	**Rearrange** sentences or paragraphs, as needed, to reflect the correct order of events.
Plot Does my narrative have a beginning, a middle, and an ending?	**Label** the three parts of your narrative.	**Add or rearrange** ideas so that the action develops, comes to a peak at the climax, and then wraps up in the conclusion.
Descriptive Details Have I used precise words and phrases and sensory details?	**Highlight** precise words and phrases and sensory details.	Analyze sentences where there is no highlighting. **Replace** vague terms. **Add** words that appeal to readers' senses.
Conclusion Do I share my thoughts, feelings, and reflections in the conclusion?	**Make brackets** ({ }) around the conclusion.	**Add** a sentence that reflects on the experience or event and clarifies your message.

APPLY TO YOUR DRAFT

Consider the following as you look for opportunities to improve your writing.

- Make sure that your narrative builds toward and stays focused on your message.

- Make sure that your descriptions are effective, precise, and detailed.

- Maintain a consistent point of view, and correct any errors in grammar and punctuation.

Peer Review in Action

Once you have finished revising your nonfiction narrative, you will exchange papers with a partner in a **peer review.** During a peer review, you will give suggestions to improve your partner's draft.

Read the introduction from a student's draft and examine the comments made by his peer reviewer to see how it's done.

First Draft

Tyler: The Boy Who Won't Quit
by Devin Harkness, Owen Middle School

My brother Tyler is always moving. He has a hard time controlling his muscles. And sometimes it seems as if he is always knocking things over. When Tyler sets his mind to something, he doesn't quit.

Is your brother younger or older than you? That detail would help me picture him.

Can you tell why? Being more specific will help me understand your brother's challenges.

Now read the revised introduction. Notice how the writer has improved the draft by revising based on his peer reviewer's comments.

Revision

What's funny, wiggly, and messy all at once? That would be my big brother Tyler. Tyler loves a good joke. And he is *always* moving. He can't really help it because he was born with cerebral palsy. He has a hard time controlling his muscles. You just never know when one of his arms is going to go whooshing past and knock something over. That's where the messy part comes in. But aside from all of that, when Tyler sets his mind to something, he never quits.

Thanks! Now I can picture him: I know what he's like.

Much better! The details really help me understand his challenges.

APPLY TO YOUR DRAFT

During your peer review, give each other specific suggestions for how you could make your narrative easier to follow and more interesting to readers. Use your revision guide to help you.

When receiving feedback from your partner, listen attentively and ask questions to make sure you fully understand the revision suggestions.

4 EDIT YOUR NONFICTION NARRATIVE

Apply the finishing touches to your draft. Edit your draft to check for proper use of standard English conventions and to correct any misspellings or grammatical errors.

Interactive Writing Lesson: Writing Narratives

Watch Your Language!

USE TRANSITIONS AND TIME-ORDER WORDS

Precise words and phrases add life to your writing. **Transitions** and **time-order words** help create and reveal structure. They connect events and explain exactly when they occur.

Read the following excerpts from "A Schoolgirl's Diary."

> My first diary entry appeared on 3 January 2009, about two weeks before Fazlullah's deadline. . . . In my next entry, I wrote about how school was the center of my life. . . .

The time-order words *first, before,* and *next* clarify and connect events: Malala's first diary entry, the deadline closing schools to girls, and a second entry about the importance of school to Malala.

APPLY TO YOUR DRAFT

Now apply what you've learned about transitions and time-order words to your own work.

1. Underline words indicating time order, and check sentences that announce a change in events. If no words have been underlined, add time-order words or transitions to clarify events.

2. Exchange drafts with a peer and review for transitions and time-order words.

Transitions

Using a variety of transitions will keep readers interested. Examples include:

- **The first thing that morning, . . .**
- Later, right after school, . . .
- **Finally, when supper was over, . . .**

5 PUBLISH YOUR NARRATIVE

Share It!

The prompt asks you to provide your nonfiction narrative for publication in a magazine. You may also use your narrative as inspiration for other projects.

Ways to Share

- Present your narrative as an **inspirational speech** to your classmates.
- **Write a letter** to a person featured in your narrative. Explain how that person inspires you.
- **Create a podcast** about people who never give up. See the next task for tips on how.

Produce and Present a Podcast

You have written a nonfiction narrative about never giving up. Now you and a group of classmates will use the material in your narratives to create an 8- to 10-minute **podcast** about people who refuse to quit.

Plan Your Podcast Presentation

With your group, agree on the overall message and tone of the podcast. Then, work individually to script two-minute presentations of your own narratives.

When you've finished, work as a group to combine your individual narratives into a single script:

- Create an introduction and conclusion to the podcast, focusing on your group's overall message.

- Create transitional segments to connect your individual presentations to each other.

- Assign roles, ensuring that everyone has a part to read in the podcast.

Use the chart to take notes as you and your group plan the podcast.

> **Consider Voice and Tone**
>
> Make sure that the voice and tone of your final script matches the message you want to send.

QUESTIONS TO ASK	ANSWERS AND NOTES
How do we want to make our listeners feel? For example: thoughtful? inspired? joyful?	
How are our narratives alike? How do they differ? How does this knowledge help us create transitions between our segments?	
How do we wrap up the podcast? What final thought(s) do we want to share with listeners?	

Practice with Your Group

A podcast does not include visuals, so you have to rely on the audio alone to convey your message. It will be important to practice speaking from your script before you record.

Use this guide as each group member practices his or her speaking part. Give specific suggestions for improvement.

SPEAKING GOAL	NOTES FOR IMPROVEMENT
Speak smoothly, without stumbling over any words.	
Speak loudly and clearly.	
Vary volume and speed of speech for effect.	

Record Your Podcast

You can record your podcast with a smartphone or a computer. Work with your teacher to coordinate the equipment and arrange a time and place to record.

Use these tips to keep your podcast on track.

- Record in a quiet place.

- Don't turn pages, rustle paper, or make noises while recording.

- If you use music or sound effects, make sure that they add to your message without creating distractions.

- Use free editing software to edit your recording.

© Houghton Mifflin Harcourt Publishing Company

Reflect & Extend

Here are some other ways to show your understanding of the ideas in Unit 2.

Reflect on the Essential Question

What keeps people from giving up?

Has your answer to the question changed after reading the texts in the unit? Discuss your ideas.

You can use these sentence starters to help you reflect on your learning.

- **I wonder about . . .**
- **I was surprised by . . .**
- **My ideas changed because . . .**

Project-Based Learning
↳ Create an Inspirational Poster

You've read about people who've refused to give up, despite the challenges they faced. Now, create an inspirational poster that encourages people not to give up, no matter what.

Here are some questions to ask yourself as you get started.

- Who is the target audience for my poster?
- What message would I like my poster to convey?
- What image will best communicate that message?
- What statement or quotation will best support my message?

Media Projects

To find help with this task online, access **Create an Inspirational Poster.**

Writing
↳ Write a Self-Help Article

The world is full of self-help books and articles—works that explain everything from how to win friends to how to start a business. Think about what you would include in a self-help article that explains how teens can keep going when times get tough. What advice would you give? Use the chart to develop ideas you might include in your article.

ASK YOURSELF	MY NOTES
What **challenges** lead teens to throw up their hands and quit trying to succeed?	
How would learning to **persist,** to keep trying no matter what, help a teenager?	
What steps should a teen follow to find the **fortitude** to keep trying?	

Ed

Get hooked by the unit topic.

Stream to Start Video

ESSENTIAL QUESTION:

? **How do you find courage in the face of fear?**

Finding Courage

"I learned that courage was not the absence of fear, but the triumph over it."
—Nelson Mandela

Analyze the Image

Which of the two riders is more courageous? Why do you think so?

Spark Your Learning

Here's a chance to spark your learning about the ideas in **Unit 3: Finding Courage.**

As you read, you can use the **Response Log** (page R3) to track your thinking about the Essential Question.

?

Make the Connection

When's the last time you read a story or watched a show in which one of the characters was brave and courageous? Describe or sketch that character.

Think About the Essential Question

How do you find courage in the face of fear? What inspires people to act bravely, even when they're terribly afraid? Explain your ideas.

Prove It!

Turn to a partner and use one of the words in a sentence describing an action that you consider courageous.

Sound Like an Expert

You can use these Academic Vocabulary words to write and talk about the topics and themes in the unit. Which of these words do you already feel comfortable using when speaking or writing?

	I can use it!	I understand it.	I'll look it up.
evident	☐	☐	☐
factor	☐	☐	☐
indicate	☐	☐	☐
similar	☐	☐	☐
specific	☐	☐	☐

© Houghton Mifflin Harcourt Publishing Company

Preview the Texts

Look over the images, titles, and descriptions of the texts in the unit. Mark the title of the text that interests you most.

from **The Breadwinner**

Novel by **Deborah Ellis**

Life seems cruel and almost impossible for Parvana's family, but Parvana's newfound courage may save them all.

Life Doesn't Frighten Me

Poem by **Maya Angelou**

Sometimes the world can seem like a terribly frightening place—even in our own imaginations.

Fears and Phobias

Informational Text by **kidshealth.org**

What causes us to feel afraid? And how should we respond when our own fears get the best of us?

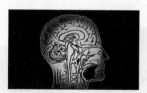

Wired for Fear

Video by the **California Science Center**

What in the world is happening in our brains when we feel afraid?

Embarrassed? Blame Your Brain

Informational Text by **Jennifer Connor-Smith**

Find out why we all feel embarrassed now and then—sometimes for the silliest of reasons.

The Ravine

Short Story by **Graham Salisbury**

A boy drowned in the ravine a couple of weeks ago. His body's never been found. So why are Vinny and his friends headed there?

from **Into the Air**

Graphic Biography by **Robert Burleigh, illustrated** by **Bill Wylie**

Their gliders keep crashing, dashing the Wright Brothers' hopes to achieve human flight. What gives them the courage to keep trying?

from **The Wright Brothers: How They Invented the Airplane**

Biography by **Russell Freedman**

Every attempt to fly has failed, yet the Wrights won't give up. Why?

I Wonder . . .

Name a childhood fear that you're now brave enough to face. How did you develop the courage to face that fear?

from

The Breadwinner

Novel by **Deborah Ellis**

ESSENTIAL QUESTION:
How do you find courage in the face of fear?

Engage Your Brain

Choose one or more of these activities to start connecting with the story you're about to read.

Everyone's an Expert

Do some research to learn about life for girls and women in Afghanistan.

- What rules, regulations, and customs govern their daily lives?

- How do their lives compare with your own?

Ready To Go "Adulting"?

With a partner, discuss and list the many duties of adulthood.

- Put a plus sign (+) next to things you'd like to do; add a minus sign (–) next to things you wouldn't like to do.

- Discuss why you rated each item as you did.

Share and Toss

With a group, share facts that you *already* know about Afghanistan.

- Gather in a circle with one member of the group holding a foam ball. Have this person report a fact about Afghanistan or "pass," and then toss the ball to someone else.

- Have that person report a different fact or "pass," tossing the ball to another member of the group.

- When your group has run out of facts, summarize the information you've learned.

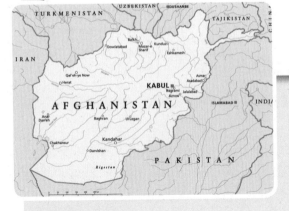

Analyze Character and Plot

A fictional **character** is any person, animal, or imaginary creature that takes part in a story's **plot**, or its series of events. Here are some ways that character and plot interact:

- A character's circumstances help set the plot in motion.

- Characters respond to events by acting and interacting with other characters. They may also change their own thoughts and feelings in response to events.

- Characters' responses, in turn, shape the plot as it develops.

Analyze Character and Setting

A story's **setting** is the time and place in which the action occurs. The setting in historical fiction is likely to be in the past, and it generally includes information about the culture of a particular place.

The setting of *The Breadwinner*—Afghanistan during a time of harsh rule—influences how characters develop. Note how the story's characters respond to the setting, including its rules for how women and men should dress and behave.

Focus on Genre
↳ Historical Fiction

- includes the basic elements of fiction: setting, character, plot, conflict, and theme

- is set in the past and includes real places and real events of historical importance

- is a type of realistic fiction in which fictional characters behave like real people and use human abilities to cope with life's challenges

CHARACTER	FEATURES OF SETTING	CHARACTER'S RESPONSE	MY IDEAS ABOUT THE CHARACTER
Parvana			
Nooria			
Mother			

Annotation in Action

Here is an example of how one reader noted information about the setting in *The Breadwinner*. As you read, highlight passages that suggest ideas about the story's time and place.

"If anybody asks about you, we'll say that you have gone to stay with an aunt in Kunduz," Mother said.

"But no one will ask about you."

At these words, Parvana turned her head sharply to glare at her sister.

Parvana's mother thinks no one will find out that she's not in Kunduz. It must be a long way away.

Expand Your Vocabulary

Put a check mark next to the vocabulary words that you feel comfortable using when speaking or writing.

solution
responsibility
stammer
fume

Turn to a partner and talk about the vocabulary words you already know. Then, use as many words as you can in a paragraph about the courage it takes to do something you don't want to do. As you read *The Breadwinner*, use the definitions in the side column to learn the vocabulary words you don't already know.

Background

Deborah Ellis (b. 1960) wrote *The Breadwinner* after interviewing Afghan women and girls in a refugee camp in Pakistan. In this excerpt, 11-year-old Parvana lives with her family in Kabul, Afghanistan, in the 1990s. Parvana's family, like others, has suffered under harsh government rule. Parvana's father has been imprisoned, and her older brother, Hossain, has been killed. With no men to help, Parvana's family must find a way to survive.

from The Breadwinner

Novel by **Deborah Ellis**

Life seems cruel and almost impossible for Parvana's family, but Parvana's newfound courage may save them all.

NOTICE & NOTE
As you read, use the side margins to make notes about the text.

1   They were going to turn her into a boy.

2   "As a boy, you'll be able to move in and out of the market, buy what we need, and no one will stop you," Mother said.

3   "It's a perfect **solution**," Mrs. Weera said.

4   "You'll be our cousin from Jalalabad," Nooria said, "come to stay with us while our father is away."

5   Parvana stared at the three of them. It was as though they were speaking a foreign language, and she didn't have a clue what they were saying.

6   "If anybody asks about you, we'll say that you have gone to stay with an aunt in Kunduz,"[1] Mother said.

7   "But no one will ask about you."

solution
(sə-lōō′shən) *n.* A *solution* is a way of handling a problem.

---

[1] **Kunduz** (kōōn′dōōz): the capital city of Kunduz Province in northern Afghanistan, situated north of Kabul.

Annotate: Mark details in
paragraph 8 that help describe
the setting in which Parvana lives.

Infer: How might this setting
affect the story's characters?

8   At these words, Parvana turned her head sharply to glare
at her sister. If ever there was a time to say something mean,
this was it, but she couldn't think of anything. After all, what
Nooria said was true. None of her friends had seen her since
the Taliban closed the schools. Her relatives were scattered to
different parts of the country, even to different countries. There
was no one to ask about her.

9   "You'll wear Hossain's clothes." Mother's voice caught, and
for a moment it seemed as though she would cry, but she got
control of herself again.

10   "They will be a bit big for you, but we can make some
adjustments if we have to." She glanced over at Mrs. Weera.
"Those clothes have been idle long enough. It's time they were
put to use."

11   Parvana guessed Mrs. Weera and her mother had been
talking long and hard while she was asleep. She was glad of that.
Her mother already looked better. But that didn't mean she was
ready to give in.

12   "It won't work," she said. "I won't look like a boy. I have
long hair."

13   Nooria opened the cupboard door, took out the sewing kit
and slowly opened it up. It looked to Parvana as if Nooria was
having too much fun as she lifted out the scissors and snapped
them open and shut a few times.

14   "You're not cutting my hair!" Parvana's hands flew up to her
head.

15   "How else will you look like a boy?" Mother asked.

16   "Cut Nooria's hair! She's the oldest! It's her **responsibility** to look after me, not my responsibility to look after her!"

17   "No one would believe me to be a boy," Nooria said calmly, looking down at her body. Nooria being calm just made Parvana madder.

18   "I'll look like that soon," Parvana said.

19   "You wish."

20   "We'll deal with that when the time comes," Mother said quickly, heading off the fight she knew was coming. "Until then, we have no choice. Someone has to be able to go outside, and you are the one most likely to look like a boy."

21   Parvana thought about it. Her fingers reached up her back to see how long her hair had grown.

22   "It has to be your decision," Mrs. Weera said. "We can force you to cut off your hair, but you're still the one who has to go outside and act the part. We know this is a big thing we're asking, but I think you can do it. How about it?"

23   Parvana realized Mrs. Weera was right. They could hold her down and cut off her hair, but for anything more, they needed her cooperation. In the end, it really was her decision.

24   Somehow, knowing that made it easier to agree.

25   "All right," she said. "I'll do it."

26   "Well done," said Mrs. Weera. "That's the spirit."

27   Nooria snapped the scissors again. "I'll cut your hair," she said.

28   "I'll cut it," Mother said, taking the scissors away. "Let's do it now, Parvana. Thinking about it won't make it any easier."

responsibility

(rĭ-spŏnˊsə-bĭlˊĭ-tē) *n.* A *responsibility* is a duty, obligation, or burden.

NOTICE & NOTE
WORDS OF THE WISER

When you notice a wiser character giving advice, you've found a **Words of the Wiser** signpost.

Notice & Note: In paragraphs 20–26, Parvana's mother expects obedience, but Mrs. Weera offers an insight. What insight does she offer Parvana? Mark this detail.

Cite Evidence: What's the life lesson and how might it affect Parvana?

29   Parvana and her mother went into the washroom where the cement floor would make it easier to clean up the cut-off hair. Mother took Hossain's clothes in with them.

30   "Do you want to watch?" Mother asked, nodding toward the mirror.

31   Parvana shook her head, then changed her mind. If this was the last she would see of her hair, then she wanted to see it for as long as she could.

32   Mother worked quickly. First she cut off a huge chunk in a straight line at her neck. She held it up for Parvana to see.

33   "I have a lovely piece of ribbon packed away," she said. "We'll tie this up with it, and you can keep it."

34   Parvana looked at the hair in her mother's hand. While it was on her head, it had seemed important. It didn't seem important any more.

35   "No, thanks," said Parvana. "Throw it away."

36   Her mother's lips tightened. "If you're going to sulk about it," she said, and she tossed the hair down to the floor.

37   As more and more hair fell away, Parvana began to feel like a different person. Her whole face showed. What was left of her hair was short and shaggy. It curled in a soft fringe around her ears. There were no long parts to fall into her eyes, to become tangled on a windy day, to take forever to dry when she got caught in the rain.

38   Her forehead seemed bigger. Her eyes seemed bigger, too, maybe because she was opening them so wide to be able to see everything. Her ears seemed to stick out from her head.

39   They look a little funny, Parvana thought, but a nice sort of funny.

40   I have a nice face, she decided.

41   Mother rubbed her hands brusquely[2] over Parvana's head to rub away any stray hairs.

42   "Change your clothes," she said. Then she left the washroom.

43   All alone, Parvana's hand crept up to the top of her head. Touching her hair gingerly[3] at first, she soon rubbed the palm of her hand all over her head. Her new hair felt both bristly and soft. It tickled the skin on her hand.

44   I like it, she thought, and she smiled.

---

[2] **brusquely** (brŭsk´lē): abruptly or curtly.
[3] **gingerly** (jĭn´jər-lē): cautiously or carefully.

45   She took off her own clothes and put on her brother's. Hossain's shalwar kameez[4] was pale green, both the loose shirt and the baggy trousers. The shirt hung down very low, and the trousers were too long, but by rolling them up at the waist, they were all right.

46   There was a pocket sewn into the left side of the shirt, near the chest. It was just big enough to hold money and maybe a few candies, if she ever had candies again. There was another pocket on the front. It was nice to have pockets. Her girl clothes didn't have any.

47   "Parvana, haven't you changed yet?"

48   Parvana stopped looking at herself in the mirror and joined her family.

49   The first face she saw was Maryam's. Her little sister looked as if she couldn't quite figure out who had walked into the room.

50   "It's me, Maryam," Parvana said.

51   "Parvana!" Maryam laughed as she recognized her.

52   "Hossain," her mother whispered.

53   "You look less ugly as a boy than you do as a girl," Nooria said quickly. If Mother started remembering Hossain, she'd just start crying again.

54   "You look fine," said Mrs. Weera.

55   "Put this on." Mother handed Parvana a cap. Parvana put it on her head. It was a white cap with beautiful embroidery all over it. Maybe she'd never wear her special red shalwar kameez again, but she had a new cap to take its place.

---

4 shalwar kameez (shäl´vär kə-mēz´): a type of long, loose shirt and pants, worn by both men and women.

ANALYZE CHARACTER AND PLOT

Annotate: Reread paragraphs 46–53. In paragraph 53, mark what Nooria says in response to Parvana's disguise. Then, mark what Nooria is thinking.

Infer: What do you learn about Nooria here?

ANALYZE CHARACTER AND SETTING

Annotate: Mark the words in paragraphs 56–59 that refer to the story's cultural setting.

Synthesize: How do you explain the relationship between the setting and Parvana's reaction in paragraph 59?

ANALYZE CHARACTER AND PLOT

Annotate: Mark the words in paragraphs 63–64 that show what Parvana is feeling or thinking.

Draw Conclusions: What is revealed about Parvana's character in these paragraphs?

56 "Here's some money," her mother said. "Buy what you were not able to buy yesterday." She placed a pattu[5] around Parvana's shoulder. It was her father's. "Hurry back."

57 Parvana tucked the money into her new pocket. She slipped her feet into her sandals, then reached for her chador.[6]

58 "You won't be needing that," Nooria said.

59 Parvana had forgotten. Suddenly she was scared. Everyone would see her face! They would know she wasn't a boy!

60 She turned around to plead with her mother. "Don't make me do this!"

61 "You see?" Nooria said in her nastiest voice. "I told you she was too scared."

62 "It's easy to call someone else scared when you're safe inside your home all the time!" Parvana shot back. She spun around and went outside, slamming the door behind her.

63 Out on the street, she kept waiting for people to point at her and call her a fake. No one did. No one paid any attention to her at all. The more she was ignored, the more confident she felt.

64 When she had gone into the market with her father, she had kept silent and covered up her face as much as possible. She had tried her best to be invisible. Now, with her face open to the sunshine, she was invisible in another way. She was just

---

[5] **pattu** (pə´tōō): a gray or brown woolen shawl worn by Afghan men and boys.
[6] **chador** (chä-dôr´): a cloth worn by women and girls to cover their hair and shoulders.

Don't forget to
Notice & Note as you
read the text.
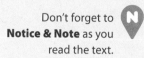

one more boy on the street. She was nothing worth paying attention to.

65　　When she came to the shop that sold tea, rice and other groceries, she hesitated for a slight moment, then walked boldly through the door. I'm a boy, she kept saying to herself. It gave her courage.

66　　"What do you want?" the grocer asked.

67　　"Some . . . some tea," Parvana **stammered** out.

68　　"How much? What kind?" The grocer was gruff, but it was ordinary bad-mood gruff, not gruff out of anger that there was a girl in his shop.

69　　Parvana pointed to the brand of tea they usually had at home. "Is that the cheapest?"

70　　"This one is the cheapest." He showed her another one.

71　　"I'll take the cheapest one. I also need five pounds of rice."

72　　"Don't tell me. You want the cheapest kind. Big spender."

73　　Parvana left the shop with rice and tea, feeling very proud of herself. "I can do this!" she whispered.

74　　Onions were cheap at the vegetable stand. She bought a few.

75　　"Look what I got!" Parvana exclaimed, as she burst through the door of her home. "I did it! I did the shopping, and nobody bothered me."

76　　"Parvana!" Maryam ran to her and gave her a hug. Parvana hugged her back as best she could with her arms full of groceries.

stammer

(stăm´ər) *v.* To *stammer* is to speak with involuntary pauses or repetitions.

ANALYZE CHARACTER AND PLOT

Annotate: How does the grocer respond to Parvana? Mark what he says in lines 69–72.

Infer: Describe what the grocer thinks of Parvana. What do his words reveal?

77   Mother was back on the toshak,[7] facing the wall, her back to the room. Ali sat beside her, patting her and saying, "Ma-ma-ma," trying to get her attention.

78   Nooria took the groceries from Parvana and handed her the water bucket.

79   "As long as you've got your sandals on," she said.

80   "What's wrong with Mother now?"

81   "Shhh! Not so loud! Do you want her to hear you? She got upset after seeing you in Hossain's clothes. Can you blame her? Also, Mrs. Weera went home, and that's made her sad. Now, please go and get water."

82   "I got water yesterday!"

83   "I had a lot of cleaning to do. Ali was almost out of diapers. Would you rather wash diapers than fetch the water?"

84   Parvana fetched the water.

85   "Keep those clothes on," Nooria said when Parvana returned. "I've been thinking about this. If you're going to be a boy outside, you should be a boy inside, too. What if someone comes by?"

86   That made sense to Parvana. "What about Mother? Won't it upset her to see me in Hossain's clothes all the time?"

87   "She'll have to get used to it."

88   For the first time, Parvana noticed the tired lines on Nooria's face. She looked much older than seventeen. "I'll help you with supper," she offered.

89   "You? Help? All you'd do is get in my way."

90   Parvana **fumed**. It was impossible to be nice to Nooria!

91   Mother got up for supper and made an effort to be cheerful. She complimented Parvana on her shopping success, but seemed to have a hard time looking at her.

92   Later that night, when they were all stretched out for sleep, Ali fussed a little.

93   "Go to sleep, Hossain," Parvana heard her mother say. "Go to sleep, my son."

---

[7] **toshak** (tō´shŏk): a narrow mattress used in many Afghan homes instead of chairs or beds.

fume
(fyo͞om) *v.* To *fume* about something is to feel or show displeasure or resentment.

ESSENTIAL QUESTION:
How do you find courage in the face of fear?

Review your notes and add your thoughts to your Response Log.

TURN AND TALK

With a partner, list the things you'd both be willing to give up for the sake of others. Then, list things you wouldn't be willing to give up. How might Parvana react to your lists?

Assessment Practice

Answer these questions before moving on to the **Analyze the Text** section.

1. Select the sentence that shows the problem the family is trying to solve.

   (A) "'As a boy, you'll be able to move in and out of the market, buy what we need, and no one will stop you,' Mother said." (paragraph 2)

   (B) "None of her friends had seen her since the Taliban closed the schools." (paragraph 8)

   (C) "Her relatives were scattered to different parts of the country, even to different countries." (paragraph 8)

   (D) "It was impossible to be nice to Nooria!" (paragraph 90)

2. Select **two** sentences that show that Parvana's changing appearance is beginning to affect her outlook.

   (A) "As more and more hair fell away, Parvana began to feel like a different person." (paragraph 37)

   (B) "What was left of her hair was short and shaggy." (paragraph 37)

   (C) "Her ears seemed to stick out from her head." (paragraph 38)

   (D) "I have a nice face, she decided." (paragraph 40)

   (E) "Mother rubbed her hands brusquely over Parvana's head to rub away any stray hairs." (paragraph 41)

3. Which of the following ideas is true?

   (A) The family forces Parvana to disguise herself as a boy.

   (B) Parvana treasures her long hair after Mother cuts it off.

   (C) Parvana feels proud that she bought food at the market.

   (D) Mother is delighted that Parvana reminds her of Hossain.

☺Ed
Test-Taking Strategies

Analyze the Text

Support your responses with evidence from the text.

(1) ANALYZE How does the author use elements of both culture and setting in paragraphs 64–72 to help further the plot?

(2) COMPARE Think about Parvana's character at the beginning of the excerpt (paragraphs 1–16) and near the end (paragraphs 85–88). What changes do you notice about Parvana over this time, and how do they affect the plot?

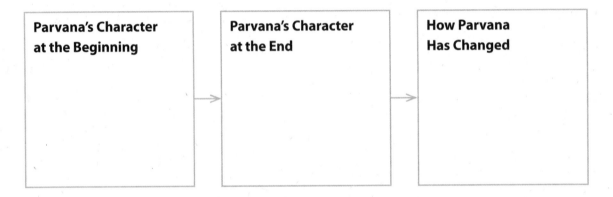

Parvana's Character at the Beginning	Parvana's Character at the End	How Parvana Has Changed

(3) EVALUATE How effectively has the author used setting to develop Parvana and other characters?

(4) INTERPRET Review paragraphs 91–93 at the end of the excerpt. What does the author reveal about Mother, and how might this information affect the plot?

(5) ANALYZE What **Words of the Wiser** are delivered by Nooria in paragraphs 85–87? What are the consequences for Parvana and Mother?

(6) PREDICT Review Parvana's observations about appearing in public in paragraphs 63–73. In your own words, describe her **Aha Moment.** What does she realize? How might this understanding help her in the future?

Choices

Here are some other ways to demonstrate your understanding of the ideas in this lesson.

Writing
↳ Explain Parvana to a Friend

Write a brief essay to help one of your peers understand the strengths of Parvana's character, given her culture and living conditions. Consider her personality, the struggles she faces, her actions, and any changes she undergoes.

- Include a claim, provide your reasoning, and support your reasons with evidence from the text.

- Use a formal style and structure, and include a conclusion that follows from and supports your argument.

As you write and discuss, be sure to use the **Academic Vocabulary** words.

evident
factor
indicate
similar
specific

Speaking & Listening
↳ Compare Media

An animated version of *The Breadwinner* is available through some streaming services. In a small group, find and view the segment that portrays events in the excerpt you just read. Then, discuss similarities and differences between the two versions.

- How did your reading experience differ from that of viewing the film?

- What similarities were there in the two experiences?

- What are the advantages and disadvantages of each form of media, text and film?

Media
↳ Give a Multimedia Presentation

Deborah Ellis has donated money from book sales to help fund education projects for Afghan women and children. Investigate an organization that delivers aid to people in your own community. Then, give a presentation that uses both text and visual elements to share what you learned about the organization with your class.

- Make sure your presentation follows a logical organization and includes facts and details to support each point.

- Pay attention to your speaking rate, enunciation, and volume.

- Maintain eye contact with your audience, and use natural gestures while you speak.

- Invite and answer questions.

Expand Your Vocabulary

PRACTICE AND APPLY

Answer the questions to show your understanding of the vocabulary words. Choose the letter of the better answer to each question.

1. Which of the following is most likely to cause someone to **fume?**

   a. an act of kindness   **b.** an insulting comment

2. Which of the following is an example of a **responsibility?**

   a. feeding a pet   **b.** playing a game

3. Which of the following is likely to need a **solution?**

   a. a problem   **b.** an airplane

4. Which of the following is an example of a **stammer?**

   a. speaking with repetitive sounds and pauses   **b.** walking with uneven steps

Vocabulary Strategy
↳ **Parts of Speech**

For a clear understanding of a word's meaning, determine the word's **part of speech,** or the function it performs in a sentence.

Review paragraphs 89–90 to see how the word *fume* is used in the selection. Here, the word's part of speech is a verb, but *fume* can also be used as a noun, meaning "gas" or "smoke." For words with **multiple meanings,** such as *fume,* compare the word's usage to the various dictionary definitions and their corresponding parts of speech to determine the correct meaning.

> ☺**Ed**
>
> **Interactive Vocabulary Lesson: Using Reference Sources**

PRACTICE AND APPLY

Work with a partner to determine the meanings of *responsibility, solution,* and *stammer* in *The Breadwinner.* Together, use a dictionary to determine each word's part of speech and its meaning. Finally, write original sentences for *fume, responsibility, solution,* and *stammer.*

1. *(fume)* _____

2. *(responsibility)* _____

3. *(solution)* _____

4. *(stammer)* _____

Watch Your Language!

Capitalization of Proper Nouns

Proper nouns name a specific person, place, thing, or idea and are capitalized to help distinguish them from common nouns. In *The Breadwinner,* proper nouns are used in the following ways:

Interactive Grammar Lesson: Capital Letters

- to name specific people

  Parvana realized Mrs. Weera was right.

- to name specific places, such as cities

  "You'll be our cousin from Jalalabad," Nooria said, "come to stay with us while our father is away."

- to name a specific thing, in this case, the title of the novel

  The Breadwinner

PRACTICE AND APPLY

Write your own sentences, following the examples from *The Breadwinner*. Your sentences can be about how Parvana faces challenges or ways in which you or someone else found courage in the face of fear.

First, complete the chart by listing common and proper nouns for people, places, and things that you can use in your sentences. Then, write your sentences using nouns from your list.

	PEOPLE	PLACES	THINGS
Common Nouns:			
Sentence:			
Proper Nouns:			
Sentence:			

Life Doesn't Frighten Me

Poem by **Maya Angelou**

Engage Your Brain

Choose one or both activities to start connecting with the poem you're about to read.

Childhood Fears

Think about things that frightened you in childhood, both real or imaginary. Sketch something that you feared, with a brief caption explaining your sketch.

New Student Handbook

Middle school can be a scary place, especially for new students. With a small group, develop ideas for a "handbook" about how new students might build the courage to face fears about middle school.

- Think about common fears, such as worries about getting to class.

- Discuss ways to deal with each fear.

- Then, list the topics your handbook would cover, and share your ideas with other groups.

Explain Speaker

"Life Doesn't Frighten Me" is a **lyric poem,** a type of poem in which a single speaker expresses personal ideas and feelings.

- A poem's **speaker,** the voice that "talks" to the reader, may be a fictional character.

- Lyric poems are usually written from a first-person point of view.

- Use of first-person pronouns does not mean that the poet is the speaker.

- Clues in the poem can help you identify the speaker and the speaker's situation.

Use a chart like this to help you make inferences about and explain the poem's speaker.

© Houghton Mifflin Harcourt Publishing Company

Focus on Genre
↳ **Lyric Poetry**

- usually short to convey emotional intensity

- usually written in first-person point of view to express the speaker's thoughts and feelings

- often uses repetition, refrain, and rhyme to create a melodic quality

- includes many forms, such as sonnets, odes, and elegies

MY QUESTIONS	INFERENCES AND EVIDENCE FROM THE POEM
Who is speaking? How do I know?	
What ideas and feelings does the speaker communicate? Why?	

Analyze Structure: Repetition and Refrain

Poets use structure and poetic elements to create mood and reinforce meaning. Often a poet will repeat certain words, sounds, or even syllables in a poem. This device is called **repetition,** and it helps emphasize important ideas, convey the speaker's attitude, reveal the author's purpose, and give the poem a musical quality.

One kind of repetition is **refrain**—a phrase, line, or set of phrases or lines repeated regularly throughout the poem.

As you read the lyric poem "Life Doesn't Frighten Me," listen for the refrain, and think about how it conveys information about the speaker's voice and the poem's mood and message.

Annotation in Action

Here are one reader's notes about the refrain in "Life Doesn't Frighten Me." As you read, note how the poet uses the refrain to help draw attention to the poem's message.

> Shadows on the wall
> Noises down the hall
> Life doesn't frighten me at all
> Bad dogs barking loud
> Big ghosts in a cloud
> Life doesn't frighten me at all

The speaker keeps saying she's not afraid of life. Why not?

Background

Maya Angelou (1928–2014) was born Marguerite Annie Johnson in St. Louis, Missouri. Though a childhood trauma led her to stop speaking for five and a half years, Angelou grew up to pursue a career as a singer and actor. She later turned to writing as her main form of expression, and in 1970, her best-selling autobiography, *I Know Why the Caged Bird Sings,* made her an international literary star. She is widely admired as a fearless and inspiring voice.

Life Doesn't Frighten Me

Poem by **Maya Angelou**

Sometimes the world can seem like a terribly frightening place—even in our own imaginations.

NOTICE & NOTE
As you read, use the side margins to make notes about the text.

Shadows on the wall
Noises down the hall
Life doesn't frighten me at all
Bad dogs barking loud
5   Big ghosts in a cloud
Life doesn't frighten me at all.

Mean old Mother Goose
Lions on the loose
They don't frighten me at all
10 Dragons breathing flame
On my counterpane[1]
That doesn't frighten me at all.

EXPLAIN SPEAKER

Annotate: Mark words and phrases in lines 1–12 that give you clues about the identity of the speaker.

Infer: Who do you think the speaker is in this poem? Why?

---

[1] **counterpane:** a bedspread.

Annotate: In lines 13–21, mark the phrase that is used again and again in the poem.

Interpret: What is the purpose of the repeated phrase? What idea does it emphasize in this stanza?

I go boo
Make them shoo
15 I make fun
Way they run
I won't cry
So they fly
I just smile
20 They go wild
Life doesn't frighten me at all.

Tough guys in a fight
All alone at night
Life doesn't frighten me at all.

25 Panthers in the park
Strangers in the dark
No, they don't frighten me at all.

That new classroom where
Boys all pull my hair
30 (Kissy little girls
With their hair in curls)
They don't frighten me at all.

Don't show me frogs and snakes
And listen for my scream,
35 If I'm afraid at all
It's only in my dreams.

I've got a magic charm
That I keep up my sleeve,
I can walk the ocean floor
40 And never have to breathe.

Life doesn't frighten me at all
Not at all
Not at all.
Life doesn't frighten me at all.

?

ESSENTIAL QUESTION:

How do you find courage in the face of fear?

Review your notes and add your thoughts to your Response Log.

TURN AND TALK

Turn to a partner and discuss fears that are common in childhood. What advice would the poem's speaker give to children experiencing any of these fears?

Assessment Practice

Answer these questions before moving on to the **Analyze the Text** section.

1. This question has two parts. First answer **Part A**. Then, answer **Part B**.

   Part A

   What inference can you make about the speaker's response to fears?

   - (A) The speaker goes back to sleep.
   - (B) The speaker stays inside at night.
   - (C) The speaker smiles and makes fun of fears.
   - (D) The speaker does not read or listen to scary stories.

   Part B

   What excerpt from the poem most clearly supports the answer in Part A?

   - (A) "Mean old Mother Goose / Lions on the loose" (lines 7–8)
   - (B) "I just smile / They go wild" (lines 19–20)
   - (C) "Tough guys in a fight / All alone at night" (lines 22–23)
   - (D) "If I'm afraid at all / It's only in my dreams." (lines 35–36)

2. Select **two** excerpts that show that using your imagination is an important topic in the poem.

   - (A) "Bad dogs barking loud / Big ghosts in a cloud" (lines 4–5)
   - (B) "I make fun / Way they run" (lines 15–16)
   - (C) "(Kissy little girls / With their hair in curls)" (lines 30–31)
   - (D) "I can walk the ocean floor / And never have to breathe." (lines 39–40)
   - (E) "Life doesn't frighten me at all / Not at all / Not at all." (lines 41–43)

Test-Taking Strategies

Analyze the Text

Support your responses with evidence from the text.

(1) DRAW CONCLUSIONS Review lines 1–9 and lines 37–40. What conclusions can you draw about the speaker's age, personality, and point of view?

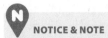

NOTICE & NOTE

Review what you **noticed and noted** as you read the text. Your annotations can help you answer these questions.

(2) ANALYZE Reread lines 1–21. Which scary things are clearly imaginary? Which are possibly real? How does the variety of scary things—and the speaker's response to them—contribute to the poem's theme?

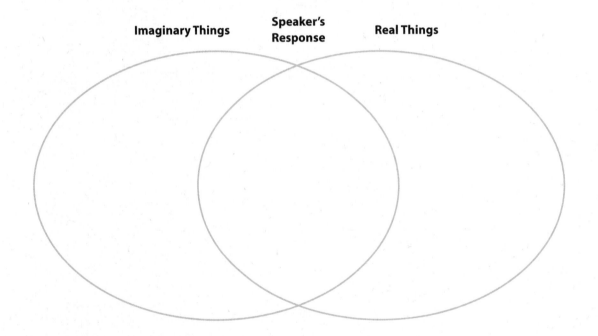

Imaginary Things   Speaker's Response   Real Things

(3) EVALUATE Read aloud lines 1–24. Notice the change to shorter line lengths in the third stanza. What effect does this change have on your reading?

(4) SYNTHESIZE Explain how the poet uses the refrain "Life doesn't frighten me at all," repeating it again and again, to help convey the meaning of the poem. Do you think the speaker of the poem is truly unafraid? Why or why not?

(5) ANALYZE Review all the things that the speaker claims not to fear. What is the effect of naming them?

Choices

Here are some other ways to demonstrate your understanding of the ideas in this lesson.

Writing
↳ Compose a Lyric Poem

Maya Angelou's "Life Doesn't Frighten Me" lists a number of childhood fears and describes how the poem's speaker finds the courage to face those fears. Write your own lyric poem about facing childhood fears.

- Write your poem from the point of view of a fictional speaker.

- Include the use of repetition and a refrain.

- Suggest ways to face a fear.

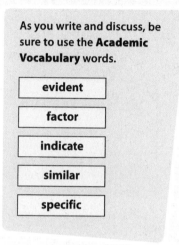

As you write and discuss, be sure to use the **Academic Vocabulary** words.

evident
factor
indicate
similar
specific

Speaking & Listening
↳ Present a Poem

With a partner, prepare a choral reading of "Life Doesn't Frighten Me."

- Decide who will read which lines or stanzas of the poem.

- Practice reading the poem, adjusting the rhythm and pacing of your reading according to different line lengths in the poem.

- Make eye contact with your audience, and use facial expressions and natural gestures to convey the meaning of the poem.

- Practice your choral reading until you can present the poem smoothly. Then, read it aloud to a small group or the class.

Research
↳ Compare and Contrast Two Versions of a Poem

With a partner, investigate the poem that Maya Angelou delivered at the 1993 presidential inauguration.

- First, find a copy of the poem and read it silently. Then, watch a video of Angelou delivering the poem.

- Compare and contrast your reading experience with your listening and viewing experience: discuss similarities and differences in the two experiences.

MENTOR TEXT

Fears and Phobias

Informational Text by **kidshealth.org**

Engage Your Brain

Choose one or both activities to start connecting with the text you're about to read.

Scary—Yet Fun

What activities do you enjoy *because* they scare you? List a few, noting why you enjoy each one. Then, sketch your favorite, trying to capture what it is that makes that activity scary—as well as why you enjoy it.

That *Was* Brave!

Think about a time you were frightened by something, yet felt brave enough to face your fear. Then, complete the following sentences to trace and describe what happened:

- I was frightened by _____.

- At first, I felt _____.

- I wanted to _____.

- But then I _____.

- And finally, I _____.

© Houghton Mifflin Harcourt Publishing Company • Image Credits: ©Jacob Lund/Adobe Stock

Analyze Structure

Text features are design elements that highlight the organization and important details in an informational text. These elements often draw attention to a text's central idea, topics, and supporting evidence.

TEXT FEATURE	EXAMPLE
A **heading** or **subheading** announces a new topic or section.	## What Is Fear? Fear is one of the most basic human emotions. It is programmed into the nervous system and works like an instinct.
A **sidebar,** or **boxed feature,** contains information related to a main topic.	*Some people find the rush of fear exciting. They might seek out the thrill of extreme sports and savor the scariest horror flicks.*
Colored type emphasizes important terms and ideas.	A tiny brain structure called the **amygdala** (pronounced: uh-mig-duh-luh) keeps track of experiences that trigger strong emotions.

Focus on Genre

↳ **Informational Text**

- provides factual information
- includes evidence to support ideas
- contains text features
- includes many forms, such as news articles and essays

Cite Evidence

To support analysis of any text, you need to **cite evidence,** or provide specific information, including details, facts, statistics, quotations, and examples.

- To gather support for an inference or conclusion, note significant words and details throughout the text.

- To analyze organization, mark words that signal a pattern, such as *because* or *as a result* for cause-and-effect.

- To determine and summarize the text's central idea, cite details from different sections of the text, in the correct order. Do not include your own opinions or views in your summary.

Annotation in Action

Here are one reader's notes about structure in "Fears and Phobias."
As you read, notice how the author uses text features to help
introduce important ideas.

What Is Fear?

Fear is one of the most basic human emotions. It is
programmed into the nervous system and works like an
instinct. From the time we're infants, we are equipped with
the survival instincts necessary to respond with fear when
we sense danger or feel unsafe.

*subheading—
introduces topic of fear*

*ideas and details
about fear*

Expand Your Vocabulary

Put a check mark next to the vocabulary words that you feel
comfortable using when speaking or writing.

activate	☐
trigger	☐
turbulence	☐
immaturity	☐

Turn to a partner and talk about the vocabulary
words you already know. Then, use as many words
as you can in a paragraph about the causes of fear.
As you read "Fears and Phobias," use the definitions
in the side column to learn the vocabulary words
you don't already know.

Background

Most people experience fear now and then; fear is an
ordinary part of life. Some fears may be overcome quickly;
others may continue for a lifetime. Science explains why
we experience fear and why our fears sometimes seem
out of control. Whether it is a fear of spiders, a fear of the
dark, or a fear of elevators, using science to understand our
responses to fear is the first step toward conquering it.

Fears and Phobias

Informational Text by **kidshealth.org**

What causes us to feel afraid? And how should we respond when our own fears get the best of us?

1 The roller coaster hesitates for a split second at the peak of its steep track after a long, slow climb. You know what's about to happen—and there's no way to avoid it now. It's time to hang onto the handrail, palms sweating, heart racing, and brace yourself for the wild ride down.

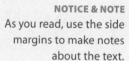

Text in Focus Video

Learn more about the text's structure.

ANALYZE STRUCTURE

Annotate: Mark two details in paragraphs 2–4 that answer the question in the subheading.

Analyze: Does the writer say that fear is helpful, or is it unhelpful?

What Is Fear?

2 Fear is one of the most basic human emotions. It is programmed into the nervous system and works like an instinct. From the time we're infants, we are equipped with the survival instincts necessary to respond with fear when we sense danger or feel unsafe.

3 Fear helps protect us. It makes us alert to danger and prepares us to deal with it. Feeling afraid is very natural—

© Houghton Mifflin Harcourt Publishing Company • Image Credits: ©Bert123/Shutterstock; (bg) ©run4it/Shutterstock

and helpful—in some situations. Fear can be like a warning, a signal that cautions us to be careful.

4 Like all emotions, fear can be mild, medium, or intense, depending on the situation and the person. A feeling of fear can be brief or it can last longer.

How Fear Works

5 When we sense danger, the brain reacts instantly, sending signals that **activate** the nervous system. This causes physical responses, such as a faster heartbeat, rapid breathing, and an increase in blood pressure. Blood pumps to muscle groups to prepare the body for physical action (such as running or fighting). Skin sweats to keep the body cool. Some people might notice sensations in the stomach, head, chest, legs, or hands. These physical sensations of fear can be mild or strong.

6 This response is known as "fight or flight" because that is exactly what the body is preparing itself to do: fight off the danger or run fast to get away. The body stays in this state of fight-flight until the brain receives an "all clear" message and turns off the response.

7 Sometimes fear is **triggered** by something that is startling or unexpected (like a loud noise), even if it's not actually dangerous. That's because the fear reaction is activated instantly—a few seconds faster than the thinking part of the brain can process or evaluate what's happening. As soon as the brain gets enough information to realize there's no danger ("Oh, it's just a balloon bursting—whew!"), it turns off the fear reaction. All this can happen in seconds.

activate
(ăk′tə-vāt′) *v.* To *activate* something means to cause it to start working.

trigger
(trĭg′ər) *v.* To *trigger* something means to cause it to begin.

ANALYZE STRUCTURE

Annotate: Mark the most important idea in the boxed feature "Fear or Fun?"

Connect: How does the information in this feature relate to what you have read so far?

FEAR OR FUN?

Some people find the rush of fear exciting. They might seek out the thrill of extreme sports and savor the scariest horror flicks. Others do not like the experience of feeling afraid or taking risks. During the scariest moments of a roller coaster ride one person might think, "I'll never get on this thing again—that is, if I make it out alive!" while another person thinks, "This is awesome! As soon as it's over, I'm getting back on!"

© Houghton Mifflin Harcourt Publishing Company • Image Credits: ©run4it/Shutterstock

Fears People Have

8   Fear is the word we use to describe our emotional reaction to something that seems dangerous. But the word "fear" is used in another way, too: to name something a person often feels afraid of.

9   People fear things or situations that make them feel unsafe or unsure. For instance, someone who isn't a strong swimmer might have a fear of deep water. In this case, the fear is helpful because it cautions the person to stay safe. Someone could overcome this fear by learning how to swim safely.

10   A fear can be healthy if it cautions a person to stay safe around something that could be dangerous. But sometimes a fear is unnecessary and causes more caution than the situation calls for.

11   Many people have a fear of public speaking. Whether it's giving a report in class, speaking at an assembly, or reciting lines in the school play, speaking in front of others is one of the most common fears people have.

12   People tend to avoid the situations or things they fear. But this doesn't help them overcome fear—in fact, it can be the reverse. Avoiding something scary reinforces a fear and keeps it strong.

13   People can overcome unnecessary fears by giving themselves the chance to learn about and gradually get used to the thing or situation they're afraid of. For example, people

CITE EVIDENCE

Annotate: In paragraphs 8–13, mark an example of a healthy fear and an example of an unnecessary fear.

Compare: How are healthy fears different from unnecessary fears?

(bg) ©run4it/Shutterstock

turbulence

(tûr′byə-ləns) *n*. In flying, *turbulence* is an interruption in the flow of wind that causes planes to rise, fall, or sway in a rough way.

who fly despite a fear of flying can become used to unfamiliar sensations like takeoff or **turbulence**. They learn what to expect and have a chance to watch what others do to relax and enjoy the flight. Gradually (and safely) facing fear helps someone overcome it.

Fears During Childhood

14 Certain fears are normal during childhood. That's because fear can be a natural reaction to feeling unsure and vulnerable— and much of what children experience is new and unfamiliar.

15 Young kids often have fears of the dark, being alone, strangers, and monsters or other scary imaginary creatures. School-aged kids might be afraid when it's stormy or at a first sleepover. As they grow and learn, with the support of adults, most kids are able to slowly conquer these fears and outgrow them.

16 Some kids are more sensitive to fears and may have a tough time overcoming them. When fears last beyond the expected age, it might be a sign that someone is overly fearful, worried, or anxious. People whose fears are too intense or last too long might need help and support to overcome them.

Phobias

17   A phobia is an intense fear reaction to a particular thing or a situation. With a phobia, the fear is out of proportion to the potential danger. But to the person with the phobia, the danger feels real because the fear is so very strong.

18   Phobias cause people to worry about, dread, feel upset by, and avoid the things or situations they fear because the physical sensations of fear can be so intense. So having a phobia can interfere with normal activities. A person with a phobia of dogs might feel afraid to walk to school in case he or she sees a dog on the way. Someone with an elevator phobia might avoid a field trip if it involves going on an elevator.

19   A girl with a phobia of thunderstorms might be afraid to go to school if the weather forecast predicts a storm. She might feel terrible distress and fear when the sky turns cloudy. A guy with social phobia experiences intense fear of public speaking or interacting, and may be afraid to answer questions in class, give a report, or speak to classmates in the lunchroom.

20   It can be exhausting and upsetting to feel the intense fear that goes with having a phobia. It can be disappointing to miss out on opportunities because fear is holding you back. And it can be confusing and embarrassing to feel afraid of things that others seem to have no problem with.

21   Sometimes, people get teased about their fears. Even if the person doing the teasing doesn't mean to be unkind and unfair, teasing only makes the situation worse.

What Causes Phobias?

22   Some phobias develop when someone has a scary experience with a particular thing or situation. A tiny brain structure called the **amygdala** (pronounced: uh-mig-duh-luh) keeps track of experiences that trigger strong emotions. Once a certain thing or situation triggers a strong fear reaction, the amygdala warns the person by triggering a fear reaction every time he or she encounters (or even thinks about) that thing or situation.

23   Someone might develop a bee phobia after being stung during a particularly scary situation. For that person, looking at a photograph of a bee, seeing a bee from a distance, or even walking near flowers where there *could* be a bee can all trigger the phobia.

24   Sometimes, though, there may be no single event that causes a particular phobia. Some people may be more sensitive

CITE EVIDENCE

Annotate: In paragraph 17, mark the definition of *phobia*.

Connect: How might a phobia affect someone? Cite evidence from paragraphs 18–21 in your response.

Close Read Screencast
Listen to a modeled close read of this text.

 **NOTICE & NOTE**
WORD GAPS

When you notice vocabulary that is unfamiliar, you've found a **Word Gaps** signpost.

Notice & Note: Mark the word in purple type.

Analyze: Can you find clues to help you understand the word?

to fears because of personality traits they are born with, certain genes[1] they've inherited, or situations they've experienced. People who have had strong childhood fears or anxiety may be more likely to have one or more phobias.

25   Having a phobia isn't a sign of weakness or **immaturity**. It's a response the brain has learned in an attempt to protect the person. It's as if the brain's alert system triggers a false alarm, generating intense fear that is out of proportion to the situation. Because the fear signal is so intense, the person is convinced the danger is greater than it actually is.

Overcoming Phobias

26   People can learn to overcome phobias by gradually facing their fears. This is not easy at first. It takes willingness and bravery. Sometimes people need the help of a therapist[2] to guide them through the process.

27   Overcoming a phobia usually starts with making a long list of the person's fears in least-to-worst order. For example, with a dog phobia, the list might start with the things the person is least afraid of, such as looking at a photo of a dog. It will then work all the way up to worst fears, such as standing next to someone who's petting a dog, petting a dog on a leash, and walking a dog.

28   Gradually, and with support, the person tries each fear situation on the list—one at a time, starting with the least fear. The person isn't forced to do anything and works on each fear until he or she feels comfortable, taking as long as needed.

29   A therapist could also show someone with a dog phobia how to approach, pet, and walk a dog, and help the person to try it, too. The person may expect terrible things to happen when near a dog. Talking about this can help, too. When people find that what they fear doesn't actually turn out to be true, it can be a great relief.

30   A therapist might also teach relaxation practices such as specific ways of breathing, muscle relaxation training, or soothing self-talk. These can help people feel comfortable and bold enough to face the fears on their list.

31   As somebody gets used to a feared object or situation, the brain adjusts how it responds and the phobia is overcome.

© Houghton Mifflin Harcourt Publishing Company • Image Credits: ©run4it/Shutterstock

immaturity
(ĭm´ə-tyŏŏr´ĭ-tē) *n. Immaturity* is the state of not being fully developed or grown.

CITE EVIDENCE

Annotate: Mark details in paragraph 26 that explain how someone may overcome a phobia.

Interpret: Choose one of the strategies for overcoming fear discussed in paragraphs 27–32. Then, explain whether it seems effective, citing text evidence in your response.

---

[1] **genes** (jēnz): the parts of cells that give a living thing its physical characteristics and make it grow and develop; a person's genes come from his or her parents and other blood relatives.

[2] **therapist** (thĕr´ə-pĭst): a person who is skilled in treating mental or physical illness.

32   Often, the hardest part of overcoming a phobia is getting started. Once a person decides to go for it—and gets the right coaching and support—it can be surprising how quickly fear can melt away.

TURN AND TALK

Work with a partner to identify why phobias can be so difficult to overcome. How might a childhood fear develop into a phobia?

ESSENTIAL QUESTION:
How do you find courage in the face of fear?

Review your notes and add your thoughts to your Response Log.

Assessment Practice

Answer these questions before moving on to the **Analyze the Text** section.

1. How does paragraph 10 contribute to the development of the author's ideas?

   (A) It warns that a fear can turn into a phobia.

   (B) It explains that fears are usually overreactions.

   (C) It notes that people avoid danger only if they feel fear.

   (D) It informs readers that fears can be both good and bad.

2. In paragraph 27, why does the author include information about dog phobias?

   (A) to describe a physical reaction to fear

   (B) to persuade readers to seek help for their fears

   (C) to show that phobias are the result of a single event

   (D) to give a specific example of how a fear could be overcome

3. Select **two** ideas that are supported by evidence in the selection.

   (A) Fears can be overcome with help and support.

   (B) Fear is natural and serves an important purpose.

   (C) Adults suffer from the sensation of fear more than children.

   (D) People stay in fight-or-flight mode because fear is activated instantly.

   (E) People develop fears only about situations that are dangerous or unsafe.

Test-Taking Strategies

Analyze the Text

Support your responses with evidence from the text.

(1) ANALYZE Examine paragraphs 2–4. How do they fit into the overall structure of the article?

(2) INTERPRET What does the term "fight-flight" refer to? How do the clues in paragraph 6 help you close a **Word Gap** and figure out the meaning of the term?

(3) INTERPRET What additional information does the boxed feature provide? How does it add to your understanding of the article?

(4) CITE EVIDENCE What causes phobias? Cite evidence from the text that explains where phobias come from.

(5) SUMMARIZE How does someone overcome a phobia? Describe and explain each step.

NOTICE & NOTE

Review what you **noticed and noted** as you read the text. Your annotations can help you answer these questions.

Steps to Overcoming a Phobia

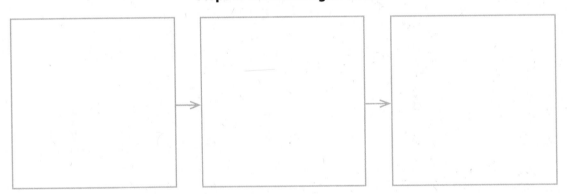

(6) SUMMARIZE What is a central idea of the text? Explain whether the author believes it is worthwhile to try to overcome phobias and why.

Choices

Here are some other ways to demonstrate your understanding of the ideas in this lesson.

Writing

↳ Fears vs. Phobias

Write a three- to four-paragraph essay in which you compare and contrast fears and phobias.

- Introduce the topic and express your central idea on fears and phobias.

- Then, tell about similarities and differences between fears and phobias. Include details from the text to support your ideas.

- Use transitional words and phrases, such as *also, as a result, for example,* and *on the other hand,* to help clarify relationships among ideas in your essay.

- In your final paragraph, state your conclusion.

As you write and discuss, be sure to use the **Academic Vocabulary** words.

evident
factor
indicate
similar
specific

Social & Emotional Learning

↳ Overcoming Fear

Hold a small group discussion about whether the information in "Fears and Phobias" can help someone overcome a fear.

- As a group, review the text and decide which information is relevant to the discussion. Use the subheadings to help you locate information.

- Listen closely to each other, and take notes on ideas and details that relate to the topic.

- Together, review the ideas and suggest which ones can help someone overcome a fear.

Research

↳ Learn About People Who Have Overcome Phobias

Well-known people have not allowed phobias to prevent them from accomplishing great things. Research these well-known figures who have suffered from phobias. Record what you learn in the chart.

WELL-KNOWN PEOPLE	PHOBIA
George Washington	
Oprah Winfrey	
Winston Churchill	

Expand Your Vocabulary

PRACTICE AND APPLY

Answer the questions to show your understanding of the
vocabulary words. Choose the better answer to each question.

1. Which of the following is an example of **immaturity?**

   a. explaining why you are upset   **b.** crying when you don't get your way

2. Which of the following is an example of **activate?**

   a. unplugging a computer   **b.** pressing the "on" button

3. Which canoe trip involves **turbulence?**

   a. canoeing on a calm lake   **b.** canoeing on a rushing river

4. Which of these is more likely to **trigger** an allergy?

   a. getting stung by a bee   **b.** reading about bees

Vocabulary Strategy
↳ **Prefixes That Mean "Not"**

A **prefix** is a word part that appears at the beginning of a base word
to form a new word. Many prefixes that mean "not" come from Latin.
One example appears in the vocabulary word *immaturity* (*im* + *maturity*).
Other prefixes that mean "not" include *in-*, *mis-*, *non-*, and *un-*.

☺ **Ed**

**Interactive Vocabulary
Lesson: Common Roots,
Prefixes, and Suffixes**

PRACTICE AND APPLY

First, identify the prefix that means "not" in each boldface word. Then,
state the meaning of the boldface word in your own words.

1. Not having Sunday hours at the library is **inconvenient** for people
   who work during the week.

   _____

2. A **nonviolent** protest would help the group avoid a confrontation.

   _____

3. Denying a citizen the right to vote is **undemocratic.**

   _____

4. The careless reporter **misquoted** the mayor's remarks.

   _____

Watch Your Language!

Dashes

Writers use dashes to interrupt their thoughts abruptly or to emphasize important ideas. A stylistic choice—used in both literary and informational texts—dashes add variety and voice.

Interactive Grammar Lesson: Dashes and Parentheses

In "Fears and Phobias" dashes are used in the following ways:

- to mark sharp turns in thought

  But this doesn't help them overcome fear—in fact, it can be the reverse.

- to enclose **nonrestrictive elements,** elements that are not needed to understand the basic meaning of the sentence

  Once a person decides to go for it—and gets the right coaching and support—it can be surprising how quickly fear can melt away.

- to set off an expression that summarizes or illustrates a statement that precedes it

  That's because the fear reaction is activated instantly—a few seconds faster than the thinking part of the brain can process or evaluate what's happening.

PRACTICE AND APPLY

Write your own sentences with dashes, using the examples from "Fears and Phobias" as models.

_____

_____

_____

_____

_____

MEDIA

MEDIA

Wired for Fear

Video by the **California Science Center**

Engage Your Brain

Think about a time when you were frightened or startled. Did your heart start racing? Did you start sweating? Describe to a partner what frightened you and how your body reacted to it.

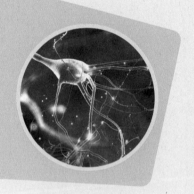

Background

"Fear is a full-body experience." This is how the website Goose Bumps! The Science of Fear introduces the topic "Fear and the Brain." This website includes a collection of videos, articles, and images about sensory information (what we see, hear, taste, smell, touch) that alerts us to what might be harmful. The section "Wired for Fear" includes a video that provides an animated version of how the brain processes fear reactions.

Analyze Media

The **purpose,** or intent, of any video or digital text is to inform, entertain, persuade, or express the feelings or thoughts of the creator. To meet the purpose, the video's creator uses words as well as visual and sound elements to convey information.

Focus on Genre
↳**Media**

- conveys a message
- targets a specific audience
- is created for a specific purpose
- includes TV broadcasts, videos, newspapers, magazines, and the Internet

Visual elements, or images, can help viewers understand **technical terms,** which are the words and phrases used in a particular profession or field of study.

STILLS	images that are motionless, such as illustrations or photographs
ANIMATION	images that appear to move and seem alive; created through drawings, computer graphics, or photographs

Sound elements include what you hear in a video.

MUSIC	sounds created by singing, playing instruments, or using computer-generated tones; creates a mood
NARRATION	the words as well as the expression and quality of voice used by the narrator

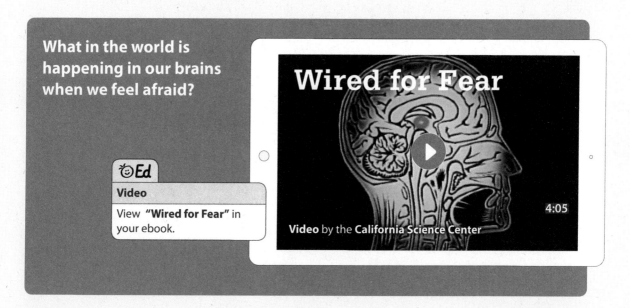

What in the world is happening in our brains when we feel afraid?

☺**Ed**

Video

View **"Wired for Fear"** in your ebook.

Wired for Fear

4:05

Video by the **California Science Center**

Analyze Media

Support your responses with evidence from the video.

ESSENTIAL QUESTION:
How do you find courage in the face of fear?

?

(1) **SUMMARIZE** Describe how the video explains what the hiker experiences.

(2) **CAUSE/EFFECT** Review the sequence that uses the animated model. What are some ways our bodies respond when the amygdala senses danger? What parts of the brain activate these responses?

(3) **ANALYZE** Explain the title "Wired for Fear." Why does the video use flashing lights and graphics that show movement in the animated model of how the brain processes potential danger?

(4) **SYNTHESIZE** Think about what you learned about fear while reading "Fears and Phobias." How does the video add to your understanding of fear?

(5) **EVALUATE** Which is more effective in explaining how fear works and why we experience it, the article or the video? Consider strengths and weaknesses of both the article and the video. Then, decide which is more effective. Explain your reasoning.

	STRENGTHS	WEAKNESSES
"Fears and Phobias"		
"Wired for Fear"		

Choices

Here are some other ways to demonstrate your understanding of the ideas in this lesson.

Writing
↳ Integrate Information

Using information from both "Wired for Fear" and "Fears and Phobias," explain two or three aspects of fear.

- Choose which aspects of fear you will explain. Review both sources and any notes you may have taken.

- Decide how to organize your information logically. What does the reader need to know in order to understand what comes next?

- Start each paragraph with a topic sentence. In each paragraph, cite at least one fact from the video and one from the text to support your point.

As you write and discuss, be sure to use the **Academic Vocabulary** words.

evident

factor

indicate

similar

specific

Media
↳ Produce a Podcast

With a partner, produce a podcast review of the video "Wired for Fear."

- Make notes about visual and sound elements in the video that made both positive and negative impressions.

- Explain how each element clarifies the topic, using examples. Present ideas for additional information that could have been included, drawing on other videos or sources as needed.

- Record your review with a partner, using a conversational approach and clear enunciation. Share your podcast with a larger group.

Research
↳ Discover the Power of Fear

Fear can have a dramatic impact on the body. In fact, there are accounts of people performing superhuman feats when faced with fear, such as lifting a car off of someone after an accident. With a partner, find such a story and share it with the class.

EVENT	DETAILS

Collaborate & Compare

ESSENTIAL QUESTION:
? **How do you find courage in the face of fear?**

Compare Across Genres

You're about to read an article and short story that share certain ideas about the lives of teens. As you read, notice how the ideas relate to your own experiences, as well as to the experiences of other young people. Then, look for ways that the ideas in the two texts relate to each other.

A

Embarrassed?
Blame Your Brain

Informational Text by
Jennifer Connor-Smith
pages 224–229

B

The Ravine

Short Story
by **Graham Salisbury**
pages 237–247

After you have read both selections, you'll get a chance to share your own ideas by holding a panel discussion to present research. You'll follow these steps:

- Develop Research Questions
- Gather the Information
- Share What You Learn

Embarrassed?

Blame Your Brain

Informational Text by **Jennifer Connor-Smith**

Engage Your Brain

Choose one or both activities to start connecting with the text you're about to read.

An Embarrassing List

Get with a partner and discuss common things that people find embarrassing, such as dropping a book or singing in public. Then, help your peers develop the courage to face embarrassment by listing four or five things they should never feel embarrassed about.

Take a Vote

People find lots of things embarrassing, but should they? Discover what your classmates think.

- Fill out five index cards, listing one situation that people find embarrassing on each card. Make sure that each card is suited to classroom discussion; if not, throw it out.

- Collect the cards, shuffle them, and read each one aloud to the group.

- Vote for the least embarrassing situation or action, and tally the votes.

Analyze Structure

Authors of informational texts organize facts and examples carefully. As you read "Embarrassed? Blame Your Brain," use a chart similar to this one to note examples of each organizational structure.

STRUCTURE	WHAT IT DOES	EXAMPLES
Definition	explains a topic's key characteristics and/or distinguishes it from similar topics or ideas	
Classification	organizes objects, ideas, or information into groups based on common characteristics	
Advantage and Disadvantage	evaluates a topic or proposal by analyzing both its positive and negative aspects	

Determine Meanings

Use the following to help you determine figurative, connotative, and technical meanings:

Text features often include information about technical meanings. Graphics often provide visual explanations of terms, and footnotes provide definitions and explanations.

Context, surrounding words and sentences, often provides clues about figurative and connotative meanings. **Figurative language** uses words in an imaginative way to help express and clarify ideas. **Connotations** are ideas and feelings associated with a word.

As you read, look for clues about figurative language and technical and connotative meanings.

Annotation in Action

Here are one reader's notes about structure in "Embarrassed? Blame Your Brain." As you read, look for ways that the author uses definition, classification, or advantage and disadvantage to help you understand each idea.

It's All in Your Head

Sometime during middle school, changes in brain activity transform how we see the world. Spending time with other kids becomes a top priority. Hormones power up the brain's reward system, making hanging out with friends more fun than ever before. But these changes come with a down side. Fitting in becomes essential.

Changes in our brains affect us.

Advantage: fun.

Disadvantage: we want to fit in.

Expand Your Vocabulary

Put a check mark next to the vocabulary words that you feel comfortable using when speaking or writing.

essential	☐
amplify	☐
generate	☐
humiliation	☐

Turn to a partner and talk about the vocabulary words you already know. Then, use as many words as you can in a paragraph about why people sometimes feel embarrassed. As you read "Embarrassed? Blame Your Brain," use the definitions in the side column to learn the vocabulary words you don't already know.

Background

We all sometimes base decisions on peer pressure, rather than on logic. Psychological research reveals that these snap decisions can have complex, confusing roots. In the following article, science writer and clinical psychologist **Jennifer Connor-Smith** explains why teenagers naturally develop a strong and sometimes overwhelming fear of embarrassment.

Embarrassed?

Blame Your Brain

Informational Text by **Jennifer Connor-Smith**

Find out why we all feel embarrassed now and then—sometimes for the silliest of reasons.

NOTICE & NOTE
As you read, use the side margins to make notes about the text.

DETERMINE MEANINGS

Annotate: Mark the figurative language in the second sentence of the first paragraph.

Infer: Determine the meaning of the phrase, using the surrounding text as clues.

1   Remember when you could pick your nose in public or run outside in your underpants without a second thought? These days, you flood with embarrassment if your dad sings in front of your friends or you drop a tray in the cafeteria.

2   What changed? Not the rules about nose picking or your father's singing voice, but your brain.

It's All in Your Head

3   Sometime during middle school, changes in brain activity transform how we see the world. Spending time with other kids becomes a top priority. Hormones[1] power up the brain's reward system, making hanging out with friends more fun

---

[1] **hormones:** chemical messengers that travel through the blood.

than ever before. But these changes come with a down side. Fitting in becomes **essential**. Threat-detection systems focus on what other people think and scan for any hints of disapproval. Hormones push the brain's shame and self-consciousness systems into overdrive.

4   Because of these brain changes, teens start reacting more strongly to social problems. Scientists don't know this *just* from surviving middle school—they have evidence from laboratory research. During a challenge like giving a speech, teens release more stress hormones and have higher blood pressure than kids

Don't forget to **Notice & Note** as you read the text.

essential

(ĭ-sĕn´shǝl) *adj.* Something *essential* is so important that you can't do without it.

DETERMINE MEANINGS

Annotate: In the graphic, mark the technical terms.

Interpret: Which part of the brain both rewards us and makes us want to fight or run away?

FEELINGS CENTRAL

A Quick Tour of Key Brain Regions Certain feelings and reactions take place in specific brain regions. Here are some regions associated with the emotional highs and lows of our social lives.

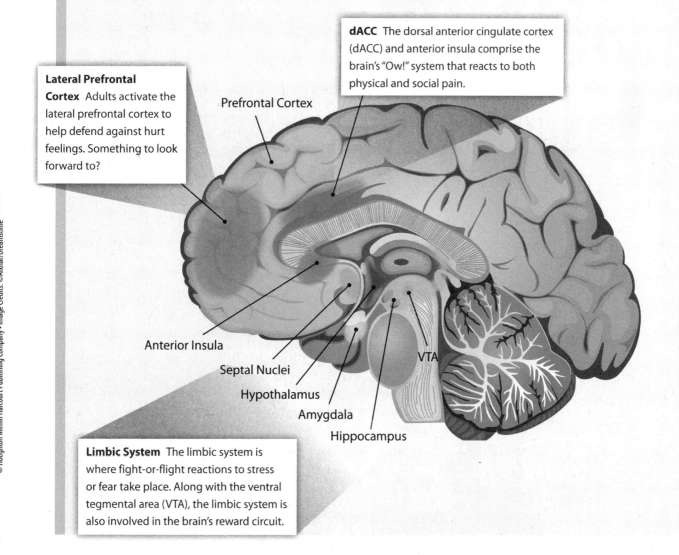

dACC The dorsal anterior cingulate cortex (dACC) and anterior insula comprise the brain's "Ow!" system that reacts to both physical and social pain.

Lateral Prefrontal Cortex Adults activate the lateral prefrontal cortex to help defend against hurt feelings. Something to look forward to?

Prefrontal Cortex

Anterior Insula

Septal Nuclei

Hypothalamus

Amygdala

Hippocampus

VTA

Limbic System The limbic system is where fight-or-flight reactions to stress or fear take place. Along with the ventral tegmental area (VTA), the limbic system is also involved in the brain's reward circuit.

or adults. Teens don't even have to tackle a challenge to feel stressed. Even being watched over a video monitor makes teens sweat more than adults.

Words Do Hurt Like Sticks and Stones

ANALYZE STRUCTURE

Annotate: Mark the subhead.

Analyze: Which main organizational pattern is the author using? How can you tell?

5   Why do we use pain words, like "hurt feelings" and "broken hearted," to talk about problems with other people? Maybe because our brains react to physical pain and social rejection in the same way. Psychologists explore this connection between physical and social pain by measuring brain activity while people play a computer game called Cyberball.

6   In Cyberball, research participants play a game of catch online with two other players. At least, that's what they believe is happening. In reality, the other "players" are fake, just part of the game's programming. The game starts fair, with the players programmed to share the ball with the research participant. Then, with no warning, the players start throwing the ball only to each other, leaving the research participant out completely.

7   No big surprise—teens in these Cyberball experiments feel sad and rejected. The surprising part? Rejection activates the same brain systems that physical pain triggers. Brain scans show that rejection fires up the "Ow!" part of our brain that makes pain upsetting. Without this pain-response system, we would recognize physical pain, but it wouldn't bother us. This physical pain system also responds to many kinds of social pain, like thinking about a breakup or being called boring.

8   Some people have especially reactive pain-response systems. A stronger "Ow!" brain response in the lab translates to people feeling more rejected, self-conscious, and sad in real life. Differences in pain-system reactivity may help explain why rejection hurts teenagers more than young kids. In Cyberball experiments comparing children to teens, teens activate brain systems related to pain and sadness more strongly.

Embarrassment Has an Unfair Advantage

Don't forget to **Notice & Note** as you read the text.

9   Our thoughts and feelings depend on the balance between many different brain systems. Activity in one system can **amplify** or cancel out activity in another. Because our brains take more than two decades to develop, some brain systems come online sooner than others. Unfortunately, the systems that trigger embarrassment and fear of rejection fire up years before the systems that tame bad feelings.

10   Imagine a tug-of-war with fear of rejection, the desire to fit in, and self-consciousness all pulling on the same side. With nothing pulling against them, they easily drag in all sorts of bad feelings. This imbalance means even small problems, like tripping in the hallway, can trigger a wave of embarrassment.

11   Brain scans reveal that adults unleash a powerful defender to pull the brain back into balance. Adult brains quickly fire up systems to soothe anxiety and **generate** positive thoughts. These systems help balance out concern about what other people think, so adults feel less hurt and embarrassed by rejection.

12   Wouldn't it be better if we could just turn off hurt feelings, embarrassment, and the desire to fit in? Probably not. Before modern society, people needed to belong to a group to survive. Without a group, people couldn't find enough food or protect themselves. Fear of rejection forced people to behave well enough for the community to keep them around.

13   Our lives don't depend on social acceptance anymore, but social pain is still helpful. Fear of rejection pulls on the right side in the tug-of-war against mean or selfish behavior. Shame punishes us for lying or cheating, even if we don't get caught. Social pain hurts, but it also makes us nicer. Brain scans show that teens with strong pain-response systems give more support to other kids.

14   Unfortunately, knowing the benefits of social pain won't save you from a flash of **humiliation** when your mom reminds you to take a "potty break" in front of your friends. But you can take comfort in reminding yourself that the pain makes you a better person. Maybe even one less likely to embarrass your own kids someday.

amplify
(ăm´plə´fī) *v.* To *amplify* something is to make it stronger or more intense.

generate
(jĕn´ə-rāt´) *v.* To *generate* is to create and develop something.

NOTICE & NOTE
CONTRASTS AND CONTRADICTIONS

When you notice a contrast between what you would expect and what you observe happening, you've found a **Contrasts and Contradictions** signpost.

Notice & Note: In paragraph 12, mark a fact about fear that contrasts with our usual views.

Analyze: Why did the author point out this contrast?

humiliation
(hyoō-mĭl´ē-ā´shən) *n.* A feeling of *humiliation* is even more intense than a feeling of embarrassment.

Annotate: Mark the two steps listed in the boxed feature.

Analyze: How does numbering these steps help you better understand the text?

ESSENTIAL QUESTION:

How do you find courage in the face of fear?

Review your notes and add your thoughts to your Response Log.

NEED HELP?

Your heart pounds, your face flames red, and your stomach feels like you've swallowed a live octopus. Meltdown mode doesn't come with an off switch—you need to hack your brain. Here are two steps you can take.

1. **Deactivate the alarm.** Your brain treats social slipups like a threat to survival, preparing your body to fight. You can't directly shut down this threat alert system, but you can trick your brain into doing it. Slow, deep breathing informs your brain the emergency has passed. Just relax your shoulders, fill your lungs completely, and exhale slowly. Your brain will respond by slowing your heart and reducing stress hormones.

2. **Disagree with yourself.** Stress floods your brain with negative thoughts. Imagining awful possibilities is your brain's attempt to protect you. The solution? Don't believe everything you think. If you wouldn't say it to a friend, find something more reasonable to say to yourself. In the moment, this boosts your mood. Over time, it rewires your brain. Brain cells forge new connections each time you talk back to negative thoughts. Eventually, realizing problems aren't so bad becomes automatic, just like riding a bike.

TURN AND TALK

Turn to a partner and discuss all of the reasons that the two of you *hate* to feel embarrassed. Then, consider the article's points about how embarrassment can be a good thing. Is the author right about that? Why or why not?

Assessment Practice

Answer these questions before moving on to the **Analyze the Text** section.

1. Which sentence states a main idea of the selection?

   (A) Adolescent brains focus on negative experiences.

   (B) It would be better if we all could turn off hurt feelings.

   (C) The brain treats bad feelings like a game of tug-of-war.

   (D) Brain changes cause teens to have strong reactions to social situations.

2. This question has two parts. First answer **Part A**. Then, answer **Part B**.

   Part A

   How does the author support the claim that the brain reacts similarly to physical pain and to social rejection?

   (A) The author includes quotes from interviews with teens.

   (B) The author includes particular research about this topic.

   (C) The author includes a graphic of important brain regions.

   (D) The author includes personal anecdotes illustrating the point.

   Part B

   Select the text that provides relevant support for the answer in Part A.

   (A) "During a challenge like giving a speech, teens release more stress hormones and have higher blood pressure than kids or adults." (paragraph 4)

   (B) "Even being watched over a video monitor makes teens sweat more than adults." (paragraph 4)

   (C) "No big surprise—teens in these Cyberball experiments feel sad and rejected. The surprising part? Rejection activates the same brain systems that physical pain triggers." (paragraph 7)

   (D) "Some people have especially reactive pain-response systems." (paragraph 8)

   ☺Ed
   Test-Taking Strategies

Analyze the Text

Support your responses with evidence from the text.

(1) **SUMMARIZE** How do the Cyberball experiments contribute to our understanding of the connection between physical and social pain in teens?

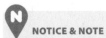

NOTICE & NOTE

Review what you noticed and noted as you read the text. Your annotations can help you answer these questions.

(2) **CRITIQUE** Why does the author consider some forms of embarrassment good for us, a **Contrast and Contradiction** from what we might expect? Do you agree with this view?

Negative Aspects of Embarrassment	Positive Aspects of Embarrassment

My View of Embarrassment

(3) **PREDICT** Review the subheading "Words Do Hurt Like Sticks and Stones." What would you predict about the ideas in this section of the text? Summarize the section and explain whether your prediction was accurate.

(4) **ANALYZE** Review the graphic of the brain included in the text. What ideas from the text does the graphic help illustrate?

(5) **ANALYZE** Reread paragraphs 9–11 and notice the word *anxiety*. Using clues from the text, fill in a word gap by providing your own definition of *anxiety*, and give an example of when someone might experience it.

Choices

Here are some other ways to demonstrate your understanding of the ideas in this lesson.

Writing
↳ **Report on Research**

Find out more about the Cyberball study the author discusses in the text. Keep track of your sources in a chart like the one shown.

URL/ SOURCE	PARAPHRASED OR QUOTED INFORMATION

When you've finished your research, write a brief summary of what you've learned. Remember to use quotation marks around text taken word-for-word from a source.

As you write and discuss, be sure to use the **Academic Vocabulary** words.

evident	similar

factor	specific

indicate

Speaking & Listening
↳ **Driven by Fear?**

Discuss how fear drives people's actions. In a small group, ask for and discuss ideas from group members, and identify points of agreement and disagreement.

- How did the information presented in the text contribute to your understanding of fear?

- Is there a difference between how you might respond to a genuine danger and how you might respond to the possibility of embarrassing yourself?

- What is going on in your brain when you're in a potentially embarrassing situation?

Social & Emotional Learning
↳ **Advertise a Service**

Use what you've learned from the selection to create an advertisement for a service that helps young people overcome their fears of embarrassment.

- Start with an attention-getting slogan or question.

- Then, include bulleted statements summarizing how your service works. Support your statements with text evidence.

- End with a call to action that encourages young people to hire you.

Expand Your Vocabulary

PRACTICE AND APPLY

To show your understanding of the vocabulary words, answer each question, using the vocabulary word in a complete sentence.

1. What is an **essential** part of your morning routine?

   _____

2. Why would a band playing outdoors need to **amplify** its instruments?

   _____

3. What is a good way to **generate** ideas for a weekend activity?

   _____

4. How does **humiliation** make someone feel?

   _____

Vocabulary Strategy

↳ Synonyms and Antonyms

Understanding **word relationships** can help you better understand certain words. A **synonym** has the same meaning as another word, and an **antonym** has the opposite or nearly the opposite meaning. Write a synonym and an antonym for each of the following words, using a print or online resource, if needed.

☺Ed

Interactive Vocabulary Lesson: Synonyms and Antonyms

WORD	SYNONYM	ANTONYM
amplify	*enlarge*	*reduce*
essential		
generate		
humiliation		

PRACTICE AND APPLY

Write sentences using a synonym or antonym for each of these words:

1. reactive (synonym) _____

2. imbalance (antonym) _____

3. rewires (synonym) _____

Watch Your Language!

Commas

Commas are used to clarify meaning. They may separate items in a **series,** as well as the parts of a **compound sentence.** They also set off phrases, words, or clauses that appear at the beginning of sentences, **introductory elements,** and they set off **nonrestrictive** or **parenthetical** elements.

> **ⓔ Ed**
>
> **Interactive Grammar Lesson: Commas with Sentence Interrupters**

These examples from the article show how commas are used in each of these ways.

1. Imagine a tug-of-war with <u>fear of rejection, the desire to fit in,</u> and self-consciousness all pulling on the same side. (a series or list)

2. <u>Our lives don't depend on social acceptance any more,</u> but <u>social pain is still helpful.</u> (compound sentence)

3. <u>Because of these brain changes,</u> teens start reacting more strongly to social problems. (introductory element)

4. Then, <u>with no warning,</u> the players start throwing the ball only to each other, leaving the research participant out completely. (nonrestrictive or parenthetical element)

PRACTICE AND APPLY

Write four sentences about the article, using commas in each of the ways described above. Indicate each comma's function in your sentences.

_____

_____

_____

_____

_____

_____

_____

The Ravine

Short Story by **Graham Salisbury**

Engage Your Brain

Choose one or both activities to start connecting with the story you're about to read.

I Double-Dog Dare You

Have you ever been dared to do something foolish or unsafe? What happened? Did you choose to take the dare or did you walk away? Briefly describe what happened, explaining what gave you the courage to make your choice.

Inspire an "Outsider"

Sometimes it's easy to feel like an "outsider," even when you're with friends. Think about what outsiders might need to hear to think better of themselves. Then, think about what "insiders" need to know. Finally, based on your thoughts, design an inspirational poster.

Analyze Character

In realistic fiction, characters—like real people—have personalities and motivations, and experience life-changing events. The **setting,** or the time and place in which the action occurs, often helps draw attention to the traits, motivations, and development of the characters.

- **Character traits** are a character's qualities, including physical traits or expressions of personality.

- **Character motivations** are the reasons a character acts, feels, or thinks in a certain way.

- **Character development** is how a character changes over the course of a story, often as a result of interactions with other characters.

As you read "The Ravine," note how the story's characters respond to events, the setting, and each other.

Focus on Genre
↳**Short Story**

- includes the basic elements of fiction—setting, characters, plot, conflict, and theme

- may center on one particular moment or event

- can be read in one sitting

Make Inferences

An **inference** is a logical guess based on facts and one's own knowledge and experience. To support an inference, **cite evidence,** or provide examples from the text. Here is one way you might make an inference about Joe-Boy, a character in "The Ravine."

EVIDENCE FROM THE STORY	MY OWN KNOWLEDGE	INFERENCE
Joe-Boy is Vinny's "best friend." He teases Vinny for being afraid.	Sometimes friends tease each other in a friendly way, but Joe-Boy's teasing seems mean.	They may be friends, but Joe-Boy may be unkind—or even mean.

Annotation in Action

Here are one reader's notes about how the setting in "The Ravine" affects a character's motivations. As you read, note how each character responds to the setting and to other characters.

> The fifteen-foot ledge was not the problem. It was the one above it, the one you had to work up to, the big one, where you had to take a deadly zigzag trail that climbed up and away from the waterfall, then cut back and forth to a foot-wide ledge something more like fifty feet up.
> That was the problem.

He's afraid to climb to the higher ledge, "the problem." He also may not want his friends to know that he's afraid.

Expand Your Vocabulary

Put a check mark next to the vocabulary words that you feel comfortable using when speaking or writing.

murky	☐
rivulet	☐
cascade	☐
precipice	☐

Turn to a partner and talk about the vocabulary words you already know. Then, use as many words as you can in a paragraph describing a scene from nature. As you read "The Ravine," use the definitions in the side column to learn the vocabulary words you don't already know.

Background

Graham Salisbury (b. 1944) was born in Pennsylvania but grew up in Hawaii. His father was killed in World War II. Raised by a distant mother, Salisbury lacked guidance. His characters explore choices similar to those he faced— making and keeping friends and learning honesty and courage. Their struggles, like Salisbury's, also take place in a Hawaiian setting. Among his many writing awards are the Boston Globe/Horn Book award and a School Library Journal Best Book of the Year award.

B

The Ravine

Short Story by **Graham Salisbury**

A boy drowned in the ravine a couple of weeks ago. His body's never been found. So why are Vinny and his friends headed there?

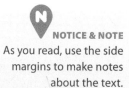

N
NOTICE & NOTE
As you read, use the side margins to make notes about the text.

😊 **Ed**

Close Read Screencast

Listen to a modeled close read of this text.

1   When Vinny and three others dropped down into the ravine,[1] they entered a jungle thick with tangled trees and rumors of what might have happened to the dead boy's body.

2   The muddy trail was slick and, in places where it had fallen away, flat-out dangerous. The cool breeze that swept the Hawaiian hillside pastures above died early in the descent.

3   There were four of them—Vinny; his best friend, Joe-Boy; Mo, who was afraid of nothing; and Joe-Boy's *haole*[2] girlfriend, Starlene—all fifteen. It was a Tuesday in July, two weeks and a day after the boy had drowned. If, in fact, that's what had happened to him.

MAKE INFERENCES

Annotate: Mark details in paragraphs 1–3 that hint that this setting is frightening.

Analyze: Why might four teens hike into a setting like this?

---

[1] **ravine** (rə-vēn´): a deep, narrow valley made by running water.
[2] **haole** (hou´lē): in Hawaii, a White person or non-native Hawaiian.

Annotate: In paragraphs 5–12, mark each of Vinny's reactions to what Joe-Boy says.

Infer: What do Vinny's reactions tell you about him? What is he afraid to admit to Joe-Boy? How do you know?

NOTICE & NOTE
AGAIN AND AGAIN

When you notice certain events, images, or words being repeated in a portion of a story, you've found an **Again and Again** signpost.

Notice & Note: Mark the words and phrases that are repeated in paragraphs 15–21.

Analyze: Why might the author be repeating these terms again and again?

4   Vinny slipped, and dropped his towel in the mud. He picked it up and tried to brush it off, but instead smeared the mud spot around until the towel resembled something someone's dog had slept on. "Tst," he said.

5   Joe-Boy, hiking down just behind him, laughed. "Hey, Vinny, just think, that kid walked where you walking."

6   "Shuddup," Vinny said.

7   "You prob'ly stepping right where his foot was."

8   Vinny moved to the edge of the trail, where the ravine fell through a twisted jungle of gnarly trees and underbrush to the stream far below. He could see Starlene and Mo farther ahead, their heads bobbing as they walked, both almost down to the pond where the boy had died.

9   "Hey," Joe-Boy went on, "maybe you going be the one to find his body."

10   "You don't cut it out, Joe-Boy, I going . . . I going . . . "

11   "What, cry?"

12   Vinny scowled. Sometimes Joe-Boy was a big fat babooze.

13   They slid down the trail. Mud oozed between Vinny's toes. He grabbed at roots and branches to keep from falling. Mo and Starlene were out of sight now, the trail ahead having cut back.

14   Joe-Boy said, "You going jump in the water and go down and your hand going touch his face, stuck under the rocks. *Ha ha ha . . . a ha ha ha!*"

15   Vinny winced. He didn't want to be here. It was too soon, way too soon. Two weeks and one day.

16   He saw a footprint in the mud and stepped around it.

17   The dead boy had jumped and had never come back up. Four search and rescue divers hunted for two days straight and never found him. Not a trace. Gave Vinny the creeps. It didn't make sense. The pond wasn't that big.

18   He wondered why it didn't seem to bother anyone else. Maybe it did and they just didn't want to say.

19   Butchie was the kid's name. Only fourteen.

20   Fourteen.

21   Two weeks and one day ago he was walking down this trail. Now nobody could find him.

22   The jungle crushed in, reaching over the trail, and Vinny brushed leafy branches aside. The roar of the waterfall got louder, louder.

23   Starlene said it was the goddess that took him, the one that lives in the stone down by the road. She did that every now and then, Starlene said, took somebody when she got lonely. Took him and kept him. Vinny had heard that legend before, but he'd never believed in it.

Don't forget to **Notice & Note** as you read the selection.

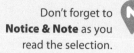

24   Now he didn't know what he believed.

25   The body had to be stuck down there. But still, four divers and they couldn't find it?

26   Vinny decided he'd better believe in the legend. If he didn't, the goddess might get mad and send him bad luck. Or maybe take *him*, too.

27   *Stopstopstop! Don't think like that.*

28   "Come on," Joe-Boy said, nudging Vinny from behind. "Hurry it up."

29   Just then Starlene whooped, her voice bouncing around the walls of the ravine.

30   "Let's go," Joe-Boy said. "They there already."

31   Moments later, Vinny jumped up onto a large boulder at the edge of the pond. Starlene was swimming out in the brown water. It wasn't **murky** brown, but clean and clear to a depth of maybe three or four feet. Because of the waterfall you had to yell if you wanted to say something. The whole place smelled of mud and ginger and iron.

32   Starlene swam across to the waterfall on the far side of the pond and ducked under it, then climbed out and edged along the rock wall behind it, moving slowly, like a spider. Above, sun-sparkling stream water spilled over the lip of a one-hundred-foot drop.

ANALYZE CHARACTER

Annotate: Mark each of Vinny's thoughts in paragraphs 24–28.

Describe: What do his thoughts indicate about what he's like? How would you describe him?

murky
(mur´kē) *adj.* Something *murky* is dark, obscure, and gloomy.

33 Mo and Joe-Boy threw their towels onto the rocks and dove into the pond. Vinny watched, his muddy towel hooked around his neck. Reluctantly, he let it fall, then dove in after them.

34 The cold mountain water tasted tangy. Was it because the boy's body was down there decomposing?[3] He spit it out.

35 He followed Joe-Boy and Mo to the waterfall and ducked under it. They climbed up onto the rock ledge, just as Starlene had done, then spidered their way over to where you could climb to a small ledge about fifteen feet up. They took their time because the hand and footholds were slimy with moss.

36 Starlene jumped first. Her shriek echoed off the rocky cliff, then died in the dense green jungle.

37 Mo jumped, then Joe-Boy, then Vinny.

38 The fifteen-foot ledge was not the problem.

39 It was the one above it, the one you had to work up to, the big one, where you had to take a deadly zigzag trail that climbed up and away from the waterfall, then cut back and forth to a foot-wide ledge something more like fifty feet up.

40 That was the problem.

41 That was where the boy had jumped from.

42 Joe-Boy and Starlene swam out to the middle of the pond. Mo swam back under the waterfall and climbed once again to the fifteen-foot ledge.

43 Vinny started to swim out toward Joe-Boy but stopped when he saw Starlene put her arms around him. She kissed him. They sank under for a long time, then came back up, still kissing.

44 Vinny turned away and swam back over to the other side of the pond, where he'd first gotten in. His mother would kill him if she ever heard about where he'd come. After the boy drowned, or was taken by the goddess, or whatever happened to him, she said never to come to this pond again. Ever. It was off-limits. Permanently.

45 But not his dad. He said, "You fall off a horse, you get back on, right? Or else you going be scared of it all your life."

46 His mother scoffed and waved him off. "Don't listen to him, Vinny, listen to me. Don't go there. That pond is haunted." Which had made his dad laugh.

47 But Vinny promised he'd stay away.

48 But then Starlene and Joe-Boy said, "Come with us anyway. You let your mommy run your life, or what?" And Vinny said, "But what if I get caught?" And Joe-Boy said, "So?"

49 Vinny mashed his lips. He was so weak. Couldn't even say no. But if he'd said, "I can't go, my mother won't like it," they

MAKE INFERENCES

Annotate: Reread paragraphs 39–44, marking each of Vinny's responses to Joe-Boy and Starlene.

Infer: Why might Vinny respond as he does?

ANALYZE CHARACTER

Annotate: Reread paragraphs 46–50 and mark each line of dialogue, noting the speaker.

Analyze: Who has the greatest influence on Vinny? What conflicts does he face?

[3] **decomposing** (dē′kəm-pōz′ĭng): starting to decay and fall apart.

would have laughed him right off the island. No, he had to go. No choice.

Don't forget to **Notice & Note** as you read the selection.

50   So he'd come along, and so far it was fine. He'd even gone in the water. Everyone was happy. All he had to do now was wait it out and go home and hope his mother never heard about it.

51   When he looked up, Starlene was gone.

52   He glanced around the pond until he spotted her starting up the zigzag trail to the fifty-foot ledge. She was moving slowly, hanging on to roots and branches on the upside of the cliff. He couldn't believe she was going there. He wanted to yell, *Hey, Starlene, that's where he* died!

53   But she already knew that.

54   Mo jumped from the lower ledge, yelling, "Banzaiiii!" An explosion of coffee-colored water erupted when he hit.

55   Joe-Boy swam over to where Starlene had gotten out. He waved to Vinny, grinning like a fool, then followed Starlene up the zigzag trail.

56   Now Starlene was twenty-five, thirty feet up. Vinny watched her for a while, then lost sight of her when she slipped behind a wall of jungle that blocked his view. A few minutes later she popped back out, now almost at the top, where the trail ended, where there was nothing but mud and a few plants to grab on to if you slipped, plants that would rip right out of the ground, plants that wouldn't stop you if you fell, nothing but your screams between you and the rocks below.

MAKE INFERENCES

Annotate: In paragraphs 56–57, mark Vinny's descriptions of what Starlene is like. Then, mark the thoughts that show his worry.

Infer: How does Vinny feel about Starlene?

57   Vinny's stomach tingled just watching her. He couldn't imagine what it must feel like to be up there, especially if you were afraid of heights, like he was. *She has no fear*, Vinny thought, *no fear at all. Pleasepleaseplease, Starlene. I don't want to see you die.*

58   Starlene crept forward, making her way to the end of the trail, where the small ledge was.

59   Joe-Boy popped out of the jungle behind her. He stopped, waiting for her to jump before going on.

60   Vinny held his breath.

ANALYZE CHARACTER

Annotate: In paragraphs 61–69, mark each description of Starlene's actions.

Analyze: Based on her actions, how would you describe Starlene? How accurate is Vinny's view of her?

61   Starlene, in her cutoff jeans and soaked T-shirt, stood perfectly still, her arms at her sides. Vinny suddenly felt like hugging her. Why, he couldn't tell. *Starlene, please.*

62   She reached behind her and took a wide leaf from a plant, then eased down and scooped up a finger of mud. She made a brown cross on her forehead, then wiped her muddy fingers on her jeans.

63   She waited.

64   Was she thinking about the dead boy?

65   She stuck the stem end of the leaf in her mouth, leaving the rest of it to hang out. When she jumped, the leaf would flap up and cover her nose and keep water from rushing into it. An old island trick.

66   She jumped.

67   Down, down.

68   Almost in slow motion, it seemed at first, then faster and faster. She fell feetfirst, arms flapping to keep balance so she wouldn't land on her back, or stomach, which would probably almost kill her.

69   Just before she hit, she crossed her arms over her chest and vanished within a small explosion of rusty water.

70   Vinny stood, not breathing at all, praying.

71   Ten seconds. Twenty, thirty . . .

72   She came back up, laughing.

73   *She shouldn't make fun that way,* Vinny thought. It was dangerous, disrespectful. It was asking for it.

74   Vinny looked up when he heard Joe-Boy shout, "Hey, Vinny, watch how a man does it! Look!"

75   Joe-Boy scooped up some mud and drew a stroke of lightning across his chest. When he jumped, he threw himself out, face and body parallel to the pond, his arms and legs spread out. *He's crazy*, Vinny thought, *absolutely insane*. At the last second Joe-Boy folded into a ball and hit. *Ca-roomp!* He came up whooping and yelling, "*Wooo!* So *good*! Come on, Vinny, it's hot!"

76   Vinny faked a laugh. He waved, shouting, "Naah, the water's too cold!"

77   Now Mo was heading up the zigzag trail—Mo, who hardly ever said a word and would do anything anyone ever challenged him to do. *Come on, Mo, not you, too.*

78   Vinny knew then that he would have to jump.

79   Jump, or never live it down.

80   Mo jumped in the same way Joe-Boy had, man-style, splayed out in a suicide fall. He came up grinning.

81   Starlene and Joe-Boy turned toward Vinny.

82   Vinny got up and hiked around the edge of the pond, walking in the muddy shallows, looking at a school of small brown-backed fish near a ginger patch.

83   Maybe they'd forget about him.

84   Starlene torpedoed over, swimming underwater. Her body glittered in the small amount of sunlight that penetrated the trees around the rim of the ravine. When she came up, she broke the surface smoothly, gracefully, like a swan. Her blond hair sleeked back like river grass.

85   She smiled a sweet smile. "Joe-Boy says you're afraid to jump. I didn't believe him. He's wrong, right?"

86   Vinny said quickly, "Of course he's wrong. I just don't want to, that's all. The water's cold."

87   "Naah, it's nice."

88   Vinny looked away. On the other side of the pond Joe-Boy and Mo were on the cliff behind the waterfall.

89   "Joe-Boy says your mom told you not to come here. Is that true?"

90   Vinny nodded. "Yeah. Stupid, but she thinks it's haunted."

91   "She's right."

92   "What?"

93   "That boy didn't die, Vinny. The stone goddess took him. He's in a good place right now. He's her prince."

94   Vinny scowled. He couldn't tell if Starlene was teasing him or if she really believed that. He said, "Yeah, prob'ly."

95   "Are you going to jump, or is Joe-Boy right?"

96   "Joe-Boy's an idiot. Sure I'm going to jump."

MAKE INFERENCES

Annotate: Mark the description of Mo in paragraphs 77–79.

Infer: Why might Vinny feel that he'll have to jump if Mo jumps? What would make him feel that he would "never live it down" if he doesn't jump?

ANALYZE CHARACTER

Annotate: In paragraphs 85–96, mark what Starlene says to Vinny.

Analyze: What do Starlene's words say about her? What do Vinny's responses tell you about him?

97   Starlene grinned, staring at Vinny a little too long. "He is an idiot, isn't he? But I love him."

98   "Yeah, well . . ."

99   "Go to it, big boy. I'll be watching."

100   Starlene sank down and swam out into the pond.

101   *Ca-ripes.*

102   Vinny ripped a hank[4] of white ginger from the ginger patch and smelled it, and prayed he'd still be alive after the sun went down.

103   He took his time climbing the zigzag trail. When he got to the part where the jungle hid him from view, he stopped and smelled the ginger again. So sweet and alive it made Vinny wish for all he was worth that he was climbing out of the ravine right now, heading home.

104   But of course, there was no way he could do that.

105   Not before jumping.

106   He tossed the ginger onto the muddy trail and continued on. He slipped once or twice, maybe three times. He didn't keep track. He was too numb now, too caught up in the insane thing he was about to do. He'd never been this far up the trail before. Once he'd tried to go all the way, but couldn't. It made him dizzy.

107   When he stepped out and the jungle opened into a huge bowl where he could look down, way, way down, he could see their three heads in the water, heads with arms moving slowly to keep them afloat, and a few bright rays of sunlight pouring down onto them, and when he saw this, his stomach fluttered and rose. Something sour came up and he spit it out.

108   It made him wobble to look down. He closed his eyes. His whole body trembled. The trail was no wider than the length of his foot. And it was wet and muddy from little **rivulets** of water that bled from the side of the cliff.

109   The next few steps were the hardest he'd ever taken in his life. He tried not to look down, but he couldn't help it. His gaze was drawn there. He struggled to push back an urge to fly, just jump off and fly. He could almost see himself spiraling down like a glider, or a bird, or a leaf.

---

[4] **hank** (hăngk): a coiled or looped bundle of something, such as rope or yarn.

ANALYZE CHARACTER

Annotate: In paragraphs 107–110, mark descriptions of the story's setting.

Infer: What do Vinny's responses to the setting tell you about him?

rivulet
(rĭv´yə-lĭt) *n.* A *rivulet* is a small brook or stream.

Don't forget to
Notice & Note as you
read the selection.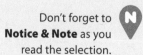

110   His hands shook as if he were freezing. He wondered, *Had the dead boy felt this way?* Or had he felt brave, like Starlene or Joe-Boy, or Mo, who seemed to feel nothing.

111   Somebody from below shouted, but Vinny couldn't make it out over the waterfall, roaring down just feet beyond the ledge where he would soon be standing, **cascading** past so close its mist dampened the air he breathed.

112   *The dead boy had just come to the ravine to have fun,* Vinny thought. Just a regular kid like himself, come to swim and be with his friends, then go home and eat macaroni and cheese and watch TV, maybe play with his dog or wander around after dark.

113   But he'd done none of that.

114   Where was he?

115   Inch by inch Vinny made it to the ledge. He stood, swaying slightly, the tips of his toes one small movement from the **precipice**.

116   Far below, Joe-Boy waved his arm back and forth. It was dreamy to see—back and forth, back and forth. He looked so small down there.

117   For a moment Vinny's mind went blank, as if he were in some trance, some dream where he could so easily lean out and fall, and think or feel nothing.

118   A breeze picked up and moved the trees on the ridge-line, but not a breath of it reached the fifty-foot ledge.

119   Vinny thought he heard a voice, small and distant. Yes. Something inside him, a tiny voice pleading, *Don't do it. Walk away. Just turn and go and walk back down.*

120   " . . . I can't," Vinny whispered.

121   *You can, you can, you can. Walk back down.*

122   Vinny waited.

123   And waited.

124   Joe-Boy yelled, then Starlene, both of them waving.

125   Then something very strange happened.

126   Vinny felt at peace. Completely and totally calm and at peace. He had not made up his mind about jumping. But something else inside him had.

127   Thoughts and feelings swarmed, stinging him: *Jump! Jump! Jump! Jump!*

128   But deep inside, where the peace was, where his mind wasn't, he would not jump. He would walk back down.

129   *No! No, no, no!*

130   Vinny eased down and fingered up some mud and made a cross on his chest, big and bold. He grabbed a leaf, stuck it in his mouth. *Be calm, be calm. Don't look down.*

131   After a long pause he spit the leaf out and rubbed the cross to a blur.

cascade

(kăs-kād´) *v.* Something that can *cascade* will fall, pour, or rush in stages, like a waterfall over steep rocks.

Text in Focus Video

Learn more about visualizing the characters, setting, and events.

precipice

(prĕs´ə-pĭs) *n.* A *precipice* is an overhanging or extremely steep area of rock.

ANALYZE CHARACTER

Annotate: In paragraphs 119–130, underline each thought that encourages Vinny not to jump. Then, mark evidence of the feelings created by those thoughts.

Analyze: What fear is Vinny overcoming? What does this tell you about him?

Annotate: In paragraphs 132–133, mark words that indicate how the group leaves the ravine.

Infer: What does this suggest about the group and how they feel about Vinny?

132   They walked out of the ravine in silence, Starlene, Joe-Boy, and Mo far ahead of him. They hadn't said a word since he'd come down off the trail. He knew what they were thinking. He knew, he knew, he knew.

133   At the same time the peace was still there. He had no idea what it was. But he prayed it wouldn't leave him now, prayed it wouldn't go away, would never go away, because in there, in that place where the peace was, it didn't matter what they thought.

134   Vinny emerged from the ravine into a brilliance that surprised him. Joe-Boy, Starlene, and Mo were now almost down to the road.

135   Vinny breathed deeply, and looked up and out over the island. He saw, from there, a land that rolled away like honey, easing down a descent of rich Kikuyu grass pasture-land, flowing from there over vast highlands of brown and green, then, finally, falling massively to the coast and flat blue sea. He'd never seen anything like it.

136   Had it always been here? This view of the island?

137   He stared and stared, then sat, taking it in.

138   He'd never seen anything so beautiful in all his life.

?

ESSENTIAL QUESTION:

How do you find courage in the face of fear?

Review your notes and add your thoughts to your Response Log.

TURN AND TALK

Rank each of the story's four main characters according to how much you like or dislike each one. Then, turn to a partner and discuss your rankings. Whom do you most like and why? Whom do you dislike and why?

Assessment Practice

Answer these questions before moving on to the **Analyze the Text** section.

1. Read the excerpt. Then answer the question.

> Inch by inch Vinny made it to the ledge. He stood, swaying slightly, the tips of his toes one small movement from the precipice. (paragraph 115)

   What does the phrase "inch by inch" in this excerpt suggest?

   (A) Vinny is nervous.

   (B) Vinny is enjoying the suspense.

   (C) Vinny is braver than his friends think he is.

   (D) Vinny has made up his mind about what to do.

2. Which **two** sentences support the idea that teens care about what their peers think of them?

   (A) "Threat-detection systems focus on what other people think and scan for any hints of disapproval." ("Embarrassed? Blame Your Brain," paragraph 3)

   (B) "Fear of rejection forced people to behave well enough for the community to keep them around." ("Embarrassed? Blame Your Brain," paragraph 12)

   (C) "He wondered why it didn't seem to bother anyone else." ("The Ravine," paragraph 18)

   (D) "But if he'd said, 'I can't go, my mother won't like it,' they would have laughed him right off the island." ("The Ravine," paragraph 49)

   (E) "Vinny knew then that he would have to jump." ("The Ravine," paragraph 78)

☺**Ed**

Test-Taking Strategies

Analyze the Text

Support your responses with evidence from the text.

(1) **SUMMARIZE** Review paragraphs 23–27. In your own words, summarize the legend about the goddess. Explain how this aspect of the story's cultural setting influences Vinny.

(2) **DRAW CONCLUSIONS** Review paragraphs 31–39. What are some examples of language the author uses to describe the setting? Why is the setting important to the story?

(3) **MAKE INFERENCES** Before jumping, the characters perform certain rituals. Reread paragraphs 61–80 to review how they prepare to jump. What inferences can you make about the characters' feelings and their reasons for these rituals?

(4) **ANALYZE** Consider Vinny's feelings and actions throughout the story. How is Vinny different by the end of the story? How is he the same?

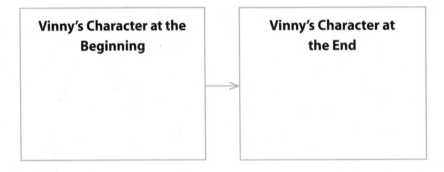

Vinny's Character at the Beginning	Vinny's Character at the End

How Vinny Is Different	How Vinny Is the Same

(5) **ANALYZE** Review paragraphs 84–100. What question does Starlene ask Vinny **Again and Again?** What does this question reveal about Starlene?

Choices

Here are some other ways to demonstrate your understanding of the ideas in this lesson.

Writing
↳ Compare and Contrast

Write a brief essay in which you compare and contrast Vinny with one of the other characters in "The Ravine."

- Introduce your essay by describing the character traits of Vinny and the other character you have selected.

- Then, explain similarities and differences between the two characters. Include details from the text.

- In your final paragraph, state your conclusion about the two.

Research
↳ Investigate Hawaiian Sports

Hawaii is known not only for its beautiful beaches, volcanoes, and waterfalls, but also for the culture of its people. Do some research to explore the history of a few sports played in Hawaii. Make sure your sources are reliable and credible, such as a respected university or an established media outlet.

> As you write and discuss, be sure to use the **Academic Vocabulary** words.
>
> | evident | similar |
> |---|---|
> | factor | specific |
> | indicate | |

Social & Emotional Learning
↳ Coward or Hero?

With a small group, discuss your opinions about Vinny's actions in "The Ravine." Consider the perspectives of Vinny and his friends. Can Vinny be characterized as a coward, a hero, or something else?

- Identify the thoughts and actions that help you understand Vinny.

- Then, discuss Vinny's motivations and what those motivations reveal.

- Listen closely to each other, and end your discussion by reviewing each of the ideas expressed about Vinny's character. List those ideas.

SPORT	INFORMATION ABOUT SPORT / SIGNIFICANCE
lele kawa (diving)	
he'e nalu (surfing)	
he'e hōlua (mountain surfing)	
'o'o ihe (spear throwing)	

Expand Your Vocabulary

PRACTICE AND APPLY

With a partner, discuss and write an answer to each of the following questions to show your understanding of the vocabulary words.

| murky | rivulet | cascade | precipice |

1. Which vocabulary word goes with *cloudy* and *dark?* Why?

    _____

2. Which vocabulary word goes with *edge?* Why?

    _____

3. Which vocabulary word goes with *trickle?* Why?

    _____

4. Which vocabulary word goes with *pouring?* Why?

    _____

Vocabulary Strategy
↳Context Clues

One way to figure out the meaning of an unfamiliar word is to use **context clues,** or hints in the surrounding text. Look at the following example:

Interactive Vocabulary Lesson: Using Context Clues

> **And it was wet and muddy from little rivulets of water that bled from the side of the cliff.**

To figure out the meaning of *rivulets*, look for clues in the surrounding words and ideas. Then, use a dictionary to confirm your guess.

PRACTICE AND APPLY

Examine the context clues for the following words in "The Ravine," and complete this chart.

WORD	LOCATION OF CONTEXT CLUES	MY GUESSED DEFINITION	DICTIONARY DEFINITION
winced	(paragraphs 14–15)		
scoffed	(paragraphs 45–46)		
parallel	(paragraph 75)		

Watch Your Language!

Varying Sentence Patterns

A **simple sentence** expresses a single, complete thought: *They took their time*. However, you can use connecting words and phrases called **subordinating conjunctions** to connect and clarify ideas, forming **complex sentences.** Complex sentences include answers to questions such as *How? Where? When? Why? For how long? How much? To what extent?* and *Under what condition?*

Why did Joe-Boy, Mo, and Vinny take their time?

> They took their time <u>because</u> the hand and footholds were slimy with moss. (paragraph 35)

😊 Ed

Interactive Grammar Lesson: Conjunctions and Interjections

COMMON SUBORDINATING CONJUNCTIONS					
after	as long as	because	in order that	though	whenever
although	as much as	before	since	unless	where
as	as soon as	how	so that	until	wherever
as if	as though	if	than	when	while

PRACTICE AND APPLY

Write three pairs of related simple sentences. Then, use a subordinating conjunction to connect the sentences in each pair. When you have finished, share your new complex sentences with a partner and work together to create a few more complex sentences.

_____

_____

_____

_____

_____

_____

Compare Across Genres

When you compare two or more texts on the same topic, you **synthesize** information from the texts, building your understanding of key ideas. It's often helpful to compare texts from different **genres,** or types of writing.

In a small group, complete the Venn diagram with similarities and differences in what you learned about responses to the fear of embarrassment in "Embarrassed?" and "The Ravine." Consider themes and central ideas shared by the texts. One example is provided.

"Embarrassed?"   Both   "The Ravine"

fear of embarrassment can be overwhelming

Analyze the Texts

Discuss these questions in your group.

1. **CONNECT** What similar ideas about fear of embarrassment do the article and the short story share? Cite evidence in your anwer.

2. **EVALUATE** Based on what you read in the article, how would you expect Vinny to resolve his dilemma in the short story? How does your expectation compare to what he actually does?

3. **INFER** According to the article, whose brain, Vinny's or Joe-Boy's, behaves more like the brain of an adult? Cite evidence in your answer.

4. **SYNTHESIZE** What theme or message about how young people approach fear can you synthesize from the two texts? What theme or message do they share?

Research and Share

Now your group can continue exploring the main ideas in these texts by collaborating to present research in a panel discussion. Follow these steps:

(1) DEVELOP RESEARCH QUESTIONS In your group, brainstorm questions you'd like answered about young peoples' fear of embarrassment. Make sure that everyone contributes ideas to the list. Circle the most interesting questions. Then, assign each of the circled questions to group members for research. When those questions have been answered, your group will have gathered plenty of information to present in a panel discussion.

(2) GATHER INFORMATION As you begin to research your individual question or questions from the list, check that your sources are reliable and credible.

- A **reliable** source comes from an expert on the topic or someone with firsthand experience.
- A **credible** source presents ideas fairly and accurately, avoiding bias (unfairly favoring one view), hyperbole (exaggeration), and stereotype (overgeneralizing a characteristic, such as saying that all teenagers are reckless).

Take notes from two or more sources for each question, paraphrasing and summarizing key information that provides an answer. You can use this framework to synthesize what you learn:

My question:	
Source 1 information:	Source 2 information:
Ideas the two sources share that answer my question:	

(3) SHARE WHAT YOU LEARN Once research is complete, everyone in your group will have become an expert on a different aspect of the topic. Gather together and share what you have learned. Listen to what others have to say, ask questions to request and clarify information, and build on the ideas of others as you discuss the topic. Use your research notes to back up your views with text evidence.

Collaborate & Compare

ESSENTIAL QUESTION:
How do you find courage in the face of fear?

Compare Presentations

You're about to read two very different biographies that show similar events in the lives of two famous Americans. As you read, notice the key ideas each author wants readers to understand.

A

from
Into the Air

Graphic Biography by Robert Burleigh

Illustrated by Bill Wylie
pages 258–267

B

from
The Wright Brothers:
How They Invented the Airplane

Biography
by Russell Freedman
pages 275–281

After you have read both selections, you'll have an opportunity to discuss and present your ideas about them. You'll follow these steps:

- Gather Information
- Discuss
- Share What You Learn

from
Into the Air

Graphic Biography by **Robert Burleigh**
Illustrated by **Bill Wylie**

Engage Your Brain

Choose one or both activities to start connecting with the biography you're about to read.

Who Were They and Why Did They Matter?

Carry out some quick research about the Wright Brothers and the history of their work, noting why it was so important. Then, gather into small groups and share what you've learned. Which points should everyone in the group remember?

A Comic Book Scene

Think about a time that you were trying to accomplish something—no matter how small it may have been—and were about to give up, yet didn't. What gave you the courage to keep going? Sketch or describe a few frames in comic-book style to illustrate your experience.

Analyze Structure of Informational Texts

Certain informational texts present information through multiple modes, or ways of expression. For example, the biography you are about to read uses both written text and comic-book style illustrations. These print and graphic features work together to introduce, illustrate, and elaborate ideas. Note these features and their purposes as you read:

GRAPHIC FEATURE	DESCRIPTION
CAPTION	a text box that provides narration; text may be set in all capital letters
SPEECH BALLOON	a balloon shape containing dialogue— what a character says aloud
THOUGHT BUBBLE	a cloud-shaped graphic that tells what a character is thinking
IMAGE PANEL	an illustration, often set within a border or frame

Focus on Genre
↳**Graphic Biography**

- uses illustrations and text to present information

- includes the basic elements of biography—a true account of someone's life—as told by another person; written from a third-person point of view

- includes facts and descriptions of events, people, and experiences that shape subjects' lives

Determine Central Idea

In a graphic biography, details in print and graphic features convey the text's **key ideas,** or important points. You can use key ideas to make inferences about a text's **central,** or **main idea,** which may not be stated directly. Look for a summary of key ideas in the **afterword,** a section sometimes found at the end of a text. To find the central idea:

- Examine details in each print feature.

- Study illustrations that accompany the text; then, reread the text.

- Use details from the text and illustrations to make inferences about the idea or message being conveyed about the topic.

Annotation in Action

In the model, you can see one reader's notes about a key idea in *Into the Air*. As you read, note how the text and graphic features communicate additional ideas.

Day after difficult day, discouraged but not defeated, the Wrights carry the damaged glider back to the campsite, repair it, and try again.

Wow. These guys just won't give up.

Expand Your Vocabulary

Put a check mark next to the vocabulary words that you feel comfortable using when speaking or writing.

discourage	☐
defeat	☐
lap	☐
table	☐
preserve	☐
demonstration	☐

Turn to a partner and talk about the vocabulary words you already know. Then, use as many words as you can in a paragraph about building or creating something you've never built or created before. As you read *Into the Air,* use the definitions in the side column to learn the vocabulary words you don't already know.

Background

As boys, brothers Orville and Wilbur Wright were fascinated by flight. In the late 1800s, they honed their mechanical skills at their bicycle sales and repair shop in Ohio, and later studied the work of Otto Lilienthal, who had built a glider with bat-like wings. The following excerpt, by author **Robert Burleigh** and illustrator **Bill Wylie**, tells about events that begin in 1901, as the Wrights try to build a glider for longer flights—an important step toward powered flight.

from

Into the Air

Graphic Biography by **Robert Burleigh**
Illustrated by **Bill Wylie**

NOTICE & NOTE
As you read, use the side margins to make notes about the text.

Their gliders keep crashing, dashing the Wright Brothers' hopes to achieve human flight. What gives them the courage to keep trying?

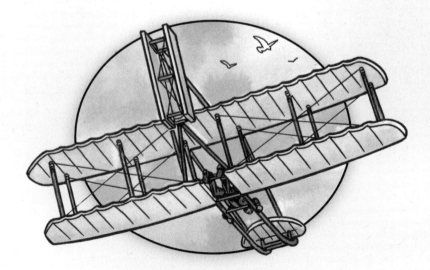

Don't forget to
Notice & Note as you
read the selection.

discourage

(dĭ-skûrˈĭj) *v.* To *discourage* is to take away hope or confidence.

defeat

(dĭ-fētˈ) *v.* To *defeat* a person or his or her efforts is to prevent his or her success.

ANALYZE STRUCTURE OF INFORMATIONAL TEXTS

Annotate: Mark the print and graphic features on this page.

Identify: Name the types of features and explain the purpose of each.

---

¹ glider: an aircraft that relies on gravity and air currents, rather than an engine, for flight; early experiments in glider flight were essential to developing motorized aircraft.

© Houghton Mifflin Harcourt Publishing Company

lap

(lăp) *v.* To *lap* is to wash against something gently.

table

(tā′bəl) *n.* An orderly arrangement of data, especially one in which the data are arranged in columns and rows in a rectangular form.

DETERMINE CENTRAL IDEA

Annotate: Mark details in the text and illustrations that express any doubts the brothers share.

Infer: How do these details work together to express an idea?

---

[2] **Lilienthal's air-pressure tables:** a set of calculations produced by German aviation pioneer Otto Lilienthal used in the design of aircraft wings.

ANALYZE STRUCTURE OF INFORMATIONAL TEXTS

Annotate: Study the two illustration panels on this page. Mark the background illustration and the inset illustration.

Compare: How do the illustrations work together and on their own to tell this part of the story?

³ **hit rock bottom:** to reach the most bleak and hopeless moment.

Annotate: Mark the print and graphic details on this page that refer to asking and answering questions.

Draw Conclusions: What inferences can you make from these details?

Don't forget to
Notice & Note as you
read the selection.

DETERMINE CENTRAL IDEA

Annotate: Mark details in the text that indicate how the brothers work and what they're learning.

Infer: What do these details reveal about the importance of their work?

preserve
(prĭ-zûrv´) *v.* To *preserve* something is to keep it or save it.

Annotate: Mark the details that help describe the brothers' new glider design.

Analyze: How do the print and graphic features work together to help you understand the design?

NOTICE & NOTE
BIG QUESTIONS

When you read informational text, you should take a **Questioning Stance**, which means that you pay close attention to information, without automatically accepting it.

Notice & Note: Mark the text that helps you answer this **Big Question:** What did the author think I already knew? Explain.

Afterword

1 The Wright brothers' story did not end at Kitty Hawk. As the brothers well knew, there was more work to be done on the airplane. Some of the problems still to be resolved included making the takeoff simpler, learning to execute complete turns in the air, and designing the plane so that the pilot could fly sitting up. In 1904 and 1905, the brothers used an empty pasture near their home in Dayton for many additional experiments and tests.

2 Meanwhile, only slowly did people in the United States and abroad become aware of the Wright brothers and the importance of their invention. For several years, the American government showed no interest in the Wrights' flying machine.

3 Finally, in 1908, the brothers were able to convince the government that flight was possible and useful. During the same year, Wilbur went to Europe and gave a series of flying **demonstrations** that made him and Orville instant celebrities.

4 Wilbur died of an illness in 1912. But Orville, who died in 1948, lived to see "the age of flight" expand in ways that he and his brother never foresaw. Today there is a sixty-foot high monument to the Wright Brothers at Kill Devil Hills, North Carolina. But perhaps the real monuments to the vision, courage, and dedication of Wilbur and Orville Wright are the airplanes you see above you, flying back and forth across the country, every day.

demonstration
(dĕm´ən-strā´shən) *n.* A *demonstration* is a presentation meant to show how something works.

?

ESSENTIAL QUESTION:

How do you find courage in the face of fear?

Review your notes and add your thoughts to your Response Log.

TURN AND TALK

With a partner, select a favorite panel of the graphic biography. Then, work together to describe everything that happens in that panel, as if you were explaining what happens to someone unable to see the images.

Assessment Practice

Answer these questions before moving on to the **Analyze the Text** section.

1. How do the illustrations of the Wright brothers' experiments support a central idea of the text?

    (A) by showing outdated technology

    (B) by showing that the Wright brothers did not get along

    (C) by showing that the Wright brothers never doubted themselves

    (D) by showing that testing ideas was important to the Wright brothers' work

2. Which sentences from the text show that the Wright brothers worked hard to develop and promote their flying machine, despite many challenges?

    (A) " 'I'm beginning to think people won't fly for a thousand years!' " (page 261)

    (B) "Back at Kitty Hawk in the fall of 1902, the Wrights solve the problem of controlling their gliding machine." (page 265)

    (C) "Finally, in 1908, the brothers were able to convince the government that flight was possible and useful." (page 266, paragraph 3)

    (D) "Today there is a sixty-foot high monument to the Wright brothers at Kill Devil Hills, North Carolina." (page 266, paragraph 4)

3. Which of the following best describes the main purpose of the afterword?

    (A) It predicts ways that flight will be improved in the future.

    (B) It summarizes events following the Wrights' first successful flight.

    (C) It provides an explanation of information appearing earlier in the selection.

    (D) It states opinions about the failures to recognize the Wrights' accomplishments.

Test-Taking Strategies

Analyze the Text

Support your responses with evidence from the text.

1 **SUMMARIZE** Review the print and graphic features on the first page of the selection. How do these elements help you understand the ideas in the story?

FEATURE	HOW THE FEATURE HELPS CONVEY THE STORY'S IDEAS
Caption	
Speech balloon	
Thought bubble	
Image panel	

2 **ANALYZE** Review the caption that begins, "Late into the nights" on page 260. What idea does the caption help explain?

3 **INFER** Review the speech balloons appearing in the train illustration on page 261. What idea does this dialogue help explain?

4 **COMPARE** Review the illustrations on the last four pages of the selection, starting with page 262. Then, compare them to the illustrations on the first three pages. How do the illustrations on the last four pages convey a change in mood and communicate a central idea of the text?

5 **INTERPRET** Reread the afterword. What in this section challenges, changes, or confirms what you already know? Explain your answer to this **Big Question** and tell how it affects your overall understanding of the Wright brothers.

Choices

Here are some other ways to demonstrate your understanding of the ideas in this lesson.

Writing
↳**Write a Summary**

Write a three- to four-paragraph objective summary of *Into the Air*.

- Use your own words to summarize the selection's print and graphic content.

- Use your annotations and analysis to make an inference about the selection's central idea.

- Include details and evidence that support the central idea.

- Exclude your own opinions and judgments in your summary.

- Use adverbs and adverbial clauses to clarify your ideas.

As you write and discuss, be sure to use the **Academic Vocabulary** words.

evident	similar
factor	specific
indicate	

Research
↳**Investigate Advances in Flight**

At the end of this excerpt, the Wright brothers have yet to achieve their ultimate goal of powered flight. One of the Wrights' biggest achievements was to inspire others to make new discoveries. Investigate advances in flight that followed those of the Wright brothers. Who made these advances? Why were they important? Record what you learn in the chart.

Speaking & Listening
↳**Discuss with a Small Group**

With a group, discuss the purpose of each type of print and graphic feature in the selection.

- Review the chart you filled out as you read.

- Discuss how each element contributes to your understanding of the selection.

- Take notes, paraphrasing what's been said to show you understand the perspectives of other members of your group.

- Participate actively: listen closely, pose and answer questions, and ask for opinions.

FLIGHT PIONEERS	ACHIEVEMENTS AND THEIR IMPORTANCE

Expand Your Vocabulary

PRACTICE AND APPLY

Complete each sentence in a way that shows the meaning of the vocabulary word.

1. The waves **lap** gently because the weather is _____ .

2. In science class, I created a **table** to _____ .

3. He gave a **demonstration** of his new invention so _____ .

4. The weather might **defeat** the campers if _____ .

5. She tried to **discourage** the puppy from _____ .

6. We **preserve** artwork so that _____ .

Vocabulary Strategy
↳Multiple-Meaning Words

Some words, **multiple-meaning words,** have more than one meaning. Their definitions are often suggested by **context,** words and sentences that surround them. To determine a multiple-meaning word's definition, use context to make a logical guess. Then, use a print or digital dictionary to confirm the definition.

> ☺Ed
>
> **Interactive Vocabulary Lesson: Words with Multiple Meanings**

PRACTICE AND APPLY

Use a print or digital dictionary to look up the different meanings of *lap, preserve,* and *table.* Then, choose one definition for each of the three words and write original sentences using those words. Include context clues to help a reader determine each word's meaning.

1. *(lap)* _____

2. *(preserve)* _____

3. *(table)* _____

Watch Your Language!

Adverbs and Adverb Clauses

Interactive Grammar
Lesson: The Adverb

Recall that **adverbs** modify, or describe, verbs, adjectives, or other adverbs. An **adverb clause** is a subordinate clause that functions as an adverb, telling more about the time, manner, place, or cause of an event. Writers also use adverbs and adverb clauses to transition from idea to idea, and they use **conjunctive adverbs** to connect and clarify ideas. Here are a few examples of conjunctive adverbs:

however	meanwhile	nonetheless
therefore	moreover	then
finally	furthermore	otherwise

Here are examples of a conjunctive adverb and an adverb used in *Into the Air:*

> <u>Meanwhile</u>, only <u>slowly</u> did people in the United States and abroad become aware of the Wright brothers and the importance of their invention.

The conjunctive adverb *meanwhile* creates a transition from an earlier idea, while the adverb *slowly* modifies the verb phrase *did become*, clarifying the manner in which people were becoming aware of the brothers.

"ADVERBS, ADJECTIVES, CONJUNCTIONS, CLAUSES...
I'LL NEVER LEARN TO SPEAK ENGLISH!"

PRACTICE AND APPLY

Write your own sentences about what kept the Wright brothers from giving up, using conjunctive adverbs to connect ideas or transition from idea to idea.

_____

_____

_____

_____

_____

from

The Wright Brothers: How They Invented the Airplane

Biography by **Russell Freedman**

Engage Your Brain

Choose one or both activities to start connecting with the biography you're about to read.

An Epic Failure

Carry out some research to discover at least four designs, images, or video clips of failed attempts to build a flying machine before the Wright brothers. Identify the most epic fail. Sketch or describe it, noting what you learned.

Would You Fly It?

Join a partner in a discussion of reasons that you would and would not like to design, build, test, and personally fly your own flying machine. What would be exciting about your attempt? What would be frightening about it? List the pros and cons that you and your partner identify.

Analyze Structure of Informational Texts

A text's **structure,** its **pattern of organization,** helps clarify information for readers. As you read, note examples of the organizational patterns listed below.

ORGANIZATIONAL PATTERNS	
definition	defines new terms or technical language within the text
classification	sorts ideas into groups and then describes characteristics
chronological order	relates information in time-order sequence
cause and effect	explains a cause-and-effect relationship
advantage and disadvantage	presents the pros and cons of an idea, position, or quality
key idea and supporting details	establishes a key idea and supports it with details as evidence

Focus on Genre
↳**Biography**

- uses text and sometimes photographs or illustrations to tell a true-life story about a person or group of people
- written in third person; may include direct quotations, including the words of the subject or subjects
- includes facts and descriptions of events, people, and experiences that shaped the subject or subjects' lives

Determine Key Ideas

Key ideas are important ideas the author wants readers to understand. Sometimes these ideas are not stated directly, but are implied, or suggested by details. As you read, determine key ideas by following these steps:

- Identify the topic of each paragraph or section.
- Note details, including descriptions, facts, and quotations.
- Ask yourself what key idea the details convey about the topic.

Annotation in Action

Here are one reader's notes about a chronological structure in *The Wright Brothers*. As you read, note other organizational patterns, such as definition, cause and effect, and key ideas and supporting details.

> The brothers returned to Kitty Hawk on July 10, 1901. This year they wanted to be closer to their launching site at Kill Devil Hills, so they loaded their camping equipment, glider parts, and some lumber into a beach cart, drove it 4 miles south, and set up camp a few hundred feet from the bottom of Big Hill.

The Wright Brothers have been to Kitty Hawk before, but this time, they're setting up camp close to the launch site.

Expand Your Vocabulary

Put a check mark next to the vocabulary words that you feel comfortable using when speaking or writing.

experiment	☐
prediction	☐
accurate	☐
calculate	☐
apparatus	☐

Turn to a partner and talk about the vocabulary words you already know. Then, use as many words as you can in a paragraph about scientific research you've heard about. As you read *The Wright Brothers: How They Invented the Airplane*, use the definitions in the side column to learn the vocabulary words you don't already know.

Background

Russell Freedman (1929–2018) specialized in nonfiction storytelling, especially biographies. He wrote numerous works for young people, including *Freedom Walkers: The Story of the Montgomery Bus Boycott* and *Becoming Ben Franklin: How a Candle-Maker's Son Helped Light the Flame of Liberty*. He won a Newbery Medal—a prize seldom given for nonfiction—for his 1988 biography of Abraham Lincoln, *Lincoln: A Photobiography*.

from The Wright Brothers:

How They Invented the Airplane

Biography by **Russell Freedman**

NOTICE & NOTE
As you read, use the
side margins to make
notes about the text.

Every attempt to fly has failed, yet the Wrights keep trying. Why?

The brothers returned to Kitty Hawk on July 10, 1901. This year they wanted to be closer to their launching site[1] at Kill Devil Hills, so they loaded their camping equipment, glider parts, and some lumber into a beach cart, drove it 4 miles south, and set up camp a few hundred feet from the bottom of Big Hill. Again they lived in a tent, but they also put up a large wooden shed to use as a workshop and hangar[2] for the new glider. This year they would share their camp with visitors. Their friend Octave Chanute and two associates joined the Wrights for a few days to observe their **experiments** and to test a new glider that Chanute had recently designed.

ANALYZE STRUCTURE OF INFORMATIONAL TEXTS

Annotate: Mark references to chronology in paragraph 1.

Analyze: What do these references help you understand?

experiment
(ĭk-spĕr´ə-mənt) n. An *experiment* is a test to determine if an idea is true or to see if a device works.

---

[1] **site:** the place or setting where something happens.
[2] **hangar:** a shelter for storing aircraft.

© Houghton Mifflin Harcourt Publishing Company • Image Credits: Library of Congress Prints & Photographs Division

2   Once again, Wilbur acted as pilot. Some of his glides were
as good or better than the year before, and yet one problem
after another cropped up.[3] They had designed the glider's wings
according to air-pressure tables published by Otto Lilienthal,
but the wings didn't have nearly the lifting power[4] the Wrights
had expected. To make matters worse, the forward elevator,
controlling up-and-down movements, wasn't as effective as they
had hoped.

3   Puzzled and dejected, they closed their camp at the end
of August, sooner than they had planned, and went back
to Dayton.

4   "We doubted that we would ever resume our experiments,"
Wilbur wrote later. "When we looked at the time and money
which we had expended, and considered the progress made and
the distance yet to go, we considered our experiments a failure.
At this time I made the **prediction** that man would sometime
fly, but that it would not be in our lifetime."

5   The experiments that Wilbur and Orville had carried out
with their latest glider in 1901 were far from encouraging.
Reflecting on their problems, Wilbur observed: "We saw that
the calculations upon which all flying machines had been based
were unreliable,[5] and that all were simply groping in the dark.[6]
Having set out with absolute faith in the existing scientific data,
we were driven to doubt one thing after another, till finally,

prediction
(prĭ-dĭk´shən) n. A prediction is a
guess about what will happen.

**ANALYZE STRUCTURE OF
INFORMATIONAL TEXTS**

Annotate: Mark the words in
paragraph 5 that refer to the
disadvantages of the data.

Cause and Effect: What decision
did the Wright brothers make
about data, and why did they
make it?

---

[3] **cropped up:** happened suddenly or unexpectedly.

[4] **lifting power:** the force that holds the glider in the air; most of the lift is produced by
airflow over the wings.

[5] **calculations . . . unreliable:** a reference to the data in the air-pressure tables produced
by German aviation pioneer Otto Lilienthal. The Wrights had used this data to design the
wings of their glider.

[6] **groping in the dark:** looking for answers without much guidance.

after two years of experiment, we cast it all aside, and decided to rely entirely on our own investigations."

6   In the gaslit workroom[7] behind their bicycle shop, Wilbur and Orville began to compile their own data. They wanted to test different types of wing surfaces and obtain **accurate** air-pressure tables. To do this, they built a wind tunnel—a wooden box 6 feet long with a glass viewing window on top and a fan at one end. It wasn't the world's first wind tunnel, but it would be the first to yield valuable results for the construction of a practical airplane.

7   The materials needed to make model wings, or *airfoils*, and the tools to shape them were right at hand. Using tin shears, hammers, files, and a soldering iron, the brothers fashioned as many as two hundred miniature wings out of tin, galvanized iron, steel, solder, and wax. They made wings that were thick or thin, curved or flat, wings with rounded tips and pointed tips, slender wings and stubby wings. They attached these experimental airfoils to balances made of bicycle spokes and old hacksaw blades. Then they tested the wings in their wind tunnel to see how they behaved in a moving airstream.

8   For several weeks they were absorbed in painstaking and systematic lab work—testing, measuring, and **calculating** as they tried to unlock the secrets of an aircraft wing. The work was tedious. It was repetitious. Yet they would look back on that winter as a time of great excitement, when each new day promised discoveries waiting to be made. "Wilbur and I could hardly wait for morning to come," Orville declared, "to get at something that interested us. *That's* happiness."

9   The Wrights knew that they were exploring uncharted territory with their wind-tunnel tests. Each new bit of data jotted down in their notebooks added to their understanding of how an airfoil works. Gradually they replaced the calculations of others with facts and figures of their own. Their doubts vanished, and their faith in themselves grew. When their lab tests were finally completed, they felt confident that they could calculate in advance the performance of an aircraft's wings with far greater accuracy than had ever before been possible.

10   Armed with this new knowledge, they designed their biggest glider yet. Its wings, longer and narrower than before, measured 32 feet from tip to tip and 5 feet from front to rear.

Don't forget to **Notice & Note** as you read the text.
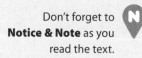

accurate
(ăk´yər-ĭt) *adj.* Something *accurate* is correct.

Text in Focus Video

Learn more about understanding technical language.

calculate
(kăl´kyə-lāt´) *v.* To *calculate* is to figure out an answer by using math.

DETERMINE KEY IDEAS

Annotate: Mark the key idea of paragraph 8.

Analyze: How do details in the paragraph support this key idea?

---

[7] **gaslit workroom:** indoor lighting came from gas-fueled lamps, which were dimmer than the electric lights used today.

Annotate: What does the
numeric information in paragraph
10 reveal? Mark the places where
the author provides numeric
information.

Draw Conclusions: What is
the purpose of including these
numbers?

For the first time, the new glider had a tail—two 6-foot-high vertical fins, designed to help stabilize the machine during turns. The hip cradle[8] developed the year before to control wing warping[9] was retained. The craft weighed just under 120 pounds.

11   With growing anticipation, Wilbur and Orville prepared for their 1902 trip to the Outer Banks. "They really ought to get away for a while," Katharine wrote to her father. "Will is thin and nervous and so is Orv. They will be all right when they get down in the sand where the salt breezes blow. . . . They think that life at Kitty Hawk cures all ills, you know.

12   "The flying machine is in process of making now. Will spins the sewing machine around by the hour while Orv squats around marking the places to sew [the cotton wing covering]. There is no place in the house to live but I'll be lonesome enough by this time next week and wish I could have some of their racket around."

13   The brothers reached the Outer Banks at the end of August with their trunks, baggage, and crates carrying the glider parts.

14   By the middle of September they had assembled their new glider and were ready to try it out. This year they took turns in the pilot's position, giving Orville a chance to fly for the first time. To begin with, they were very cautious. They would launch the machine from the slope on Big Hill and glide only a short distance as they practiced working the controls. Steering to the right or left was accomplished by warping the wings, with the glider always turning toward the lower wing. Up-and-down movements were controlled by the forward elevator.

15   In a few days they made dozens of short but successful test glides. At this point, things looked more promising than ever. The only mishap occurred one afternoon when Orville was at the controls. That evening he recorded the incident in his diary:

16   "I was sailing along smoothly without any trouble . . . when I noticed that one wing was getting a little too high and that the machine was slowly sliding off in the opposite direction. . . . The next thing I knew was that the wing was very high in the air, a great deal higher than before, and I thought I must have worked the twisting **apparatus** the wrong way. Thinking of nothing else . . . I threw the wingtips to their greatest angle. By this time I found suddenly that I was making a descent backwards toward the low wing, from a height of 25

apparatus
(ăp´ə-răt´əs) *n.* An *apparatus* is a piece of equipment.

---

[8] **hip cradle:** a device that allowed the pilot to lie down and use hip movement to control the rudder and wings.

[9] **wing warping:** the Wright brothers' discovery of how they could twist the ends of the wings in order to balance and control the aircraft.

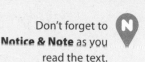

or 30 feet. . . . The result was a heap of flying machine, cloth and sticks in a heap, with me in the center without a bruise or scratch. The experiments thereupon suddenly came to a close till repairs can be made. In spite of this sad catastrophe we are tonight in a hilarious mood as a result of the encouraging performance of the machine."

17   A few days' labor made the glider as good as new. It wasn't seriously damaged again during hundreds of test glides, and it repeatedly withstood rough landings at full speed. Wilbur and Orville became more and more confident. "Our new machine is a very great improvement over anything we had built before and over anything anyone has built," Wilbur told his father. "Everything is so much more satisfactory that we now believe that the flying problem is really nearing its solution."

18   And yet the solution was not yet quite at hand. As they continued their test flights, a baffling new problem arose. On most flights, the glider performed almost perfectly. But every so often—in about one flight out of fifty—it would spin out of control as the pilot tried to level off after a turn.

19   Lying in bed one sleepless night, Orville figured out what the problem was. The fixed tail worked perfectly well most of the time. During some turns, however—when the airspeed was low and the pilot failed to level off soon enough—pressure was built up on the tail, throwing the glider off balance and into a spin. That's just what happened to Orville the day of his accident. The cure was to make the tail movable—like a ship's rudder or a bird's tail.

VOCABULARY

Resources: The word *catastrophe* might be difficult to understand. Look it up in a dictionary to discover each of its meanings.

Analyze: Why would Orville describe what happened as a catastrophe?

[LC-W85-85]

NOTICE & NOTE
QUOTED WORDS

When you notice the author has quoted the opinions or conclusions of an expert or someone who participated in or witnessed an event, you've found a **Quoted Words** signpost.

Annotate: Mark the quotation in paragraph 21.

Analyze: Why was the quotation included and what did it add?

?

ESSENTIAL QUESTION:

How do you find courage in the face of fear?

Review your notes and add your thoughts to your Response Log.

20   The next morning at breakfast, Orville told Wilbur about his idea. After thinking it over for a few minutes, Wilbur agreed. Then he offered an idea of his own. Why not connect the new movable tail to the wing-warping wires? This would allow the pilot to twist the wings and turn the tail at the same time, simply by shifting his hips. With the wings and tail coordinated, the glider would always make a smooth banked turn.

21   They removed the original tail and installed a movable single-vaned tail[10] 5 feet high. From then on, there were no more problems. The movable tail rudder finally gave the Wright brothers complete control of their glider. "With this improvement our serious troubles ended," wrote Wilbur, "and thereafter we devoted ourselves to the work of gaining skill by continued practice."

22   Wilbur and Orville made hundreds of perfectly controlled glides in 1902. They proved that their laboratory tests were accurate. The next step was to build a powered airplane. "Before leaving camp," Orville wrote, "we were already at work on the general design of a new machine which we proposed to propel with a motor."

TURN AND TALK

With a partner, talk about why the Wrights may have never let a fear of failure stop them. How did the two respond each time they failed?

---

[10] **single-vaned tail:** the one-piece plate that extends from the back end of the aircraft for stability and control.

Assessment Practice

Answer these questions before moving on to the **Analyze the Text** section.

1. How does paragraph 4 contribute to the development of the author's idea that the Wright brothers faced many obstacles?

   (A) by showing how much money the Wright brothers had spent

   (B) by explaining that the Wright brothers gave up their experiments

   (C) by describing other people's predictions for the Wright brothers' work

   (D) by providing a direct quotation from Wilbur Wright about losing hope

2. What key idea in paragraph 8 is supported by what Orville says?

   (A) The Wright brothers' work took many days to complete.

   (B) The Wright brothers' work was scientific and methodical.

   (C) The Wright brothers' work was exciting because it interested them.

   (D) The Wright brothers' work often led to sleepless nights of discovery.

3. What central idea about the Wright brothers is shared by *Into the Air* and *The Wright Brothers: How They Invented the Airplane*?

   (A) The Wright brothers are considered to be geniuses.

   (B) The Wright brothers' friends and family helped them test their airplane.

   (C) The Wright brothers worked hard to design and test their airplane, despite many setbacks.

   (D) The Wright brothers based their design for a flying machine on the data of other inventors.

Test-Taking Strategies

Analyze the Text

Support your responses with evidence from the text.

(1) **ANALYZE** Review paragraph 6. How does the author define *wind tunnel?* How does the description of a wind tunnel affect your understanding of the text?

(2) **CAUSE AND EFFECT** Review paragraph 9. What effect did the wind tunnel tests have on the Wright brothers and their work?

(3) **IDENTIFY PATTERNS** Review paragraph 18. What pattern of organization does the author use to structure information? How does the organization add to your understanding of the selection?

(4) **CITE EVIDENCE** Review paragraphs 19–21. What details does the author provide about how the brothers work together? What key idea is suggested by these details?

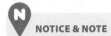

NOTICE & NOTE

Review what you **noticed and noted** as you read the text. Your annotations can help you answer these questions.

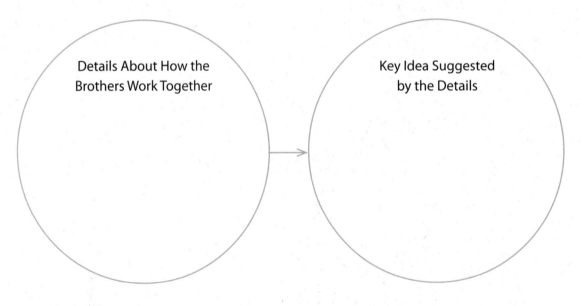

Details About How the Brothers Work Together

Key Idea Suggested by the Details

(5) **ANALYZE** Review the use of **Quoted Words** throughout the selection. How do the quotations help you understand the key ideas in the selection?

Choices

Here are some other ways to demonstrate your understanding of the ideas in this lesson.

Writing
↳What Happened?

Review paragraphs 13–22; then, write a three-paragraph summary of that section.

- State key ideas and supporting details found in the section.

- Paraphrase ideas by stating them in your own words.

- Use transitions and introductory elements.

- Do not include personal opinions or judgments in your summary.

> As you write and discuss, be sure to use the **Academic Vocabulary** words.
>
> | evident | similar |
> |---------|---------|
> | factor | specific |
> | indicate | |

Speaking & Listening
↳Find the Main Idea

Have a group discussion to determine a possible central or main idea for the selection.

- Remind group members that you are not looking for a topic. Instead, you are looking for a message that is central to the text.

- Provide support for your ideas by citing text evidence.

- Review the ideas together. Listen closely and actively to each other.

- Ask questions to clarify points. Respond appropriately.

Social & Emotional Learning
↳Never Give Up

At the time that the Wrights were building and crashing their gliders, people sometimes said, "if human beings were meant to fly, they'd have been born with wings." If the Wrights had listened to them, they'd never have flown.

Hold a small group discussion about what it takes to stand up to failure, time and time again, especially when people doubt that you'll ever succeed.

- List your group's ideas about how to stick to a goal, even when it seems impossible.

- Share your group's ideas with the class.

Expand Your Vocabulary

PRACTICE AND APPLY

Answer the questions to show your understanding of the vocabulary words.

1. Why is it important to be **accurate** when you **calculate** how much water to take on a trip through the desert?

2. What type of **apparatus** could be used to measure weight?

3. What is one possible purpose of an **experiment?**

4. Why is it useful to make a **prediction** before taking a risk?

Vocabulary Strategy
↳Resources

In *The Wright Brothers: How They Invented the Airplane,* the author uses technical and scientific language to describe how the Wrights developed their glider. Sometimes, writers provide definitions or context clues to help readers determine the meaning of technical terms. But if you need more help to understand a technical term or subject in your reading, turn to online and print resources for additional information.

A **standard dictionary** will tell you a word's definitions, pronunciation, syllabication, parts of speech, history, and origin. A **specialized dictionary** focuses on terms related to a particular field of study or work. An **encyclopedia** includes facts and background information on many subjects. Finally, many professional and technical organizations host websites that may be useful in defining terminology.

☺Ed

Interactive Vocabulary Lesson: Using Reference Sources

PRACTICE AND APPLY

Use context clues in the selection, as well as online and print resources, to define these terms: *air pressure* (paragraphs 2 and 6), *forward elevator* (paragraphs 2 and 14), and *airfoil* (paragraphs 7 and 9). Cite the resources you used to write your definitions. Share your definitions with a classmate and compare results.

Watch Your Language!

Transitions and Commas

Transitions are words and phrases that link and clarify relationships among ideas. Commas often set off transitions from other parts of a sentence:

☺**Ed**

Interactive Grammar Lesson: Commas with Compound Sentences

> <u>From then on</u>, there were no more problems.

Commas are also useful in **compound sentences**—sentences that consist of two or more independent clauses. Commas are also needed in **complex sentences**—sentences that combine an independent clause with one or more dependent clauses:

> Their doubts vanished, and their faith in themselves grew.

> When their lab tests were finally completed, they felt confident that they could calculate in advance the performance of an aircraft's wings with far greater accuracy than had ever before been possible.

PRACTICE AND APPLY

Write your own sentences with transitions and commas, using the examples from the selection as models. Your sentences should be about a topic related to the Wright brothers.

When you have finished, share your sentences with a partner and compare your use of transitions and commas.

_____

_____

_____

_____

_____

_____

_____

_____

Compare Presentations

The two selections you have read focus on some of the same events in the lives of Wilbur and Orville Wright. You will now compare **key ideas,** and will **integrate** the information to determine a **central idea** shared by the two.

In this task, you will need to make **inferences,** logical guesses based on facts and your own knowledge, to determine the authors' messages. Evidence from the text should support each inference.

In a small group, complete a chart like the one below. Analyze each scene or event listed in the first column, considering each author's purpose and tone, and infer the key ideas in each selection.

Scene/Event	Key Ideas: *Into the Air*	Key Ideas: *The Wright Brothers*
Summer 1901		
Wind Tunnel Experiments		
Fall 1902		

Analyze the Texts

Discuss these questions in your group.

(1) **COMPARE** Think about the Wright brothers' quotations and dialogue in each text. How are these words presented in each biography? Describe similarities and differences.

(2) **INFER** What do the frustrations experienced by the brothers in the summer of 1901 say about what they were like and what was important to them?

(3) **EVALUATE** Between the two selections, which is more effective in communicating facts? Ideas? Moods and emotions? Explain.

(4) **SYNTHESIZE** What have you learned from these sources about trying hard and not giving up?

Discuss and Present

Now, your group can continue exploring the ideas in these texts by collaborating on a presentation to give to your class. Follow these steps:

(1) **GATHER INFORMATION** In your group, review and then list the key events that are described in both texts.

(2) **DISCUSS** Examine the similarities and differences in how each event is presented in the texts. Ask:

- How do the authors use **text** to describe this event?
  - Between the two selections, how is the text similar?
  - Between the two selections, how does the text differ?
- How do the authors use **images** to describe this event?
  - Between the two selections, how are the images similar?
  - Between the two selections, how do the images differ?
- What is the **key idea** of this event, as presented in each selection?
  - Between the two selections, how are the ideas similar?
  - Between the two selections, how do the ideas differ?

As you discuss, remember to listen to what others say, to ask questions to request and clarify information, and to build on the ideas of others. Use the chart below to take notes. As a group, determine what you think is the central idea shared by the two selections.

Scene/Event:	
Similarities:	Differences:
Key Idea:	Key Idea:

(3) **SHARE WHAT YOU LEARN** Now you can share your group's findings with the rest of the class. Begin by stating what your group thinks is the central idea expressed by the two selections. Use your notes to remember important points to talk about. Speak clearly and loudly enough for others to hear. Remember to invite the class to ask questions. Answer questions respectfully.

Reader's Choice

Continue your exploration of the Essential Question by doing some independent reading on finding courage. Read the titles and descriptions shown. Then mark the texts that interest you.

? **ESSENTIAL QUESTION:**
How do you find courage in the face of fear?

Short Reads Available on ☺Ed

These texts are available in your ebook. Choose one to read and rate. Then defend your rating to the class.

Horrors
Poem by **Lewis Carroll**

What are those terrible things that go bump in the night?

Rate It ☆☆☆☆☆

Vanquishing the Hungry Chinese Zombie
Short Story by **Claudine Gueh**

A girl faces terror to protect her parents and the family store.

Rate It ☆☆☆☆☆

Running into Danger on an Alaskan Trail
Narrative Nonfiction by **Cinthia Ritchie**

A long-distance runner has a terrifying encounter with a bear.

Rate It ☆☆☆☆☆

Face Your Fears: Choking Under Pressure Is Every Athlete's Worst Nightmare
Informational Text by **Dana Hudepohl**

How do athletes handle fear and stress while dealing with the pressure to succeed at competitive sports?

Rate It ☆☆☆☆☆

Long Reads

Here are three recommended books that connect to this unit topic. For additional options, ask your teacher, school librarian, or peers. Which titles spark your interest?

Dragonwings

Novel by **Laurence Yep**

Moon Shadow travels from China to San Francisco to get to know his father. Together, they face challenges and take risks, all while navigating the difficulties of immigrant life.

The Parker Inheritance

Novel by **Varian Johnson**

Candice and Brandon dive into a mystery embedded in their town's history. While deciphering the clues, they begin to unravel the unspoken secrets of their own families.

The Breadwinner

Novel by **Deborah Ellis**

After Parvana's father is arrested by the Taliban, her family may face starvation. Parvana must transform herself—in unexpected ways—to become the breadwinner for her family.

Extension
↳ Connect & Create

WHAT HAPPENED NEXT? Create a plot diagram outlining critical events in one of the texts, capturing each step of a character's journey as that character develops the courage to face a fear. Include a brief explanation of each event in your diagram, using the following structure: exposition, rising action, climax, falling action, and resolution.

WATCH OUT, HOLLYWOOD! With a partner, create a storyboard describing a scene in one of the texts that shows what helped a person or character develop courage. Work together to identify a scene, and then create your storyboard. Be sure to capture—

- details of the setting,

- the scene's events,

- dialogue and directions to actors, and

- your ideas about what was so helpful to the person or character.

 NOTICE & NOTE

- Pick one of the texts and annotate the Notice & Note signposts you find.

- Then, use the **Notice & Note Writing Frames** to help you write about the significance of the signposts.

- Compare your findings with those of other students who read the same text.

Notice & Note Writing Frames

Write an Informative Essay

Writing Prompt

Using ideas, information, and examples from multiple texts in this unit, write an informative essay for your community newspaper explaining how people find the courage to face their fears.

Manage your time carefully so that you can

- review the texts in the unit and plan your essay;
- write your essay; and
- revise and edit your essay.

Be sure to

- provide an introduction that includes a clear controlling idea or thesis statement;
- support your main ideas with relevant evidence from sources;
- organize information in a logical way, using a formal style that includes precise language and vocabulary specific to your audience and purpose;
- end with a satisfying conclusion.

> ### Review the
> ### Mentor Text
>
> For an example of a well-written informative essay that you can use as a mentor text and source for your essay, review:
>
> - **"Fears and Phobias"** (pages 205–211)
>
> Review your notes and annotations about this text. Think about the techniques the author uses to make the work interesting, convincing, clear, and informative.

Consider Your Sources

Review the list of texts in the unit and choose at least three that you may want to use as support for your informative essay.

As you review potential sources, consult the notes you made on your **Response Log** and make additional notes about ideas that might be useful in your essay. Include source titles and page numbers to help you provide accurate citations when you refer to these texts.

UNIT 3 SOURCES

- [ ] *from* **The Breadwinner**
- [ ] **Life Doesn't Frighten Me**
- [ ] **Fears and Phobias**
- [ ] **Wired for Fear** MEDIA
- [ ] **Embarrassed? Blame Your Brain**
- [ ] **The Ravine**
- [ ] *from* **Into the Air**
- [ ] *from* **The Wright Brothers**

Analyze the Prompt

Review the prompt to make sure you understand the assignment.

Mark the sentence in the prompt that identifies the topic of your informative essay. Rephrase this sentence in your own words.

Next, look for words that indicate the purpose and audience for your essay, and write a sentence describing each.

What is my topic? What is my writing task?

What is my purpose?

Who is my audience?

Find a Purpose

Common purposes of an informative essay are

- to **provide factual information**
- to **explain a topic or idea**
- to **motivate an audience**
- to **educate readers**

Review the Rubric

Your informative essay will be scored using a rubric. As you write, focus on the characteristics as described in the chart. You will learn more about these characteristics as you work through the lesson.

PURPOSE, FOCUS, AND ORGANIZATION	EVIDENCE AND ELABORATION	CONVENTIONS OF STANDARD ENGLISH
The response includes: • A strongly maintained controlling idea • Transitions that logically connect ideas • A logical progression of ideas • Appropriate style and tone	The response includes: • Effective use of evidence and sources • Effective use of elaboration • Clear and effective expression of ideas • Appropriate, domain-specific vocabulary • Varied sentence structure	The response may include the following: • Some minor errors in usage but no patterns of errors • Correct punctuation, capitalization, sentence formation, and spelling • Command of basic conventions

1 PLAN YOUR INFORMATIVE ESSAY

Help with Planning

Consult **Interactive Writing Lesson: Writing Informative Texts.**

Gather Ideas

Determine the ideas you'd like to include, using strategies such as discussing the topic with classmates, doing background reading, or thinking about how your own experiences relate to the topic. Use a chart like the one below to take notes. Include any source titles and page numbers in your notes.

IDEAS FROM DISCUSSION	IDEAS FROM BACKGROUND READING	IDEAS FROM PERSONAL EXPERIENCE

Develop a Central or Controlling Idea

Use your notes to develop a clear and concise **central** or **controlling idea,** or thesis statement. State it in your own words.

NOTES ABOUT A POSSIBLE CONTROLLING IDEA	CONTROLLING IDEA

Identify Main Ideas and Supporting Evidence

After developing your central or controlling idea, think about main ideas to include. A main idea may be explicitly expressed in a topic sentence, or it may be implied, or suggested, by details. Use the chart below to organize main ideas and the evidence that supports each idea.

IDEA:	IDEA:	IDEA:
SUPPORTING EVIDENCE	**SUPPORTING EVIDENCE**	**SUPPORTING EVIDENCE**

Organize Ideas

Organize your ideas and supporting details in a way that logically supports your central or controlling idea. Keep in mind that a well-written essay has a compelling introduction and a satisfying conclusion. Use a **formal tone** throughout your essay. Use the table below to help you organize your ideas and add coherence to your writing.

FIND SUPPORTING EVIDENCE

Supporting evidence tells more about a main idea. Include:

- facts
- examples
- quotations
- statistics
- personal experiences

INTRODUCTION	• Clearly state your central or controlling idea. • Grab readers' attention; include a vivid description or a thought-provoking quotation, for example.
BODY PARAGRAPHS	• Present each main idea in its own paragraph. • Cite evidence that supports your ideas. • Be sure that evidence is relevant and credible.
CONCLUSION	• Restate the central or controlling idea. • Clearly tie ideas together. • Leave readers with a final thought that will stick with them.

2 DEVELOP A DRAFT

Drafting can be challenging. It can be helpful to examine how professional authors craft cohesive informative essays and to use similar techniques in your own writing.

Write a Compelling Introduction

EXAMINE THE MENTOR TEXT

Notice how the author of "Fears and Phobias" vividly describes the experience of riding a roller coaster to grab readers' attention.

Fears and Phobias
Informational Text | kidshealth.org

The author directly **addresses readers** to grab their attention.

The roller coaster hesitates for a split second at the peak of its steep track after a long, slow climb. You know what's about to happen—and there's no way to avoid it now. It's time to hang onto the handrail, palms sweating, heart racing, and brace yourself for the wild ride down.

Vivid **descriptions** help readers connect with the experience.

APPLY TO YOUR DRAFT

In your introduction, include an experience to which most readers can relate. Think of **sensory details,** words or phrases that appeal to readers' senses, that you can use to bring the experience to life.

Try These Suggestions

Review your notes with these questions in mind:

- Which experience will most readers relate to?
- What sensory details can I use to bring the experience to life?
- What is the best way to get readers' attention?

Experiences to Which Readers Might Relate		
Sensory Words that Describe the Experiences		

Use a Formal Style

EXAMINE THE MENTOR TEXT

The author of "Fears and Phobias" uses a formal style, which is appropriate for the purpose and audience.

Drafting Online

Check your assignment list for a writing task from your teacher.

The author uses **formal language** as well as **vocabulary** that is specific to the topic.

> When we sense danger, the brain reacts instantly, sending signals that activate the nervous system. This causes physical responses, such as a faster heartbeat, rapid breathing, and an increase in blood pressure.

The author uses **precise language** to describe physical responses to danger.

APPLY TO YOUR DRAFT

Use this chart to practice using specific vocabulary and precise language for your essay.

WHAT VOCABULARY IS SPECIFIC TO THE TOPIC?	WHAT PRECISE LANGUAGE DESCRIBES THE TOPIC?
IS THERE A MORE FORMAL WAY TO SAY ANY OF THESE THINGS? IF SO, WRITE THEM BELOW.	

REVISE YOUR INFORMATIVE ESSAY

Experienced writers know the importance of revision. Review your essay and consider how you can improve it. Use the guide to help you revise your essay.

REVISION GUIDE		
ASK YOURSELF	**PROVE IT**	**REVISE IT**
Introduction Does my introduction grab the reader's attention?	**Place brackets ({ })** around the introduction. **Highlight** words or phrases that grab attention.	**Add** an interesting fact, example, or quotation. **Introduce** vivid descriptions.
Central or Controlling Idea Does my introduction clearly state the purpose?	**Underline** the central or controlling idea, or thesis statement.	**Revise** so that your central or controlling idea is clearly stated.
Supporting Details Do I support each main idea with evidence?	**Circle** main ideas. **Highlight** supporting evidence for each main idea, using different colors.	**Add** facts, details, examples, or quotations to support ideas.
Organization Are paragraphs organized logically and do transitions clearly connect ideas?	**Highlight** transitional words within and between paragraphs.	**Rearrange** sentences or paragraphs to organize ideas logically. **Add** transitions.
Tone Is my essay written in a formal style?	**Mark** informal language, including slang.	**Replace** informal words and phrases. **Add** precise language and vocabulary specific to your topic.
Conclusion Does my conclusion support the topic?	**Place brackets ({ })** around the conclusion. **Underline** words or phrases that refer to the topic.	**Add** a statement that summarizes the main ideas.

APPLY TO YOUR DRAFT

Consider the following as you look for opportunities to improve your writing.

- Make sure your essay has a clear central or controlling idea.
- Avoid informal language.
- Use specific terms.
- Add examples to increase interest and elaborate upon your ideas.

Peer Review in Action

Once you have finished revising your informative essay, you will exchange papers with a partner in a **peer review.** During a peer review, you will give suggestions to improve your partner's draft.

Read the paragraph from a student's draft and examine the comments made by her peer reviewer.

Help with Revision

Find a **Peer Review Guide** and **Student Models** online.

First Draft

When Fear Becomes Irrational
By Rose Hsu, Valley Middle School

There are tons of phobias. One is being scared of public places. I feel this way sometimes. I worry about getting stuck in a public place, like a line at the airport. Untreated, this phobia can drive people into isolation.

Is there a specific name for this phobia?

Don't use informal expressions like "tons of" and the word "I" in a formal essay.

Can you identify more examples?

Now read the revised paragraph below. Notice how the writer has improved her draft by making revisions based on her peer reviewer's comments.

Revision

When Fear Becomes Irrational
By Rose Hsu, Valley Middle School

Experts put phobias into different categories. One category is agoraphobia, or a fear of being trapped in public places. Someone who suffers from agoraphobia irrationally fears not being able to escape a public place, like a line at the airport, a bustling shopping mall, a busy subway car, or a crowded concert. Untreated, this phobia can drive people into isolation.

Well done! With words like "experts," "category," and "agoraphobia," the tone is formal now.

The new examples add nice, elaborative details. Great job!

APPLY TO YOUR DRAFT

During your peer review, give each other specific suggestions for how you could make your essays clearer or more informative. Use your revision guide to help you.

When receiving feedback from your partner, listen attentively and ask questions to make sure you fully understand the revision suggestions.

EDIT YOUR INFORMATIVE ESSAY

Edit your final draft to check for proper use of standard English conventions and to correct any errors.

Watch Your Language!

USE COMPOUND AND COMPLEX SENTENCES

A **compound sentence** consists of two or more independent clauses connected with commas or dashes and coordinating conjunctions. Here's an example from "Fears and Phobias":

> You know what's about to happen—<u>and</u> there's no way to avoid it now.

A **complex sentence** consists of one independent clause and at least one dependent clause. Here's an example:

> When fears last beyond the expected age, it might be a sign that someone is overly fearful, worried, or anxious.

APPLY TO YOUR DRAFT

Now apply what you've learned to your own work.

1. Highlight simple sentences in pink, compound sentences in blue, and complex sentences in yellow.

2. Work with a peer to analyze your paper. Have you included a variety of sentence patterns?

3. Revise for sentence variety. Consider revising simple sentences to form compound or complex sentences.

Interactive Grammar Lesson:

Simple Sentences and Compound Sentences

Words to Know

Common **coordinating conjunctions** are *and, but, or, nor, yet* and *for.*

Many **dependent clauses** start with words such as *when, until, who, where, because,* or *so that.*

Ways to Share

- Recast your essay as an **advice column.** Use a question-and-answer format to convey ideas.

- **Write a blog post** on a class or school website to tell others about what you learned. Invite online comments and discussion.

- **Create a presentation** based on your essay. See the next task for tips on how.

5 PUBLISH YOUR INFORMATIVE ESSAY

Share It!

The prompt asks you to present information in an essay for a community newspaper. You may also use your essay about how people deal with their fears as inspiration for other projects.

© Houghton Mifflin Harcourt Publishing Company

Give a Presentation

Imagine that you are invited to adapt the information in your essay into a multimedia presentation for your classmates. Plan and create a presentation and then present it to the class.

Adapt Your Essay for Presentation

Review your informative essay. Then, use the chart below to guide you as you adapt your essay and create a script and presentation materials.

Convey Your Message

- Use formal language, just like the written essay does.

- Audio effects or visuals should enhance the message, not distract from it.

PRESENTATION ELEMENTS	NOTES
Title and Introduction How will you capture the attention of listeners? Is there a more engaging way to state your central or controlling idea?	
Audience What information will your audience already know? What information should you add or exclude?	
Effective Language and Organization Do you need to simplify parts of your text? Should you add transitions such as *first, second, in addition,* and *finally?* How can you use accessible, formal English?	
Audio and/or Visual Effects What sounds, images, or graphics would help clarify ideas or add interest? What text should appear on screen?	

Practice with a Partner

Once you've completed the draft of your script, practice with a partner. Give each other feedback on visuals that may be irrelevant or difficult to understand.

Use this guide as you practice your presentation. Give each other specific suggestions for improvement.

Active Listening

As you work with your partner, remember to:

- Listen closely and don't interrupt.
- Ask relevant questions.
- Provide clear and thoughtful answers.

PRESENTATION GOAL	NOTES FOR IMPROVEMENT
Practice pronouncing difficult words and phrases. Repeat challenging sections a few times until you can say them clearly.	
Make sure you speak comfortably, slowly, and loudly and clearly enough that classmates will understand your points.	
Connect with your listeners by using good posture, speaking expressively, and focusing on audience members as you speak.	

Deliver Your Presentation

Use the advice you received during practice to make final changes to your presentation. Then, using effective techniques, present it to your classmates. Invite questions and comments.

- Speak directly to the audience.
- After your presentation, acknowledge each question from the audience, and answer it to the best of your ability.
- If you don't understand a question, ask the speaker for clarification.

Share It!

- **Conduct a class discussion.** Talk about similarities and differences that came to light about how people face their fears.
- **Choose visuals from your presentations and make memes or posters about facing fears.**
- **Evaluate the presentations.** Consider speaker's tone and volume, formality, effectiveness of visuals, and so on. Provide constructive feedback.

Interactive Speaking & Listening Lesson: Giving a Presentation

Reflect & Extend

Here are some other ways to show your understanding of the ideas in Unit 3.

Reflect on the Essential Question ?

How do you find courage in the face of fear?

Has your answer to the question changed after reading the texts in the unit? Discuss your ideas.

You can use these sentence starters to help you reflect on your learning.

- **I still wonder whether . . .**
- **I want to learn more about . . .**
- **I don't understand . . .**

Project-Based Learning
↳ Create a Vlog

You've read about ways that people discover the courage to face their fears. Now, create a vlog that gives advice on how to overcome a fear.

Here are some questions to ask yourself as you get started.

- What are some ways to overcome a fear?
- How might I present each of those ways in a vlog?
- What video and audio elements would I like to include?
- What details should be in my vlog's storyboard?

 Ed

Media Projects

To find help with this task online, access **Create a Vlog.**

Writing
↳ Write a Short Story

The world is filled with stories about people gaining the courage to face their fears. It's time to add one of your own! Write a story about a character who faces a fear and finds courage enough to overcome it. Your story can be realistic, historical, science fiction, or anything you want it to be. Use the chart to jot down your ideas. Then, write your story.

ASK YOURSELF	MY NOTES
Where and when will my story be **set?**	
What **traits** will my characters have? What will they be like?	
What **conflict** will my central character face? External? Internal? A combination of the two?	
What will happen? How will the conflict be **resolved**?	

⏺Ed

Get hooked by the unit topic.

Stream to Start Video

Through an Animal's Eyes

*"I have wished that I could . . .
look out onto the world through
the eyes, with the mind,
of a chimpanzee."*

—Jane Goodall

Analyze the Image

How do you interpret the expression
you see in this animal's eyes?

Spark Your Learning

Here's a chance to spark your learning about ideas in **Unit 4: Through an Animal's Eyes.**

As you read, you can use the **Response Log** (page R4) to track your thinking about the Essential Question.

Make the Connection

What was the last animal you really paid attention to? Take a few moments to consider what your knowledge of that animal might teach you about human life. Then, list your ideas in the box below.

Think About the
Essential Question

What can you learn from seeing the world through an animal's eyes? People and animals live in very different worlds. What might we learn about our own lives if we pay attention to how animals see and understand the world? Explain your ideas.

Prove It!

Turn to a partner and use one of the words in a sentence about what we might learn by paying attention to animals.

Sound Like an Expert

You can use these Academic Vocabulary words to write and talk about the topics and themes in the unit. How many of these words do you already feel comfortable using when speaking or writing?

	I can use it!	I understand it.	I'll look it up.
benefit	☐	☐	☐
distinct	☐	☐	☐
environment	☐	☐	☐
illustrate	☐	☐	☐
respond	☐	☐	☐

Preview the Texts

Look over the images, titles, and descriptions of the texts in the unit. Mark the title of the text that interests you most.

from **Pax**

Novel by **Sara Pennypacker**

A pet fox takes a mysterious and disturbing drive with his boy and the boy's father. Where are they headed and why?

Zoo

Science Fiction by **Edward Hoch**

Professor Hugo's Interplanetary Zoo makes a quick stop in Chicago, but which of his "creatures" are actually on display?

from **Animal Snoops: The Wondrous World of Wildlife Spies**

Informational Text by **Peter Christie**

Not only do wild animals snoop on each other, but they also use what they hear and see to figure out how to behave.

Animal Wisdom

Poem by **Nancy Wood**

What wisdom might turtles, bears, eagles, and people share about what's missing from each other's lives?

The Last Wolf

Poem by **Mary TallMountain**

The very last wolf, after wandering the streets of a shattered city, has an important question for us all.

Wild Animals Aren't Pets

Argument by **USA TODAY**

Why in the world do we let people own wild animals? This selection claims that it's a bad idea—for both the animals and their owners.

Let People Own Exotic Animals

Argument by **Zuzana Kukol**

Should people be allowed to keep lions, tigers, bears, elephants, and other large animals in private collections? This author thinks so.

I Wonder . . .

Pick a type of animal that interests you, and think about the things that it notices every day. How does this animal's view of the world differ from your own? Explain your ideas.

from **Pax**

Novel by **Sara Pennypacker**

ESSENTIAL QUESTION:

What can you learn from seeing the world through an animal's eyes?

Engage Your Brain

Choose one or more of these activities to start connecting with the novel excerpt you are about to read.

Are You as Clever as a Fox?

Many clichés and expressions refer to foxes. In a small group, discuss the meaning of each of these phrases:

- as sly as a fox
- crazy like a fox
- like a fox in a henhouse

What do these expressions reveal about what we think of foxes?

A Fox's Life

Do some quick online research to learn more about foxes.

- Where do they usually live?
- What threats do they face?

Share what you learn with the class.

A Dog's (or Cat's) Life

Pick any event from your day. Now imagine that you're a dog or cat. What would matter to you? Describe the event from the point of view of a dog or cat.

Analyze Point of View

Perspective is a character's attitude and way of looking at events. **Point of view,** on the other hand, is the vantage point from which the voice telling the story, the story's **narrator,** relates events.

In **first-person point of view,** the narrator is a character in the story. In **third-person point of view,** the narrator is not a character. Third-person narrators may be **omniscient,** knowing everything, or **limited,** knowing only certain aspects of the story.

Use the diagram below to help you determine which third-person point of view is used in *Pax.*

Focus on Genre
↳ **Novel**

- includes the basic elements of fiction—plot, characters, conflict, setting, point of view, and theme
- is longer than a short story or novella and is often organized into chapters
- provides authors with the length to develop plot and characters thoroughly

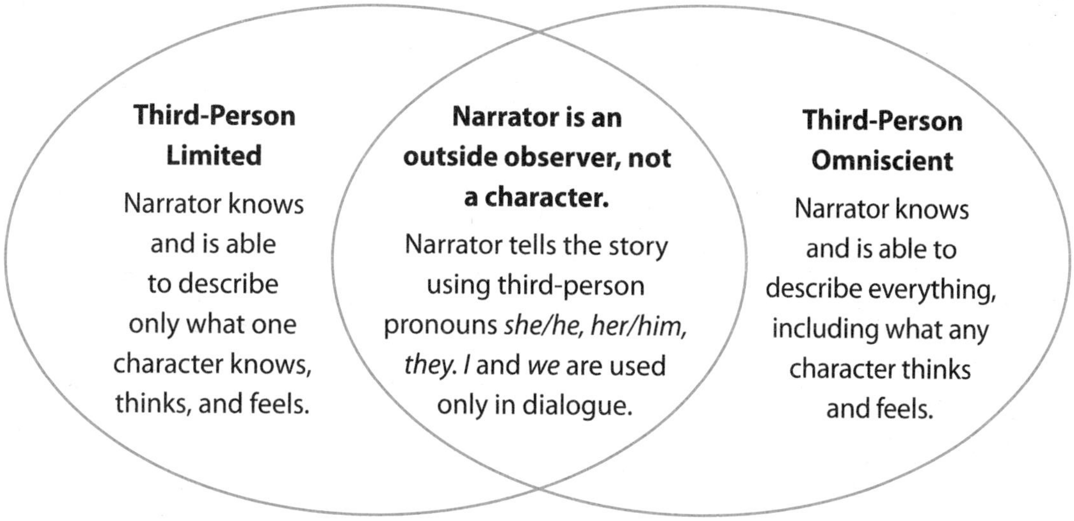

Third-Person Limited

Narrator knows and is able to describe only what one character knows, thinks, and feels.

Narrator is an outside observer, not a character.

Narrator tells the story using third-person pronouns *she/he, her/him, they.* *I* and *we* are used only in dialogue.

Third-Person Omniscient

Narrator knows and is able to describe everything, including what any character thinks and feels.

Analyze Word Choice

Authors carefully choose words and details that help develop the **voice**—the unique personality or sensibility—of a character or a narrator, as well as the story's **mood,** the story's feeling or atmosphere.

As you read, note specific word choices that help create the voice of the excerpt's main character as well as the story's mood.

Annotation in Action

Here are one reader's notes on this excerpt from *Pax*. As you read, mark words or phrases that reveal the story's point of view.

> The fox felt the car slow before the boy did, as he felt everything first. Through the pads of his paws, along his spine, in the sensitive whiskers at his wrists. By the vibrations, he learned also that the road had grown coarser. He stretched up from his boy's lap and sniffed at threads of scent leaking in through the window, which told him they were now traveling into woodlands.

The narrator is showing what the fox knows—just by using touch and smell.

Expand Your Vocabulary

Put a check mark next to the vocabulary words that you feel comfortable using when speaking or writing.

sensitive	☐
anxiety	☐
injury	☐
displease	☐

Turn to a partner and talk about the vocabulary words you already know. Then, use as many words as you can in a paragraph about caring for an animal. As you read the excerpt from *Pax*, use the definitions in the side column to learn the vocabulary words you don't already know.

Background

Sara Pennypacker (b. 1951) recalls feeling very shy as a child. She spent her time making art and reading and writing stories—activities she still enjoys as an adult. She is the author of many books, including the *Clementine* series and *Summer of the Gypsy Moths*. Honors for her books include a Golden Kite Award and a Christopher's Medal.

from **Pax**

Novel by **Sara Pennypacker**

A pet fox takes a mysterious and disturbing drive with his boy and the boy's father. Where are they headed and why?

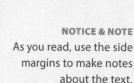

NOTICE & NOTE
As you read, use the side margins to make notes about the text.

1   The fox felt the car slow before the boy did, as he felt everything first. Through the pads of his paws, along his spine, in the **sensitive** whiskers at his wrists. By the vibrations, he learned also that the road had grown coarser. He stretched up from his boy's lap and sniffed at threads of scent leaking in through the window, which told him they were now traveling into woodlands. The sharp odors of pine—wood, bark, cones, and needles—slivered through the air like blades, but beneath that, the fox recognized softer clover and wild garlic and ferns, and also a hundred things he had never encountered before but that smelled green and urgent.

2   The boy sensed something now, too. He pulled his pet back to him and gripped his baseball glove more tightly.

3   The boy's **anxiety** surprised the fox. The few times they had traveled in the car before, the boy had been calm or even excited. The fox nudged his muzzle into the glove's webbing, although he hated the leather smell. His boy always laughed when he did this. He would close the glove around his pet's head, play-wrestling, and in this way the fox would distract him.

sensitive
(sĕn′sĭ-tĭv) *adj.* Something *sensitive* is able to perceive small differences or changes.

anxiety
(ăng-zī′ĭ-tē) *n. Anxiety* is a feeling of uneasiness, fear, or worry.

Shutterstock

Pax   **309**

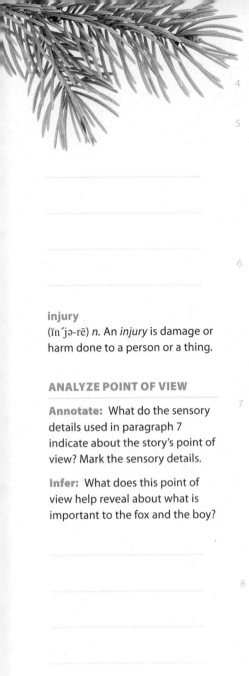

4 But today the boy lifted his pet and buried his face in the fox's white ruff, pressing hard.

5 It was then that the fox realized his boy was crying. He twisted around to study his face to be sure. Yes, crying—although without a sound, something the fox had never known him to do. The boy hadn't shed tears for a very long time, but the fox remembered: always before he had cried out, as if to demand that attention be paid to the curious occurrence of salty water streaming from his eyes.

6 The fox licked at the tears and then grew more confused. There was no scent of blood. He squirmed out of the boy's arms to inspect his human more carefully, alarmed that he could have failed to notice an **injury,** although his sense of smell was never wrong. No, no blood; not even the under-skin pooling of a bruise or the marrow leak of a cracked bone,[1] which had happened once.

7 The car pulled to the right, and the suitcase beside them shifted. By its scent, the fox knew it held the boy's clothing and the things from his room he handled most often: the photo he kept on top of his bureau and the items he hid in the bottom drawer. He pawed at a corner, hoping to pry the suitcase open enough for the boy's weak nose to smell these favored things and be comforted. But just then the car slowed again, this time to a rumbling crawl. The boy slumped forward, his head in his hands.

8 The fox's heartbeat climbed and the brushy hairs of his tail lifted. The charred[2] metal scent of the father's new clothing was burning his throat. He leaped to the window and scratched at it. Sometimes at home his boy would raise a similar glass wall if he did this. He always felt better when the glass wall was lifted.

9 Instead, the boy pulled him down onto his lap again and spoke to his father in a begging tone. The fox had learned the meaning of many human words, and he heard him use one of them now: "NO." Often the "no" word was linked to one of the two names he knew: his own and his boy's. He listened carefully, but today it was just the "NO," pleaded to the father over and over.

10 The car juddered[3] to a full stop and tilted off to the right, a cloud of dust rising beyond the window. The father reached over the seat again, and after saying something to his son in a

injury
(ĭn´jə-rē) *n.* An *injury* is damage or harm done to a person or a thing.

ANALYZE POINT OF VIEW

Annotate: What do the sensory details used in paragraph 7 indicate about the story's point of view? Mark the sensory details.

Infer: What does this point of view help reveal about what is important to the fox and the boy?

---

[1] **marrow leak of a cracked bone:** *marrow* is the thick, dark substance at the core of a bone, which is exposed when a bone is broken or cracked open.

[2] **charred** (chärd): burned or scorched.

[3] **juddered** (jŭd´ərd): shook or vibrated rapidly.

soft voice that didn't match his hard lie scent,[4] he grasped the fox by the scruff of the neck.

 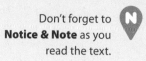

11   His boy did not resist, so the fox did not resist. He hung limp and vulnerable[5] in the man's grasp, although he was now frightened enough to nip. He would not **displease** his humans today. The father opened the car door and strode over gravel and patchy weeds to the edge of a wood. The boy got out and followed.

displease
(dĭs-plēz´) v. To *displease* someone is to cause annoyance or irritation.

12   The father set the fox down, and the fox bounded out of his reach. He locked his gaze on his two humans, surprised to notice that they were nearly the same height now. The boy had grown very tall recently.

13   The father pointed to the woods. The boy looked at his father for a long moment, his eyes streaming again. And then he dried his face with the neck of his T-shirt and nodded. He reached into his jeans pocket and withdrew an old plastic soldier, the fox's favorite toy.

14   The fox came to alert, ready for the familiar game. His boy would throw the toy, and he would track it down—a feat the boy always seemed to find remarkable. He would retrieve the toy and wait with it in his mouth until the boy found him and took it back to toss again.

ANALYZE WORD CHOICE

Annotate: Mark the words in paragraphs 14–15 that help show the fox's personality and attitude toward the boy.

Analyze: How do the author's word choices contribute to mood and voice?

15   And sure enough, the boy held the toy soldier aloft and then hurled it into the woods. The fox's relief—they were only here to play the game!—made him careless. He streaked toward the woods without looking back at his humans. If he had, he would have seen the boy wrench away from his father and cross his arms over his face, and he would have returned. Whatever his boy needed—protection, distraction, affection—he would have offered.

16   Instead, he set off after the toy. Finding it was slightly more difficult than usual, as there were so many other, fresher odors in the woods. But only slightly—after all, the scent of his boy was also on the toy. That scent he could find anywhere.

ANALYZE WORD CHOICE

Annotate: Mark the words and details that help establish mood and voice in paragraph 17.

Compare: How do mood and voice in paragraph 17 differ from mood and voice in paragraphs 14–15?

17   The toy soldier lay facedown at the burled root of a butternut tree, as if he had pitched himself there in despair. His rifle, its butt pressed tirelessly against his face, was buried to the hilt in leaf litter. The fox nudged the toy free, took it between his teeth, and rose on his haunches[6] to allow his boy to find him.

18   In the still woods, the only movements were bars of sunlight glinting like green glass through the leafy canopy.

---

[4] **lie-scent:** the smell that the fox detects of the father's insincerity.
[5] **vulnerable** (vŭl´nər-ə-bəl): open to harm.
[6] **haunches** (hôn´chəz): the hips, buttocks, and upper thighs of an animal.

© Houghton Mifflin Harcourt Publishing Company • Image Credits: ©Duohua F/Alamy; (inset) ©Spalnic/Shutterstock

He stretched higher. There was no sign of his boy. A prickle of worry shivered up the fox's spine. He dropped the toy and barked. There was no response. He barked again, and again was answered by only silence. If this was a new game, he did not like it.

19   He picked up the toy soldier and began to retrace his trail. As he loped out of the woods, a jay streaked in above him, shrieking. The fox froze, torn.

20   His boy was waiting to play the game. But birds! Hours upon hours he had watched birds from his pen, quivering at the sight of them slicing the sky as recklessly as the lightning he often saw on summer evenings. The freedom of their flights always mesmerized[7] him.

21   The jay called again, deeper in the forest now, but answered by a chorus of reply. For one more moment the fox hesitated, peering into the trees for another sight of the electric-blue wedge.

22   And then, behind him, he heard a car door slam shut, and then another. He bounded at full speed, heedless of the briars that tore at his cheeks. The car's engine roared to life, and the fox skidded to a stop at the edge of the road.

23   His boy rolled the window down and reached his arms out. And as the car sped away in a pelting spray of gravel, the father cried out the boy's name, *"Peter!"* And the boy cried out the only other name the fox knew.

24   *"Pax!"*

NOTICE & NOTE
MEMORY MOMENT

When you notice that the narrator has interrupted the forward progress of a story by bringing up something from the past, you've found a **Memory Moment** signpost.

Notice & Note: What does the fox recall in paragraphs 19–20? Mark this memory.

Analyze: Why might this memory be important?

?

ESSENTIAL QUESTION:

What can you learn from seeing the world through an animal's eyes?

Review your notes and add your thoughts to your Response Log.

TURN AND TALK

Get together with a partner and discuss the novel excerpt you just read. How does experiencing events from the fox's point of view affect your understanding?

---

[7] **mesmerized** (mĕz´mə-rīzd): held fixed in attention as though hypnotized.

Assessment Practice

Answer these questions before moving on to the **Analyze the Text** section.

1. Select **two** sentences that are supported by details in the selection.

   (A) The fox likes and trusts the boy's father.

   (B) The fox and the boy share a close bond.

   (C) The boy is confused by the fox's behavior.

   (D) The father is doing what's best for the boy.

   (E) The fox is curious about the smells and sounds of nature.

2. This question has two parts. First answer **Part A**, then **Part B**.

   Part A

   What emotion is the boy feeling during the car ride?

   (A) anxiety

   (B) boredom

   (C) annoyance

   (D) excitement

   Part B

   Select the sentence that best supports the answer to Part A.

   (A) "The fox felt the car slow before the boy did, as he felt everything first." (paragraph 1)

   (B) "The boy sensed something now, too." (paragraph 2)

   (C) "He pulled his pet back to him and gripped his baseball glove more tightly." (paragraph 2)

   (D) "His boy did not resist, so the fox did not resist." (paragraph 11)

Test-Taking Strategies

Analyze the Text

Support your responses with evidence from the text.

(1) **EVALUATE** Review paragraph 1. What details does the author use to describe key ideas about the fox?

(2) **ANALYZE** Review paragraph 3. What do the fox's memories suggest about the relationship between the boy and the fox? What conflict is revealed by this **Memory Moment?**

(3) **SUMMARIZE** Review paragraphs 7–9. What is the mood (or feeling) of this passage? Explain how the author's specific word choices affect voice and mood.

(4) **INTERPRET** Review paragraph 18, especially the last sentence of the paragraph. How do specific word choices help reveal the fox's confusion?

(5) **CITE EVIDENCE** Cite evidence from the text that indicates the narrator's point of view. What is the specific purpose or benefit of using this point of view in *Pax?*

NOTICE & NOTE

Review what you **noticed and noted** as you read the text. Your annotations can help you answer these questions.

PARAGRAPH NUMBER	EVIDENCE FOR POINT OF VIEW

PURPOSE OR BENEFIT

Choices

Here are some other ways to demonstrate your understanding of the ideas in this lesson.

Writing
↳ Write a Story

Write a fictional narrative from the point of view of an animal or an object.

- Think about what and how your character sees, hears, touches, smells, and tastes.

- Include setting, characters, plot, conflict, and theme.

- Check to make sure that you use complex sentences correctly. If the subject of a sentence is singular, make sure that the verb is singular; if the subject is plural, make sure that the verb is plural.

As you write and discuss, be sure to use the **Academic Vocabulary** words.

| benefit |
| distinct |
| environment |
| illustrate |
| respond |

Research
↳ People and Pets

What kinds of bonds connect people with their pets? Investigate a true story that illustrates a special bond between someone and a pet. If you'd like, use a story of your own or of someone you know. Record what you learn in the chart.

PERSON AND PET	DETAILS ABOUT THEIR BOND

Social & Emotional Learning
↳ Caring and Responsibility

In *Pax*, Peter makes a difficult choice about setting a wild animal free. Think about the choices pet owners make about caring for their pets. Then, work with a partner to present your ideas about the responsibilities of pet owners. Include images and text in your presentation, and use complex sentences correctly. Communicate your ideas effectively by maintaining eye contact and speaking at an appropriate rate and volume.

Expand Your Vocabulary

PRACTICE AND APPLY

Answer the questions to show your understanding of the vocabulary
words. Explain each answer.

1. Does someone experiencing **anxiety** feel happy or upset? Why?
   _____

2. Which is more likely to **displease** someone, a gift or an insult? Why?
   _____

3. If you had an **injury,** would you need a doctor or a teacher? Why?
   _____

4. Can a **sensitive** scientific instrument detect small changes? Why?
   _____

Vocabulary Strategy
↳ **Greek and Latin Roots**

A **root** is a word part that suggests a word's core meaning, so
knowing a root can help you understand a word. Roots are often
combined with prefixes or suffixes to form words.

**Interactive Vocabulary
Lesson: Understanding
Word Origins**

Many English words contain roots and other word parts from
older languages, including Greek and Latin. For example, *sensitive*
contains the Latin root *sens,* which means "to perceive or feel," so
you can guess that *sensitive* can mean "able to receive information
through the senses" or even "aware of the emotions of others."

PRACTICE AND APPLY

Find the word that contains the Latin root *sens* in each sentence.
Use context clues and the root's meaning to write the word's
definition. Use a dictionary to check your work.

1. That silly fable seems like complete nonsense.
   _____

2. Be careful not to trip the alarm's sensor when you walk in.
   _____

3. The group felt the same way about the issue, so they quickly reached consensus.

Watch Your Language!

Complex Sentences

A **complex sentence** includes an independent clause and one or more subordinate clauses. A subordinate clause is introduced by a subordinating conjunction, such as *because, if, since, until, when,* and *where,* and it often includes an answer to a question such as *How? Where? Why? For how long? To what extent?* and *Under what condition?*

As you write sentences, make sure that you follow the rules of good grammar. Here are some mistakes to look out for, along with ways to create complex sentences to correct them.

☺Ed

Interactive Grammar Lesson: Simple Sentences and Compound Sentences

- Run-on sentences and comma splices (two or more independent clauses either run together or joined by only a comma)

  Incorrect: **The fox licked at the tears and then grew more confused, there was no scent of blood.**

  Correct: **The fox licked at the tears and then grew more confused because there was no scent of blood.**

- Sentence fragments (a group of words that is only part of a sentence)

  Incorrect: **The boy slumped forward. His head in his hands.**

  Correct: **The boy slumped forward until his head fell into his hands.**

PRACTICE AND APPLY

Work independently to create your own complex sentences written from the point of view of the fox. Imagine what the fox experienced after the car drove away, and then describe it in your sentences. Share your sentences with a classmate, checking for use of complex sentences and correct grammar.

Zoo

Science Fiction by **Edward Hoch**

Engage Your Brain

Choose one or more of these activities to start connecting with the short story you are about to read.

An Animal for the Aliens

Select an animal you'd show off to aliens visiting Earth. Share your choice, and explain why you'd display this animal.

Do We Really Live in a Sci-Fi World?

In a small group, list features of our lives that people a hundred years ago—

- could hardly have imagined
- would immediately recognize

What *hasn't* changed? Share your ideas.

Star Attraction

Imagine it's hundreds of years in the future and you've been asked to select an alien animal to star in Earth's first "interplanetary zoo." Sketch your alien animal.

Infer Theme

A story's **theme** is its message about life or human nature. Stories may have more than one theme, and themes may be universal; they may apply to anyone, anywhere, at any time.

Authors sometimes state themes directly, but themes are often **implied,** developed through repeated ideas, words, and imagery. As you read "Zoo," note and cite evidence that conveys theme. To **infer** the story's multiple and universal themes, make logical guesses based on evidence and your own knowledge and experience.

EVIDENCE FROM THE STORY	INFERENCES ABOUT POSSIBLE THEMES

Analyze Point of View

Point of view refers to the vantage point from which the voice telling the story, the **narrator,** relates events.

- In the **first-person point of view,** the narrator is a character in the story and uses first-person pronouns such as *I, me*, and *we*. The reader knows only what that character knows.

- In a story told from the **third-person point of view,** the narrator is not a character in the story. A third-person narrator who reveals what all the characters think and feel is said to be **omniscient,** or all-knowing. A narrator who knows and reveals only what one character thinks and feels is **limited.**

As you read this story, note how its point of view affects your understanding of events and helps convey the story's theme.

Focus on Genre
↳ Science Fiction

- combines scientific information and the author's imagination to create unexpected possibilities

- generally includes a **theme**, a statement about human nature or the human experience

- is usually set in the future

- may have a surprise ending

- includes such forms as short stories and novels

Annotation in Action

Here are one reader's comments about evidence that might hint at a theme. As you read, mark details that reveal possible themes.

> The children were always good during the month of August, especially when it began to get near the twenty-third. It was on this day that Professor Hugo's Interplanetary Zoo settled down for its annual six-hour visit to the Chicago area.

Children are "good" for a whole month. Something must be really special about this "Interplanetary Zoo."

Expand Your Vocabulary

Put a check mark next to the vocabulary words that you feel comfortable using when speaking or writing.

interplanetary	☐
constantly	☐
microphone	☐
embrace	☐

Turn to a partner and talk about the vocabulary words you already know. Then, use as many words as you can in a paragraph about space travel. As you read the short story "Zoo," use the definitions in the side column to learn the vocabulary words you don't already know.

Background

Edward Hoch (1930–2008) is best known for his crime fiction and mysteries, having published more than 900 mystery stories. In this science fiction story, Hoch imagines a surprising, futuristic zoo. Throughout the history of zoos, most animals were exhibited in cages. However, zookeepers today have a greater understanding of animals' needs. Many modern zoo enclosures replicate animals' natural habitats, with the intent of making zoo animals healthier and more comfortable.

Zoo

Science Fiction by **Edward Hoch**

Professor Hugo's Interplanetary Zoo makes a quick stop in Chicago, but which of his "creatures" are actually on display?

NOTICE & NOTE

As you read, use the side margins to make notes about the text.

1   The children were always good during the month of August, especially when it began to get near the twenty-third. It was on this day that Professor Hugo's **Interplanetary** Zoo settled down for its annual six-hour visit to the Chicago area.

2   Before daybreak the crowds would form, long lines of children and adults both, each one clutching his or her dollar and waiting with wonderment to see what race of strange creatures the professor had brought this year.

3   In the past they had sometimes been treated to three-legged creatures from Venus, or tall, thin men from Mars, or even snakelike horrors from somewhere more distant. This year, as the great round ship settled slowly to Earth in the huge tri-city parking area just outside of Chicago, they watched with awe[1] as the sides slowly slid up to reveal the familiar barred cages. In them were some wild breed of nightmare—small, horselike animals that moved with quick, jerking motions and **constantly** chattered in a high-pitched tongue. The citizens of Earth clustered around as Professor Hugo's crew quickly collected the waiting dollars, and soon the good professor himself made an appearance, wearing his many-colored rainbow cape and top hat. "Peoples of Earth," he called into his **microphone**.

---

[1] **awe** (ô): a feeling of fear and wonder.

interplanetary

(ĭn´tər-plăn´ĭ-tĕr´ē) *adj. Interplanetary* means existing or occurring between planets.

INFER THEME

Annotate: Mark words and phrases in paragraphs 2–3 that describe the zoo animals.

Analyze: What do the descriptions reveal about how humans feel about the animals?

constantly

(kŏn´stənt-lē) *adv. Constantly* means something that is regularly occurring.

microphone

(mī´krə-fōn´) *n.* A *microphone* is an instrument that is often used to amplify the voice.

Annotate: Mark each noun and pronoun in paragraphs 4–5.

Analyze: Is the narrator a character in the story? From what point of view is this story told? Explain.

embrace

(ĕm-brās´) v. To embrace someone is to hug or hold the person close.

NOTICE & NOTE
AGAIN AND AGAIN

When you notice certain words being repeated, you've found an **Again and Again** signpost.

Notice & Note: Mark the phrase from earlier in the story that is repeated in the final paragraph.

Analyze: Why might the author bring this up again and again?

4   The crowd's noise died down and he continued. "Peoples of Earth, this year you see a real treat for your single dollar—the little-known horse-spider people of Kaan—brought to you across a million miles of space at great expense. Gather around, see them, study them, listen to them, tell your friends about them. But hurry! My ship can remain here only six hours!"

5   And the crowds slowly filed by, at once horrified and fascinated by these strange creatures that looked like horses but ran up the walls of their cages like spiders. "This is certainly worth a dollar," one man remarked, hurrying away. "I'm going home to get the wife."

6   All day long it went like that, until ten thousand people had filed by the barred cages set into the side of the spaceship. Then, as the six-hour limit ran out, Professor Hugo once more took the microphone in hand. "We must go now, but we will return next year on this date. And if you enjoyed our zoo this year, telephone your friends in other cities about it. We will land in New York tomorrow, and next week on to London, Paris, Rome, Hong Kong, and Tokyo. Then on to other worlds!"

7   He waved farewell to them, and as the ship rose from the ground, the Earth peoples agreed that this had been the very best Zoo yet. . . .

8   Some two months and three planets later, the silver ship of Professor Hugo settled at last onto the familiar jagged rocks of Kaan, and the odd horse-spider creatures filed quickly out of their cages. Professor Hugo was there to say a few parting words, and then they scurried[2] away in a hundred different directions, seeking their homes among the rocks.

9   In one house, the she-creature was happy to see the return of her mate and offspring.[3] She babbled a greeting in the strange tongue and hurried to **embrace** them. "It was a long time you were gone! Was it good?"

10   And the he-creature nodded. "The little one enjoyed it especially. We visited eight worlds and saw many things."

11   The little one ran up the wall of the cave. "On the place called Earth it was the best. The creatures there wear garments over their skins, and they walk on two legs."

12   "But isn't it dangerous?" asked the she-creature.

13   "No," her mate answered. "There are bars to protect us from them. We remain right in the ship. Next time you must come with us. It is well worth the nineteen commocs it costs."

14   And the little one nodded. "It was the very best Zoo ever. . . ."

---

[2] **scurry** (skûr´ē): to run with light steps; scamper.
[3] **offspring** (ôf´sprĭng): a child or children.

TURN AND TALK

Get together with a partner and discuss the ending of the story. How did the ending surprise you? What does it suggest?

ESSENTIAL QUESTION:

What can you learn from seeing the world through an animal's eyes?

Review your notes and add your thoughts to your Response Log.

Assessment Practice

Answer these questions before moving on to the **Analyze the Text** section.

1. How does paragraph 1 build suspense in the story?

- (A) by describing the crowd
- (B) by describing details of the story's setting
- (C) by describing the character of Professor Hugo
- (D) by describing the children's anticipation of the Interplanetary Zoo

2. This question has two parts. First answer **Part A**, then **Part B**.

Part A

What is one theme of the story?

- (A) Humans and other life forms share certain qualities.
- (B) The future will be different from the present.
- (C) Zoos are expensive and hard to maintain.
- (D) Aliens are dangerous and undesirable.

Part B

Select the sentence that best supports the answer to Part A.

- (A) "'But hurry! My ship can remain here only six hours!'" (paragraph 4)
- (B) "'I'm going home to get the wife.'" (paragraph 5)
- (C) "'Then on to other worlds!'" (paragraph 6)
- (D) "In one house, the she-creature was happy to see the return of her mate and offspring." (paragraph 9)

Test-Taking Strategies

Analyze the Text

Support your responses with evidence from the text.

NOTICE & NOTE

Review what you **noticed and noted** as you read the text. Your annotations can help you answer these questions.

(1) **COMPARE** How is Professor Hugo's Interplanetary Zoo like zoos that exist in our world? How does his zoo differ from ours? What do these similarities and differences help the author reveal?

(2) **INFER** How does the narrator describe the animals in the Interplanetary Zoo? How do the zoo animals describe humans? Based on these descriptions, what inferences can you draw about the story's theme?

HOW HUMANS DESCRIBE THE ZOO ANIMALS	HOW THE ZOO ANIMALS DESCRIBE HUMANS

(3) **EVALUATE** Review paragraphs 1–2 and 8–14. From which point of view is the story told? How do you know? Why do you think the author chose to tell the story this way?

(4) **DRAW CONCLUSIONS** Compare paragraphs 7 and 14. How does the author's use of repetition ("the very best Zoo yet"; "the very best Zoo ever") affect your understanding of the story?

(5) **ANALYZE** Notice the author's references to money **Again and Again,** both in a familiar currency (dollars) and an unfamiliar currency ("commocs"). Why do you think the author mentions money more than once?

Choices

Here are some other ways to demonstrate your understanding of the ideas in this lesson.

Writing
↳ What's the Point?

Think about science fiction you know, including novels, short stories, movies, or television shows. What common themes do those works share? Record your thoughts in a chart. Then, write a paragraph describing your conclusions.

TITLE OF WORK	THEME OR THEMES

As you write and discuss, be sure to use the **Academic Vocabulary** words.

benefit

distinct

environment

illustrate

respond

Media
↳ Get Ready to Film

Work in a small group to create a storyboard for a "Zoo" movie. First, discuss ways to convert "Zoo" into a movie. Then, using digital tools, if they're available, create—

- a **storyboard,** a visual map that illustrates significant moments in each scene of the movie

- set designs that highlight the interplanetary travels of Dr. Hugo

- sketches of costumes for different characters in the story

Social & Emotional Learning
↳ Such Different Points of View

In a small group, discuss why the humans and the "horse-spider people" never realize that they're each staring at intelligent, thoughtful, and caring beings.

- What might have prevented them from learning the truth about each other?

- Why were they unable to take each other's perspectives?

- How might beings with such diverse backgrounds come to understand each other?

When you've finished your discussion, write a brief paragraph summarizing your group's conclusions, and share your ideas with the class.

Expand Your Vocabulary

PRACTICE AND APPLY

Choose the better answer to each question.

1. Which of the following is a **constantly** heard sound?
   a. the hum of an engine   b. the ring of a doorbell

2. Which of the following are most likely to **embrace?**
   a. a dog and a cat   b. a parent and a child

3. Which of the following is an example of **interplanetary** travel?
   a. travel among planets   b. travel on a planet

4. Which of the following is an example of a **microphone?**
   a. a device used to transmit visual information   b. a device used to make the voice louder

Vocabulary Strategy

Greek Roots

A **root** is a word part that contains the core meaning of a word, so knowing a root can help you determine a word's meaning. Many English words contain roots from Greek and Latin. For example, in *microphone,* the base word *phone* is from a Greek root meaning "sound." The prefix *micro-* is from a Greek root meaning "small."

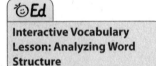
Ed

Interactive Vocabulary Lesson: Analyzing Word Structure

PRACTICE AND APPLY

Use context clues and your understanding of *micro* and *phone* to choose the word that best completes each sentence. Then, write the meaning of the word under the sentence.

symphony	cacophony	micromanaged

1. He _____ the project by questioning every tiny detail.

   _____

2. The school orchestra played a _____ by Beethoven.

   _____

3. The blaring car horns created a _____.

   _____

Watch Your Language!

Verb Tenses

A **verb** expresses an action, a condition, or a state of being. Helping verbs such as *is, could, has,* and *might* can be combined with verbs to form **verb phrases.**

The **tense** of a verb or verb phrase shows the time of the action, clarifying whether an event occurs in the present, the past, or the future.

In "Zoo," verb tenses are used in the following ways.

- to narrate past events

  In the past they had sometimes been treated to three-legged creatures from Venus. . . .

- to show that action is consistently happening in the past

  And the he-creature nodded. "The little one enjoyed it especially. We visited eight worlds and saw many things."

- to make a distinction between past-tense narration and direct quotation, or dialogue, that tells about events in the present

  "This is certainly worth a dollar," one man remarked, hurrying away. "I'm going home to get the wife."

Interactive Grammar
Lesson: Tense

GRAMMARIAN

PRACTICE AND APPLY

Write your own sentences using past and present verb tenses consistently to indicate when action takes place. Your sentences can be about animals, or you can write your own imagined scene to add to "Zoo." When you have finished, share your sentences with a partner and compare your use of verb tenses.

from
Animal Snoops:
The Wondrous World of Wildlife Spies

Informational Text by **Peter Christie**

Engage Your Brain

Choose one or more of these activities to start connecting with the informational text you are about to read.

Four Minutes and Thirty-Three Seconds

Do you notice messages in your environment as well as an animal might? For four minutes and thirty-three seconds, write down every sound you hear. What does each one tell you?

My Pet, the Spy

Have you ever suspected that a family pet has been spying on you or listening in on your conversations? Share your experience with a small group.

Mind Your Own Business!

Almost every one of us secretly listens in on conversations around us. Why? With a partner, list possible reasons.

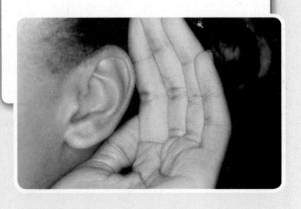

Analyze Text Structure

A text's **structure** is how its ideas are organized for readers. Ideas appear in paragraphs, often arranged under helpful headings and subheadings. Paragraphs are generally organized in distinct patterns. These may include—

- ideas and supporting details
- chronological order
- cause-effect
- compare-and-contrast
- problem-solution

The author of *Animal Snoops* uses a variety of organizational patterns and often includes **anecdotes,** short accounts of events, that both entertain readers and clarify key ideas. As you read, note the text's headings and subheadings, as well as its patterns of organization.

Analyze Central Ideas

To develop and deepen your understanding of what you read, you need to be able to analyze central ideas (sometimes called key or main ideas) and evaluate details. A **central idea** is a very important idea about a topic in the text. To analyze a central idea, note how it is developed through the use of supporting ideas and details.

SUPPORTING IDEAS	SUPPORTING DETAILS

Annotation in Action

Here is how one reader began analyzing a **central idea** in *Animal Snoops*.
As you read, note how the author presents and develops important ideas.

Deep Secrets Overheard

Tick, tick, creak.

In the eerie, deep-water gloom off the coast of Norway, an enormous sperm whale makes mysterious noises before it abruptly rakes its toothy mouth through a school of swimming squid.

Subheading says this is about being "overheard." Then, there's a sound effect.

Why would a whale make that noise? And what's overhearing it?

Expand Your Vocabulary

Put a check mark next to the vocabulary words that you feel comfortable using when speaking or writing.

eavesdrop	☐
foil	☐
predator	☐
stake	☐
intercept	☐

Turn to a partner and talk about the vocabulary words you already know. Then, use as many words as you can in a paragraph about how animals communicate. As you read the informational text from *Animal Snoops*, use the definitions in the side column to learn the vocabulary words you don't already know.

Background

Peter Christie (b. 1962) loved exploring nature in the fields and streams of his native Canada as a child. As a freelance science author and editor, he enjoys writing for young people because they are naturally curious. Young people also love a good story, and for Christie, the best science writing is about telling a story. In his explorations of animal behavior and intelligence, Christie continues to find many stories to tell.

from
Animal Snoops:
The Wondrous World of Wildlife Spies

Informational Text by **Peter Christie**

Not only do wild animals snoop on each other, but they also use what they hear and see to figure out how to behave.

NOTICE & NOTE
As you read, use the side margins to make notes about the text.

Presenting: The Bird-Brained Burglar Bust

ANALYZE TEXT STRUCTURE

Annotate: Mark the subhead.

Predict: What do you think this section will discuss? Why?

1 The house in Memphis, Tennessee, sat empty: the coast was clear for a robbery. Quickly and secretively, the three young burglars checked the windows and doors and found a way in. They piled up computers, DVD players, and other electronic equipment.

2 The thieves talked as they worked, paying no attention to the parrot, nearly motionless in its cage. Only when the crooks were ready to make their getaway did the bird finally pipe up. "JJ," it said plainly. "JJ, JJ."

3 Marshmallow—a six-year-old green parrot—had been quietly **eavesdropping.** And the private-eye parrot had learned a thing or two, including the nickname of one of the robbers: JJ.

eavesdrop
(ēvz´drŏp´) *intr.v.* To *eavesdrop* is to listen secretly to others' private conversations.

4 The burglars fled but soon realized that the parrot knew too much. "They were afraid the bird would stool[1] on them," said Billy Reilly, a local police officer. When the thieves returned to the crime scene to nab the bird, police captured them.

5 The Memphis crooks hadn't counted on Marshmallow's talents as an eavesdropper. Why would they? Few people imagine that animals can be highly skilled spies and snoops. Yet nature is filled with them.

6 More and more, scientists are discovering that creatures—from bugs to baboons—are experts at watching, listening, and prying into the lives of other animals. While Marshmallow's eavesdropping helped to **foil** human criminals, wild spies work for their own benefit. Spying can be the best or fastest way to find food or a mate, or get early warning of a **predator.**

7 Until recently, researchers preferred to think of communication between animals as similar to two people talking privately. But wildlife sounds and signals are often loud or bright enough that it is easy for others to listen in. It's like having conversations on social media that every one of your friends—and maybe some of your enemies—can read.

8 Animal messages are often detected by audiences that were not meant to get wind of[2] them. Hungry gopher snakes, for example, use foot-drumming signals between kangaroo rats to locate a snaky snack. Female chickadees listen in on singing contests of territorial males when choosing a mate.

9 Biologists call it eavesdropping. It sounds sneaky, but it works well. And some animals are doubly sneaky, changing their behavior when they expect to be overheard. The animal communication network is far more complicated than researchers used to believe.

10 The **stakes** in wild spy games are high. Eavesdropping can determine whether animals mate, find a home, or enjoy a sneaky life instead of meeting sudden death. It can reveal whom they should trust and even affect the evolution of songs and signals.

11 Naturally clever secret agents learn things from snooping that help them survive and pass their genes to the next generation. It's one more tool that crafty creatures use to understand the world around them.

---

[1] **stool:** a slang term meaning to tell on someone else, especially to spy on someone or to inform the police; to be a stool pigeon.
[2] **get wind of:** to learn of or find out about.

The Hungry Spy: Spying and Prying Predators

Don't forget to **Notice & Note** as you read the text.

12 The path home was one the eastern chipmunk had traveled a hundred times before: under the ferns to the narrow tunnel into his burrow. The small animal ran briskly through the quiet Pennsylvania forest.

13 Suddenly, a flash and a sting. The startled chipmunk jumped. Dried leaves scattered. A sharp pain seared his haunches.[3] Scrambling away, he glimpsed the motionless length of a timber rattlesnake.

14 The ambush had succeeded. The deadly serpent had lain coiled and still for many hours, waiting. Even now, after striking, the snake was in no hurry. She would track down the chipmunk's lifeless body after her venom had done its work.

ANALYZE CENTRAL IDEAS

Annotate: Mark details in paragraphs 13–16 that describe how the snake hunts its prey.

Identify Patterns: How does the snake use its senses to hunt?

15 Patience is among the most practiced skills of a rattlesnake. Snooping is another. Before choosing an ambush site, timber rattlesnakes study the habits of their prey. Using their highly sensitive, flickering tongues, the snakes use scent clues to reveal the routines of rodents and other tasty animals.

16 Their tongues are so remarkable that they also pry into the hunting habits of other rattlesnakes. Scenting the difference between a recently fed rattlesnake and a hungry one, they use the clues to hide where another snake has dined and the hunting is likely to be successful.

17 For many animals, snooping and spying can mean the difference between a full stomach and starvation. Some creatures, like the rattlesnake, spy on the habits of their prey. Others **intercept** private communication—and think of the signals as a call to supper.

intercept
(ĭn′tər-sĕpt′) *v.* To *intercept* is to stop or interrupt something.

---

[3] **haunches** (hônch′əz): the hips, buttocks, and upper thighs of an animal.

ANALYZE TEXT STRUCTURE

Annotate: Reread this section's subheading. Then, mark a key idea in paragraphs 18–19 that the subheading suggests.

Analyze: How would you describe the organizational pattern used to develop this idea?

18   *Photinus* fireflies, for instance, broadcast their mating messages with a light show. These plant-eating beetles flash luminescent[4] abdomens to wow potential mates on warm North American summer nights.

19   A bigger relative is named *Photuris*. They also blink biological tail lights during courtship, but are not always looking for a mate. These fireflies are predators that eat their smaller *Photinus* cousins. They spy on their blinking prey and follow the flashing beacon to a nighttime meal.

A flashing **Photinus** firefly looks good to his mate—but he looks delicious to his **Photuris** cousin!

ANALYZE TEXT STRUCTURE

Annotate: Mark the sound effects in paragraphs 20–22. What do these effects convey?

Evaluate: How does this anecdote use humor to help you understand the text's important ideas?

20   In the still-frigid early spring of northern Europe, a male moor frog begins his tuneless chorus: *Waug, waug, waug.*

21   Not minding that the ice has barely loosed its grip on the pond edge, the frog has emerged from wintering beneath marsh-bottom muck. He's all set to attract female moor frogs the moment they wake from chilly months of sleep.

22   *Waug, waug, waug* . . . **WHAM!**

23   With a lightning strike, the long, lance-like bill of a white stork jabs through the marsh grass and snatches up the singing frog. In an instant, the tireless music-maker becomes the dinner of a spy.

24   White storks are master eavesdroppers. They rely on the songs of moor frogs to guide them when they're hunting. The birds are so skillful that they can stealthily follow frog sounds to within two or three strides of an unsuspecting singer.

25   Some spies can intercept signals sent by plants. Bright flowers invite bees and other animals to come for a meal of pollen or nectar (and to pollinate the plants at the same time).

[4] **luminescent** (lōō′mə-nĕs′ənt): brightly lit up.

Don't forget to **Notice & Note** as you read the text.

Scientists believe that the most symmetrical flowers—where each half mirrors the other like two sides of a face—help bees and birds recognize them as healthy, with top-quality pollen and nectar.

26 But crab spiders are deadly spies: they love to eat honeybees and know all about this flower-bee communication system. These sneaky spiders build their bee-trapping webs next to good-looking, symmetrical blooms that bees are more likely to visit.

Deep Secrets Overheard

Tick, tick, creak.

27 In the eerie, deep-water gloom off the coast of Norway, an enormous sperm whale makes mysterious noises before it abruptly rakes its toothy mouth through a school of swimming squid.

28 Scientists believe the whale is using echolocation[5]—in the same way bats use echoes of their ultrasonic[6] chirps to "see" in the dark. The whale's ticks and creaks help it zero in on prey.

ANALYZE CENTRAL IDEAS

Annotate: Mark the definition of *symmetrical* in paragraph 25.

Summarize: Summarize how crab spiders use symmetrical flowers to hunt honeybees.

---

[5] **echolocation** (ĕk´ō-lō-kā´shən): a system used by some animals to locate objects around them; the animals produce high-pitched sounds and "listen" for the sounds to come back.

[6] **ultrasonic** (ŭl´trə-sŏn´ĭk): not able to be heard by humans; above the range of sound waves that humans can hear.

29 But the sounds may also help distant sperm whales to find a good meal. The whales' echolocation sounds travel far, farther than the length of Manhattan Island. Sly sperm whales may eavesdrop to learn where another whale is hunting successfully, and drop by for lunch.

Live and Let Die: Spying and Prying to Stay Alive

30 The tiny antelope jerked his head up to listen.

31 He was a Gunther's dik-dik, a miniature antelope no larger than a Labrador dog. The tall grasses of the East African savannah[7] surrounded him like a curtain: he was well hidden from leopards and hyenas, but predators were also concealed from him. Through the chattering of birds and insects, the dik-dik recognized a familiar sound: *Gwaa, gwaa, gwaa.*

32 The insistent cry had an electric effect on the dik-dik. He leaped and bolted through the grass. The fleeing animal glimpsed the source of the sound—on a nearby tree sat a white-bellied go-away bird, sentinel of the savannah. Beyond it, barely visible above the grass, were the large black ears of a hunting wild dog.

33 Go-away birds are known for their noisy alarm call; the *gwaa* is thought by some to sound like a person shouting "g'away." These social birds feed together in chattering groups. A loud, urgent *gwaa* cry is a signal to other go-away birds that an eagle, wild dog, or other predator has been spotted nearby.

34 Many of these dangerous hunters also eat dik-diks. The wary antelopes use every trick in the book to avoid becoming a meal—including eavesdropping on go-away bird communication. Unable to see far on the grassy savannah, dik-diks rely on the birds, which spot approaching predators from treetop lookouts.

35 For many animals, spying is a life-and-death business. Creatures that catch warning signals meant for others may stay one step ahead of enemies.

---

[7] **savannah** (sə-văn´ə): a flat grassland environment located in or near the tropics.

Assessment Practice

Answer these questions before moving on to the **Analyze the Text** section.

1. Why does the author include the anecdote about the frog and the stork in paragraphs 20–24?

   (A) to describe how the moor frog attracts a mate

   (B) to persuade readers to learn more about white storks

   (C) to show how eavesdropping provides an animal with prey

   (D) to persuade readers that the moor frog should be protected

2. This question has two parts. First answer **Part A**, then **Part B**.

   Part A

   What is a central idea of the text?

   (A) Parrots and storks are expert snoops.

   (B) Animal snooping can determine life or death for animals.

   (C) Creatures watch and listen only discreetly to other animals.

   (D) Animal sounds are for communicating only within the same species.

   Part B

   Select the sentence that best supports the answer to Part A.

   (A) "Few people imagine that animals can be highly skilled spies and snoops." (paragraph 5)

   (B) "White storks are master eavesdroppers." (paragraph 24)

   (C) "These social birds feed together in chattering groups." (paragraph 33)

   (D) "Creatures that catch warning signals meant for others may stay one step ahead of enemies." (paragraph 35)

   ☺Ed
   Test-Taking Strategies

Analyze the Text

Support your responses with evidence from the text.

(1) ANALYZE The author opens the text with an anecdote about a pet parrot. Explain the author's purpose for including this anecdote.

(2) SUMMARIZE Review paragraphs 6–9. Write a brief summary of important ideas from this section of the text. You can refer to the chart you used as you read.

NOTICE & NOTE

Review what you **noticed and noted** as you read the text. Your annotations can help you answer these questions.

Paragraph #	Paragraph's Important Ideas
6	
7	
8	
9	

(3) INFER The author refers to the animals in the text as spies and snoops. What does he mean by this?

(4) SYNTHESIZE What important idea does the photograph of the firefly and its caption (following paragraph 19) help you understand?

(5) ANALYZE Reread paragraph 29 and note how the author describes how far a whale's echolocation sound travels. Why does the author describe distance this way? Make a generalization about how science writing clarifies facts, such as **Numbers and Stats,** for readers who aren't scientists.

Choices

Here are some other ways to demonstrate your understanding of the ideas in this lesson.

Writing
↳ Field Research

Information about wild animals often comes from people who watch and study them in their natural habitats. Choose an animal you can watch—a pet or an animal you see often. Then, observe the animal, making notes about its behavior. When you've finished, write a brief article about the animal. What did you learn from watching it?

- Organize your article effectively, including details to support each point.

- Use transition words and phrases, such as *because*, *therefore*, and *for that reason*, to clarify your ideas, and use pronouns correctly.

As you write and discuss, be sure to use the **Academic Vocabulary** words.

benefit
distinct
environment
illustrate
respond

Speaking & Listening
↳ Just How Smart Are They?

Work with a small group to discuss the behaviors of familiar animals. What conclusions about animal intelligence can you draw? Are they really as smart as we sometimes think?

- Review ideas together and ask questions of each other.

- Listen attentively to all ideas.

- Identify points of agreement and disagreement and discuss them respectfully.

Research
↳ Learn a Little More

The author discusses many different animals in the text. Choose one that interests you, and carry out research to learn a little more about it. Use the chart below to guide you as you gather information about this animal.

Animal	
What I Want to Know	
What I Discover	

Expand Your Vocabulary

PRACTICE AND APPLY

To show your understanding of the vocabulary words, describe what is alike and different about the two words in each pair.

1. **eavesdrop** and *listen* _____

2. **stake** and *reward* _____

3. **foil** and **intercept** _____

4. **predator** and *enemy* _____

Vocabulary Strategy
↳ **Latin Roots**

A **root** is a word part that contains the core meaning of the word. For example, *cept* comes from a Latin root meaning "to take." Knowing the meaning of *cept* can help you figure out that *intercept* describes the action of taking, or stopping, someone or something on the way from one place to another.

Another way to use word roots is to identify and understand **word families,** groups of words that include the same root. Many familiar words include the root *cept,* for example.

☺ *Ed*
Interactive Vocabulary Lesson: Common Roots, Prefixes, and Suffixes

PRACTICE AND APPLY

Work with a partner or small group to create a word family for *intercept.* Complete the organizer with words that share the root *cept.*

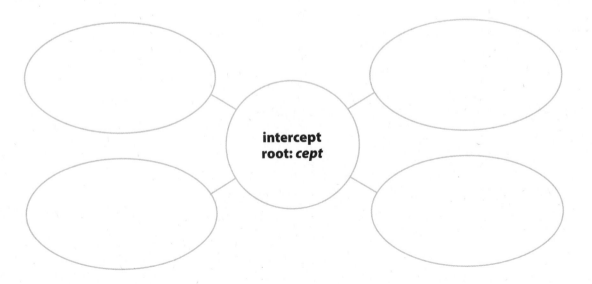

intercept
root: *cept*

© Houghton Mifflin Harcourt Publishing Company

Watch Your Language!

Pronouns

A **pronoun** is a word that is used in place of a noun or another pronoun. Personal pronouns change form, or **case,** to show how they function in sentences. The three forms are the **subjective case,** the **objective case,** and the **possessive case.**

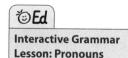

	SUBJECTIVE CASE	OBJECTIVE CASE	POSSESSIVE CASE
Singular			
First Person	I	me	my, mine
Second Person	you	you	your, yours
Third Person	she, he, it	her, him, it	her, hers, his, its
Plural			
First Person	we	us	our, ours
Second Person	you	you	your, yours
Third Person	they	them	their, theirs

Pronouns should agree with their **antecedents,** the words to which they refer, in three ways: in number, gender, and person.

The examples below include possessive pronouns that agree in number, gender, and person with their antecedents.

> <u>Go-away birds</u> are known for <u>their</u> noisy alarm call.

> The author <u>Peter Christie</u> loved exploring nature as a child in <u>his</u> native Canada.

> <u>We</u> shared <u>our</u> favorite anecdote about animal eavesdropping.

PRACTICE AND APPLY

For each sentence, choose the correct pronoun and mark its antecedent.

1. The burglars entered the house, and (he, they) stole things.

2. The thieves paid no attention to the parrot in (its, their) cage.

3. When the thieves returned, police captured (him, them).

Collaborate & Compare

ESSENTIAL QUESTION:
? *What can you learn from seeing the world through an animal's eyes?*

Compare Themes

You're about to read two poems about what wild animals might think, say, or feel, according to the poets. As you read, focus on discovering themes, or messages about life or human nature, that both poems share.

A

Animal Wisdom

Poem by Nancy Wood
pages 346–348

B

The Last Wolf

Poem by Mary TallMountain
pages 349–351

After you have read the poems, you'll get a chance to present your ideas about their themes. You'll follow these steps:

- Decide on the Most Important Details
- Create Theme Statements
- Compare and Contrast Themes
- Present to the Class

Animal Wisdom

Poem by **Nancy Wood**

The Last Wolf

Poem by **Mary TallMountain**

Engage Your Brain

Choose one or both activities to start connecting with the poems you are about to read.

I Didn't Know . . .

In one way or another, many animals, especially our animal companions, communicate with people. Can you think of a time when an animal communicated something to you? How did the animal communicate, and what did you learn? In a small group, discuss what happened.

What Would They "Say"?

List two animals that people generally don't keep as pets. Consider the characteristics of each one. Does it fly? Does it swim? Where does it live, and how does it behave? Then, think about what each animal might "say" to us, if it were able to speak. Write or sketch your response.

Analyze Personification and Imagery

Figurative language is language that has meaning beyond the literal meaning of the words. **Personification,** one type of figurative language, uses words to describe an object or animal as if it has human characteristics. Personification helps create tone and often emphasizes ideas by presenting them in new and unusual ways.

"ANIMAL WISDOM" EXAMPLE	PERSONIFICATION
Turtle crawled up on land. He said: What's missing is the ability to find contentment in a slow-paced life.	The author uses personification to express an idea about what might be missing from our lives.

Imagery consists of **sensory language,** words and phrases that appeal to readers' senses. Writers use imagery to help readers imagine how things look, sound, feel, smell, and taste.

"THE LAST WOLF" EXAMPLE	IMAGERY
and I heard his baying echoes down the steep smashed warrens of Montgomery Street and past the few ruby-crowned highrises left standing	The sensory details in these lines help the reader imagine the sounds of the wolf and view what it sees.

As you read "Animal Wisdom" and "The Last Wolf," note instances of imagery and personification. Why does the author include them? What is being communicated?

Paraphrase

Paraphrasing is restating text in your own words, which can help you **monitor comprehension** and ensure that you understand the text as you're reading. Like a summary, a paraphrase should exclude your personal opinions or judgments about the text.

ORIGINAL TEXT FROM "THE LAST WOLF"	PARAPHRASE
he laid his long gray muzzle on the spare white spread and his eyes burned yellow his small dotted eyebrows quivered	The wolf put his head on the bed and stared with intense emotion.

When you paraphrase, capture the meaning of the original text, but avoid using the text's exact wording. If you do include exact words in your paraphrase, enclose those words in quotation marks.

Annotation in Action

Here is how one reader paraphrased to better understand a stanza of "Animal Wisdom." As you read, pause often to paraphrase lines of the poem.

At first, the wild creatures were too busy
to explore their natural curiosity until
Turtle crawled up on land. He said:
What's missing is the ability
to find contentment in a slow-paced life.

A turtle talking! I wonder why.

Turtle says to slow down and be happy with a less busy life.

Background

Animals have long been a favorite focus of poets and storytellers such as **Nancy Wood** (1936–2013). She was a poet, novelist, and photographer who lived in Colorado and New Mexico, where she was inspired by Native American culture and the wilderness around her.

Mary TallMountain (1918–1994) was born in a small village in Alaska, but when her mother fell ill, she was adopted and was taken away from her life and her home. Many of TallMountain's poems and stories reflect her struggles to reconnect with nature and her lost home.

Animal Wisdom

Poem by **Nancy Wood**

What wisdom might turtles, bears, eagles, and people share about what's missing from each other's lives?

NOTICE & NOTE
As you read, use the side margins to make notes about the text.

NOTICE & NOTE
AHA MOMENT

When you notice a shift in a character's understandings, you've found an **Aha Moment** signpost.

Notice & Note: Mark what Turtle realizes.

Analyze: How might Turtle's realization change things?

At first, the wild creatures were too busy
to explore their natural curiosity until
Turtle crawled up on land. He said:
What's missing is the ability
5 to find contentment in a slow-paced life.

As the oceans receded, fish sprouted whiskers.
Certain animals grew four legs and were able
to roam from shore to shore. Bear stood
upright and looked around. He said:

10   What's missing is devotion
    to place, to give meaning to passing time.

    Mountains grew from fiery heat, while
    above them soared birds, the greatest
    of which was Eagle, to whom penetrating
15   vision was given. He said: What's missing
    is laughter so that arguments
    can be resolved without rancor.[1]

    After darkness and light settled their
    differences
20   and the creatures paired up,
    people appeared in all the corners of
    the world. They said: What's missing
    is perception.[2] They began to notice
    the beauty hidden
25   in an ordinary stone,
    the short lives of snowflakes,
    the perfection of bird wings, and
    the way a butterfly speaks
    through its fragility.[3] When they realized

30   they had something in common with animals,
    people began saying the same things.
    They defended the Earth together,
    though it was the animals who insisted
    on keeping their own names.

ANALYZE PERSONIFICATION

Annotate: Mark an example of personification in lines 6–11.

Infer: What can you infer about the bear through the poet's use of personification?

ANALYZE IMAGERY

Annotate: Mark two examples of imagery related to the natural world in lines 23–34.

Interpret: What ideas about nature does the poet convey through the use of these images?

TURN AND TALK

Get together with a partner and discuss the poem you just read. Which animal's wisdom seems most valuable to you? Why?

ESSENTIAL QUESTION:

What can you learn from seeing the world through an animal's eyes?

Review your notes and add your thoughts to your Response Log.

---

[1] **rancor** (răng´kər): long-lasting resentment or anger.
[2] **perception** (pər-sĕp´shən): the ability to understand something, usually through the senses; also insight, intuition.
[3] **fragility** (frə-jĭl´ĭ-tē): the quality of being easily broken, damaged, or destroyed; frail.

Assessment Practice

Answer these questions before moving on to the next poem.

1. Select **two** examples of personification in the poem.

   (A) "As the oceans receded, fish sprouted whiskers." (line 6)

   (B) "Certain animals grew four legs and were able / to roam from shore to shore." (lines 7–8)

   (C) "Mountains grew from fiery heat" (line 12)

   (D) "After darkness and light settled their / differences" (lines 18–19)

   (E) "the way a butterfly speaks" (line 28)

2. This question has two parts. First answer **Part A**, then **Part B**.

   Part A

   What is an important theme, or message, of the poem?

   (A) Animals have many names.

   (B) Eagles have excellent vision.

   (C) Animals understand the earth.

   (D) People know more than animals.

   Part B

   What is one way the theme, or message, is developed throughout the poem?

   (A) by personifying animals

   (B) by using rhyme and repetition

   (C) by listing animals according to their habitats

   (D) by emphasizing the differences between animals and people

   Test-Taking Strategies

B

The Last Wolf

Poem by **Mary TallMountain**

The very last wolf, after wandering the streets of a shattered city, has an important question for us all.

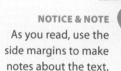

NOTICE & NOTE
As you read, use the side margins to make notes about the text.

The last wolf hurried toward me
through the ruined city
and I heard his baying echoes
down the steep smashed warrens[1]
5 of Montgomery Street and past
the few ruby-crowned highrises
left standing
their lighted elevators useless

passing the flickering red and green
10 of traffic signals
baying his way eastward
in the mystery of his wild loping gait
closer the sounds in the deadly night
through clutter and rubble of quiet blocks

PARAPHRASE

Annotate: Mark any unfamiliar words and phrases in lines 1–8. Use a dictionary to determine their meanings.

Interpret: Restate lines 1–8 in your own words. Remember to maintain the order and meaning of the original text.

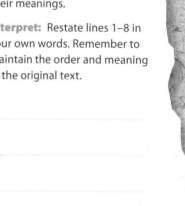

---

[1] **warrens** (wôr´ənz): overcrowded living areas.

Annotate: Mark striking examples of imagery that describe the wolf in lines 15–26.

Infer: What does this imagery suggest about how the last wolf feels?

ESSENTIAL QUESTION:

What can you learn from seeing the world through an animal's eyes?

Review your notes and add your thoughts to your Response Log.

15 I heard his voice ascending[2] the hill
and at last his low whine as he came
floor by empty floor to the room
where I sat
in my narrow bed looking west, waiting
20 I heard him snuffle[3] at the door and
I watched
he trotted across the floor
he laid his long gray muzzle
on the spare white spread
25 and his eyes burned yellow
his small dotted eyebrows quivered

Yes, I said.
I know what they have done.

TURN AND TALK

Get together with a partner and discuss the poem you just read. What do you think the wolf's message was? Why?

[2] **ascending** (ə-sĕn´dĭng): rising up.
[3] **snuffle** (snŭf´əl): sniff.

Assessment Practice

Answer these questions before moving on to the **Analyze the Texts** section.

1. Read the excerpt from the poem. Then, answer the question.

> Yes, I said. / I know what they have done. (lines 27–28)

What inference can you make about what has happened to the city in "The Last Wolf"?

- (A) It has been rebuilt.
- (B) People have ruined it.
- (C) Animals have attacked it.
- (D) An earthquake has destroyed it.

2. Which of the following is noted in the poem?

- (A) All of the city's buildings have been destroyed.
- (B) The speaker doesn't know what has happened.
- (C) The wolf threatens the speaker, as if it is hungry.
- (D) Lights continue working, as if people are still there.

3. What idea is shared by both this poem and the poem "Animal Wisdom"?

- (A) Animals find strength in groups or pairs.
- (B) Animals possess a strong awareness of their surroundings.
- (C) Animals and humans have been and always will be at odds.
- (D) Animals resent the damage humans have done to the planet.

☺**Ed**
Test-Taking Strategies

Analyze the Texts

Support your responses with evidence from the texts.

(1) **CITE EVIDENCE** Reread lines 1–17 of "Animal Wisdom."
How does the use of personification affect the way you
perceive the animals? Cite text evidence in your response.

NOTICE & NOTE

Review what you **noticed and
noted** as you read the texts.
Your annotations can help
you answer these questions.

(2) **INTERPRET** Paraphrase lines 29–34 of "Animal Wisdom."
Why do you think the animals "insisted on keeping their
own names"?

(3) **ANALYZE** Reread lines 1–8 of "The Last Wolf." What mood
or feeling does the imagery in these lines create?

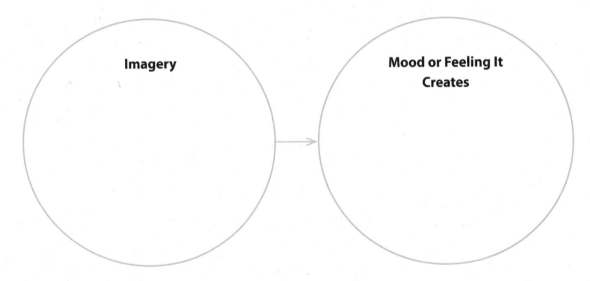

Imagery → Mood or Feeling It Creates

(4) **EVALUATE** Reread lines 9–26 of "The Last Wolf." How does
the poet's use of figurative language and details suggest
that the wolf is intelligent? Is this use effective? Cite text
evidence.

(5) **ANALYZE** State in your own words the meaning of the last
two lines of "The Last Wolf." How do these lines reflect an
Aha Moment for the poem's speaker, a realization on the
speaker's part? How might the lines affect a reader?

Choices

Here are some other ways to demonstrate your understanding of the ideas in this lesson.

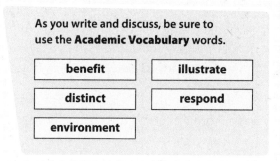

As you write and discuss, be sure to use the **Academic Vocabulary** words.

benefit	illustrate
distinct	respond
environment	

Speaking & Listening
↳ Views of Wildlife

Hold a discussion on how the animals in the poems demonstrate their intelligence and what this suggests about each poet's view of wildlife.

- Discuss how animal intelligence is presented in each poem. Cite evidence to support your ideas.

- Take notes about your ideas and other students' thoughts.

- As a group, identify points of agreement or disagreement, and then draw a conclusion on how each poet feels about wildlife.

Research
↳ Discover the Truth About Wolves

The action of Mary TallMountain's poem takes place in a "ruined city," which is not a place one would expect to find a wolf. Do some quick research to discover a few facts about wolves.

Media
↳ What Did You See? Hear? Feel?

In a small group, create illustrations to share your interpretation of key images from the poems.

- With your group, choose three images that struck you as especially memorable. Then, create an illustration for each image, using digital tools, if they're available.

- Indicate the sense to which each image appeals, and note its meaning.

- When you've finished, present your illustrations. Then, discuss how the experience of reading the poems compares with the experience of viewing the images that each group created.

QUESTIONS	ANSWERS
Where do wolves usually live?	
What do wolves eat?	
My own questions:	

Compare Themes

"Animal Wisdom" and "The Last Wolf" are poems about animals, nature, and human beings. Although the poems share similar topics, they may express different **themes,** or messages about life or human nature.

Infer each poem's theme based on significant details. With your group, complete a chart, citing evidence.

	ANIMAL WISDOM	**THE LAST WOLF**
Key Statements		
Significant Events		
Memorable Images		
Impact of Figurative Language		

Analyze the Texts

Discuss answers to these questions with your group.

1. **COMPARE** With your group, review the images and figurative language you cited in your chart. What are the impacts of the imagery and language? Explain.

2. **INFER** Both poems contain themes about how humans relate to the natural world. Compare these themes.

3. **EVALUATE** In "Animal Wisdom," the animals speak as humans do. In "The Last Wolf," the wolf communicates without speaking. Which portrayal seems more effective? Why?

4. **INTERPRET** Reflect on how, according to the poems, human beings benefit from the wisdom of animals. Cite evidence from the poems to support your ideas.

Collaborate and Present

Now your group can continue exploring the ideas in these texts by identifying and comparing their themes. Follow these steps:

1 **DECIDE ON THE MOST IMPORTANT DETAILS** With your group, review your chart to identify the most important details from each poem. Identify points you agree on, and resolve disagreements through discussion, basing your decisions on evidence from the texts.

2 **CREATE THEME STATEMENTS** State a theme for each poem, using complete sentences. Remember, it is up to you and your group to infer the themes based on details. You can use a chart like the one shown here to determine the theme each writer suggests.

DETAIL	DETAIL	DETAIL

THEME, OR MESSAGE ABOUT LIFE OR HUMAN NATURE

3 **COMPARE AND CONTRAST THEMES** With your group, discuss similarities and differences in the themes of the poems. Listen actively to the members of your group, take notes, and ask the group to clarify any points you do not understand. Identify points of agreement or disagreement before you present your ideas.

4 **PRESENT TO THE CLASS** Now it is time to present your ideas. State your conclusions about the themes of the poems. Discuss points of similarity and difference in themes. You may adapt the charts you created or use other visuals to help convey your ideas and information to the class.

Collaborate & Compare

ESSENTIAL QUESTION:
? **What can you learn from seeing the world through an animal's eyes?**

Evaluate and Compare Arguments

You're about to read two arguments about whether people should own wild animals. As you read, focus on the reasoning and evidence used by each author. Think about which points make sense to you and which do not. Then, consider the strength of the evidence presented to support each point.

MENTER TEXT

A CAUTION EXOTIC ANIMALS

Wild Animals Aren't Pets

Argument by USA TODAY
pages 360–362

MENTER TEXT

B

Let People Own Exotic Animals

Argument by Zuzana Kukol
pages 363–365

After you've read both arguments, you'll hold a debate about the topic. You'll follow these steps:

- Assign Roles
- Form Two Teams
- Research and Prepare Notes
- Hold the Debate

Get Ready

Wild Animals Aren't Pets
Argument by **USA TODAY**

Let People Own Exotic Animals
Argument by **Zuzana Kukol**

Engage Your Brain

Choose one or both activities to start connecting with the arguments you are about to read.

Wildly Different Views

The first selection you're about to read argues that people should *not* be allowed to own wild, sometimes dangerous, animals. The second selection argues that responsible people *should* be allowed to own these animals. Before you read, take a quick poll. Discuss possible pros and cons of each position, and then take a vote.

Just the Facts, Ma'am

Imagine what it'd be like to own and care for a wild animal, such as a lion, a monkey, a wolf, or a bear. First, identify a wild animal. Then, complete the following sentence frames for that animal:

- It'd be wonderful to own and care for a _____ because _____.

- It'd be terrible to own and care for a _____ because _____.

Analyze Arguments

"Wild Animals Aren't Pets" and "Let People Own Exotic Animals" present opposing arguments. A written **argument** expresses a position, or makes a **claim** about an issue or problem, and supports that position with reasoning and evidence.

TYPES OF REASONING		EXAMPLES
Deductive	uses a generally accepted idea to draw a conclusion about a specific situation	Many people are allergic to cats. Allison sneezes when she's around cats. Therefore, Allison is allergic to cats.
Inductive	uses a set of specific examples to draw a general conclusion	We studied fifteen people who sneeze around cats. Each one was allergic to cats. Therefore, many people are allergic to cats.

Focus on Genre
↳ **Argument**

- makes a claim or takes a position on an issue
- supports a claim with reasons and evidence (facts, statistics, quotations, and examples)
- presents counterarguments to address objections
- may appeal to *logos*, or logic; to *ethos*, or credibility; or to *pathos*, or emotion

Evaluate Arguments

To evaluate an argument, identify any **logical fallacies,** errors in reasoning that weaken the argument, and evaluate the strength of supporting evidence. Remember to distinguish **facts,** which can be proven or observed, from **opinions,** which are personal beliefs that may or may not be supported by facts.

COMMON TYPES OF FALLACIES		EXAMPLES
Ad Hominem	attempts to discredit an idea by attacking a person or group associated with it	Only childish people enjoy animated films.
Bandwagon Appeal	appeals to an idea's popularity, rather than to its logical support	You should vote for this proposal because everyone else likes it.
Red Herring	evades the issue by using arguments and evidence that fail to address it	Sure, I broke the vase, but you didn't like it anyway.
False Analogy	compares two subjects, ignoring critical differences between them	Rachel loved French, so she'll probably love German, too.
Non Sequitur	draws a conclusion that doesn't follow logically from the previous statement	Last year, 7.5 million teens had the flu, but only a few were hurt while texting and walking, so we shouldn't worry about safety while texting.

Annotation in Action

In the model, you can see one reader's notes evaluating reasoning in "Wild Animals Aren't Pets." As you read, analyze and evaluate how the author tries to convince readers to agree with the claim.

> Until recently, though, few people knew how easy it is to own a wild animal as a pet. Or how potentially tragic.
>
> But just as a 2007 raid on property owned by football star Michael Vick laid bare the little known and cruel world of dogfighting, a story that unfolded in a small Ohio city recently opened the public's eyes to the little known, distressing world of "exotic" pets.

What does this have to do with owning wild animals? Is this a false analogy?

Expand Your Vocabulary

Put a check mark next to the vocabulary words that you feel comfortable using when speaking or writing.

exotic	☐
dictate	☐
exempt	☐
regulate	☐

Turn to a partner and talk about the vocabulary words you already know. Then, use as many words as you can in a paragraph about wild animals. As you read the arguments "Wild Animals Aren't Pets" and "Let People Own Exotic Animals," use the definitions in the side column to learn the vocabulary words you don't already know.

Background

Although many states have laws that prohibit owning a wild animal, thousands of people in the United States keep animals such as wolves, pythons, crocodiles, and bears as pets. Some people want to make it illegal to own these kinds of animals.

In 2012, in Zanesville, Ohio, Terry Thompson set free his collection of exotic animals. Most of them had to be killed on sight to protect nearby residents. In the aftermath of this tragedy, **Zuzana Kukol** wrote "Let People Own Exotic Animals," arguing that private ownership of wild animals should still be permitted. "Tigers," Kukol has said, "are better than dogs. They don't bark."

NOTICE & NOTE
As you read, use the side margins to make notes about the text.

🙂**Ed**

Text in Focus Video

Learn more about comparing arguments.

ANALYZE ARGUMENTS

Annotate: Mark the claim in the title.

Analyze: Do you think it's effective to state the claim in this location? Why or why not?

exotic
(ĭg-zŏt´ĭk) *adj.* An *exotic* pet is rare or unusual.

dictate
(dĭk´tāt´) *v.* To *dictate* is to require or to command.

Wild Animals Aren't Pets

Argument by **USA TODAY**

Why do we let people own wild animals? This selection claims that it's a bad idea.

1   In many states, anyone with a few hundred dollars and a yen[1] for the unusual can own a python, a black bear or a big cat as a "pet." For $8,000 a baby white tiger can be yours. Sometimes, wild animals are even offered free: "Siberian tigers looking for a good home," read an ad in the *Animal Finder's Guide*.

2   Until recently, though, few people knew how easy it is to own a wild animal as a pet. Or how potentially tragic.

3   But just as a 2007 raid on property owned by football star Michael Vick laid bare the little known and cruel world of dogfighting, a story that unfolded in a small Ohio city recently opened the public's eyes to the little known, distressing world of **"exotic"** pets. We're not suggesting that people who own these animals are cruel. Many surely love them. But public safety, common sense and compassion for animals all **dictate** the same conclusion: Wild animals are not pets.

4   If that weren't already obvious, it became more so when collector Terry Thompson opened the cages on his Zanesville

---

[1] **yen** (yĕn): a strong desire or inclination.

farm, springing dozens of lions, tigers, bears and other wild creatures before killing himself. With animals running loose and darkness closing in, authorities arrived with no good choices to protect the public. They shot all but a handful of the animals as the nation watched, transfixed and horrified.

5   Owners of "exotic" animals claim they rarely maim or kill. But is the death rate really the point?

6   In 2009, a 2-year-old Florida girl was strangled by a 12-foot-long Burmese python, a family pet that had gotten out of its aquarium. That same year, a Connecticut woman was mauled and disfigured by a neighbor's pet chimp. Last year, a caretaker was mauled to death by a bear owned by a Cleveland collector. In Zanesville, it was the animals themselves, including 18 rare Bengal tigers, who became innocent victims.

7   Trade in these beautiful creatures thrives in the USA, where thousands are bred and sold through classified ads or at auctions centered in Indiana, Missouri and Tennessee. There's too little to stop it.

8   A 2003 federal law, which forbids the interstate transport of certain big cats, has stopped much of the trade on the Internet, according to the Humane Society of the U.S. But monkeys, baboons and other primates were left out, and measures to plug that hole have twice stalled in Congress.

9   Only collectors who exhibit animals need a federal license. Those, such as Thompson, who keep the animals as "pets" are left alone, unless states intervene. And many do not. Eight—Alabama, Idaho, Ohio, Nevada, North Carolina, South Carolina, West Virginia and Wisconsin—have no rules, and in 13 others the laws are lax, according to Born Free USA, which has lobbied for years for stronger laws.

10   After the Cleveland bear-mauling, then-Ohio Gov. Ted Strickland issued an emergency order to ban possession of wild animals. While it **exempted** current owners, Thompson might have been forced to give up his menagerie[2] because he had been cited for animal cruelty. We'll never know. Strickland's successor, John Kasich, let the order expire.

TURN AND TALK

Get together with a partner and discuss the argument you just read. What's your opinion?

Close Read Screencast

Listen to a modeled close read of this text.

NOTICE & NOTE
EXTREME OR ABSOLUTE LANGUAGE

When you notice language that leaves no room for doubt, you've found an **Extreme or Absolute Language** signpost.

Notice & Note: Mark language describing the actions of the authorities in paragraph 4.

Analyze: Why did the author use this language?

EVALUATE ARGUMENTS

Annotate: In paragraph 9, mark the states that do not have rules about keeping wild animals as pets.

Analyze: Does this evidence support the claim? Explain.

exempt
(ĭg-zĕmpt´): *adj.* A person who is *exempt* is excused from following a law or duty others must obey.

ESSENTIAL QUESTION:
What can you learn from seeing the world through an animal's eyes?

Review your notes and add your thoughts to your Response Log.

---

[2] **menagerie** (mə-năj´ə-rē): a collection of live wild animals, often kept for showing to the public.

Assessment Practice

Answer these questions before moving on to the next selection.

1. This question has two parts. First answer **Part A**, then **Part B**.

Part A

How does the author best support the claim that wild animals should not be kept as pets?

- (A) The author cites a law that bans possession of wild animals.
- (B) The author lists states that do not regulate keeping wild animals as pets.
- (C) The author says that most wild animals are given away for free to owners.
- (D) The author gives examples of wild animals kept as pets that hurt or killed people.

Part B

Select the sentence from the text that provides relevant support for the answer in Part A.

- (A) "For $8,000 a baby white tiger can be yours." (paragraph 1)
- (B) "That same year, a Connecticut woman was mauled and disfigured by a neighbor's pet chimp." (paragraph 6)
- (C) "Only collectors who exhibit animals need a federal license." (paragraph 9)
- (D) "Strickland's successor, John Kasich, let the order expire." (paragraph 10)

2. Which sentence from the text suggests that the author will offer a counterargument to an opposing claim?

- (A) Until recently, though, few people knew how easy it is to own a wild animal as a pet." (paragraph 2)
- (B) "We're not suggesting that people who own these animals are cruel." (paragraph 3)
- (C) "Many surely love them." (paragraph 3)
- (D) "Owners of 'exotic' animals claim they rarely maim or kill." (paragraph 5)

Test-Taking Strategies

Let People Own Exotic Animals

Argument by **Zuzana Kukol**

Should people be allowed to keep lions, tigers, bears, elephants, and other large animals in private collections? This author thinks so.

© Houghton Mifflin Harcourt Publishing Company • Image Credits: ©Lewis Whyld/PA Images/Alamy

1 The recent tragedy in Zanesville, Ohio brought back the question of whether private ownership of wild and exotic animals should be legal.

2 The simple answer is yes. Responsible private ownership of exotic animals should be legal if animal welfare is taken care of. Terry Thompson didn't represent the typical responsible owner. He had a criminal record and animal abuse charges. What Thompson did was selfish and insane; we cannot **regulate** insanity.

3 People keep exotic animals for commercial[1] reasons and as pets. Most exotic animals—such as big cats, bears or apes—are in commercial, federally inspected facilities. These animals are born in captivity, and not "stolen" from the wild. Captive breeding eliminates the pressure on wild populations, and also serves as a backup in case the animals go extinct.[2]

---

[1] **commercial** (kə-mûr´shəl): of or relating to commerce or trade.
[2] **extinct** (ĭk-stĭngkt´): no longer existing or living.

NOTICE & NOTE
As you read, use the side margins to make notes about the text.

ANALYZE ARGUMENTS

Annotate: Mark the claim.

Interpret: What reasons are used to support the claim?

regulate
(rĕg´yə-lāt´) *v.* To *regulate* is to control according to a rule, principle, or law.

⊙ *Ed*

Close Read Screencast

Listen to a modeled close read of this text.

EVALUATE ARGUMENTS

Annotate: Mark the claim and evidence provided in paragraph 4.

Evaluate: Is this argument convincing? Why or why not?

ESSENTIAL QUESTION:

What can you learn from seeing the world through an animal's eyes?

Review your notes and add your thoughts to your Response Log.

4   Dangers from exotic animals are low. On average in the United States, only 3.25 people per year are killed by captive big cats, snakes, elephants and bears. Most of these fatalities are owners, family members, friends and trainers voluntarily on the property where the animals were kept. Meanwhile, traffic accidents kill about 125 people per day.

5   If we have the freedom to choose what car to buy, where to live, or what domestic animal to have, why shouldn't we have the same freedom to choose what species of wild or exotic animal to own and to love?

6   Would the Ohio situation be any different if the animals were owned by a government and their caretaker released them? Is this really about private ownership, or is it about certain people's personal issues with exotics in captivity?

7   If society overreacts and bans exotics because of actions of a few deranged[3] individuals, then we need to ban kids, as that is the only way to totally stop child abuse, and we need to ban humans, because that is the only way to stop murder. Silly, isn't it?

TURN AND TALK

Get together with a partner and discuss the argument you just read. Did you find it convincing? Why or why not?

---

[3] **deranged** (dĭ-rānj′d): mentally unbalanced; insane.

Assessment Practice

Answer these questions before moving on to the **Analyze the Texts** section.

1. This question has two parts. First answer **Part A**, then **Part B**.

   Part A

   What is the central claim presented in "Let People Own Exotic Animals"?

   (A) Exotic animals make good pets.

   (B) Captive breeding helps save wild populations.

   (C) Ownership of exotic animals should be strictly regulated.

   (D) Responsible private ownership of exotic pets should be permitted if the animals are properly cared for.

   Part B

   Select the fact that best supports the answer in Part A.

   (A) "What Thompson did was selfish and insane; we cannot regulate insanity." (paragraph 2)

   (B) "People keep exotic animals for commercial reasons and as pets." (paragraph 3)

   (C) "On average in the United States, only 3.25 people per year are killed by captive big cats, snakes, elephants and bears." (paragraph 4)

   (D) "Meanwhile, traffic accidents kill about 125 people per day." (paragraph 4)

2. Select **two** ways that both the author of this article and the author of "Wild Animals Aren't Pets" support their claims.

   (A) They both refute opposing claims.

   (B) They both draw on personal experience.

   (C) They both use strong, emotional language.

   (D) They both claim that animals pose a health risk.

   (E) They both discuss interstate transport of big cats.

Test-Taking Strategies

Analyze the Texts

Support your responses with evidence from the texts.

NOTICE & NOTE

Review what you **noticed and noted** as you read the texts. Your annotations can help you answer these questions.

(1) COMPARE How do the two authors' purposes differ?

(2) ANALYZE Paragraphs 2–3 of "Let People Own Exotic Animals" claim that responsible ownership of exotic animals is a good thing. What form of reasoning is being used to defend this claim? How can you tell?

(3) ANALYZE Reread paragraph 4 in "Wild Animals Aren't Pets." What specific evidence does the writer use to support the argument that people should not be allowed to own exotic animals? Explain how the evidence is or is not directly related to the claim.

(4) ANALYZE Review paragraph 4 in "Let People Own Exotic Animals." What specific evidence does the writer use to support the argument that people should be allowed to own exotic animals? Explain how the evidence is or is not directly related to the claim.

(5) ANALYZE Find examples of **Extreme or Absolute Language** in "Wild Animals Aren't Pets" or "Let People Own Exotic Animals." Do these word choices strengthen or weaken the author's argument? Explain.

	Title: _____ **Examples of Extreme or Absolute Language**	
Strengths of Extreme or Absolute Language		**Weaknesses of Extreme or Absolute Language**

Choices

Here are some other ways to demonstrate your understanding of the ideas in this lesson.

Writing
↳ Take a Stand

Take a position, pro or con, about owning an exotic animal. Then, write a formal letter to a newspaper or government official, supporting your position.

- Use appropriate vocabulary and a formal tone in your letter.

- Clearly state your claim in the opening paragraph.

- In the next paragraphs, provide reasons and evidence that support your position. Be sure to include solid, fact-based supporting evidence.

- In your final paragraph, state your conclusion about owning an exotic animal.

Research
↳ Do You *Really* Want One?

Investigate an exotic animal that you are interested in. What are the pros and cons of owning the animal as a pet? Gather information from a variety of sources and record what you learn in the chart.

> As you write and discuss, be sure to use the **Academic Vocabulary** words.
>
> | | |
> |---|---|
> | benefit | illustrate |
> | distinct | respond |
> | environment | |

Social & Emotional Learning
↳ Create a PSA

Work with a small group to create a Public Service Announcement (PSA) poster, video, or blog post supporting an opinion about whether people should be allowed to own exotic animals.

- As you work, stay focused on the task, avoid personal conflicts, and make constructive choices.

- Include images and evidence to support your group's position.

When you've finished, present the PSA.

EXOTIC ANIMAL:	
PROS OF OWNING AS A PET	**CONS OF OWNING AS A PET**

Expand Your Vocabulary

PRACTICE AND APPLY

To show your understanding of the vocabulary words, choose the correct response to each question.

1. Which of the following could be described as **exotic?**

   a. a pair of sneakers

   b. a rare type of flower

2. Which of the following is something a school might **dictate?**

   a. students' hobbies

   b. the length of recess

3. What might cause someone to be **exempt** from soccer practice?

   a. a previous absence

   b. an injury

4. Which of the following might a government **regulate?**

   a. how fast people drive

   b. what people eat for dinner

Vocabulary Strategy
↳**Word Origins**

Knowing the origin and historical development of a word, also known as its **etymology,** gives you a deeper understanding of the word. When you study a word's history and origin, you can find out when, where, and how the word came to be.

> **ʊ̃Ed**
> **Interactive Vocabulary Lesson: Etymologies**

PRACTICE AND APPLY

Using print and online resources, determine each word's syllabication and pronunciation. Then, identify the word's etymology and current meaning.

WORD	SYLLABICATION / PRONUNCIATION	ETYMOLOGY / CURRENT MEANING
dictate		
exempt		
exotic		
regulate		

Watch Your Language!

The Correct Word

Many common words with similar spellings and pronunciations are easily confused. Use a dictionary to discover the meanings of the following examples.

advice / advise	
lie / lay	
passed / past	
than / then	
two / too / to	
their / there / they're	

Knowing the correct word, including its spelling, is critical for clear communication—as a writer and as a reader.

PRACTICE AND APPLY

Choose the word that correctly completes each sentence. You may use a dictionary if you'd like.

1. Gena did not (accept/except) Mindy's offer of a ride to school.

2. I will not discuss this any (farther/further) until I speak to my family.

3. A lawyer will (advice/advise) you of your rights.

4. The old bridge did not look like it could (bare/bear) the weight of the truck.

5. Russell slammed his foot on the (brake/break) to avoid hitting the ducks crossing the road in front of him.

6. The judge's ruling today will have a significant (affect/effect) on similar cases waiting to be heard.

7. Malia (passed/past) the library on her way to the store.

8. We would rather see a movie (than/then) go to the park.

Evaluate and Compare Arguments

To **evaluate** and **compare** arguments on the same issue, analyze the arguments, comparing their strengths. **Trace and evaluate** each argument: identify its claim, follow its reasoning, and determine the strength of its evidence. Then, decide which argument is more convincing.

As a group, identify key points and evidence from both texts.

- Examine supporting evidence—facts, reasons, examples, and statistics. Does the evidence logically support the claim?

- Look for persuasive language. Are the writers appealing to a reader's emotions (*pathos*), to logic (*logos*), or to both?

	WILD ANIMALS AREN'T PETS	LET PEOPLE OWN EXOTIC ANIMALS
Claim		
Evidence and Support		
Persuasive Language		
Why/Why Not Convincing?		

Analyze the Texts

Discuss these questions in your group.

1. **COMPARE** Summarize each author's claim and supporting evidence. Does each author include enough evidence?

2. **EVALUATE** Identify examples of opinions in each text. Do these opinions strengthen or weaken the argument?

3. **CRITIQUE** Which argument seems more convincing? Why?

Research and Debate

Plan a **debate** about whether people should be permitted to sell exotic animals to private owners. Follow these steps.

1. **ASSIGN ROLES** Select one person to be the **moderator,** who presents the debate's topic and goals, keeps track of time, and introduces and thanks participants. Choose another person to be the **note taker,** who keeps track of points made during the debate.

2. **FORM TWO TEAMS** One team will argue the affirmative side of the issue (pro), and the other team will argue the negative side (con). Within your team, assign speaking roles to each member.

3. **RESEARCH AND PREPARE NOTES** Search the texts you've read as well as print and online sources for valid reasons and evidence to support your claim. Integrate the information from other sources with your own support. Remember to anticipate opposing claims and gather evidence to counter those claims.

4. **HOLD THE DEBATE** The moderator states the topic, introduces the participants, and announces whose turn it is to speak.

SPEAKER	TASK	TIME
Affirmative Speaker 1	Present the claim and evidence for the affirmative (pro) side.	5 minutes
Negative Speaker 1	Ask questions prompting the other team to address flaws in its argument.	3 minutes
Affirmative Speaker 2	Respond to questions and counter the concerns of the opposition.	3 minutes
Negative Speaker 2	Present the claim and evidence for the negative (con) side.	5 minutes
Affirmative Speaker 3	Ask questions prompting the other team to address flaws in its argument.	3 minutes
Negative Speaker 3	Respond to questions and counter the concerns of the opposition.	3 minutes
Affirmative Speaker 4	Summarize the claim and evidence for the affirmative side, explaining why the reasoning is more valid than the opposition's.	3 minutes
Negative Speaker 4	Summarize the claim and evidence for the negative side, explaining why the reasoning is more valid than the opposition's.	3 minutes

Reader's Choice

Continue your exploration of the Essential Question by doing some independent reading on what we might learn from the animals around us. Read the titles and descriptions shown. Then mark the texts that interest you.

? **ESSENTIAL QUESTION:**
What can you learn from seeing the world through an animal's eyes?

Short Reads Available on Ed

These texts are available in your ebook. Choose one to read and rate. Then defend your rating to the class.

The Caterpillar
Poem by **Robert Graves**

A poet sees the world through the eyes of a caterpillar.

Rate It

The Pod
Short Story by **Maureen Crane Wartski**

A teenager recovering from a serious accident discovers empathy for a stranded animal.

Rate It

The Flying Cat
Poem by **Naomi Shihab Nye**

What happens when a pet owner prepares to take her cat on a plane?

Rate It

Tribute to the Dog
Speech by **George Graham Vest**

A famous speech wins a case for a sheep farmer whose dog was shot and killed.

Rate It

Views on Zoos
Arguments

What's your position on whether zoos should exist?

Rate It

Long Reads

Here are three recommended books that connect to this unit topic. For additional options, ask your teacher, school librarian, or peers. Which titles spark your interest?

Julie of the Wolves

Novel by **Jean Craighead George**

Miyax has run away from a dangerous situation at home. Desperate to survive the wild Alaskan tundra, she seeks the help of a wolf pack.

Primates: The Fearless Science of Jane Goodall, Dian Fossey, and Biruté Galdikas

Graphic Nonfiction by **Jim Ottaviani and Maris Wicks**

Three ground-breaking female scientists make remarkable contributions to the study of primates.

Pax

Novel by **Sara Pennypacker**

Peter's best friend is his pet fox, Pax, but he's forced to release him back into the wild when his father leaves to work for the Army. Lonely, worried, and threatened by war, Peter strikes out to find his old friend.

Extension

↳ Connect & Create

SELL IT Work with a partner to create a media campaign to "sell" your favorite Reader's Choice text to your classmates. First, discuss how to interest someone. Then, plan and craft your campaign. What will it include? Posters? Social media posts? Critical reviews? Include artwork, images, and text in your campaign.

INTERACTIVE WEB PAGE Identify a short, but critical, section of one of the texts. Then, create content that might be used in an interactive web page exploring and explaining that section.

- Introduce the section you've selected by explaining its importance, and describe how it fits into the rest of the text.

- Point out any uses of figurative language or allusions to other texts, and clarify their meanings and significance.

- Include a running commentary of your opinions, questions, and views, if you'd like.

NOTICE & NOTE

- Pick one of the texts and annotate the Notice & Note signposts you find.

- Then, use the **Notice & Note Writing Frames** to help you write about the significance of the signposts.

- Compare your findings with those of other students who read the same text.

 Ed

Notice & Note Writing Frames

Write an Argument

Writing Prompt

You have been asked to write an editorial for your school newspaper. Using ideas, information, and examples from multiple texts in this unit, write an argumentative essay, supported by research, in which you support or oppose allowing people to keep wild animals as pets.

Manage your time carefully so that you can

- review the texts in the unit;
- plan your essay and gather evidence;
- write your essay; and
- revise and edit your essay.

Be sure to

- clearly state the claim of your argument;
- address alternate or opposing claims;
- use and cite evidence from multiple sources; and
- avoid relying too much on one source.

Review the Mentor Texts

For two examples of arguments you can use as mentor texts and as sources for your essay, review:

- **"Wild Animals Aren't Pets"** (pages 360–362)
- **"Let People Own Exotic Animals"** (pages 363–365)

Review your notes and annotations about these texts carefully. Think about the techniques the authors use to make their arguments convincing.

Consider Your Sources

Review the list of texts in the unit and choose at least three that you may want to use as inspiration or support for your argument.

As you review potential sources, consult the notes you made on your **Response Log** and make additional notes about ideas that might be useful as you write. Include titles and page numbers to help you provide accurate text evidence and citations from these texts.

UNIT 4 SOURCES

- [ ] *from* **Pax**
- [ ] **Zoo**
- [ ] **Animal Snoops: The Wondrous World of Wildlife Spies**
- [ ] **Animal Wisdom**
- [ ] **The Last Wolf**
- [ ] **Wild Animals Aren't Pets**
- [ ] **Let People Own Exotic Animals**

Analyze the Prompt

Review the prompt to make sure you understand what you are required to do.

Mark the part of the sentence in the prompt that identifies the topic of your argument. Rephrase the topic in your own words.

Look for words that indicate your essay's topic, purpose, and audience. Then, write a sentence describing each.

What is my topic?

What is my purpose?

Who is my audience?

Consider Your Audience

Consider the following:

- Who will read my essay?
- What do my readers already know about the topic?
- What reasons might they have to disagree with my position?

Review the Rubric

Your argument will be scored using a rubric. As you write, focus on the characteristics as described in the chart. You will learn more about these characteristics as you work through the lesson.

PURPOSE, FOCUS, AND ORGANIZATION	EVIDENCE AND ELABORATION	CONVENTIONS OF STANDARD ENGLISH
The response includes: - A strongly maintained claim - Effective responses to alternate or opposing claims - A variety of transitions to connect ideas - A logical progression of ideas - Appropriate style and tone	The response includes: - Integrated, thorough, and relevant evidence - Precise, accurate references to sources, and citations according to an accepted style - Effective use of a variety of elaborative techniques - Clear and effective expression of ideas - Academic and domain-specific vocabulary - Varied sentence structure	The response may include the following: - Some minor errors in usage but no patterns of errors - Correct punctuation, capitalization, sentence formation, and spelling - Command of basic conventions

1 PLAN YOUR ARGUMENT

Develop a Claim

In an argument, the **claim** is the writer's position on an issue. A **strong claim**

- is stated clearly
- uses direct, specific language
- focuses on one idea

In the chart, identify your position. Do you think people should be allowed to keep wild animals as pets? Then, draft your claim.

Help with Planning
Consult **Interactive Writing Lesson: Writing Arguments**

SHOULD PEOPLE BE ALLOWED TO KEEP WILD ANIMALS AS PETS?	CLAIM
👍 👎	

Identify Support

A strong argument must have solid support for your claim. Support consists of reasons and evidence.

- **Reasons** explain *why* you have taken your position.

- **Evidence,** such as facts, statistics, examples, or expert opinions, back up your reasons. Evidence can come from primary and/or secondary sources.

Use the chart to outline the support for your claim. Be sure to record the title, author, and page numbers for each source.

Consider Your Sources

Gather solid evidence from credible sources.

- What are an author's or expert's qualifications?

- How current is the source? Recently published sources are usually more reliable.

- Is a website reliable? Look for websites with URLs ending in *.edu*, *.org*, and *.gov*.

CLAIM:		
Reason:	Evidence:	Source:
Reason:	Evidence:	Source:
Reason:	Evidence:	Source:

Address Opposing Claims

A good argument addresses an opposing idea by making a **counterclaim:** the writer explains why his or her claim, reasoning, and evidence is stronger. This is called **refuting** an opposing claim. Review your notes to find and list a possible opposing claim. Then, write your counterclaim to refute it.

Opposing Claim:

_____

Why My Claim Is Stronger:

_____

Organize Ideas

Organize your material in a way that will help you draft your argument. Remember that a well-written argument has **coherence:** it relies on a logical progression of ideas. Paragraph breaks and transitional words and phrases help readers understand how ideas are related.

Cite Sources

As you present reasons and evidence, list and cite your sources.

- Avoid **plagiarism**, the unauthorized use of someone else's words and ideas.

- Cite every source from which you have taken information.

- Use the citation style your teacher prefers.

- If you use someone's exact words, enclose them in quotation marks.

- If you **paraphrase**, or put someone's ideas into your own words, represent those ideas accurately, and provide a citation.

INTRODUCTION	• State your claim clearly in the first paragraph. • Grab readers' attention with an interesting question, quotation, or fact.
BODY PARAGRAPHS	• Present reasons and evidence to support your claim, devoting a paragraph to each main idea. • Include a paragraph in which you refute an opposing claim. • Use transitional words and phrases such as "To begin with . . ." and "Another good reason . . ." to link ideas.
CONCLUSION	• Restate your claim and its significance. • Close with an insight that gives readers something to think about.

2 DEVELOP A DRAFT

Now it is time to draft your essay. You can develop your writing skills by seeing how the experts do it. Read about the techniques professional writers use to craft their arguments.

Drafting Online
Check your assignment list for a writing task from your teacher.

Provide Support with Relevant Facts

EXAMINE THE MENTOR TEXT

Notice how the author of **"Let People Own Exotic Animals"** (pages 363–365) provides relevant facts to support her argument.

Let People Own Exotic Animals
Argument by Zuzana Kukol

The author supports a **reason** (in the first sentence) with a **fact.**

The author **elaborates** with a comparison that includes a fact about traffic accidents.

Dangers from exotic animals are low. On average in the United States, only 3.25 people per year are killed by captive big cats, snakes, elephants and bears. Most of these fatalities are owners, family members, friends and trainers voluntarily on the property where the animals were kept. Meanwhile, traffic accidents kill about 125 people per day.

APPLY TO YOUR DRAFT

Use this organizer to practice providing relevant facts and citing sources. Then, apply this technique to all of the evidence you will provide in your argument.

Try These Suggestions

Vary the ways you introduce and integrate sources into your writing. Try these out:

- In [Title of Text], the author states . . .
- Based on the author's findings, . . .
- The study proves/statistics prove . . .

Introduce State one reason that supports your overall claim.	
Cite List a piece of evidence to support your reason, noting its source. Include the title, author's name, and location.	
Elaborate Explain how this evidence supports the reason you listed.	

Address an Opposing Claim

EXAMINE THE MENTOR TEXT

In **"Wild Animals Aren't Pets"** (pages 360–362), the *USA TODAY* authors address an **opposing claim,** or a claim that expresses disagreement with their position.

Wild Animals
Aren't Pets
Argument by USA TODAY

The authors acknowledge a viewpoint that **opposes** their own position.

> Owners of "exotic" animals claim that they rarely maim or kill. But is the death rate really the point?
>
> In Zanesville, it was the animals themselves, including 18 rare Bengal tigers, who became innocent victims.

The authors respond with a **counterclaim** that strengthens their own argument.

APPLY TO YOUR DRAFT

As you write, be sure to refute at least one opposing claim. Use the chart to guide you as you respond to and refute this claim.

INTRODUCE

- Some people say . . .
- Opponents will claim . . .
- Granted, it's true that . . .

RESPOND AND REFUTE!

- But . . .
- . . . many experts insist . . .
- . . . there is growing evidence to support . . .

3 REVISE YOUR ARGUMENT

Experienced writers know the importance of revision. Review your argument and consider how it can be improved. Use the guide to help you revise your argument.

Help with Revision

Find a **Peer Review Guide** and **Student Models** online.

REVISION GUIDE		
ASK YOURSELF	**PROVE IT**	**REVISE IT**
Claim Is my claim clearly stated?	**Underline** your claim.	**Add** or **revise** your claim to clarify or strengthen it.
Organization Is the argument organized logically and clearly?	**Number** the paragraphs in order of importance. **Circle** transitions that connect ideas.	**Rearrange** paragraphs in order of importance. **Add** transitions to connect ideas.
Support Does the argument include strong reasons and evidence?	**Put a star** (★) next to each reason. **Highlight** evidence.	**Add** reasons and evidence, such as facts, examples, or statistics.
Sources Is each source properly cited so that I avoid plagiarism?	**Put a check mark** (✔) next to references to your sources.	**Add** missing sources and precise references to each source.
Plagiarism Does the essay avoid plagiarism?	**Highlight** any information from sources.	**Paraphrase** ideas or **enclose** direct quotations in quotation marks. **Add** references to sources.
Opposing Claims Have I refuted opposing claims?	**Underline** opposing claims. **Highlight** your counterclaims.	**Add** opposing claims and counterclaims to refute them.
Style Is the language formal?	**Cross out** (✗) any informal words and phrases.	**Replace** informal text or slang with formal words and phrases.
Conclusion Does the conclusion logically flow from my reasoning?	**Highlight** parts of the conclusion that support your claim.	**Add** or **revise** the conclusion so that it flows from the reasoning.

APPLY TO YOUR DRAFT

Consider the following as you look for opportunities to improve your writing.

- Check that your reasons and evidence relate to your claim.

- Ensure that you have cited sources accurately.

- Correct any unclear or informal language.

Peer Review in Action

Once you have finished revising your argument, you will exchange papers with a partner in a **peer review.** During a peer review, you will give suggestions to improve your partner's draft.

Read the introduction from a student's draft and examine the comments made by her peer reviewer.

First Draft

Keep Wild Animals Wild

By Felicia Campos, Riverside Middle School

People should not keep wild animals. They should live outside and away from people. Wild animals might adjust to captivity, but there's always a chance that someone will get hurt. And does a wild animal have fun living in a cage? No way. I think it would be boring.

This doesn't grab readers' attention at all. Perhaps start with a question.

Can you state stronger reasons using more formal language?

Now read the revised introduction. Notice how the writer has improved her draft based on her peer reviewer's comments.

Revision

Awesome! A catchy way to start your argument.

Keep Wild Animals Wild

By Felicia Campos, Riverside Middle School

Should a fox live in a backyard? Does a python belong in a cage in a garage? Domesticated animals can make wonderful pets, but wild animals belong in nature—where they have been living for thousands of years. Humans cannot provide wild animals with the habitats they have in nature. It's cruel to keep wild animals confined to cages inside homes or in outdoor enclosures.

Nice! Your claim is clear, formal— but not dull.

APPLY TO YOUR DRAFT

During your peer review, give each other specific suggestions for how you could make your arguments more effective. Use your revision guide to help.

When receiving feedback from your partner, listen attentively and ask questions to make sure you fully understand the revision suggestions.

4 EDIT YOUR ARGUMENT

Edit your final draft to check for proper use of standard English conventions and to correct any misspellings or grammatical errors.

 Ed
Interactive Grammar Lesson: Conjunctions and Interjections

Watch Your Language!

USE TRANSITIONS

As you know, **transitions** connect ideas and show how they are related. Transitions create coherence in writing, and coherence is vital to a strong argument.

Read the following sentences from "Wild Animals Aren't Pets."

> Owners of "exotic" animals claim they rarely maim or kill. But is the death rate really the point?

The conjunction *But* signals a transition from an opposing claim (animals rarely kill) to the writer's contrasting response (whether or not they kill isn't the real problem with owning exotic animals).

Transitions to Try

Here are some common transitional words and phrases:

- **Comparison/contrast:** *but, however, although, similarly, likewise*
- **Elaboration:** *also, in addition, too, furthermore*
- **Cause/effect:** *so, as a result, therefore*

APPLY TO YOUR DRAFT

Now apply what you've learned about transitions to your own work.

1. Read your paper aloud and underline transitions you've used.

2. Add transitional words, phrases, or clauses that will help connect ideas.

3. With a peer, review transitions in each other's work.

5 PUBLISH YOUR ARGUMENT

Share It!

The prompt asks you to provide your argument in the format of an editorial for your school newspaper. You may also use your argument as inspiration for other projects.

Ways to Share

- Imagine that you've been asked to **write a blog post** to share your opinion on an animal shelter's website.

- **Write a letter** to an organization that works with wild animals. Voice your support or your opposition to the organization's work.

- **Create a video presentation** based on your argument. See the next task for tips on how.

Present an Argument

These days, many people share their opinions in videos. Anyone with a smartphone can shoot a video. With a partner, plan, shoot, and present an editorial video in which you argue your side of the issue: Should people keep wild animals as pets?

Adapt Your Argument for Presentation

Use the chart below to guide you as you create a script for an editorial video based on your argument.

Use a Variety of Media

Your video can present information visually in a number of ways.

- photos
- video clips
- interviews with experts
- charts, tables, or graphs

ON PAPER: YOUR ESSAY	ON CAMERA: YOUR VIDEO
Introduction You worked to write a catchy introduction. How will your video grab viewers' attention in the first 30 seconds?	**Intro**
Readers Are the viewers the same people who read the essay? If so, how will you keep their interest? If not, how do you need to change your message?	**Viewers**
Structure and Language Will your script use the same logic as your essay? Will your tone be formal or more conversational?	**Structure and Tone**
Title Your essay has a title. How will you display it onscreen?	**Graphics**
Evidence Your essay contains facts, data, and other evidence. How will you present this information in a memorable way on video?	**Images and Data**
Conclusion The outro is the end of a video. How will you adapt your conclusion to leave viewers thinking?	**Outro**

Practice with a Partner

Presenting on video is like a performance. Be sure to rehearse, or practice, your presentation. Before you shoot the video, take turns reading drafts of your script aloud with your partner.

Use this checklist to polish your presentation skills. Then, as you rehearse, give specific, helpful feedback on presentation style and the clarity of the argument. Check off each item after you and your partner have considered it.

Active Listening

Effective listeners listen actively. Active listeners—

- give a presenter their full attention
- think critically to break down the claims, reasons, and evidence
- provide specific feedback to strengthen arguments
- paraphrase the presenter's ideas during feedback
- ask questions to clarify any confusing parts

	CHECKLIST FOR EFFECTIVE PRESENTATION TECHNIQUES
✔	Speak loudly and pronounce words clearly.
✔	Vary your pace, vocal pitch, and tone.
✔	Look directly at the camera frequently.
✔	Refer to onscreen text, images, and data.
✔	Use authentic gestures and facial expressions.
✔	Stay calm, relaxed, and confident.

Record Your Presentation

Use the video app on a smartphone, tablet, or computer to record your video. Work with your teacher to arrange for equipment and a time and place to shoot your video.

Use these tips to help with filming.

- Stand or sit in front of a plain background.
- Don't fidget with your script, whether it's print or electronic.
- Make sure your face is well lit.
- Use video editing software to add graphics, audio, and effects.

Share It!

- Have a viewing party and then **hold a debate** about the issue.
- Imagine that your presentation is a documentary on TV. **Create a 30-second ad** to promote your documentary.
- Visit the website of an animal rights organization. **Discuss** with classmates the similarities and differences between the organization's views and your own.

Interactive Speaking & Listening Lesson: Giving a Presentation

Reflect & Extend

Here are some other ways to show your understanding of the ideas in Unit 4.

Reflect on the Essential Question

What can you learn from seeing the world through an animal's eyes?

Has your answer to the question changed after reading the texts in the unit? Discuss your ideas.

You can use these sentence starters to help you reflect on your learning.

- **I think differently because . . .**
- **I want to learn more about . . .**
- **I still don't understand . . .**

Writing
Write a Literary Essay

You've been exploring what we can learn by seeing the world through an animal's eyes. Now it's time to write an essay about what animals might learn by seeing the world through *our* eyes. Write an essay explaining your thoughts about how human beings view the world. Use the chart to develop your ideas.

ASK YOURSELF	NOTES
How does our view of the world differ from that of the animals around us?	
What about us seems most exciting to you? What seems most confusing?	
Which of the ideas you've listed interests you the most? Why?	
What would help your audience best understand us? Why?	

Project-Based Learning
Create a Song

You've read about animals and what we might learn from them. Now, create lyrics for a song that portrays an animal's personality and its view of the world.

Here are some questions to ask yourself as you get started.

- Which animal would I like to write lyrics about?
- What sensory words and images can I use to describe this animal?
- If my animal could talk, what might it most want to say?

Ed

Media Projects

To find help with this task online, access **Create a Song.**

😊 Ed

Get hooked by the unit topic.

Stream to Start Video

ESSENTIAL QUESTION:

What does it take to be a survivor?

Surviving the Unthinkable

"Through every kind of disaster and setback and catastrophe. We are survivors."
—Robert Fulghum

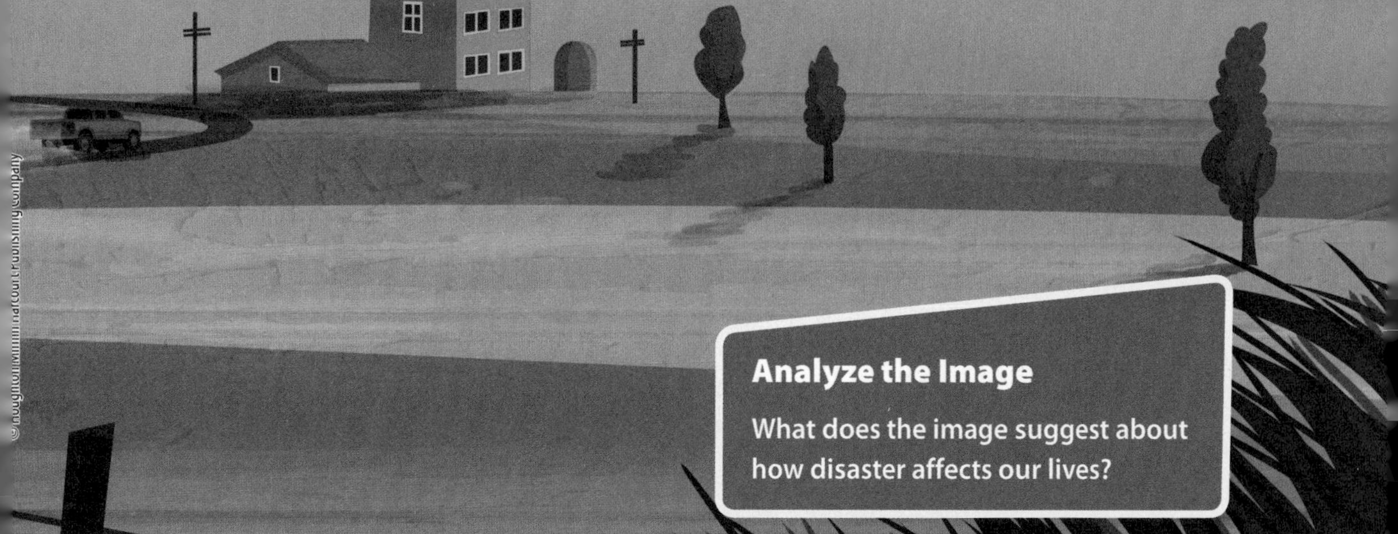

Analyze the Image

What does the image suggest about how disaster affects our lives?

Spark Your Learning

Here's a chance to spark your learning about ideas in **Unit 5: Surviving the Unthinkable.**

As you read, you can use the **Response Log** (page R5) to track your thinking about the Essential Question.

?

Make the Connection

Believe it or not, everyone has survived something. It may have been a tough day at school. It may have been moving to an unfamiliar city. Think about a moment that you or someone you know showed what it is to be a survivor. Explain what happened.

_____

_____

_____

_____

Think About the Essential Question

What does it take to be a survivor?
All around the world, people withstand disasters, from droughts and flooding to wars and shipwrecks. Something helps them get by. What qualities help people survive, no matter how difficult conditions become? List your ideas.

_____

_____

_____

_____

✓

Prove It!
Turn to a partner and use one of the words in a sentence about survival.

Sound Like an Expert

You can use these Academic Vocabulary words to write and talk about the topics and themes in the unit. Which of these words do you already feel comfortable using when speaking or writing?

	I can use it!	I understand it.	I'll look it up.
circumstance	☐	☐	☐
constraint	☐	☐	☐
impact	☐	☐	☐
injure	☐	☐	☐
significant	☐	☐	☐

Preview the Texts

Look over the images, titles, and descriptions of the texts in the unit. Mark the title of the text that interests you most.

from A Long Walk to Water

Novel by **Linda Sue Park**

It's just another day for Salva Dut, but war suddenly arrives. Armed soldiers begin leading his entire village away. Where are they being taken? What will happen?

Salva's Story

Documentary by **POVRoseMedia**

Find out more about Salva Dut's life, including his move to the United States and his efforts to help provide clean water to Sudan.

Into the Lifeboat
from Titanic Survivor

Memoir by **Violet Jessop**

Follow Violet Jessop as she makes her way to a lifeboat in those desperate minutes before the Titanic goes down.

from After the Hurricane

Poem by **Rita Williams-Garcia**

Parts of New Orleans are suddenly underwater, and people are left without food, power, or shelter. What will the poem's speaker—and other members of the high school band—do to get by?

from Ninth Ward

Novel by **Jewell Parker Rhodes**

After the hurricane passes, Lanesha and her friend TaShon are trapped on a roof. They're hot, thirsty, and staring out at the floodwaters where their neighborhood once stood.

I Wonder . . .

Sometimes survival is a matter of having the right attitude about facing a challenge or threat. What do you think that attitude would be? Write or sketch your answer.

from

A Long Walk to Water

Novel by **Linda Sue Park**

Engage Your Brain

Choose one or more of these activities to start connecting with the story you're about to read.

A Long Walk

Imagine that you were going to take a long walk, a journey to somewhere out there in the world. Where would you go? Write or sketch your response.

Saying Goodbye

Think about someone with whom you'd never want to lose contact— someone you'd never want to leave behind. If you were forced to part ways, knowing that you'd never see each other again, what would you say to this person? Write a text message to share your thoughts about leaving.

Leaving Home

How would you feel if you had to leave your home, family, and community without any warning? What might you miss the most? Discuss your thoughts with a partner.

Analyze Setting and Character

A **character** is a person, animal, or imaginary creature that takes part in a story's plot. Characters, like real people, have personalities and motivations for their actions.

A story's **setting,** or the time and place in which the action occurs, influences the development of the characters. Elements of setting include geographic location, historical period, season, time of day, and culture.

Analyze Structure

To analyze the structure of a story, pay close attention to how the author combines different literary elements—plot, conflict, setting—to form the story. Also note the story's **point of view,** the perspective of its narrator, and think about the order of events in the plot. Most stories are structured using chronological—or time—order; some stories include **flashbacks,** descriptions of prior events, or **foreshadowing,** hints about events to come.

As you read, use the following strategies to check your understanding.

STRATEGY	BENEFIT
Question	Develop and ask questions as you read to clarify your understanding of various story elements.
Connect	Use background knowledge, including any information in footnotes or in a selection's introduction, to help you understand the text.
Reread	Reread passages you don't understand—slowly or out loud—to aid comprehension.
Annotate	Mark specific words that will help you understand important aspects of the story.

Focus on Genre
↳ **Historical Fiction**

- has the basic features of fiction, including plot, characters, conflict, setting, and theme

- is set in the past and includes real places and real events of historical importance

- may be based on actual people who lived during the work's historical and cultural setting and who dealt with the setting's challenges in remarkable ways

Annotation in Action

Here is how one reader noted details of the setting in *A Long Walk to Water*. As you read, pay attention to how aspects of the story's setting affect its characters.

> *BOOM!*
>
> Salva turned and looked. Behind him, a huge black cloud of smoke rose. Flames darted out of its base. Overhead, a jet plane veered away like a sleek evil bird.
>
> In the smoke and dust, he couldn't see the school building anymore.

Images suggest that there's been an explosion.

Maybe a wartime bombing?

Expand Your Vocabulary

Put a check mark next to the vocabulary words that you feel comfortable using when speaking or writing.

veer	☐
hesitate	☐
collapse	☐
scurry	☐
shoulder	☐

Turn to a partner and talk about the vocabulary words you already know. Then, use as many words as you can in a paragraph about taking a long trip. As you read *A Long Walk to Water,* use the definitions in the side column to learn the vocabulary words you don't already know.

Background

Linda Sue Park (b. 1960) has written several books for young people. *A Long Walk to Water* is historical fiction based on the story of Salva Dut, who fled his home in Sudan in 1985 during a civil war. He, like many boys, was separated from his family. Eventually, he found refuge in the United States and later returned to what is now the country of South Sudan. To aid the people of his homeland, he formed an organization that drills wells to provide them with clean water.

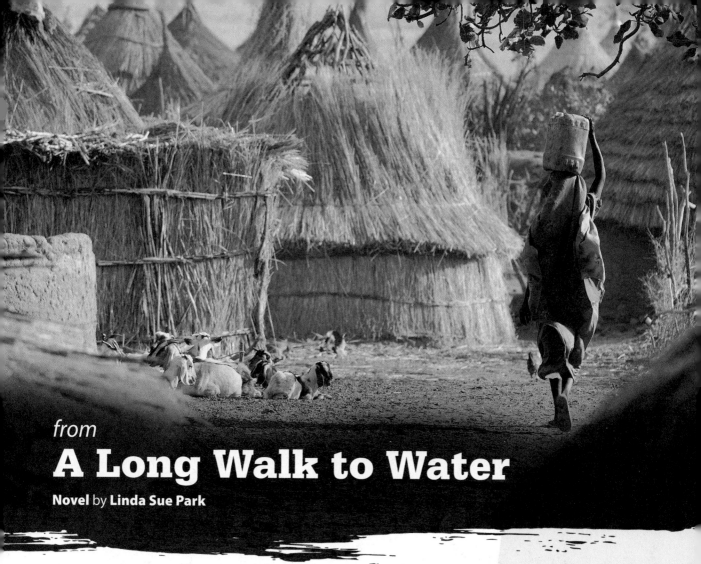

from
A Long Walk to Water
Novel by **Linda Sue Park**

NOTICE & NOTE **N**
As you read, use the side margins to make notes about the text.

It's just another day for Salva Dut, but war suddenly arrives. Armed soldiers begin leading his entire village away. Where are they being taken? What will happen?

1   *B*OOM!

2   Salva turned and looked. Behind him, a huge black cloud of smoke rose. Flames darted out of its base. Overhead, a jet plane **veered** away like a sleek evil bird.

3   In the smoke and dust, he couldn't see the school building anymore. He tripped and almost fell. No more looking back; it slowed him down.

4   Salva lowered his head and ran.

5   He ran until he could not run anymore. Then he walked. For hours, until the sun was nearly gone from the sky.

veer
(vîr) *v.* Something that can *veer* will swerve, or suddenly change course or direction.

Annotate: In paragraph 7, Salva thinks "in rhythm with his steps." Mark Salva's thoughts.

Analyze: What do Salva's thoughts reveal about his situation? What do they reveal about him?

6   Other people were walking, too. There were so many of them that they couldn't all be from the school village; they must have come from the whole area.

7   As Salva walked, the same thoughts kept going through his head in rhythm with his steps. *Where are we going? Where is my family? When will I see them again?*

8   The people stopped walking when it grew too dark to see the path. At first, everyone stood around uncertainly, speaking in tense whispers or silent with fear.

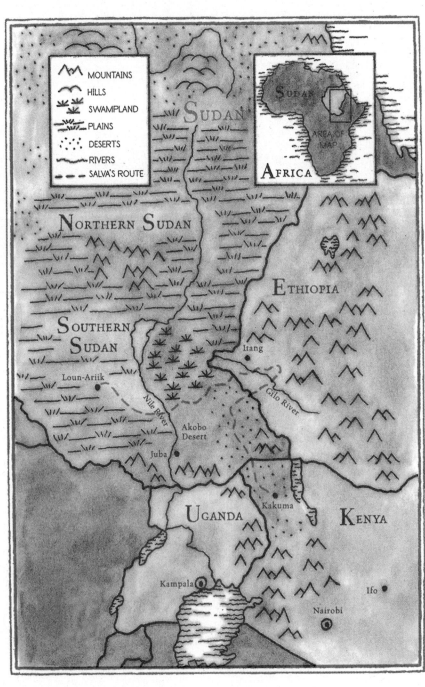

Map of Sudan, 1985

Don't forget to
Notice & Note as you
read the text.

9   Then some of the men gathered and talked for a few moments. One of them called out, "Villages—group yourselves by villages. You will find someone you know."

10   Salva wandered around until he heard the words "Loun-Ariik! The village of Loun-Ariik, here!"

11   Relief flooded through him. That was his village! He hurried toward the sound of the voice.

12   A dozen or so people stood in a loose group at the side of the road. Salva scanned their faces. There was no one from his family. He recognized a few people—a woman with a baby, two men, a teenage girl—but no one he knew well. Still, it was comforting to see them.

13   They spent the night right there by the road, the men taking shifts to keep watch.[1] The next morning, they began walking again. Salva stayed in the midst of the crowd with the other villagers from Loun-Ariik.

14   In the early afternoon, he saw a large group of soldiers up ahead.

ANALYZE SETTING AND CHARACTER

Annotate: Mark the words in paragraphs 9–11 related to setting; then, mark words that describe Salva's thoughts and actions.

Connect: How does Salva's reaction to the setting help you understand his character?

---

[1] **taking shifts to keep watch:** the men take turns watching for dangerous wild animals, including lions, as well as dangerous people, such as fighters with weapons.

© Houghton Mifflin Harcourt Publishing Company • Image Credits: ©Tyler Hicks/Getty Images; (border) ©APOSTOLI100/

© Houghton Mifflin Harcourt Publishing Company

NOTICE & NOTE
TOUGH QUESTIONS

When you notice characters asking questions that reveal their internal struggles, you've found a **Tough Questions** signpost.

Notice & Note: In paragraph 17, mark the question Salva has asked before.

Evaluate: What does this question make you wonder about?

_____

_____

_____

hesitate
(hĕz´ĭ-tāt´) *v. To hesitate* is to pause or wait in uncertainty.

_____

_____

_____

_____

_____

15   Word passed through the crowd: "It's the rebels." The rebels—those who were fighting against the government.[2]

16   Salva passed several rebel soldiers waiting by the side of the road. Each of them held a big gun. Their guns were not pointed at the crowd, but even so, the soldiers seemed fierce and watchful. Some of the rebels then joined the back of the line; now the villagers were surrounded.

17   *What are they going to do to us? Where is my family?*

18   Late in the day, the villagers arrived at the rebel camp. The soldiers ordered them to separate into two groups—men in one group, women and children and the elderly in the other. Teenage boys, it seemed, were considered men, for boys who looked to be only a few years older than Salva were joining the men's group.

19   Salva **hesitated** for a moment. He was only eleven, but he was the son of an important family. He was Salva Mawien Dut Ariik, from the village named for his grandfather. His father always told him to act like a man—to follow the example of his older brothers and, in turn, set a good example for Kuol.[3]

---

[2]   **those who were fighting against the government:** in Sudan's civil war, government soldiers fought against opposition groups that wanted to seize control of territory and take over the Sudanese government.
[3]   **Kuol:** Salva's younger brother.

20   Salva took a few steps toward the men.

21   "Hey!"

22   A soldier approached Salva and raised his gun.

23   Salva froze. All he could see was the gun's huge barrel, black and gleaming, as it moved toward his face.

24   The end of the barrel touched his chin.

25   Salva felt his knees turn to water. He closed his eyes.

26   *If I die now, I will never see my family again.*

27   Somehow, this thought strengthened him enough to keep him from **collapsing** in terror.

28   He took a deep breath and opened his eyes.

29   The soldier was holding the gun with only one hand. He was not *aiming* it; he was using it to lift Salva's chin so he could get a better look at his face.

30   "Over there," the soldier said. He moved the gun and pointed it toward the group of women and children.

31   "You are not a man yet. Don't be in such a hurry!" He laughed and clapped Salva on the shoulder.

32   Salva **scurried** over to the women's side.

---

33   The next morning, the rebels moved on from the camp. The village men were forced to carry supplies: guns and mortars, shells, radio equipment.[4] Salva watched as one man protested that he did not want to go with the rebels. A soldier hit him in the face with the butt of a gun.[5] The man fell to the ground, bleeding.

34   After that, no one objected. The men **shouldered** the heavy equipment and left the camp.

35   Everyone else began walking again. They went in the opposite direction from the rebels, for wherever the rebels went, there was sure to be fighting.

36   Salva stayed with the group from Loun-Ariik. It was smaller now, without the men. And except for the infant, Salva was the only child.

37   That evening they found a barn in which to spend the night. Salva tossed restlessly in the itchy hay.

38   *Where are we going? Where is my family? When will I see them again?*

39   It took him a long time to fall asleep.

---

[4] **guns and mortars, shells, radio equipment:** mortars are large, portable weapons that fire explosive bombs, called shells; radio equipment is used to communicate, often in remote areas.

[5] **butt of a gun:** the thicker end of a gun, which is held in the hand, or in the case of a rifle, held up against the shoulder while firing.

Don't forget to **Notice & Note** as you read the text.

collapse
(kə-lăps´) *v.* When something is said to *collapse,* it falls down.

scurry
(skûr´ē) *v.* Something that can *scurry* will run with quick, light steps.

ANALYZE STRUCTURE

Annotate: Mark the words in paragraph 33 related to war.

Analyze: Think about how important the setting is to the plot of this story. Then, think about Salva's view of events. What does Salva's perspective—as a child watching this scene—help reveal about both the setting and the plot?

shoulder
(shōl´dər) *v.* To *shoulder* something is to carry it on one's shoulders.

© Houghton Mifflin Harcourt Publishing Company

Annotate: Mark the words in paragraphs 36–41 that show the sequence of events.

Identify: What event is revealed before Salva is fully awake?

?

ESSENTIAL QUESTION:

What does it take to be a survivor?

Review your notes and add your thoughts to your Response Log.

40 Even before he was fully awake, Salva could feel that something was wrong. He lay very still with his eyes closed, trying to sense what it might be.

41 Finally, he sat up and opened his eyes.

42 No one else was in the barn.

43 Salva stood so quickly that for a moment he felt dizzy. He rushed to the door and looked out.

44 Nobody. Nothing.

45 They had left him.

46 He was alone.

TURN AND TALK

With a partner, discuss what keeps Salva moving, despite his feelings of confusion and fear. What motivates him?

Assessment Practice

Answer these questions before moving on to the **Analyze the Text** section.

1. Read the excerpt from the selection. Then, answer the question.

> He tripped and almost fell. No more looking back; it slowed him down.
> Salva lowered his head and ran. (paragraphs 3–4)

Why does Salva begin to run?

- (A) because he is being chased
- (B) because he is late for school
- (C) because a storm is approaching
- (D) because he heard and saw an explosion

2. This question has two parts. First, answer **Part A**, then **Part B**.

Part A

Which word best describes the mood, or feeling, of the selection?

- (A) tired
- (B) fearful
- (C) excited
- (D) hopeful

Part B

Which excerpt from the selection most clearly contributes to this mood?

- (A) "Relief flooded through him." (paragraph 11)
- (B) "He was only eleven, but he was the son of an important family." (paragraph 19)
- (C) *"If I die now, I will never see my family again."* (paragraph 26)
- (D) "Finally, he sat up and opened his eyes." (paragraph 41)

Test-Taking Strategies

Analyze the Text

Support your responses with evidence from the text.

NOTICE & NOTE

Review what you **noticed and noted** as you read the text. Your annotations can help you answer these questions.

(1) **INTERPRET** How does the information that precedes the selection help you understand the setting and what is happening in the selection's opening scene (paragraphs 1–4)? Paraphrase these paragraphs to confirm your understanding.

(2) **PREDICT** Review paragraphs 3–4. What does the phrase *No more looking back* mean? How might this realization affect Salva as the novel continues?

(3) **ANALYZE** Review paragraphs 40–46. How does this scene fit into the overall structure of the story? How might the events of this scene affect what happens in the rest of the novel?

(4) **DRAW CONCLUSIONS** Review paragraphs 31–34. What might Salva have felt after he went to the women's side? How might Salva's feelings have changed after witnessing what happened to the man who did not want to go with the rebels? Explain.

(5) **EVALUATE** Review paragraphs 37–39. Identify the **Tough Questions** he asks, along with details that describe the setting. How might Salva's surroundings affect his thoughts and actions?

PARAGRAPH	DETAILS	SALVA'S THOUGHTS AND ACTIONS

Choices

Here are some other ways to demonstrate your understanding of the ideas in this lesson.

Writing
↳ Salva and the Setting

Write an essay analyzing how the setting of *A Long Walk to Water* shapes Salva's experience and character.

- Review your annotations and the information about Sudan to find a relationship between the setting and Salva's character.

- Create a clear thesis or controlling idea to guide your analysis, and support your ideas with evidence from the text.

- Use prepositions and prepositional phrases to help clarify relationships between ideas.

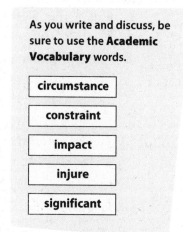

As you write and discuss, be sure to use the **Academic Vocabulary** words.

> circumstance

> constraint

> impact

> injure

> significant

Research
↳ Water for South Sudan

A Long Walk to Water is based on the life of Salva Dut, who founded the organization Water for South Sudan. Using multiple sources, discover what Water for South Sudan does. Use the chart below to guide your research.

Social & Emotional Learning
↳ Rising to the Challenge

Have a discussion about character traits needed to meet a challenge.

- As a group, review the text and list each challenge Salva faces.

- Identify character traits that help Salva rise to meet each challenge.

- Finally, discuss how someone might develop the traits you've identified.

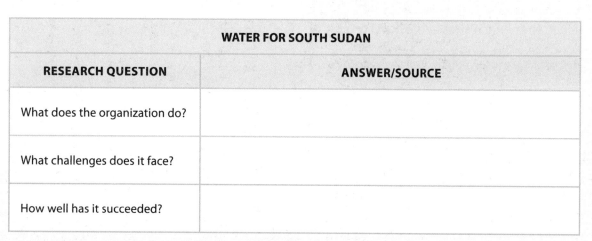

WATER FOR SOUTH SUDAN	
RESEARCH QUESTION	**ANSWER/SOURCE**
What does the organization do?	
What challenges does it face?	
How well has it succeeded?	

Expand Your Vocabulary

PRACTICE AND APPLY

To show your understanding of the vocabulary words, choose the better answer to each question.

1. Which of the following is an example of **collapse?**

   a. a falling tower   **b.** a stack of paper

2. Which of the following would cause most people to **hesitate?**

   a. skydiving   **b.** knitting

3. Which of the following is an example of **scurry?**

   a. a bear sitting down   **b.** a squirrel running

4. Which of the following would someone **shoulder?**

   a. a heavy package   **b.** a baseball

5. Which of the following is an example of **veer?**

   a. a car quickly changing direction   **b.** a thin coat of paint

Vocabulary Strategy

↳ **Vocabulary Resources**

A print or online dictionary is a useful tool for determining the meaning of a word. A dictionary includes every meaning of a word, as well as its syllabication (how it breaks into syllables), pronunciation, part of speech, and word origin.

 Ed

> **Interactive Vocabulary Lesson: Using Reference Sources**

PRACTICE AND APPLY

Look up *shouldered* in a dictionary by searching for its base word, *shoulder,* and then answer the questions.

1. What parts of speech are listed for *shoulder?* _____

2. Review the use of *shouldered* in paragraph 34. According to context, its suffix, and a dictionary, what part of speech is it? _____

3. How many syllables do *shoulder* and *shouldered* have? _____

4. What is the word origin and dictionary meaning of *shoulder* as it is used in the selection? _____

Watch Your Language!

Prepositions and Prepositional Phrases

Writers use **prepositions** and **prepositional phrases** to express where, when, and how words and ideas are related. Prepositions and prepositional phrases create variety and add clarity to sentences.

⊙**Ed**

Interactive Grammar Lessons: The Prepositional Phrase

When inserting prepositional phrases between a subject and a verb, be sure to identify the subject and verb so that they agree. A sentence with a singular subject should have a singular verb. A sentence with a plural subject should have a plural verb.

In the following sentence, *The villagers* is the subject, and *in the text* is a prepositional phrase. The subject is plural, so the verb must also be plural.

> The villagers in the text seems/seem frightened.

Study the sentence below to determine which form of *to be* is correct. First identify the subject of the sentence, and then mark the correct verb.

> Each of the students is/are required to attend.

Each is the subject of the sentence, while *of the students* is a prepositional phrase that modifies *each*. Because *each* is singular, use *is*, the singular form of the verb *to be*.

PRACTICE AND APPLY

Write your own sentences about Salva's response when he discovers that he has been left alone. Use prepositions and prepositional phrases. Check your use of prepositions and prepositional phrases with a partner.

MEDIA

Salva's Story

Documentary by **POVRoseMedia**

ESSENTIAL QUESTION:
What does it take to be a survivor?

Engage Your Brain

You're about to watch a video about Salva Dut and the reasons he returned to South Sudan as an adult.

With a partner, share what you remember about Dut from your reading of *A Long Walk to Water*. Why might someone like Dut have chosen to return to a place where he had undergone such suffering? Discuss your ideas with a partner.

Background

During a long and brutal civil war in Sudan, thousands of children fled on foot to neighboring countries. Along the way, many died. **Salva Dut** was one of the children, called the Lost Boys, who survived. In 1996, he became one of the first of the Lost Boys to resettle in the United States. The novel *A Long Walk to Water* is based on Salva Dut's life story.

Integrate Information from Media

When you **integrate information**, you bring together different pieces of information from more than one source, helping you develop a more complete understanding of a topic.

As you compare and contrast two or more works, for example, you integrate information from each of those works. Comparing and contrasing the information helps you develop a better understanding of the topic as a whole.

The video you are about to view is a **documentary** about Salva Dut. A documentary is a nonfiction film or video that tells about important people, historic places, or significant events. Documentaries present information in an engaging, visually interesting way. They may use **animated graphics,** such as maps, and **footage,** such as reenactments or film clips.

You first learned about Salva Dut in *A Long Walk to Water*. Now, watch and analyze *Salva's Story* to get a fuller understanding of his life. Then, reread the excerpt from *A Long Walk to Water*, and compare and contrast the two presentations of Dut's life and experiences. Integrate information from the two sources.

Focus on Genre
↳**Documentary**

- highlights a person, place, event, or cause
- targets a specific audience
- is created for a specific purpose
- includes TV broadcasts, videos, print newspapers and magazines, and online newspapers and magazines

Find out more about Salva Dut's life, including his move to the United States and his efforts to help provide clean water to Sudan.

☺**Ed**

Video

View *Salva's Story* in your ebook.

Salva's Story ETHIOPIA

KENYA

Analyze Media

Support your responses with evidence from the video.

NOTICE & NOTE

Review what you **noticed and noted** as you viewed the video. Your notes can help you answer these questions.

(1) **ANALYZE** How do the visual and audio features of the video help you understand Salva Dut's life? Explain how one element of the video—such as a map or the narration—helps you better understand Dut's life story.

(2) **CONNECT** Why did Salva Dut tell the filmmakers the story of visiting his father when he was ill? How did that experience shape decisions Dut made afterward?

(3) **MAKE INFERENCES** How does the video help you better understand the significance of the novel's title, *A Long Walk to Water?*

(4) **ANALYZE** What questions did you have about Salva Dut's life after you finished the excerpt from *A Long Walk to Water?* Did the video address any of your questions? Explain.

(5) **CRITIQUE** Compare and contrast the excerpt from *A Long Walk to Water* with the documentary *Salva's Story.* Which presentation did you find more effective in helping you understand Salva Dut? Explain.

	REASONS PRESENTATION IS EFFECTIVE
A Long Walk to Water	
Salva's Story	

Choices

Here are some other ways to demonstrate your understanding of the ideas in this lesson.

Writing
↳ Summary Timeline

Create a timeline summarizing the main events described in *Salva's Story*.

- Review *Salva's Story*, taking notes on events and dates.

- Create a timeline to organize the events chronologically—in the order they occurred, adding brief summaries describing each event.

- Exclude personal opinions or judgments in your summaries.

Research
↳ The Lost Boys

The video briefly describes the experiences of the Lost Boys of Sudan. What else would you like to know about the Lost Boys? Use reputable sources to answer questions you have. When you finish, share what you've found, and explain how it adds to your understanding of *Salva's Story* and *A Long Walk to Water*.

Speaking & Listening
↳ Compare and Contrast Presentation of Events

With a group, compare and contrast information in *Salva's Story* with information in *A Long Walk to Water*.

- First, outline points of difference.

- Next, outline points of similarity.

- Then, work together to compare and contrast the presentation of similar information.

Share your conclusions with the class.

RESEARCH QUESTIONS	NOTES AND SOURCES

Into the Lifeboat

from **Titanic Survivor**

Memoir by **Violet Jessop**

ESSENTIAL QUESTION:
What does it take to be a survivor?

Engage Your Brain

Choose one or more of these activities to start connecting with the memoir you're about to read.

What Do You Know?

What do you know about the *Titanic*? Where did you get your information about the ship and what happened? Discuss your answers with a partner.

Modern Marvels

Before the *Titanic* sank, many people considered the ship "a perfection" of human engineering. What modern marvels of engineering do we have today? Which one do you consider most impressive and why? Write or sketch your response.

Different Views, Same Event

In the memoir you're about to read, Violet Jessop provides a firsthand view of events aboard the *Titanic*. In a small group, select one event you each experienced firsthand, such as waiting for class to begin.

- Work alone to list significant details about the event.

- Then, reveal the detail you consider most important to your group.

- Finally, compare views. Did each of you note the same detail from your firsthand experience? Why or why not?

Determine Author's Purpose and Point of View

In a memoir, an author communicates a unique **perspective,** a combination of ideas, values, feelings, and beliefs that influence the way the author looks at a topic. This perspective helps explain the **author's purpose,** or reason for writing.

The **author's point of view,** or how the author presents information on a topic, is connected to perspective and purpose. A **subjective point of view** includes the author's opinions, feelings, and beliefs. An **objective point of view** gives only factual information and does not include opinions.

To determine an author's point of view, consider the following:

- Does the author include opinions or personal ideas that cannot be proven true? If so, why?

- Do the text's details, examples, and tone reveal the author's unique perspective on the topic? If so, how?

Focus on Genre
↳ **Memoir**

- is a form of autobiographical writing
- includes the writer's personal experiences and observations
- often has an informal or intimate tone
- presents insights into the impact of historical events on people's lives

Determine Meaning of Words and Phrases

Authors carefully choose language that helps create vivid descriptions for their readers. As you read, pause often to determine the meaning of descriptive words and phrases, including figurative language. Look at the example below.

DESCRIPTIVE LANGUAGE	MENTAL IMAGE
. . . as the ship seemed to right herself like a hurt animal with a broken back.	Similes are a kind of comparison. This simile compares the ship to an injured animal. Readers can imagine a creature, too injured to survive, that still fights to live.

Annotation in Action

Here is how one reader made notes about the meaning of phrases in "Into the Lifeboat." As you read, pause to determine the meaning of descriptive words and phrases.

> You could almost imagine this a scene of busily curious people with not very much to do. True, there were officers and men briskly getting lifeboats ready to lower, their tense faces strangely in contrast to the well ordered groups wandering about.

These people sound tense and nervous. Are they trying not to panic?

Expand Your Vocabulary

Put a check mark next to the vocabulary words that you feel comfortable using when speaking or writing.

reluctance	☐
reassure	☐
fascinate	☐
unrestrainedly	☐
agonizing	☐

Turn to a partner and talk about the vocabulary words you already know. Then, use as many words as you can in a paragraph about convincing a crowd of people to abandon a sinking ship. As you read "Into the Lifeboat," use the definitions in the side column to learn the vocabulary words you don't already know.

Background

Violet Jessop (1887–1971) was a stewardess on board the *Titanic* for its first and only voyage in 1912. Because of its state-of-the-art construction, the luxurious *Titanic* was considered practically unsinkable—so it didn't carry enough lifeboats for all of its passengers. When the ship sank, Jessop, along with most of the women and children, was rescued on one of those lifeboats. Despite surviving two other disasters aboard ships, she continued to work aboard them until 1950.

Into the Lifeboat

from **Titanic Survivor**

Memoir by **Violet Jessop**

Follow Violet Jessop as she makes her way to a lifeboat in those desperate minutes before the *Titanic* goes down.

You could almost imagine this a scene of busily curious people with not very much to do. True, there were officers and men briskly getting lifeboats ready to lower, their tense faces strangely in contrast to the well ordered groups wandering about. I felt chilly without a coat, so I went down again for something to cover my shoulders and picked up a silk eiderdown¹ from the first open cabin I came to. How strange it was to pass all those rooms lit up so brilliantly, their doors open and contents lying around in disorder. Jewels sparkled on dressing tables and a pair of silver slippers were lying just where they had been kicked off.

---

¹ **silk eiderdown** (sĭlk ī´dər-doun´): a quilt stuffed with the down, or feathers, of the eider duck.

DETERMINE AUTHOR'S PURPOSE AND POINT OF VIEW

Annotate: Reread paragraphs 2–5. Mark who was allowed to get into the lifeboats first.

Evaluate: Why would this be an important point for the author to present early in the text?

reluctance

(rǐ-lŭk´təns) *n.* Showing *reluctance* to do something means you are unwilling.

reassure

(rē´ə-shŏŏr´) *v.* To *reassure* someone is to give comfort or confidence to that person.

2   I gathered my eiderdown and went up. On my way I passed a group of officers, still in their mess jackets,[2] hands in pockets, chatting quietly on the companion square as men do who are waiting for something. They smiled at me and I waved back.

3   As I turned I ran into Jock, the bandleader and his crowd with their instruments. "Funny, they must be going to play," thought I, and at this late hour! Jock smiled in passing, looking rather pale for him, remarking, "Just going to give them a tune to cheer things up a bit," and passed on. Presently the strains of the band reached me faintly as I stood on deck watching a young woman excitedly remonstrating[3] with an embarrassed young officer. He wanted her to get into the lifeboat he was trying to fill but she refused to go without her father.

4   "He must wait," responded the officer, "till the decks are cleared of women and children."

5   Out on deck, the first arguments started over who would and who wouldn't go into the boats which appeared to be suspended miles above the yawning blackness below.

6   Nobody was anxious to move; *Titanic* seemed so steady. To justify their **reluctance,** some pointed to a light on the horizon: another ship's lights![4] People were **reassured,** content to bide their time.[5]

---

[2] **mess jacket:** a man's short, close-fitting jacket worn by the military or as part of a uniform for officers, waiters, etc.

[3] **remonstrating** (rǐ-mŏn´strāt´ǐng): to say or plead in protest or objection.

[4] **another ship's lights:** two ships were nearby, the *Carpathia* and the *Californian;* the *Carpathia* was more than 50 miles away, and the *Californian* was about 20 miles away.

[5] **bide their time:** to wait in a patient way for further developments.

7　　One boat was already being lowered with very few people in it. When this was pointed out as a shining example for backward souls by the officer near me, he got a rather alarming response as the crowd surged forward to embark. The boat was lowered very full, almost too full this time; and so on. Always, some held back in need of coaxing while a few were too eager.

8　　A steward stood waiting with his back to the bulkhead,[6] hands in his pockets. It struck me forcibly as the first time I had ever seen a steward stand thus amid a group of distinguished guests.

9　　A woman standing near me gave an approving glance as John Jacob Astor handed his wife into a boat, waving encouragingly to her as he stepped back into an ever-increasing crowd of men.

10　　Ann Turnbull,[7] still silent and unmoved, dragged a little behind me. I suggested we keep together and we stood awhile to watch. There was nothing else we could do. Dimly I heard a shot.

11　　Glancing forward I caught my breath as a white rocket shot up,[8] then another. Distress rockets! They went very high with great noise. The lights on the horizon seemed to come nearer. That cheered up the group about us, who had slowly started to fill a boat. Young officers urged them to greater speed, showing unlimited patience, I thought. Another rocket went up into the night.

12　　A few women near me started to cry loudly when they realized a parting had to take place, their husbands standing silently by. They were Poles[9] and could not understand a word of English. Surely a terrible plight, to be among a crowd in such a situation and not be able to understand anything that is being said.

13　　Boats were now being lowered more rapidly and a crowd of foreigners was brought up by a steward from the third class. They dashed eagerly as one man over to a boat, almost more than the officer could control. But he regained order and managed to get the boat away. It descended slowly, uncertainly at first, now one end up and then the other; the falls were new and difficult to handle.[10] Some men nearby

© Houghton Mifflin Harcourt Publishing Company • Image Credits: ©Paladin12/Shutterstock

---

[6] **bulkhead:** a supporting barrier or wall dividing a ship into compartments that prevents leaks and fires.

[7] **Ann Turnbull:** another stewardess aboard the *Titanic* and a friend to Jessop.

[8] **a white rocket shot up:** a large Roman candle that indicated a ship's identity and condition to other ships; at the time, it was a way to communicate over long distances.

[9] **Poles:** people from Poland.

[10] **the falls were new and difficult to handle:** lifeboat "falls" are the ropes and blocks used with a crane to lower the boat.

Text in Focus Video

Learn more about analyzing comparisons and contrasts.

NOTICE & NOTE
CONTRASTS AND CONTRADICTIONS

When you notice a sharp contrast, you've found a **Contrasts and Contradictions** signpost.

Notice & Note: In paragraph 7, mark people's contrasting reactions to loading the lifeboats.

Analyze: Why does the author note these contrasting reactions?

DETERMINE MEANING OF WORDS AND PHRASES

Annotate: Mark the author's word choices in paragraphs 11–12 that create vivid descriptions.

Connect: How do these word choices help develop the scene and reveal the author's feelings?

were throwing things over the side—deck chairs, rafts or any wooden thing lying nearby.

14   Suddenly, the crowd of people beside me parted. A man dashed to the ship's side, and before anyone could stop him, hurled himself into the descending boat. There was a murmur of amazement and disapproval.

15   I turned to say something to Ann. Looking along the length of the ship, I noticed the forward part of her was lower now, much lower! For a fraction of a second, my heart stood still, as is often the case when faith, hitherto unshaken faith, gets its first setback.

16   One of the mailmen from our sorting office joined us. His work was finished, he remarked unemotionally. "The mail is floating up to F-deck with the water," he told us.

17   I tried not to hear what he said, not wanting to believe what he accepted so stoically.[11] Instead, I listened to the faint sounds of music from Jock's men. They were playing *Nearer My God to Thee.*[12]

18   My arm was suddenly jerked and I turned to see young Mason who had been busy filling a boat. His face looked weary and tired, but he gave a bright smile as he ordered my group into the boat, calling out "Good luck!" as we stepped in, helped by his willing, guiding hand. I nearly fell over the tackle and oars[13] as I tried to assist Ann in beside me. She was suffering with her feet, I could see, and found her lifebelt got in the way of moving freely.

DETERMINE AUTHOR'S PURPOSE AND POINT OF VIEW

Annotate: Mark details in paragraphs 19–23 related to the baby Jessop holds in the lifeboat.

Explain: What message is conveyed through the details about the baby?

19   Before I could do anything, young Mason hailed me and held up something, calling as he prepared to throw it, "Look after this, will you?" and I reached out to receive somebody's forgotten baby in my arms.

20   It started to whimper as I pressed it to me, the hard cork surface of the lifebelt being anything but a comfort, poor mite. The boat was full now, full of people with dull, inquiring faces. I spoke to one woman but she shook her head, not understanding a word I said.

21   Groaning, the boat descended a fearful distance into that inky blackness beneath, intensified as the lights fell on it occasionally.

---

[11] **stoically** (stō´ĭk-əl-lē): enduring pain and hardship without showing feelings or complaining.

[12] **playing *Nearer My God to Thee:*** a 19th-century Christian hymn popularly believed to have been played as the *Titanic* sank.

[13] **tackle and oars:** lifeboat equipment and paddles.

WHITE STAR LINE

Don't forget to **Notice & Note** as you read the text.

22   "Surely it is all a dream," I thought as I looked up the side of the ship, beautifully illuminated, each deck alive with lights; the dynamos were on the top deck.[14] I tried to make myself believe it could not be true, all this. I even noticed a few people leaning over the rail, watching in an unconcerned manner; perhaps they too were persuading themselves it was a bad dream!

23   We touched the water with a terrific thud, a bone-cracking thud which started the baby crying in earnest. Somebody in the forepart ordered oars out and we slowly pulled away from the side of the ship. I noticed one of the few men in the boat rowing; he was a fireman who had evidently just come up from the stokehold,[15] his face still black with coal dust and eyes red-rimmed, wearing only a thin singlet[16] to protect him from the icy cold.

---

[14] **the dynamos were on the top deck:** dynamos were electric generators on the ship; their location helps explain why the lights remained on.
[15] **stokehold:** the area or compartment into which a ship's furnaces or boilers open.
[16] **thin singlet:** a sleeveless, tight-fitting undershirt or athletic shirt.

VOCABULARY

Context Clues: Authors often provide clues, sometimes including figurative language, about a word's meaning. A context clue can help you better understand a word, as well as the author's perspective.

Analyze: How does the figurative language in the context clue for *illuminated* help reveal both the meaning of *illuminated* and the author's feelings toward the ship?

fascinate

(făs´ə-nāt´) *v.* To *fascinate* someone means to capture the interest or attention of that person.

unrestrainedly

(ŭn´rĭ-strā´nĭd-lē) *adv.* Doing something *unrestrainedly* means doing it without control.

DETERMINE MEANING OF WORDS AND PHRASES

Annotate: Mark the figurative language in paragraph 29.

Infer: Explain the meaning of each comparison, and discuss images invoked by this language.

agonizing

(ăg´ə-nīz´ĭng) *adj.* To be in an *agonizing* state means to feel great mental suffering and worry.

24   **Fascinated**, my eyes never left the ship, as if by looking I could keep her afloat. I reflected that but four days ago I had wished to see her from afar, to be able to admire her under way; now there she was, my *Titanic*, magnificent queen of the ocean, a perfection of man's handiwork, her splendid lines outlined against the night, every light twinkling.

25   I started unconsciously to count the decks by the rows of lights. One, two, three, four, five, six; then again—one, two, three, four, five. I stopped. Surely I had miscounted. I went over them again more carefully, hushing the whimpering baby meanwhile.

26   No, I had made no mistake. There were only five decks now; then I started all over again—only four now. She was getting lower in the water, I could not any longer deny it.

27   As if all could read my mind, the women in the boat started to weep, some silently, some **unrestrainedly**. I closed my eyes and prayed, prayed for one and all but dared not think of anyone in particular. I dared not visualize those people I had just left, warm and alive as I was. I tried to busy myself with the baby, but could not refrain from looking up again. Only three decks now, and still not a list to one side or the other.[17]

28   Desperately, I turned to where that other ship's lights shone on the horizon; surely they should be getting nearer by now. It was such a long, long time since we had first seen their comforting glow. They should be with us by now, taking off those patient waiting people over there. But no, she did not seem nearer, in fact, she seemed further away. Strange!

29   A tiny breeze, the first we had felt on this calm night, blew an icy blast across my face; it felt like a knife in its penetrating coldness. I sat paralyzed with cold and misery, as I watched *Titanic* give a lurch forward. One of the huge funnels toppled off[18] like a cardboard model, falling into the sea with a fearful roar. A few cries came to us across the water, then silence, as the ship seemed to right herself like a hurt animal with a broken back. She settled for a few minutes, but one more deck of lighted ports disappeared. Then she went down by the head with a thundering roar of underwater explosions, our proud ship, our beautiful *Titanic* gone to her doom.

30   One awful moment of empty, misty blackness enveloped us in its loneliness, then an unforgettable, **agonizing** cry went up from 1500 despairing throats, a long wail and then silence and our tiny craft tossing about at the mercy of the ice field.

---

[17] **not a list to one side or the other:** no tilt of the ship.
[18] **One of the huge funnels toppled off:** a smokestack fell off.

Get with a partner, and discuss the memoir you just read. Which events or descriptions were most interesting to you? Why?

Assessment Practice

Answer these questions before moving on to the **Analyze the Text** section.

1. Which sentence best expresses the author's feelings of both pride and sadness about the ship *Titanic*?

   A "Some men nearby were throwing things over the side—deck chairs, rafts or any wooden thing lying nearby." (paragraph 13)

   B "I tried to make myself believe it could not be true, all this." (paragraph 22)

   C "Desperately, I turned to where that other ship's lights shone on the horizon; surely they should be getting nearer by now." (paragraph 28)

   D "Then she went down by the head with a thundering roar of underwater explosions, our proud ship, our beautiful *Titanic* gone to her doom." (paragraph 29)

2. Why does the author describe how she counted the rows of deck lights? (paragraphs 25–26)

   A to demonstrate how she soothed the crying baby

   B to show how she realized that the ship was truly sinking

   C to reassure herself and other passengers during the crisis

   D to explain that the bright deck lights were on as a signal for help

Test-Taking Strategies

Analyze the Text

Support your responses with evidence from the text.

NOTICE & NOTE

Review what you **noticed and noted** as you read the text. Your annotations can help you answer these questions.

1. **ANALYZE** Review the description of the "fireman" in paragraph 23. Use context clues and the sensory details to explain who this person is, and then infer what he is thinking and feeling.

2. **COMPARE** Compare the author's use of the phrase "yawning blackness below" in paragraph 5 with her reference to "that inky blackness beneath" in paragraph 21. What does the author convey about her feelings by returning to this image?

3. **EVALUATE** Reread paragraph 22. What is the author's purpose in this paragraph? How does this paragraph contribute to your understanding of the author's experience?

4. **ANALYZE** Review the figurative language used in paragraph 24. To what does the author compare the *Titanic?* How does this figurative language help you understand the author's relationship to the ship and the author's purpose in writing the memoir?

5. **ANALYZE** Which people are admired by the author? Which people are disliked by the author? How do these **Contrasts and Contradictions** help you understand the selection as a whole?

People Jessop Admires

People Jessop Dislikes

Effect on My Understanding

Choices

Here are some other ways to demonstrate your understanding of the ideas in this lesson.

Writing
↳ Posts from the Deck

Violet Jessop wrote her memoir long after her experience aboard the *Titanic*. If modern technology had been available, she might have described what was happening in real time: she might have posted what she saw, thought, felt, and heard *while* the ship went down. Identify key moments in Jessop's memoir, and then write a sequence of social media posts describing each of those moments. In your posts, try to capture Jessop's perspective, her style, and her personality.

As you write and discuss, be sure to use the **Academic Vocabulary** words.

- circumstance
- constraint
- impact
- injure
- significant

Media
↳ Present Your Ideas

Create a short video or slideshow about Violet Jessop and her experiences.

- List ideas you'd most like to share about Jessop or the sinking of the *Titanic*.

- Develop a script to express your ideas, using figurative language and detailed descriptions where appropriate.

- Locate images you can incorporate to emphasize portions of your script, without distracting from your points.

- Create and present your video or slideshow.

After you've presented, explain which format you think is more effective, a written memoir or a multimedia presentation. Evaluate the pros and cons of each format.

Research
↳ Other Survivors

Choose and investigate another *Titanic* survivor. First, list other survivors. Then, choose one to research further, using multiple sources. What happened to that person at the time of the ship's sinking? What happened afterward?

SURVIVOR'S NAME	NOTES

Expand Your Vocabulary

PRACTICE AND APPLY

To show your understanding of the vocabulary words, fill in the blank with the correct vocabulary word.

| reluctance | reassure | fascinate | unrestrainedly | agonizing |

1. The sound of crying from the sinking ship was _____ to hear.

2. Volcanoes and tsunamis _____ me.

3. _____ , she splashed paint all over the canvas.

4. With _____ , he turned in his incomplete test.

5. The coach takes time to _____ players before a game.

Vocabulary Strategy

↳ ## Context Clues

To figure out an unfamiliar word's meaning, look for **context clues,** words or phrases that provide hints about the word's meaning. Two types of context clues are **analogies** and **definitions.**

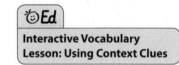

☺Ed

Interactive Vocabulary Lesson: Using Context Clues

UNFAMILIAR WORD	CONTEXT CLUE	TYPE OF CLUE	POSSIBLE MEANING
Like a bear cub losing sight of its mother, Laura was **reluctant** to part with her rescuer.	like a bear cub about to lose sight of its mother	analogy—a comparison between two things	resisting or not wanting something to happen
He felt **confounded,** or bewildered, when he learned that the ship had sunk.	bewildered	definition—words in the text define the unfamiliar word	greatly confused

PRACTICE AND APPLY

Locate *hailed* (paragraph 19) and *whimper* (paragraph 20) in the selection.

Mark context clues, and then write definitions. Use a dictionary to check your definitions.

Watch Your Language!

Commas

Commas help communicate and clarify ideas by grouping words together to form units of meaning in a sentence.

In "Into the Lifeboat," commas are used in the following ways:

- **As if all could read my mind, the women in the boat started to weep. . . . (to set off a dependent clause)**

- **Instead, I listened to the faint sounds of music from Jock's men. (to set off an introductory element)**

- **Ann Turnbull, still silent and unmoved, dragged a little behind me. (to set off a parenthetical element)**

Commas Save Lives!

Using commas or other punctuation incorrectly causes confusion and misunderstanding. For example, **comma splices** incorrectly connect two independent clauses without a conjunction such as *and* or *but*.

Incorrect:	**She agonized over leaving, she eventually did go.**
Correct:	**She agonized over leaving, but she eventually did go.**

PRACTICE AND APPLY

Write your own sentences about the selection, using commas. Use the examples from "Into the Lifeboat" as models. When you have finished, share your sentences with a partner and explain each comma you used. Then, work together to identify places that a comma might make a sentence clearer. Revise your sentences as needed for clarity.

Collaborate & Compare

Compare Across Genres

You're about to read part of a poem and a novel excerpt about the experiences of young people caught in the aftermath of Hurricane Katrina. As you read, focus on themes that the two texts share.

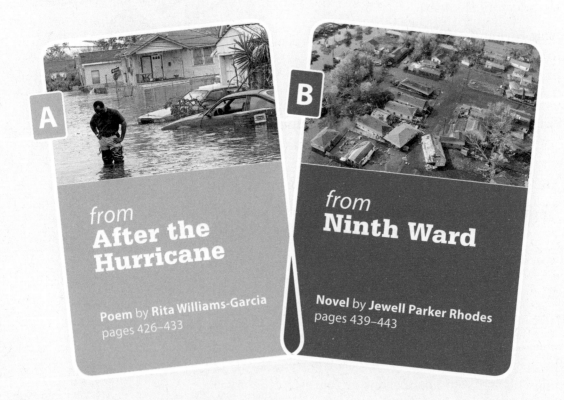

A

from
After the Hurricane

Poem by Rita Williams-Garcia
pages 426–433

B

from
Ninth Ward

Novel by Jewell Parker Rhodes
pages 439–443

After you've read both texts, you'll develop guidelines for how an organization can provide help following a natural disaster. You'll follow these steps:

- Develop a Research Question
- Gather Information
- Present Findings

from
After the Hurricane

Poem by **Rita Williams-Garcia**

Engage Your Brain

Choose one or both activities to start connecting with the poem you're about to read.

Catalog Your "Status"

Free verse poems like the one you're about to read sometimes include **catalogs,** lists of people, places, or ideas that explain or emphasize a point. Imagine that you're posting an update to your day's "status" on a social media site. What items would you include in a catalog describing your day?

Life After the Storm

Hurricanes are astonishing storms. They're both terrifying and destructive. Gather in a small group to discuss how people rebuild their lives once a hurricane has passed. Summarize your group's thoughts below.

Analyze Free Verse

Many traditional forms of poetry use regular patterns of syllables, rhyme schemes, lines, and stanzas. **Free verse,** however, has no regular patterns of line length, rhyme, or rhythm. In free verse, poets use poetic devices such as repetition, word choice, **catalogs** (lists of related words and ideas), and **alliteration** (the repetition of consonant sounds at the beginning of words) to create rhythm and express ideas. Although free verse does not have a set structure, you can understand the organization of a free verse poem by analyzing its basic structural elements.

STRUCTURAL ELEMENT	DEFINITION
line	any text appearing on one line—a sentence, a phrase, or a single word
line break	the place where a line of poetry ends; may be used to add emphasis to certain words and phrases
stanza	a group of two or more lines that forms a unit in a poem to express related ideas—as a paragraph functions in prose

To analyze free verse, ask and answer these questions as you read:

- What ideas are expressed in lines, stanzas, and in the entire poem?
- How does the use of free verse support the poem's ideas?
- What rhythms are created by repetition or line lengths?
- How do poetic devices work to create structure and organization?
- How do poetic devices contribute to the poem's message or theme?

Focus on Genre
↳**Free Verse Poetry**

- lacks regular patterns of rhyme, rhythm, or line length
- captures the sounds and rhythms of ordinary speech
- varies line length to call attention to words and ideas
- includes poetic devices— alliteration, figurative language, imagery, and rhythm

Analyze Figurative Language

Figurative language is language that communicates meanings beyond
the literal meanings of words. Authors use figurative language to
emphasize ideas, evoke emotions, create tone, and communicate theme.
Personification, simile, and metaphor are types of figurative language.
Use a chart like this one to analyze a writer's use of figurative language.

TYPE	DEFINITION	EXAMPLE, EFFECT, AND MEANING
Personification	gives human qualities to an animal, object, or idea	
Simile	uses *like* or *as* to compare two essentially unlike things	
Metaphor	compares two unlike things without using *like* or *as*	
Extended Metaphor	compares two unlike things at length and in several ways	

Annotation in Action

Here are one reader's notes about "After the Hurricane." As you
read, note the author's use of figurative language.

> this could be a disaster movie with
> helicopters whipping up sky overhead,
> Special Effects brought in to create
> Lake George and not the great Mississippi
> meeting Lake Ponchartrain.

Wow! Things must be <u>really</u> bad if she's comparing what's happening to a disaster movie.

Background

Rita Williams-Garcia (b. 1957) draws on her own experiences
to write about issues that urban teenagers face today. The
following poem focuses on the aftermath of Hurricane Katrina,
which ripped through the Gulf Coast on August 29, 2005. In the
city of New Orleans, thousands of people were left homeless,
almost 2,000 people lost their lives, and hundreds more
disappeared. Years later, parts of the city have yet to be rebuilt.

from **After the Hurricane**

Poem by **Rita Williams-Garcia**

Parts of New Orleans are suddenly underwater, and people are left without food, power, or shelter. What will the poem's speaker—and other members of the high school band—do to get by?

ANALYZE FREE VERSE

Annotate: Mark the use of repetition in lines 1–6.

Identify Patterns: How do repetition and line length affect the poem's rhythm and create emphasis?

If toilets flushed,
if babies slept,
if faucets ran,
old bodies didn't die in the sun,
5 if none of it were real,
if we weren't in it,
this could be a disaster movie with
helicopters whipping up sky overhead,
Special Effects brought in to create Lake George
10   and not the great Mississippi
        meeting Lake Pontchartrain.
Out-of-work waiters would pose as policemen,
locals as extras paid in box lunches.
For set design, dump raw sewage, trash everywhere,
15 news trucks, patrol cars, army tanks, Humvees.

Don't forget to
Notice & Note as you
read the text.
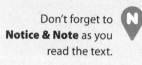

If none of it were real,
if we weren't in it,
this could be a big-budget disaster flick
King, Jasper, and I'd rent
20 after band practice
like we did last Tuesday watching *Titanic* on Grandmama's
sofa.
That Jasper could *laaaugh* at all the actors drowning
while the band played—*glub, glub, glub*—to the death.

25 But this ain't that. We're waist high in it.
Camera crews bark, "Big Mike! Get this, over here!"
"Roll tape."
"Got that?"
"Good God!"
30 "Shut it down."
This ain't hardly no picture.
We're not on location.
We're herded. Domed in,
feels like for good
35 unless you caught a bus like Ma
or Jasper's family (save Jasper).
I still want to smash a camera,
break a lens, make them stop shooting.
But King says, "No, Freddie. Gotta show it.
40 Who'd believe it without film?"

Still no running water, no food, no power, no help.
The world is here but no one's coming.
The Guard[1] is here with rifles pointed.
The Red Cross got their tables set up.
45 Weathermen, anchors,[2] reporters, meteorologists,
a fleet of black Homeland SUVs.
The world is here
but where is the water? The food? The power?
The way to Ma or Jasper's people.
50 They just herd us, split us, film us, guard us.

Close Read Screencast

**Listen to a modeled close read
of this text.**

NOTICE & NOTE
AGAIN AND AGAIN

When you notice certain images
or words being repeated in a
portion of a poem, you've found
an **Again and Again** signpost.

Notice & Note: Why is water so
significant to the speaker? Mark
words used to describe water in
lines 41–65.

Infer: Why might the author
bring this up again and again?

---

¹ **The Guard:** the National Guard of the United States, units of reserve soldiers that are
controlled by each state. The National Guard responds to both the federal (national) and
state governments for a variety of emergencies, both in this country and abroad.
² **anchors** (ăng´kərs)**:** people who organize and read the news on media newscasts
(television, radio, online); they work with a team that includes reporters and camera
operators to report the news.

No one said feed us. No one brought water.
The world is here but no one's coming.
Helicopters overhead beat up on our skies.

■ ■ ■

Miracle One.
55   King noses around the news guys,
runs back to Jasper and me.
"There's water trucks held up on the highway.
Gallons, girl! Water by the gallons.
Fresh drinking water.
60   Clean shower water.
See that, Freddie. The water company loves us.
Somebody thought to send us water."
Even with our trumpets drowned, King's chest swells.
He booms, "Brass Crew, are you with me?
65   Let's get outta here, bring back some water."

How can I leave TK and Grandmama?
How can I leave, and be happy to leave?
Watch me. Just watch me
high step on outta here
70   for the water I say I'll bring back.
Honest to God, I heard "Brass Crew" and was gone.
I heard *Elbows up,*
natural breath!
That was enough.
75   How can I leave, and be happy to leave?
Easy. As needing to breathe new air.

King's got a First Trumpet stride. Jasper walks.
I lick the salt off my bare arms,
turn to look back at the people
80   held up by canes, hugging strollers, collapsible
black and newly colored people,
women with shirts for head wraps.
Salt dries my tongue.
I turn my eyes from them and walk.
85   I don't have to tell myself
it's not a school project for Ms. LeBlanc,
"The Colored Peoples of Freddie's Diorama."[3]
Green pasted just so, around the huts just so.
The despair just right.

© Houghton Mifflin Harcourt Publishing Company

---

[3] **diorama** (dī´ə-răm´ə): a three-dimensional scene in which models of people, animals, or other objects are arranged in natural poses against a painted background.

ANALYZE FIGURATIVE LANGUAGE

Annotate: In lines 60–65, mark the use of personification.

Interpret: Why might the poet be using personification here?

ANALYZE FREE VERSE

Annotate: What questions does the speaker ask in lines 66–76? Mark the repeated questions.

Draw Conclusions: What conflict do these questions and their answers reveal?

Don't forget to
Notice & Note as you
read the text.

90   It's not my social studies diorama
depicting "Over There," across the Atlantic,
the Pacific. Bodies of water.
Way, way over there.
The refugees of the mudslides,
95   refugees of the tsunami,
refugees of Rwanda.
No. It is US. In state. In country.
Drowned but not separated by
bodies of water or by spoken language.
100   The despair is just right, no translation needed.
We are not the refugees in my social studies diorama.
We are 11th graders,
a broken brass line,
old homeowners, grandmamas, head chefs, street
105   performers, a saxophonist mourning the loss of his Selmer
horn of 43 years and wife of 38 years. We are aunties,
dry cleaners, cops' daughters, deacons, cement mixers,
auto mechanics, trombonists without trombones, quartets
scattered, communion servers, stranded freshmen, old
110   nuns, X-ray technicians, bread bakers, curators,[4] diabetics,
shrimpers,[5] dishwashers, seamstresses, brides-to-be, new
daddies, taxi drivers, principals, Cub Scouts crying, car
dealers, other dealers, hairstylists, too many babies, too
many of us to count.

ANALYZE FREE VERSE

Annotate: Catalogs, or lists of related words, give structure and rhythm to free verse. Mark the catalog in lines 102–114.

Analyze: Identify how the words in the list are related. What effect does this catalog have on the poem's meaning?

---

[4] **curators** (kyŏŏ-rā´tərz): people who manage and oversee; most often describes those who manage a museum and its collection of art or other materials.

[5] **shrimpers** (shrĭmp´ərz): people who catch shrimp—small edible sea animals with a semihard outer shell.

115 Still wearing what we had on when it hit.
When we fled,
or were wheeled, piggybacked, airlifted, carried off.
Citizens herded.
We are Ms. LeBlanc, social studies teacher, a rag wrapped
120 around her head,
And Principal Canelle. He missed that last bus.

■ ■ ■

Minor Miracle.
We walk past the Guard.
You'd think they'd see us
125 marching on outta here.
You'd think they'd stop us. Keep us domed.
But we're on the march, a broken brass line.
King, Jasper, and me, Fredericka.
King needs to lead; I need to leave.
130 Been following his lead since
band camp. Junior band. Senior band.
Box formations, flying diamonds, complicated transitions.
Jasper sticks close. A horn player, a laugher. Not a talker.
See anything to laugh about?
135 Jasper sticks close. Stays quiet. Maybe a nod.

Keeping step I would ask myself,
Aren't you ashamed? No.
Of band pride? No.
You band geek. So.
140 Aren't you ashamed? No.
You want to parade? So.
Raise your trumpet? So.
Aren't you ashamed? No.
To praise Saint Louis?
145 "Oh, when the saints go marching in?"
Aren't you ashamed? No.
Of strutting krewe[6]
On Mardi Gras? The Fourth of July?
These very streets
150 Purple and gold, bop
Stars and Stripes, bop
Aren't you ashamed?
To shake and boogie?
Aren't you ashamed?

ANALYZE FIGURATIVE LANGUAGE

Annotate: Mark the language in lines 123–133 that compares the behavior of the speaker and her friends to their behaviors in the school band.

Analyze: What idea is being developed through the poet's use of this comparison?

ANALYZE FREE VERSE

Annotate: Read lines 136–161 aloud and mark repeated words and phrases.

Analyze: How do elements of structure and meter—including line breaks, repetition, and rhythm—help convey the speaker's feelings at this point in the poem?

---

[6] **krewe** (krōō): any of several groups of people who organize and participate in the annual Mardi Gras carnival in New Orleans.

Don't forget to
Notice & Note as you
read the text.

155　To enjoy your march,
　　while Grandmama suffers
　　and no milk for TK?
　　Tell the truth. Aren't you ashamed?
　　No. I'm not ashamed.
160　I step high, elbows up.
　　Band pride.

　　King asks, "Freddie, what you thinking?"
　　I say, "I'm not thinking, King."
　　But I'm dried out on the inside.
165　Hungry talks LOUD, you know.
　　"Let's try the Beauxmart. The Food Circle. Something."

　　King knows better. He doesn't say.
　　Still, we go and find (no surprise)
　　the Beauxmart's been hit. Stripped. Smashed.
170　Forget about Food Circle and every corner grocery.
　　Nothing left but rotten milk,
　　glass shards.⁷ Loose shopping carts.
　　Jasper sighs. Grabs a cart.

　　Stomach won't shut up.
175　Talking. Knotting. Cramping. I whine,
　　"Let's go to Doolie's."
　　Again, King knows better. Still, we go,
　　almost passed right by. Didn't see it until
　　Jasper points. King sighs.
180　Check out the D in Doolie's, blown clear off.
　　The outside boarded up, chained up, locked.
　　Black and red spray-painted:
　　LOOTERS WILL BE SHOT.
　　I can't believe it.
185　Doolie who buys block tickets to home games
　　Doolie who sponsors our team bus
　　Band instruments, uniforms (all underwater),
　　Chicken bucket championships. The band eats half-price.
　　My eyes say, *Freddie, believe the spray paint:*
190　*Big Sean Doolie will shoot the looters.*
　　Yeah. Big Sean Doolie.
　　Believe.

---

⁷ **shards** (shärdz): small pieces of something that has been broken.

© Houghton Mifflin Harcourt Publishing Company • Image Credits: ©Mark Wilson/Getty Images

ANALYZE FREE VERSE

Annotate: In lines 201–208, mark repeated phrases and examples of alliteration.

Draw Conclusions: How do these elements help convey the speaker's feelings at the end of the excerpt?

King (First Trumpet) was right,
he doesn't make me (Second) like I'm second.

195 A simple, "Come on, Brass. Let's get this water."
I follow King. Jasper pushes the cart.
First, Second, Third. No bop step,
high step, no feather head shake,
no shimmy[8] front, boogie back.

200 Just walk.
"Hear that?"
Another helicopter overhead.
Another chopper stirring up the Big Empty.
Wide blades good for nothing but whirling up

205 heavy heat, heavy stink on empty streets
full of ghosts and mosquitoes.
Swat all you want. Look around.
Nothing here but us in Big Empty.

ESSENTIAL QUESTION:

What does it take to be a survivor?

Review your notes and add your thoughts to your Response Log.

TURN AND TALK

Discuss the poem's speaker, Fredericka, with a partner. What are her strengths? Her weaknesses? What advice would she give to someone in a similar situation?

---

8 **shimmy** (shĭm´ē): to do the shimmy, a dance involving rapid shaking of the body.

Assessment Practice

Answer these questions before moving on to the **Analyze the Text** section.

1. Read the excerpt from the selection. Then, answer the question.

> if none of it were real,
> if we weren't in it,
> this could be a disaster movie with
> helicopters whipping up sky overhead,
> Special Effects brought in to create Lake George
>   and not the great Mississippi
>   meeting Lake Pontchartrain. (lines 5–11)

What does the speaker mean by "if none of it were real"?

(A) Disaster movies are usually based on real events.

(B) The hurricane would make a good topic for a disaster movie.

(C) The disaster is very real, but it's so terrible that it's as if it were fictional.

(D) The hurricane never actually happened, and it is as fictional as a disaster movie.

2. This question has two parts. First, answer **Part A**, then **Part B**.

Part A

What word best describes the speaker's mood at the end of the poem?

(A) relieved

(B) hopeless

(C) frightened

(D) encouraged

Part B

What excerpt from the poem most clearly contributes to this mood?

(A) "LOOTERS WILL BE SHOT." (line 183)

(B) "A simple, 'Come on, Brass. Let's get this water.'" (line 195)

(C) "Another helicopter overhead." (line 202)

(D) "Nothing here but us in Big Empty." (line 208)

Test-Taking Strategies

Analyze the Text

Support your responses with evidence from the text.

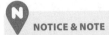
1. **INTERPRET** How does the poet use figurative language in lines 50–53 to convey meaning and tone?

2. **INFER** Identify examples of repetition in lines 66–76. How might the poet's use of repetition point to a theme in the poem?

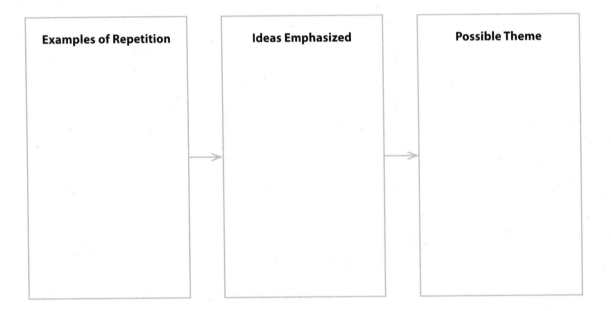

Examples of Repetition	Ideas Emphasized	Possible Theme

3. **ANALYZE** Reread lines 155–166 aloud. How do elements of free verse contribute to the pace and rhythm of the poem?

4. **DRAW CONCLUSIONS** Identify any examples of figurative language in lines 174–175. What idea might the poet be trying to express with this figurative language?

5. **ANALYZE** Identify ways in which water is mentioned throughout the poem. What ideas does the poet convey through the use of water images **Again and Again** throughout the poem?

Choices

Here are some other ways to demonstrate your understanding of the ideas in this lesson.

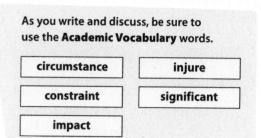

As you write and discuss, be sure to use the **Academic Vocabulary** words.

circumstance	injure
constraint	significant
impact	

Writing
↳ Write a Poem

Using "After the Hurricane" as a model, write a free verse poem describing an event that you have experienced or witnessed. Your poem can be about a disaster, an important milestone or achievement, or another experience that made an impression on you.

- Vary the length and grouping of your lines to change rhythm and meter.

- Incorporate free verse elements, such as catalogs, alliteration, and repetition.

- Include figurative language, such as similes, metaphors, and extended metaphors.

Social & Emotional Learning
↳ What Went Right?

Fredericka, the speaker in "After the Hurricane," expresses outrage and anger about how media and aid organizations react to the disaster. In a small group, list and discuss the reasons for Fredericka's anger. Then, work together to identify and analyze how King responds to her anger. What does he say? What does he do? Finally, discuss your ideas about which of the two characters, Fredericka or King, has the healthier approach to what's happening.

Speaking & Listening
↳ Responders

In a small group, discuss volunteers, professionals, and organizations that offered help in a recent disaster. What do you remember responders doing? Whom did they help? How effective were they? Use a chart like the one below to record your group's ideas. Then, share them with the class.

DISASTER:	
RESPONDERS	**DISCUSSION NOTES**

from
Ninth Ward

Novel by **Jewell Parker Rhodes**

Engage Your Brain

Choose one or more of these activities to start connecting with the story you're about to read.

Your World from Above

Close your eyes and imagine that you're viewing your neighborhood from the top of a house or tall tree. What would you see? Cars? Fences? Bicycles and toys? Write or sketch what your neighborhood would look like.

Three Very Long Days

Imagine that you and a younger friend are spending three days together—but you have no books to read, no television to watch, no games to play, and no one else to talk to. What would you do? What would you say to each other? Describe your days together.

When Things Go Wrong

When life gets difficult or frightening because things have gone wrong, people respond in very different ways. With a partner, discuss how you've seen people react to a crisis. Which reactions seem helpful? Which reactions seem to make matters worse?

Analyze Setting

The **setting** of a work of literature is the time and place of the action. In historical fiction, setting plays an especially significant role in both plot and characterization.

This story is set in one area of New Orleans during the aftermath of Hurricane Katrina. As the story's characters interact, they respond both to each other and to the setting. These interactions reveal important character traits and qualities.

Analyze Language

Mood is the feeling or atmosphere that a writer creates for readers. Descriptive words, imagery, and figurative language all influence the mood of a work. *Ninth Ward* is a first-person narrative, so the mood is created by the narrator, revealing her own feelings and character traits.

As you read, note how the narrator's use of language helps create the mood of the text, and what the mood reveals about the text's characters and theme. Use a chart like the one below.

> **Focus on Genre**
> ↳ **Historical Fiction**
>
> - is set in the past
> - includes real places and real events of historical importance
> - can be a short story or a novel
> - has the basic features of realistic fiction, including plot, characters, conflict, setting, and theme

TEXT	MOOD	MY IDEAS ABOUT CHARACTER AND THEME
TaShon lifts his head and wipes his eyes. He looks far-off.	expectant	TaShon is someone who takes time to think before speaking.

Annotation in Action

Here are one reader's notes about setting in *Ninth Ward*. As you read, note how the narrator describes the setting, revealing her own responses to it.

No land. Only sky and dirty water.

TaShon has his head buried in Spot's fur. He's crying full-out—sobbing like the world has ended and Noah hasn't landed his ark.

Sounds like a terrible place. It's as if they're trapped on a boat in the middle of the ocean— with nowhere to land.

Expand Your Vocabulary

Put a check mark next to the vocabulary words that you feel comfortable using when speaking or writing.

fortitude	☐
endure	☐
horizon	☐
angular	☐
focus	☐

Turn to a partner and talk about the vocabulary words you already know. Then, use as many words as you can in a paragraph about witnessing a flood. As you read this excerpt from *Ninth Ward*, use the definitions in the side column to learn the vocabulary words you don't already know.

Background

Jewell Parker Rhodes (b. 1954) loved to read and write as a child. *Ninth Ward* is her first published book for young people. The Ninth Ward is the largest of seventeen wards, or administrative districts, in New Orleans, and it is divided by a shipping channel and another waterway. When Hurricane Katrina struck New Orleans in 2005, the Ninth Ward received the greatest damage. Many residents died, and many others lost their homes because of the hurricane.

B

from **Ninth Ward**

Novel by **Jewell Parker Rhodes**

After the hurricane passes, Lanesha and her friend TaShon are trapped on a roof. They're hot, thirsty, and staring out at the floodwaters where their neighborhood once stood.

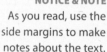

NOTICE & NOTE
As you read, use the side margins to make notes about the text.

1   No land. Only sky and dirty water.

2   TaShon has his head buried in Spot's fur. He's crying full-out—sobbing like the world has ended and Noah hasn't landed his ark.[1]

3   I want to sit and cry, too. But it's almost dawn, and I think when there's light, someone will surely find us. I also think, still dark, I've got to make sure TaShon doesn't fall off the roof into the water.

4   I feel tired, sad. Even though I expect to see her as a ghost, I know I'll still miss the flesh and blood Mama Ya-Ya.[2] The warm hands. Her making breakfast. And me resting my head upon her shoulder. I'll miss talking to her. Listening to her stories.

5   TaShon lifts his head and wipes his eyes. He looks far-off. For a minute, I think he's going to be his quiet old self, and pretend to disappear. Then, he says softly, "**Fortitude**."

6   "Strength to **endure**."

ANALYZE SETTING

Annotate: Mark words in paragraphs 1–3 that show the setting.

Identify: Which elements tell you about the place and time?

fortitude
(fôr´tĭ-tōōd) *n.* To have *fortitude* is to show strength of mind and face difficulty with courage.

endure
(ĕn-dŏŏr´) *v.* To *endure* is to carry on despite difficulty or suffering.

---

[1] **Noah hasn't landed his ark:** in the biblical flood story, Noah builds an ark, or large boat, to save his family and animals of every kind from a flood.

[2] **Mama Ya-Ya:** Lanesha's elderly caretaker who has died during the water's rise.

Ninth Ward   **439**

Annotate: Mark the words in paragraph 8 that help establish the mood of this scene.

Analyze: How would you describe the mood here?

horizon

(hə-rī′zən) *n*. The *horizon* is the intersection of the earth and sky.

angular

(ăng′gyə-lər) *adj*. Something that is angular, such as a peaked roof, has two sides that form an angle.

NOTICE & NOTE
AHA MOMENT

When you notice a sudden realization that changes a character's actions or understanding, you've found an **Aha Moment** signpost.

Notice & Note: Mark the words in paragraphs 16–19 that show Lanesha is realizing something about TaShon's character.

Analyze: How might this change things?

7   "That's right. We're going to show fortitude."

8   TaShon and I scoot closer, our arms and legs touching. I put my arms around him; he puts his arms around me. Neither of us moves. I know we are both thinking, murmuring in our minds, over and over again, "Fortitude. Fortitude. Fortitude."

9   Sunrise. As far as my eye can see, there is water.

10   The Mississippi is brown, filled with leaves, branches, and pieces of folks' lives. I see a plastic three-wheeler tangled in algae. I see a picture frame with a gap-toothed boy smiling in black and white. I see a red car, a Ford, floating.

11   Overhead, I hear a helicopter. It sounds like a lawn mower in the sky.

12   Me and TaShon start yelling, waving our hands. "Here, over here." The helicopter doesn't seem to see us. It keeps flying south. Its big bird wings circling and the roar of its engine getting softer.

13   TaShon is cursing now. I haven't the heart to say, "Watch your mouth." I'm positive the 'copter man saw us. How come he didn't stop? Lift us in the air with rope?

14   I start trembling and look around my neighborhood. The **horizon** is like none I've seen before. Just tips of houses. Tops or halves of trees. Lampposts hacked off by water. Rooftops—some flat, some **angular**—most, empty.

15   Far left, I see a man and woman sitting on a roof, their feet in the water. Two blocks east, I see what I think is an entire family. Five, six people, all different sizes, waving white sheets.[3] I hear them screaming, calling for help.

16   Where are the others? At the Superdome? Safe in Baton Rouge?[4]

17   TaShon says softly, "At least we made it out of the attic, didn't we, Lanesha?"

18   I look at TaShon. I should've known better. Should've known that there was more to see about TaShon than he ever let show. He's a butterfly, too.

19   "Yes, we did," I say. "We made it out."

20   No one is coming. All day and all night, we waited. Spot panted, slept. TaShon swatted at mosquitoes and his feet turned itchy red after he left them in the water to cool off. We are both sunburned. Funny, I didn't think black folks sunburned. But all day in the sun, no shade, has made me and TaShon red faced.

---

[3] **waving white sheets:** in wartime, soldiers wave white flags to signal their willingness to surrender to the enemy.

[4] **At the Superdome? Safe in Baton Rouge?:** the Superdome is the name of the stadium in New Orleans that sheltered Katrina refugees. Baton Rouge is Louisiana's capital, and the city to which thousands of New Orleans residents fled to escape Hurricane Katrina.

My cheeks and shoulders hurt like someone touched them with a hot iron.

21   I keep **focused** on the horizon. Above it, I search for helicopters. Below it, I search for signs of my neighbors.

22   I used to think the Mississippi was beautiful. Not anymore. Up close, it is filled with garbage; clothes and furniture, ugly catfish and eels.

23   My lips are cracked. I'm hungry. Thirsty. Tired. I tell TaShon a hundred different Bible stories—all about hope. I tell him about Moses, David and Goliath, and Noah's ark.[5] "Someone's coming," I insist. "People know we're here." But I feel Spot, if he could talk, would say, "That's a lie," then blink his big brown eyes.

24   The moon is high. TaShon is feverish and asleep. His legs, up to his knees, are bright red. His face is peeling.

25   I haven't seen any ghosts either. Are they scared?

26   I murmur, "Mama Ya-Ya, help me. Momma, help me." But the night doesn't answer. Nothing shimmers. There's no message from another world.

27   Day two since the flood. Day three since the hurricane.

28   No one has come to our rescue. There's no TV. No radio. No news from anywhere. The family that has been hollering for help is quiet now.

29   I can't make the Mississippi disappear. I can't make food and water appear. But we're going to go stir-crazy, get more and more miserable.

30   I press my head to my hand. I feel dizzy.

31   TaShon's itching, rubbing his left foot against his right leg. "Look. A rowboat."

32   I exhale. "Mr. Henri's! He liked catfish. He always gave some to Mama Ya-Ya."

33   TaShon's eyes are bright.

34   I move to the left—careful not to slip in the water, my feet angling on the roof. It's slippery. Water is in my tennis shoes. The shingles are slick with oil and gunk.

35   I can barely see the house next door. Most of it is covered with water. But a rowboat is floating, caught between our two houses and a bigger willow tree that kept it from floating down the street. It is maybe six, seven feet away. It's south, *perpendicular* to both our houses. "A sharp right angle." If it'd

Don't forget to
Notice & Note as you
read the text.
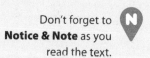

focus
(fō ́kəs) *v.* When you *focus* on something, you keep attention fixed on it.

ANALYZE LANGUAGE

Annotate: Mark the words in paragraph 23 that help show mood.

Infer: What does the mood suggest about the kind of person the narrator is?

---

[5] **Moses, David and Goliath, and Noah's ark:** in a set of stories from the Bible, Moses is directed by God to lead the Israelites out of Egypt; David is a boy who killed Goliath, a giant warrior, and later became a king; and Noah's ark is the large boat Noah built to save his family and animals from a flood.

ANALYZE SETTING

Annotate: Mark details in paragraphs 34–40 that help describe the scene.

Predict: What do these details reveal about the challenges Lanesha and TaShon now face?

been parallel, it might've floated out—at least on the north side. But the angle kept it safe.

36 "Do you think we can reach it?" asks TaShon. "The boat?"

37 I squint. The boat's rope must be floating deep, loose inside the water.

38 My arms aren't long enough to push the boat free and I'm not sure I can doggy-paddle to it.

39 "The angle's all wrong."

40 Well, right and wrong, I think. Right, 'cause being perpendicular, it didn't get swept away in the storm. Wrong, 'cause being perpendicular, it needs to be unstuck.

41 I see TaShon's shoulders sagging. Giving up.

42 How can I rescue a rowboat?

43 EVERYTHING IS MATH. Think, Lanesha.

44 I look about. There are all kinds of pieces of wood, trees floating in the water. I see a long, thin trunk floating.

45 "TaShon. We've got to catch that tree." It looks like a young willow. Just a few years old.

46 I'm sure my hands can fit around its trunk. With effort, I can hold it like a stick.

47 I lie down on my stomach, shouting, "Come on, come on!" like a lunatic to the tree. It bobs left, then right. Then turns sideways.

48 "We've got to grab it, TaShon!"

49 TaShon lies beside me on his stomach, too. We flap our hands in the water, trying to make it draw near. Trying to create another current in the muddy tide.

50 "It's coming," hollers TaShon. "It's coming."

51 "Brace yourself." Though the tree is moving slow, it'll be heavy. "Don't fall! Don't fall in."

52 I stretch my arms wide, clawing at the water, trying to move the trunk closer. I strain, feeling the pull in my shoulders. Water is lapping, almost to my chin.

53 I clutch bark. A piece cracks away in my hand.

54 "Get it, get it," TaShon screams. His arms are too short. The trunk is floating by.

55 I inch my body further, my hips and legs still touching the roof. Inhaling, I plunge forward. My arms are around the tree.

ESSENTIAL QUESTION:

What does it take to be a survivor?

Review your notes and add your thoughts to your Response Log.

TURN AND TALK

Get with a partner and discuss the story you just read. How do Lanesha and TaShon keep their hopes up, even when help seems like it'll never arrive?

Assessment Practice

Answer these questions before moving on to the **Analyze the Text** section.

1. Which excerpt suggests that Lanesha wants to be rescued?

   (A) "No land. Only sky and dirty water." (paragraph 1)

   (B) "But it's almost dawn, and I think when there's light, someone will surely find us." (paragraph 3)

   (C) "I start trembling and look around my neighborhood." (paragraph 14)

   (D) "TaShon says softly, 'At least we made it out of the attic, didn't we, Lanesha?'" (paragraph 17)

2. This question has two parts. First, answer **Part A**, then **Part B**.

   Part A

   Which theme do "After the Hurricane" and *Ninth Ward* share?

   (A) Natural disasters destroy people's lives.

   (B) Music can help people through tough times.

   (C) Young people cannot make decisions on their own.

   (D) It takes determination and courage to survive a crisis.

   Part B

   Select **two** excerpts that support the answer in Part A.

   (A) "He booms, 'Brass Crew, are you with me? / Let's get outta here, bring back some water.'" ("After the Hurricane," lines 64–65)

   (B) "I know we are both thinking, murmuring in our minds, over and over again, 'Fortitude. Fortitude. Fortitude.'" (*Ninth Ward*, paragraph 8)

   (C) "No. I'm not ashamed. / I step high, elbows up. / Band pride." ("After the Hurricane," lines 159–161)

   (D) "I say, 'I'm not thinking, King.' / But I'm dried out on the inside." ("After the Hurricane," lines 163–164)

   (E) "No one has come to our rescue. There's no TV. No radio. No news from anywhere." (*Ninth Ward*, paragraph 28)

   😊 **Ed**
   Test-Taking Strategies

Analyze the Text

Support your responses with evidence from the text.

(1) **ANALYZE** Reread paragraphs 1–3 and note details about setting and character traits. How is the historical setting related to the characters?

NOTICE & NOTE

Review what you've **noticed and noted** as you read the text. Your annotations can help you answer these questions.

(2) **DRAW CONCLUSIONS** Review the author's use of language in paragraph 8. How do mood and characterization suggest the text's theme?

(3) **SUMMARIZE** Review paragraphs 9–11. How does the text help you understand the novel's cultural setting?

(4) **COMPARE** Review paragraphs 3 and 13. How would you compare the narrator's attitude in the two passages? Explain how Lanesha's character changes over time.

Details About Narrator in Paragraph 3	Details About Narrator in Paragraph 13	Inferences About How She Has Changed

(5) **ANALYZE** Review paragraphs 36–48. What does Lanesha's **Aha Moment** reveal about their situation? Explain how Lanesha uses her realization to help TaShon overcome his sense of hopelessness.

Choices

Here are some other ways to demonstrate your understanding of the ideas in this lesson.

Writing
↳ Texts from a Rooftop

What would the narrator of *Ninth Ward* have texted to a friend if she'd had a smartphone? Imagine you're Lanesha, looking out from her rooftop, describing what she sees. Write a sequence of texts from Lanesha's point of view, directed at a friend far away.

- Use what you know about Lanesha, including her voice, personality traits, and relationship to TaShon, to describe what she sees, thinks, and feels.

- Follow spelling and grammar conventions, and use pronouns correctly. Make sure that your pronouns agree with the nouns to which they refer.

As you write and discuss, be sure to use the **Academic Vocabulary** words.

circumstance	injure
constraint	significant
impact	

Social & Emotional Learning
↳ Create a Poster

In the excerpt, Lanesha and TaShon decide to show fortitude. With a group, write your own definition of *fortitude*. Then, work together to create a poster encouraging others to develop a sense of fortitude. Illustrate your poster with your own drawings or gather images from magazines or the Internet. Use digital tools, if they're available.

Finally, present and explain your poster to the class. As other groups present, listen actively by taking notes and asking authentic questions.

Research
↳ Discover the Ninth Ward

The city of New Orleans is divided into areas called "wards." The Ninth Ward suffered badly from Hurricane Katrina. Investigate the history of the Ninth Ward, from the time before Hurricane Katrina to the present. Use a chart like the one shown to record relevant information from reliable sources.

NINTH WARD	
FACT	**SOURCE**

Expand Your Vocabulary

PRACTICE AND APPLY

Answer each question, explaining which vocabulary word is most closely related to the word in italics.

fortitude	endure	horizon
angular	focus	

1. Which vocabulary word goes with *sunset?* Why?

2. Which vocabulary word goes with *strength?* Why?

3. Which vocabulary word goes with *lasting?* Why?

4. Which vocabulary word goes with *concentrate?* Why?

5. Which vocabulary word goes with *pointed?* Why?

Vocabulary Strategy
↳ **Context Clues**

Context clues are the words and phrases surrounding a word that provide hints about its meaning. In *Ninth Ward,* the words *above it* and *below it* provide clues to the meaning of *horizon:*

☺**Ed**

Interactive Vocabulary Lesson: Using Context Clues

> I keep focused on the horizon. Above it, I search for helicopters. Below it, I search for signs of my neighbors.

PRACTICE AND APPLY

Find and list context clues for the following words and guess their meanings. Then, check your definitions in a dictionary.

WORD	CONTEXT CLUES	GUESSED DEFINITION	DEFINITION
fortitude (paragraph 5)			
endure (paragraph 6)			
angular (paragraph 14)			

Watch Your Language!

Pronouns

A **pronoun** is used in place of a noun or another pronoun.

Personal pronouns include *I, me, we, us, our, yours, she, he, they,* and *theirs,* and change form, or **case,** depending on how they function in sentences. In the independent clause, "I am hungry," *I* is in the **subjective case** and refers to the speaker. In the independent clause "Her hair is black," *her* is a **possessive pronoun,** showing whose hair is black.

Reflexive and **intensive pronouns,** such as *myself, himself, herself,* or *themselves,* reflect on or emphasize the nouns or pronouns to which they refer. In the sentence "Sheila mowed the lawn herself," *herself* is a reflexive pronoun referring to Sheila. In the sentence "The children themselves found a way to be courageous," *themselves* is an intensive pronoun emphasizing the noun *children*.

The word or words to which a pronoun refers are called **antecedents.** Pronouns must agree with their antecedents in **number, gender,** and **person.**

As you speak and write, avoid vague pronouns. In the first example below, *it* does not clearly relate to an antecedent—*it* could refer to the report, the storm, or to the flooding. In the second example, the meaning is clear:

> **The report indicated that the storm could cause flooding, and it would start soon.**

> **The report indicated that the storm could cause flooding, and the storm would start soon.**

Interactive Grammar
Lessons: Using Pronouns
Correctly

PRACTICE AND APPLY

Write sentences using each type of pronoun: personal, reflexive, and intensive. Then, share your sentences with a partner and compare your use of pronouns. Correct any vague pronouns.

_____

_____

_____

_____

Compare Across Genres

"After the Hurricane" and *Ninth Ward* use different **genres,** or types of writing, to explore the effects of Hurricane Katrina. Although the works are about a similar topic, each may express a different **theme,** or message about life or human nature. Comparing texts about a similar topic across a variety of genres can provide a deeper understanding of that topic.

With your group, complete the chart to **infer** themes based on your own knowledge and information from the text. This information may include important statements, events, and images.

	AFTER THE HURRICANE	NINTH WARD
Key Statements		
Significant Events		
Memorable Images		

Analyze the Texts

Discuss these questions in your group.

① **IDENTIFY** How are the speaker in "After the Hurricane" and the narrator in *Ninth Ward* similar?

② **COMPARE** How are the circumstances faced by the poem's speaker and the novel's narrator different? How are their responses to their circumstances different?

③ **INFER** Think about the image of helicopters in both selections. What ideas does this image suggest in each selection?

④ **DRAW CONCLUSIONS** What have you learned from these selections about what it takes to be a survivor?

Collaborate and Research

Continue exploring the ideas in the texts by developing your own guidelines for how an organization can provide help in a natural disaster. Follow these steps:

(1) **DEVELOP A RESEARCH QUESTION** In your group, brainstorm questions about how government and volunteer organizations help victims of natural disasters. Circle the most interesting questions, and then decide which group member or members will research each question.

(2) **GATHER INFORMATION** Research answers to your assigned question, avoiding plagiarism by properly citing your sources.

- **Plagiarism** is the unauthorized use of someone else's words or ideas. Plagiarism is not honest.
- Include a proper **citation** for each source you use.
- To **cite print** or **digital sources,** include author, title, and publication information, according to the style guide your teacher prefers.

Use a chart like this one to record your notes.

MY QUESTION:	
Source 1 Information: Citation:	Source 2 Information: Citation:
Ideas from the sources that answer my question:	

(3) **PRESENT FINDINGS** Share and discuss your research with your group. Use everyone's research to help develop a set of guidelines that describe how an organization can help victims of a natural disaster. Present your guidelines to the class, and include your citations.

Reader's Choice

Continue your exploration of the Essential Question by doing some independent reading on what it takes to survive a disaster. Read the titles and descriptions shown. Then mark the texts that interest you.

? **ESSENTIAL QUESTION:** *What does it take to be a survivor?*

Short Reads [Available on  Ed]

These texts are available in your ebook. Choose one to read and rate. Then defend your rating to the class.

Watcher: After Katrina, 2005

Poem by **Natasha D. Trethewey**

In the weeks following a devastating hurricane, what might you observe?

Rate It ☆☆☆☆☆

The Day I Didn't Go to the Pool

Short Story by **Leslie J. Wyatt**

An older brother must think fast in order to save his siblings.

Rate It ☆☆☆☆☆

Tuesday of the Other June

Short Story by **Norma Fox Mazer**

Relentless bullying affects all aspects of a girl's life.

Rate It ☆☆☆☆☆

In Event of Moon Disaster

Speech by **Bill Safire**

What speech would the president have given if the first moon landing had ended in disaster?

Rate It ☆☆☆☆☆

Ready: Preparing Your Pets for Emergencies Makes Sense

Informational Text by **Ready.gov**

A practical guide prepares pet owners for an emergency.

Rate It ☆☆☆☆☆

Long Reads

Here are three recommended books that connect to this unit topic. For additional options, ask your teacher, school librarian, or peers. Which titles spark your interest?

Hatchet

Novel by **Gary Paulsen**

Brian's a passenger on a small plane when something goes terribly wrong with its pilot. Brian finds himself alone in a vast, empty wilderness. His survival depends on two things: his wits and a recent gift, a small hatchet.

A Long Walk to Water

Novel by **Linda Sue Park**

Nya and Salva are both Sudanese children, but they live over twenty years apart. Based on real events and the life of Salva Dut, A Long Walk to Water tells both of their stories, describing their struggles, the dangers they face, and their eventual triumphs.

Ninth Ward

Novel by **Jewell Parker Rhodes**

As Hurricane Katrina bears down on New Orleans' Ninth Ward, twelve-year-old Lanesha—who can see ghosts—and Mama Ya-Ya have no choice but to stay and weather the storm.

Extension
↳Connect & Create

HOW WOULD YOU HAVE "SAID" IT? The Reader's Choice texts for this unit include works of fiction, nonfiction, and even a how-to article. Identify a central idea or theme from one of the texts. Then, gather with a small group, and explain the theme or central idea of the text you selected. After your explanation, discuss how *you* might have expressed that same theme or key idea. Would you have written a speech? Would you have painted a scene? Why?

BLOG A BIT Select a character from a Reader's Choice text that best illustrates the qualities of a survivor. Then, with a partner, develop a sequence of blog posts that that character might make to help others develop those qualities. Be sure to—

- Identify how the character illustrates the qualities of a survivor.

- Offer advice that the character would naturally give.

- Capture a sense of the character's voice and personality.

 NOTICE & NOTE

- Pick one of the texts and annotate the Notice & Note signposts you find.

- Then, use the **Notice & Note Writing Frames** to help you write about the significance of the signposts.

- Compare your findings with those of other students who read the same text.

Notice & Note Writing Frames

Write an Explanatory Essay

Writing Prompt

Using ideas, information, and examples from multiple texts in this unit, write an explanatory essay for a school blog in which you identify the qualities, or characteristics, of a survivor and describe why these qualities are important.

Manage your time carefully so that you can

- review the texts in the unit;
- plan your essay;
- write your essay; and
- revise and edit your essay.

Be sure to

- use and cite evidence from multiple texts;
- clearly state a central or controlling idea for your essay;
- organize your essay with smooth transitions;
- provide a strong conclusion; and
- use a formal style and an appropriate tone.

> ### Review the
> ### Mentor Text
>
> For an example of a well-written text that you can use as a mentor text, review:
>
> - **"Into the Lifeboat"** (pages 411–417)
>
> Review your notes and annotations about this text and other texts in this unit. Think about techniques the authors use to elaborate on ideas and to keep their works focused and interesting for readers.

Consider Your Sources

Review the list of texts and think about characters or real people who have survived difficult or dangerous situations. What qualities do they possess?

As you review potential sources, consult the notes you made in your **Response Log** and make additional notes about ideas that might be useful as you write your explanatory essay. Include source titles and page numbers so that you can find information again later.

UNIT 5 SOURCES

- [ ] from **A Long Walk to Water**
- [ ] **Salva's Story** `MEDIA`
- [ ] **Into the Lifeboat**
- [ ] from **After the Hurricane**
- [ ] from **Ninth Ward**

Analyze the Prompt

Analyze the prompt to make sure you understand the writing task.

Mark the sentence in the prompt that identifies the topic of your explanatory essay.

Look for words that indicate the purpose and audience for your essay, and write a sentence describing each.

Consider Your Audience

Consider these questions about your audience:

- Who will read my essay?
- What do they already know about the topic?
- How might this essay help others who face difficult or dangerous situations?

What is my topic? What is my writing task?

What is my purpose?

Who is my audience?

Review the Rubric

Your explanatory essay will be scored using a rubric. As you write, focus on the characteristics described in the chart. You will learn more about these characteristics as you work through the lesson.

PURPOSE, FOCUS, AND ORGANIZATION	DEVELOPMENT OF IDEAS	CONVENTIONS OF STANDARD ENGLISH
The response includes: • A strongly maintained controlling idea • Skillful transitions that clarify relationships among ideas • A logical progression of ideas • A satisfying introduction and conclusion • Appropriate style and tone	The response includes: • Thorough and relevant evidence • Precise references to sources • Effective use of a variety of elaborative techniques to support the central or controlling idea • Clear and effective expression of ideas • Academic and domain-specific vocabulary, where appropriate • Varied sentence structure	The response may include: • Some minor errors in usage but no patterns of errors • Effective use of punctuation, capitalization, sentence formation, and spelling • Command of basic conventions

1 PLAN YOUR EXPLANATORY ESSAY

Develop a Central or Controlling Idea

The topic of this essay is survival. To keep such a large topic manageable, focus on a single idea and three or four qualities that survivors share. After you have reviewed the texts in this unit, choose the qualities you think are most important and note them below, along with your central or controlling idea.

My central or controlling idea:	
Three or four important qualities or characteristics of survivors:	

Gather and Describe Examples

To write an effective essay, you must **describe** and **elaborate on** ideas that support your central or controlling idea.

- Use specific **examples** that "show" each quality of survivors.

- **Explain** the importance of each quality.

Use the chart to start developing support for your central or controlling idea.

Stay on Topic

As you describe and elaborate, make sure that you

- provide **relevant** details

- give information that pertains to and supports your central or controlling idea

QUALITIES OF SURVIVORS		
DESCRIPTION	**EXAMPLE**	**SOURCE**

Plan for Transitions

Review your descriptions and examples and look for connections among them. Use this chart to note the order in which you will present aspects of your topic. Take notes on how you will transition from one section to the next.

Help with Planning

Consult **Interactive Writing Lesson: Writing Informative Texts**

Quality 1:
Transition to next quality:
Quality 2:
Transition to next quality:
Quality 3:

Organize Ideas

Organize your material in a way that demonstrates coherence, a logical progression of ideas. Use the table below to help you organize your ideas.

Choose Your Structure

Essay writers can arrange paragraphs in several ways. Here are two:

- Begin with the strongest example and follow with the second strongest, and so on.
- Begin with a weaker example and build up to the most important one.

INTRODUCTION	• Grab a reader's attention with a question, an interesting quotation, or a vivid description.
	• State your central or controlling idea.
	• Give an overview of the main points you will raise.
BODY PARAGRAPHS	• Write a paragraph about each quality you have identified.
	• Cite examples so that readers understand the quality.
	• Elaborate on the significance of the quality.
CONCLUSION	• Restate your central or controlling idea, and explain its importance.
	• Close with a thought or statement that relates to and flows logically from the ideas in your essay.

2 DEVELOP A DRAFT

Now it is time to draft your essay. Looking at how experts do it is one way to develop your own writing skills. Read about the techniques that professional writers use to craft essays.

Describe and Elaborate

EXAMINE THE MENTOR TEXT

Notice how the author of "Into the Lifeboat" (pages 411–417) describes and elaborates upon the behaviors of survivors.

Into the Lifeboat

The author **describes** an extraordinary action and then notes the crowd's reaction to help **elaborate** upon its significance.

> Suddenly, the crowd of people beside me parted. A man dashed to the ship's side, and before anyone could stop him, hurled himself into the descending boat. There was a murmur of amazement and disapproval.
>
> ***
>
> Before I could do anything, young Mason hailed me and held up something, calling as he prepared to throw it, "Look after this, will you?" and I reached out to receive somebody's forgotten baby in my arms.

The author describes a simple action and then **elaborates,** revealing the seriousness of the situation.

APPLY TO YOUR DRAFT

In the chart below, use the sentence starters to practice using signal words and phrases to integrate your examples into your essay. Then use these or other approaches as you draft your essay.

Try These Suggestions

As you cite sources, keep things clear for readers:

- The first time you mention a source, state both its title and the author's name.

- In later references, you need to mention only the title *or* the author's last name to let readers know to what text you are referring.

- Use the citation style your teacher prefers.

In the excerpt from _____, the author relates _____

_____

In _____, the author's description reveals that _____

_____

The actions of _____ in the selection _____

make it clear that _____

Use Precise Language

☺ Ed

Drafting Online

Check your assignment list for a writing task from your teacher.

EXAMINE THE MENTOR TEXT

In "Into the Lifeboat," Violet Jessop uses precise language to highlight another quality of a survivor: preparedness. When Jessop first retrieves an outer garment, her action does not seem at all significant. Later, its importance becomes evident.

Early, precise details, such as feeling "chilly" and taking a "silk eiderdown," perfectly set the scene.

> I felt chilly without a coat, so I went down again for something to cover my shoulders and picked up a silk eiderdown from the first open cabin I came to.
>
> ***
>
> . . . a fireman who had evidently just come up from the stokehold . . . wearing only a thin singlet to protect him from the icy cold.

Later on, other precise language reveals that it is "icy cold," and readers realize the significance of Violet's earlier actions.

APPLY TO YOUR DRAFT

Look back at the qualities and examples you identified. In the chart, use precise language to tell when and/or why each of your qualities helps a person survive.

Quality 1:

Is vital when . . .

Is vital because . . .

Quality 2:

Is vital when . . .

Is vital because . . .

Quality 3:

Is vital when . . .

Is vital because . . .

3 REVISE YOUR ESSAY

All writers benefit from revising their ideas and language. Not even the professionals get it right the first time. Use the guide to help you revise your essay.

☺ **Ed**

Help with Revision

Find a **Peer Review Guide** and **Student Models** online.

REVISION GUIDE		
ASK YOURSELF	**PROVE IT**	**REVISE IT**
Introduction Does my introduction clearly state the central or controlling idea?	**Highlight** the central or controlling idea.	**Add** a central or controlling idea or **revise** the introduction to clarify or strengthen the idea.
Organization Are the paragraphs organized logically?	**Label** your qualities **1, 2, 3.**	**Rearrange** paragraphs to improve the flow of ideas.
Transitions Do transitions connect ideas adequately and logically?	**Circle** transitions. **Draw arrows** to show what ideas each transition connects.	**Add** or **revise** transitions so that ideas are clearly connected.
Supporting Details Do I include specific examples to illustrate each quality of a survivor? Do I include elaboration to clarify each example?	**Highlight** the example or examples for each quality. **Underline** elaboration that clarifies each example.	**Add** or **revise** examples. **Add** elaboration to clarify the significance of each example.
Style Do I consistently use a formal style and an objective tone?	**Underline** instances of informal or biased language.	**Replace** informal words and phrases. **Revise** to eliminate biased language.
Conclusion Does my conclusion follow from and connect to my essay's introduction, ideas, and examples?	**Highlight** the parts of the conclusion that state and support your central or controlling idea.	**Add** or **revise** the conclusion so that it supports and follows from the ideas in your essay.

APPLY TO YOUR DRAFT

Consider the following as you look for opportunities to improve your writing.

- Make sure that your central or controlling idea is specific and clearly stated.

- Check to ensure that your style and tone are consistent, confirming that you used formal language.

- Make sure that you used precise language to express your ideas.

Peer Review in Action

Once you have finished revising your argument, you will exchange papers with a partner in a **peer review.** During a peer review, you will give suggestions to improve your partner's draft.

Read the introduction from a student's draft and examine the comments made by a peer reviewer.

First Draft

Surviving the Unimaginable
by David Johnson, Riverside Middle School

I don't know how some people survive super dangerous situations. But I think they have special qualities, such as being determined, observant, and lucky. We can learn about these qualities from the stories that survivors tell about their frightening experiences. Then if we find ourselves in a tough spot, we can try to find these qualities within us.

To avoid a subjective and informal tone, use he, she, and they instead of I and we.

Avoid informal and slang expressions such as "super dangerous."

Your central idea is spread throughout the paragraph. Instead, state the idea concisely in one statement.

Now read the revised introduction below. Notice how the writer has improved the draft by making revisions based on the peer reviewer's comments.

Revision

If someone stumbles into a dangerous situation, will that person survive? The answer depends, in part, on what that person is like. Survival requires determination, a keen sense of observation, and luck. Although many different kinds of situations are dangerous, these three qualities can help someone survive.

Good job clarifying your central idea.

Nicely done! Now the tone and style are appropriate.

APPLY TO YOUR DRAFT

During your peer review, give each other specific suggestions for how you could make your essays clearer and more effective. Use the revision guide to help you.

When receiving feedback from your partner, listen carefully and ask questions to make sure you understand the revision suggestions.

4 EDIT YOUR ESSAY

Edit your final draft to check for proper use of standard English conventions and to correct any misspellings or grammatical errors.

Ed

Interactive Writing Lesson: Writing Informative Texts: Formal Style

Watch Your Language!

CONSISTENCY IN STYLE AND TONE

Style refers to how something is said. **Tone** is the writer's attitude toward a subject. Writing that has a consistent style and tone allows readers to focus on important ideas and content.

Read the following paragraph from "Into the Lifeboat."

> Fascinated, my eyes never left the ship. . . . [N]ow there she was, my *Titanic*, magnificent queen of the ocean, a perfection of man's handiwork, her splendid lines outlined against the night, every light twinkling.

Evaluate Style and Tone

Consider these elements as you evaluate the style and tone of your essay:

- Word choice
- Sentence structure
- Use of imagery
- Perspective and point of view

Well-chosen imagery lets readers know that the writer is both a fascinated observer and an agonized participant. The tone is solemn and respectful. Consistent style and tone keep readers focused on the magnificence of the ship and the horror of its sinking.

APPLY TO YOUR DRAFT

Now apply what you've learned about consistency in style and tone to your own work.

1. Read your essay aloud, marking words that seem out of place.

2. Fix inconsistencies in style and tone by replacing informal words with choices more suited to your essay's overall style.

3. Exchange drafts with a peer and review each other's work for consistency in style and tone.

5 PUBLISH YOUR ESSAY

Share It!

The prompt asks you to provide your ideas in the form of an essay for a school blog. You may also use your essay as inspiration for other projects.

Ways to Share

- **Hold a class debate** about the qualities of survivors. Try to agree on the three most important qualities.

- **Record a podcast** based on your essay. Invite listeners to share additional examples related to the qualities you chose.

- **Deliver a speech** about what it takes to survive. Use it to inspire your peers.

Reflect & Extend

Here are some other ways to show your understanding of the ideas in Unit 5.

Reflect on the Essential Question ?

What does it take to be a survivor?

Has your answer to the question changed after reading the texts in the unit? Discuss your ideas.

You can use these sentence starters to help you reflect on your learning.

- **I feel differently now because . . .**
- **I want to learn more about . . .**
- **I still don't understand . . .**

Writing
↳ Compare and Contrast Accounts

Find another account of a situation you've read about, such as the sinking of the *Titanic,* Hurricane Katrina, or the Lost Boys of Sudan. Compare and contrast the two accounts.

Project-Based Learning
↳ Create an Infographic

You've learned a lot about people who survive the unthinkable. Now, create an infographic to help others survive a natural disaster or emergency.

Use these steps to develop your infographic:

- Choose the type of disaster or emergency you'd like to help people face—and survive.

- Carry out some initial research to learn what professional organizations have to say about preparing for the type of disaster or emergency you've selected.

- Create your infographic, using text, images, and graphics, to guide people to a clear understanding of what they should do, should that disaster strike.

Media Projects

To find help with this task online, access **Create an Infographic.**

ASK YOURSELF	MY NOTES
How are the accounts' purposes similar? How do they differ?	
What similarities and differences are there in tone and use of language?	
How do the perspectives of the two accounts affect your understanding?	
How did reading two versions improve your understanding?	

UNIT 6

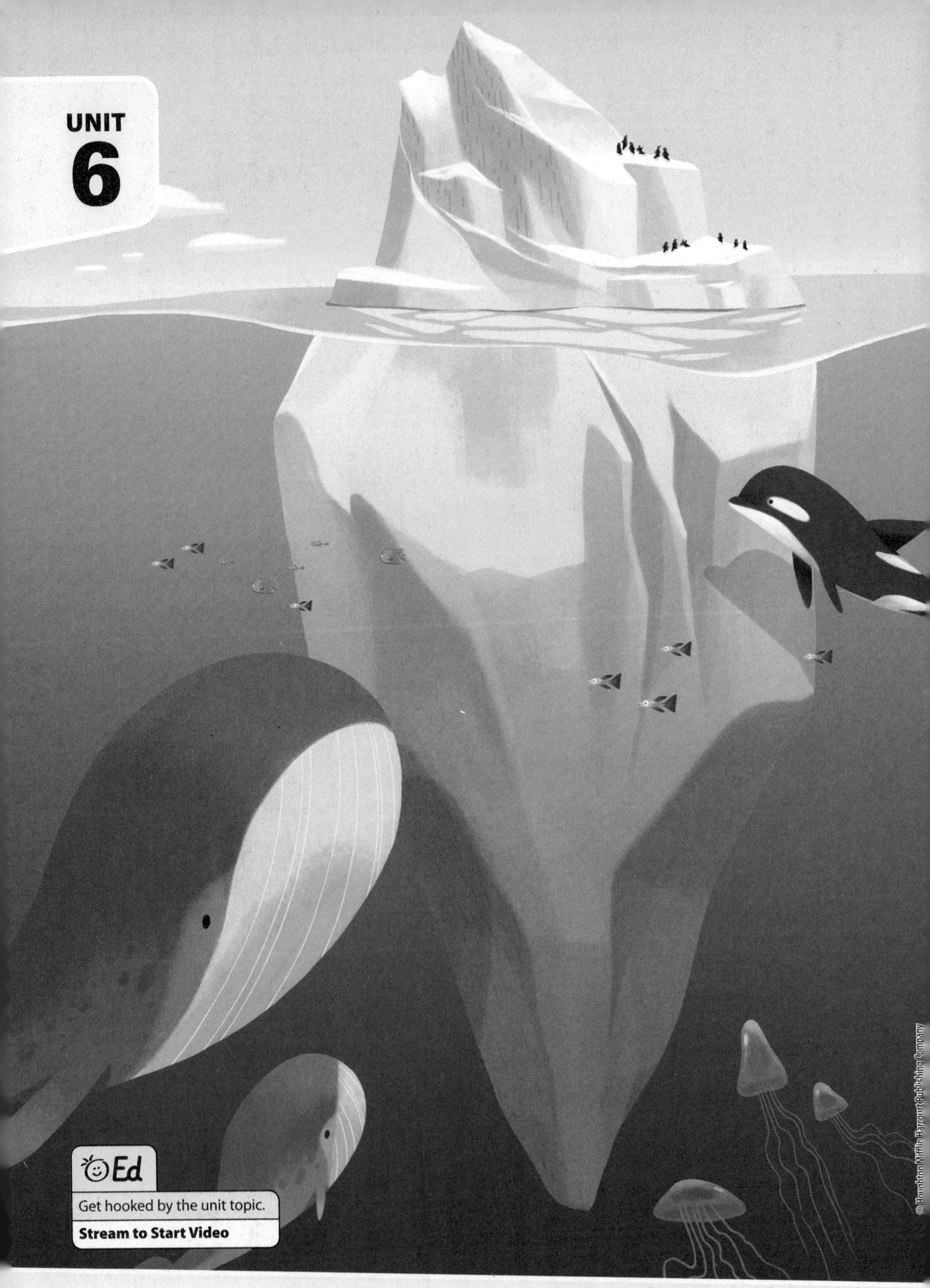

Get hooked by the unit topic.

Stream to Start Video

ESSENTIAL QUESTION:

What hidden truths about people and the world are revealed in stories?

Hidden Truths

"The destiny of the world is determined less by battles that are lost and won than by the stories it loves and believes in."
—Harold Goddard

Analyze the Image

What hidden truths are revealed in this image?

Spark Your Learning

Here's a chance to spark your learning about ideas in **Unit 6: Hidden Truths.**

As you read, you can use the **Response Log** (page R6) to track your thinking about the Essential Question.

Make the Connection

When was the last time you told a story? It may have been a story about something that happened to you or to someone you know. Think about why you told *that* story. Then, in the box below, list your ideas about why we tell stories at all.

Think About the Essential Question ?

What hidden truths about people and the world are revealed in stories?
People everywhere around the world love a good story. Why? What is it about stories that makes us want to hear, read, or watch them unfold on stage or screen? Explain your ideas about why stories are so important to us.

Prove It!

Turn to a partner and use one of the words in a sentence about things we learn from stories that we read or hear.

Sound Like an Expert ✓

You can use these Academic Vocabulary words to write and talk about the topics and themes in the unit. Which of these words do you already feel comfortable using when speaking or writing?

	I can use it!	I understand it.	I'll look it up.
emphasize	☐	☐	☐
occur	☐	☐	☐
period	☐	☐	☐
relevant	☐	☐	☐
tradition	☐	☐	☐

Preview the Texts

Look over the images, titles, and descriptions of the texts in the unit. Mark the title of the text that interests you most.

from Storytelling

Book Introduction
by **Josepha Sherman**

From scary stories told around campfires to stories meant to warn kings, human beings have been telling tales for a very, very long time. Why?

The Prince and the Pauper

by **Mark Twain**
Drama by **Joellen Bland**

The future king of England swaps outfits with one of the country's poorest subjects. Both wind up where they least expect to be.

Archetype

Poem by **Margarita Engle**

Almost every one of us loves a fairy tale or two. What might a favorite fairy tale reveal about who we are?

Fairy-tale Logic

Poem by **A. E. Stallings**

Every fairy tale tells its own story, yet there's something terribly similar about what every one of them has to say. What might that message be?

The Boatman's Flute

Folktale retold by **Sherry Garland**

A beautiful young woman falls in love with the music of a boatman's flute. She's sure she'd love the boatman, too, but she's never even seen his face.

The Mouse Bride

Folktale
retold by **Heather Forest**

A father sends his three sons off to find wives. When the sons return, he sends them back to test each of their sweethearts three times.

I Wonder . . .

What do the stories we love actually tell us about life and human nature? Write or sketch your answer.

from

Storytelling

Book Introduction by **Josepha Sherman**

Engage Your Brain

Choose one or more of these activities to start connecting with the book introduction you're about to read.

Four Little Words

Once upon a time.... You've heard or read those four little words plenty of times in your life. You know what follows them: the beginning of a story. Just for fun, start with those four little words, and finish the sentence with the opening line of a story all your own.

Story Catalog

Think about all of the stories you told today. One may have been about an adventure with a friend. Another may have been a brief little snippet about how you lost a book or couldn't find one of your shoes. List every story you remember telling. Then, next to each story on your list, explain why you told it.

Favorites

With a group, share examples of your favorite types of stories. Include stories you've read, stories you've watched, stories in songs, or stories you simply like to tell. Discuss why these types of stories appeal to you—and why you think they're likely to appeal to others.

Analyze Informational Texts

Nonfiction writers organize and present facts and ideas in a variety of ways. Analyzing sections of texts, including their organizational patterns, will help deepen your understanding of the works and their central ideas.

The selection you are about to read is a **book introduction**—a feature that provides background information and suggests a writer's purpose and perspective. As you read, analyze how the author introduces, presents, elaborates upon, and organizes information.

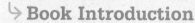

Focus on Genre

↳ **Book Introduction**

- appears before the main text
- introduces readers to the author's ideas and the purpose of the main text
- includes ideas and supporting evidence

ORGANIZATION	DESCRIPTION
Definition/Description	explains and describes new terms or ideas
Cause and Effect	explains cause-and-effect relationships
Classification	organizes by topic or type of idea
Key Ideas and Supporting Details	establishes ideas and supports them with evidence

Analyze Central Ideas

A **central idea** is a **main idea** of the text, and it is supported by key ideas. Authors may state these ideas **explicitly,** or directly. However, they may also suggest them **implicitly,** or indirectly. In such cases, readers must make **inferences**—logical guesses based on prior knowledge and the text's evidence, including facts, definitions, details, or quotations.

As you read the following text, use its evidence and structure to make inferences about its central and key ideas.

Annotation in Action

Here is an example of how one reader noted an important idea in the excerpt from *Storytelling*. As you read, remember to note other important ideas.

> Once a story has begun, there is something deep within the human psyche that must hear what will happen next. The pull of the story is universal. There is no known culture without some form of storytelling, and the craving to know "what comes next" has been felt by every human being, regardless of age, gender, culture, or century.

important point about why we love to hear stories all the way through

Expand Your Vocabulary

Put a check mark next to the vocabulary words that you feel comfortable using when speaking or writing.

universal	☐
integral	☐
invariably	☐
trance	☐
nurture	☐
chastise	☐
adversity	☐

Turn to a partner and talk about the vocabulary words you already know. Then, use as many words as you can in a paragraph about why we tell stories. As you read the excerpt from *Storytelling*, use the definitions in the side column to learn the vocabulary words you don't already know.

Background

Author and folklore expert **Josepha Sherman** (1946–2012) became interested in folktales at an early age. She loved to compare and retell folktales from around the world. Her works include *Trickster Tales: Forty Folk Stories from Around the World* and *The Shining Falcon,* which is based on Russian folklore and was awarded the 1990 Compton Cook Award for best fantasy fiction. The excerpt you are about to read is from the introduction to an encyclopedia of mythology and folklore that Sherman edited.

from
Storytelling
Book Introduction by **Josepha Sherman**

From scary stories told around campfires to stories meant to warn kings, human beings have been telling tales for a very, very long time. Why?

NOTICE & NOTE
As you read, use the side margins to make notes about the text.

Once Upon a Time . . .

1   . . . there was a story. Story openings take a number of forms: "once there was," "once there was not," "once, in the long ago days," and many others. But no matter what shape the opening words take, the result is always the same—listeners are hooked.

2   Once a story has begun, there is something deep within the human psyche[1] that must hear what will happen next. The pull of the story is **universal.** There is no known culture without some form of storytelling, and the craving[2] to know "what comes next" has been felt by every human being, regardless of age, gender, culture, or century.

universal
(yoo′nə-vûr′səl) *adj.* Something that is *universal* affects every member of a group.

---

[1] **psyche** (sī′kē): the mind, spirit, or soul.
[2] **craving** (krā′vĭng): an overwhelming urge or desire.

3   Storytelling is present in many aspects of human life. Stories are told by grandparents, parents, and other family members. Professional storytellers share their tales at fairs, festivals, schools, libraries, and other sites. Stories are **integral** to the mediums of television, film, opera, and theater, and storytelling sessions sometimes take place in the business world at special meetings. Campfire tales are meant to make campers shiver. And urban legends, contemporary folktales that usually are attributed to a "friend of a friend," are told and retold. No matter how unlikely the tale may be, the teller **invariably** insists, "It's *true!*"

Why Tell Stories?

4   The real question may be how can one *not* tell stories? Every conversation is rife[3] with information-packed stories of what the teller has been doing recently. People share stories they have heard from others, retell stories they have read, and even rehash things they have seen on television. Anyone who chooses to formalize this sharing takes on the role of the "storyteller."

---

[3] **rife** (rīf): prevalent or in widespread use.

integral

(ĭn-tĕ′grəl) *adj.* Something that is *integral* is necessary or essential for completeness.

invariably

(ĭn-vâr′ē-ə-blē) *adv.* Something that happens *invariably* occurs again and again or constantly.

© Houghton Mifflin Harcourt Publishing Company • Image Credits: ©Ian Gavan/Getty Images; (border) ©Nicetoseeya/

5   The most wonderful gift of story is the bonding of a group. Held close under the spell of a story, the group breathes as one. The shared experience softens the edges between individuals and brings everyone closer in the warmth of the moment. Together, the members of the group enter a "story **trance**." Storytellers benefit, in turn, as they experience the heartwarming feeling of holding the audience's attention and **nurturing** the group by sharing a beloved tale.

6   Many stories also serve the community in a broader sense. All societies use stories to pass on group values. Wrapped in the sweet pill of an entertaining story, a moral goes down easily. Stories also can be useful tools that allow individuals to **chastise** or expose negative behaviors without overtly speaking the truth. The Liberian storyteller Won-Ldy Paye related how Anansi spider stories have been used to "say without saying" in front of a chief. If the chief has behaved in a greedy manner, the storyteller shows Anansi in this incorrect behavior. Everyone knows whom the storyteller is talking about. The chief hears, and he knows, too.

7   Many families draw "catch-phrases" from their favorite stories, with which they can quickly refer to a story in the course of their daily lives. A phrase, such as "It don't take long to look at a horseshoe,"[4] can bring family members back to the original story, as well as remind them of the moral of the tale.

8   Communities and families also may wrap their history in stories in order to remember details of events long past. A moment in time can be preserved by creating a story and telling it a few times. The story format bundles the facts into a neatly tied packet that is more readily stored and retrieved[5] than a number of separate details.

9   Stories also help to broaden awareness of other cultures. The folktale genre, in particular, reflects many traditions and helps to familiarize people with world cultures.

10   Stories also can be used for educational purposes. Stories can help to develop a child's literary sensibilities, and listening to tales impresses a sense of story structure into a child's mind. Stories aid in stretching vocabulary, and children who are able to tell stories often gain advanced verbal ability and an increased sense of self-worth.

Don't forget to **Notice & Note** as you read the text.

trance
(trăns) *n.* When someone is in a *trance*, that person is in a daze or is daydreaming.

nurture
(nûr´chər) *v.* To *nurture* is to provide love, affection, nourishment, or something else necessary for development.

chastise
(chăs-tīz´) *v.* To *chastise* is to punish or criticize.

ANALYZE CENTRAL IDEAS

Annotate: Mark the ideas that are stated explicitly, or directly, in paragraph 7.

Infer: What inference can you make about why families use catch-phrases?

ANALYZE INFORMATIONAL TEXTS

Annotate: Mark an important idea in paragraph 10.

Summarize: What details support that idea? What organizational pattern is the author using?

---

[4] **"It don't take long to look at a horseshoe":** In an old story, a blacksmith warns a boy not to touch a hot metal horseshoe. The boy picks up the horseshoe, then quickly drops it in surprise and pain. When the blacksmith asks if the boy burned himself, the boy quickly says, "No, it just don't take me long to look at a horseshoe."
[5] **retrieve** (rĭ-trēv´): to get back or regain possession of something.

NOTICE & NOTE
QUOTED WORDS

When you notice the author citing other people to provide support for a point, you've found a **Quoted Words** signpost.

Notice & Note: Reread paragraphs 10–11. Which words in paragraph 11 tell you that an expert has been cited? Mark the words.

Analyze: Why is this person cited and what does this add?

adversity
(ăd-vûr´sĭ-tē) *n. Adversity* is misfortune or hardship.

11   Storytelling provides other growth opportunities, as stories help listeners to see through another's eyes and to share the protagonist's[6] feelings of anger, fear, or love—all from a safe place. The Austrian-born American writer and child psychologist Bruno Bettelheim explained that stories are important to children because battling difficulties through story can help them face real-life troubles. Stories provide role models who show us how to face demons and overcome **adversity.**

12   Perhaps best of all, stories stretch the imagination. The teller takes the listener to distant places where remarkable things happen. And once stretched, an imagination stays stretched.

?

ESSENTIAL QUESTION:

What hidden truths about people and the world are revealed in stories?

Review your notes and add your thoughts to your Response Log.

TURN AND TALK

With a partner, identify a passage or idea that was difficult to understand. Then, discuss it together, working to clarify its meaning.

---

[6] **protagonist** (prō-tăg´ĭ-nĭst): the leading character in a work of fiction, such as a novel or play.

Assessment Practice

Answer these questions before moving on to the **Analyze the Text** section.

1. Which **two** sentences explain the benefits and rewards of storytelling?

   A "The pull of the story is universal." (paragraph 2)

   B "Storytelling is present in many aspects of human life." (paragraph 3)

   C "The most wonderful gift of story is the bonding of a group." (paragraph 5)

   D "Everyone knows whom the storyteller is talking about." (paragraph 6)

   E "Communities and families also may wrap their history in stories in order to remember details of events long past." (paragraph 8)

2. How does paragraph 3 contribute to the development of the author's ideas?

   A by persuading readers to see more movies

   B by describing how to disprove urban legends

   C by explaining that there are three kinds of storytelling

   D by providing examples of how storytelling is part of everyone's life

3. Which sentence states an important idea of the introduction?

   A Actors make the best storytellers.

   B Storytelling is part of being human.

   C Actors were more skilled in the past.

   D Storytelling is more about entertainment than education.

Test-Taking Strategies

Analyze the Text

Support your responses with evidence from the text.

NOTICE & NOTE

Review what you **noticed and noted** as you read the text. Your annotations can help you answer these questions.

(1) **CITE EVIDENCE** Review paragraph 3. What key idea is presented in the paragraph? Cite evidence from the paragraph that supports the idea. How does the author organize the information in this paragraph?

EVIDENCE FROM PARAGRAPH 3	IDEA	ORGANIZATION

(2) **PREDICT** Reread the heading before paragraph 4. Based on the heading, what is the author's purpose for that section of the introduction? What ideas does the heading suggest the section will discuss?

(3) **EVALUATE** Review paragraphs 4–10. How does the author structure ideas in the text? How does this section fit into the overall structure of the selection?

(4) **INTERPRET** Use your annotations and what you've learned from this selection to summarize the text and determine a central idea.

(5) **ANALYZE** Review the **Quoted Words** in paragraph 6. How do the words and ideas of the expert add to the author's points about storytelling?

Choices

Here are some other ways to demonstrate your understanding of the ideas in this lesson.

As you write and discuss, be sure to use the **Academic Vocabulary** words.

| emphasize |
| occur |
| period |
| relevant |
| tradition |

Writing
↳ ## A Guide for Storytellers

Professional storytellers know how to keep an audience interested. Come up with a set of guidelines about how to tell stories to children so that they'll stay interested. Record your guidelines in the chart.

GUIDELINE	DETAILS

Speaking & Listening
↳ ## Hey, What Did it Say?

Work in a small group to identify and discuss the text's most important ideas.

- Work together to identify important ideas from the text, making sure that you can paraphrase each one, or put it into your own words.

- Ensure that every group member participates fully.

- Listen closely and respectfully to all ideas, and make sure that you understand the perspectives of all members of your group, especially those that differ from your own.

Social & Emotional Learning
↳ ## Write a Speech

Join a small group and develop a three-paragraph speech about how storytelling can help people make responsible decisions.

- Draw upon ideas stated explicitly and implicitly in *Storytelling*.

- Make sure that you cite both the author and the selection in your speech.

- Include complex sentences in your speech.

Expand Your Vocabulary

PRACTICE AND APPLY

Answer the questions to show your understanding of the vocabulary words.

1. Do you think everyone **invariably** faces **adversity?** Explain.

   _____

2. Would you ever **chastise** a friend or sibling? Explain.

   _____

3. Are stories **integral** to movies? Explain.

   _____

4. How would you **nurture** a new pet?

   _____

5. What might a person in a **trance** look like?

   _____

6. Name a **universal** idea, behavior, or experience. Explain.

   _____

Vocabulary Strategy
↳ **Context Clues**

Context clues are hints about a word's meaning that you can find in surrounding words, sentences, and paragraphs. Take a look at the following passage:

**Interactive Vocabulary
Lesson: Using Context Clues**

> **The pull of the story is <u>universal</u>. There is no known culture without some form of storytelling, and the craving to know "what comes next" has been felt by every human being. . . .**

The phrases "no known culture without" and "felt by every human being" provide clues that *universal* means "applying to everyone."

PRACTICE AND APPLY

Identify context clues that help explain the meaning of the words *trance* (paragraph 5) and *chastise* (paragraph 6). Record the clues and explain how they hint at the meaning of each word.

© Houghton Mifflin Harcourt Publishing Company

Watch Your Language!

Complex Sentences

**Interactive Grammar
Lesson: Simple Sentences
and Compound Sentences**

Writers use **complex sentences** to help clarify and connect ideas. Using complex sentences will add sentence variety and improve the flow and coherence of your writing.

- A **simple sentence** includes one independent clause and expresses a single, complete thought.

- A **compound sentence** includes two or more independent clauses.

- A **complex sentence** includes an independent clause and at least one dependent clause. A dependent clause always begins with a **subordinating conjunction,** such as *if, although, after, as, before, because, once, since, when,* and *unless.*

  Parents and grandparents sometimes share stories of their lives because they want us to avoid their mistakes.

  If the chief has behaved in a greedy manner, the storyteller shows Anansi in this incorrect behavior.

PRACTICE AND APPLY

Write your own complex sentences about the ideas explored in the selection or the importance of stories in your own life. When you have finished, compare your sentences with a partner's.

_____

_____

_____

_____

_____

_____

_____

The Prince and the Pauper

by **Mark Twain**

dramatized by **Joellen Bland**

ESSENTIAL QUESTION:
What hidden truths about people and the world are revealed in stories?

Engage Your Brain

Choose one or more of these activities to start connecting with the drama you're about to read.

Handbook for a King or Queen

What advice would you give to a child who's about to become the leader of a country? Write or sketch your response.

Stage Directions

Stage directions describe settings, actions, and how actors speak. Write stage directions describing something you did today so that an actor would know *exactly* how to perform it.

Oh, Those Royals

With a group, share what you know about England's kings, queens, princes, and princesses.

- What names do you know?

- Which of their actions can you recall?

Share your group's responses with the class.

© Houghton Mifflin Harcourt Publishing Company • Image Credits: (t) ©ferrantraite/E+/Getty Images; (c) ©nelen/

Analyze Elements of Drama

A **playwright**—a person who writes a play—uses the elements of drama to tell a story. One element, a **cast of characters,** lists each character in the drama. Important characters develop over the course of the drama, just as they do in other types of fiction.

Together, **scenes** (short episodes) and **acts** (a collection of scenes) form the basic structure of a drama's plot. As the play moves from one scene to the next, the plot unfolds and develops. Plays typically have one or more acts and several scenes.

Stage directions, which are often set in italics in a script, provide instructions to the actors, director, and stage crew. Stage directions reveal important information about characters and setting.

Dialogue is the conversation between two or more characters. Through dialogue, characters express their own thoughts, feelings, and motivations. Dialogue also reveals how characters respond and react to other characters and events in the play.

As you read, look for ways that the playwright uses the elements of drama to develop characters and plot.

Focus on Genre
 Drama

- includes a script, or the text of the play
- provides a cast of characters—a list of all characters in the play
- is divided into one or more large sections called acts and smaller sections called scenes
- tells a story through dialogue, the spoken words of characters
- includes stage directions that give instructions about performing the drama

Analyze Theme

In a play, the elements of drama come together to suggest a **theme**—a lesson about life or human nature. Playwrights introduce or expand upon important ideas through dialogue and descriptions of characters' actions. Readers can make inferences about theme based on these dramatic elements.

DIALOGUE	IDEA	POSSIBLE THEME
Tom. I have always dreamed of seeing a real Prince! . . . **1st Guard.** Mind your manners, you young beggar! (paragraphs 6–7)	Citizens are kept away from members of the royal household.	People in power should know more about the people they rule.

Annotation in Action

Here are one reader's notes about stage directions in *The Prince and the Pauper*. As you read, note other elements of drama, including dialogue, scenes, and characters.

> **Setting:** *Westminster Palace, England. Gates leading to courtyard are at right. Slightly to the left, off courtyard and inside gates, interior of palace anteroom is visible. There is a couch with a rich robe draped on it, screen at rear, bellcord, mirror, chairs, and a table with bowl of nuts, and a large golden seal on it. Piece of armor hangs on one wall. Exits are rear and downstage.*
>
> Palace, nice clothes, cord with bell to call servants, gold, armor: this is a <u>really</u> fancy room.

Expand Your Vocabulary

Put a check mark next to the vocabulary words that you feel comfortable using when speaking or writing.

wistfully	☐
anxiously	☐
discreetly	☐
rueful	☐
jest	☐
perplexed	☐

Turn to a partner and talk about the vocabulary words you already know. Then, use as many words as you can in a paragraph describing someone's actions or appearance. As you read *The Prince and the Pauper*, use the definitions in the side column to learn the vocabulary words you don't already know.

Background

Mark Twain (1835–1910) is one of America's most beloved writers. Born Samuel Clemens, he adopted his pen name when he began his writing career. He is well known for his novels *The Adventures of Tom Sawyer* and *Adventures of Huckleberry Finn*. Twain's *The Prince and the Pauper* concerns Prince Edward, King Henry VIII's son, who became king in 1547 at the age of nine. This adaptation is by **Joellen Bland,** who has been writing scripted versions of classic stories for more than 30 years.

The Prince and the Pauper

by **Mark Twain**
dramatized by **Joellen Bland**

The future king of England swaps outfits with one of the country's poorest subjects. Both wind up where they least expect to be.

NOTICE & NOTE
As you read, use the side margins to make notes about the text.

CHARACTERS

Edward, Prince of Wales
Tom Canty, the Pauper
Lord Hertford
Lord St. John
King Henry VIII
Herald
Miles Hendon
John Canty, Tom's father
Hugo, a young thief
Two Women

Justice
Constable
Jailer
Sir Hugh Hendon
Two Prisoners
Two Guards
Three Pages
Lords and Ladies
Villagers

ANALYZE ELEMENTS OF DRAMA

Annotate: Mark the characters that are given specific names.

Infer: Why do you think some characters are given names, while others are not?

❦ Scene 1 ❦

1   **Time:** *1547.*

2   **Setting:** *Westminster Palace, England. Gates leading to courtyard are at right. Slightly to the left, off courtyard and inside gates, interior of palace anteroom[1] is visible. There is a couch with a rich robe draped on it, screen at rear, bellcord, mirror, chairs, and a table with bowl of nuts, and a large golden seal on it. Piece of armor hangs on one wall. Exits are rear and downstage.*

3   **At Curtain Rise:** Two Guards—*one at right, one at left—stand in front of gates, and several* Villagers *hover nearby, straining to see into courtyard where* Prince *may be seen through fence, playing.* Two Women *enter right.*

4   **1st Woman.** I have walked all morning just to have a glimpse of Westminster Palace.

5   **2nd Woman.** Maybe if we can get near enough to the gates, we can have a glimpse of the young Prince. (Tom Canty, *dirty and ragged, comes out of crowd and steps close to gates.*)

6   **Tom.** I have always dreamed of seeing a real Prince! (*Excited, he presses his nose against gates.*)

7   **1st Guard.** Mind your manners, you young beggar! (*Seizes* Tom *by collar and sends him sprawling into crowd.* Villagers *laugh, as* Tom *slowly gets to his feet.*)

8   **Prince** (*rushing to gates*). How dare you treat a poor subject of the King in such a manner! Open the gates and let him in! (*As* Villagers *see* Prince, *they take off their hats and bow low.*)

9   **Villagers** (*shouting together*). Long live the Prince of Wales! (Guards *open gates and* Tom *slowly passes through, as if in a dream.*)

10 **Prince** (*to* Tom). You look tired, and you have been treated cruelly. I am Edward, Prince of Wales. What is your name?

11 **Tom** (*looking around in awe*). Tom Canty, Your Highness.

12 **Prince.** Come into the palace with me, Tom. (Prince *leads* Tom *into anteroom.* Villagers *pantomime[2] conversation, and all but a few exit.*) Where do you live, Tom?

13 **Tom.** In the city, Your Highness, in Offal Court.

14 **Prince.** Offal Court?[3] That is an odd name. Do you have parents?

ANALYZE THEME

Annotate: Mark the dialogue in paragraphs 6–12.

Infer: What does this conversation reveal about the character of the Prince? What important ideas are introduced?

☺Ed

Text in Focus Video

Learn more about reading stage directions.

---

[1] **anteroom** (ăn´tē-rōōm´): an outer room that leads to another room and is often used as a waiting room.

[2] **pantomime** (păn´tə-mīm´): to communicate by gestures and facial expressions.

[3] **Offal Court:** a place very poor people lived, named after the waste products from butchering animals.

482   UNIT 6   **ANALYZE & APPLY**

15 **Tom.** Yes, Your Highness.

16 **Prince.** How does your father treat you?

17 **Tom.** If it please you, Your Highness, when I am not able to beg a penny for our supper, he treats me to beatings.

18 **Prince** *(shocked).* What! Beatings? My father is not a calm man, but he does not beat me. *(looks at* Tom *thoughtfully)* You speak well and have an easy grace. Have you been schooled?

19 **Tom.** Very little, Your Highness. A good priest who shares our house in Offal Court has taught me from his books.

20 **Prince.** Do you have a pleasant life in Offal Court?

21 **Tom.** Pleasant enough, Your Highness, save when I am hungry. We have Punch and Judy shows,[4] and sometimes we lads have fights in the street.

22 **Prince** *(eagerly).* I should like that. Tell me more.

23 **Tom.** In summer, we run races and swim in the river, and we love to wallow in the mud.

24 **Prince** *(sighing, **wistfully**).* If I could wear your clothes and play in the mud just once, with no one to forbid me, I think I could give up the crown!

25 **Tom** *(shaking his head).* And if I could wear your fine clothes just once, Your Highness . . .

26 **Prince.** Would you like that? Come, then. We shall change places. You can take off your rags and put on my clothes—and I will put on yours. *(He leads* Tom *behind screen, and they return shortly, each wearing the other's clothes.)* Let's look at ourselves in this mirror. *(leads* Tom *to mirror)*

27 **Tom.** Oh, Your Highness, it is not proper for me to wear such clothes.

28 **Prince** *(excitedly, as he looks in mirror).* Heavens, do you not see it? We look like brothers! We have the same features and bearing.[5] If we went about together, dressed alike, there is no one who could say which is the Prince of Wales and which is Tom Canty!

29 **Tom** *(drawing back and rubbing his hand).* Your Highness, I am frightened. . . .

30 **Prince.** Do not worry. *(seeing* Tom *rub his hand)* Is that a bruise on your hand?

wistfully
(wĭst′fəl-ē) *adv.* When you think of something *wistfully*, you do so with sadness and longing.

ANALYZE ELEMENTS OF DRAMA

Annotate: Mark the stage directions in paragraphs 26–29.

Draw Conclusions: What is the purpose of these directions? How do they help you understand the scene?

---

[4] **Punch and Judy shows:** famous puppet show originating in 16th-century Italy, featuring Mr. Punch and his wife, Judy, who are always fighting.
[5] **features and bearing:** parts of the face and ways of standing or walking.

Tom. Yes, but it is a slight thing, Your Highness.

Prince (angrily). It was shameful and cruel of that guard to strike you. Do not stir a step until I come back. I command you! (He picks up golden Seal of England[6] and carefully puts it into piece of armor. He then dashes out to gates.) Open! Unbar the gates at once! (2nd Guard opens gates, and as Prince runs out, in rags, 1st Guard seizes him, boxes him on the ear, and knocks him to the ground.)

1st Guard. Take that, you little beggar, for the trouble you have made for me with the Prince. (Villagers roar with laughter.)

Prince (picking himself up, turning on Guard furiously). I am Prince of Wales! You shall hang for laying your hand on me!

1st Guard (presenting arms; mockingly). I salute Your Gracious Highness! (Then, angrily, 1st Guard shoves Prince roughly aside.) Be off, you mad bag of rags! (Prince is surrounded by Villagers, who hustle him off.)

Villagers (ad lib,[7] as they exit, shouting). Make way for His Royal Highness! Make way for the Prince of Wales! Hail to the Prince! (etc.)

Tom (admiring himself in mirror). If only the boys in Offal Court could see me! They will not believe me when I tell them about this. (looks around **anxiously**) But where is the Prince?

(Looks cautiously into courtyard. Two Guards immediately snap to attention and salute. He quickly ducks back into anteroom as Lords Hertford and St. John enter at rear.)

Hertford (going toward Tom, then stopping and bowing low). My Lord, you look distressed. What is wrong?

Tom (trembling). Oh, I beg of you, be merciful. I am no Prince, but poor Tom Canty of Offal Court. Please let me see the Prince, and he will give my rags back to me and let me go unhurt. (kneeling) Please, be merciful and spare me!

Hertford (puzzled and disturbed). Your Highness, on your knees? To me? (bows quickly, then, aside to St. John) The Prince has gone mad! We must inform the King. (to Tom) A moment, your Highness. (Hertford and St. John exit rear.)

Tom. Oh, there is no hope for me now. They will hang me for certain! (Hertford and St. John re-enter, supporting King. Tom watches in awe as they help him to couch, where he sinks down wearily.)

---

anxiously

(ăngk´shəs-lē) adv. To do something anxiously is to do it nervously, as if worried.

ANALYZE THEME

Annotate: Mark the stage directions and dialogue in paragraphs 38–40 that reveal Hertford's attitude toward Tom.

Analyze: What explains Hertford's behavior and attitude? What themes does this interaction suggest?

---

[6] **Seal of England:** a device used to stamp a special design, usually a picture of the ruler, onto a document, thus indicating that it has royal approval.

[7] **ad lib:** talk together about what is going on, but without an actual script.

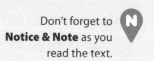

42 **King** (*beckoning* Tom *close to him*). Now, my son, Edward, my prince. What is this? Do you mean to deceive me, the King, your father, who loves you and treats you so kindly?

43 **Tom** (*dropping to his knees*). You are the King? Then I have no hope!

44 **King** (*stunned*). My child, you are not well. Do not break your father's old heart. Say you know me.

45 **Tom.** Yes, you are my lord the King, whom God preserve.

46 **King.** True, that is right. Now, you will not deny that you are Prince of Wales, as they say you did just a while ago?

47 **Tom.** I beg you, Your Grace, believe me. I am the lowest of your subjects, being born a pauper, and it is by a great mistake that I am here. I am too young to die. Oh, please, spare me, sire!

48 **King** (*amazed*). Die? Do not talk so, my child. You shall not die.

49 **Tom** (*gratefully*). God save you, my king! And now, may I go?

50 **King.** Go? Where would you go?

51 **Tom.** Back to the alley where I was born and bred to misery.

52 **King.** My poor child, rest your head here. (*He holds* Tom's *head and pats his shoulder, then turns to* Hertford *and* St. John.) Alas, I am old and ill, and my son is mad. But this shall pass. Mad or sane, he is my heir and shall rule England. Tomorrow he shall be installed and confirmed in his princely dignity! Bring the Great Seal!

53 **Hertford** (*bowing low*). Please, Your Majesty, you took the Great Seal from the Chancellor two days ago to give to His Highness the Prince.

54 **King.** So I did. (*to* Tom) My child, tell me, where is the Great Seal?

55 **Tom** (*trembling*). Indeed, my lord, I do not know.

56 **King.** Ah, your affliction[8] hangs heavily upon you. 'Tis no matter. You will remember later. Listen, carefully! (*gently, but firmly*) I command you to hide your affliction in all ways that be within your power. You shall deny to no one that you are the true prince, and if your memory should fail you upon any occasion of state, you shall be advised by your uncle, the Lord Hertford.

57 **Tom** (*resigned*). The King has spoken. The King shall be obeyed.

58 **King.** And now, my child, I go to rest. (*He stands weakly, and* Hertford *leads him off, rear.*)

ANALYZE ELEMENTS OF DRAMA

Annotate: Mark words and phrases in paragraphs 44–52 that show what Tom and the King want from one another.

Analyze: What are Tom and the King trying to accomplish? What element(s) of drama does the playwright use to express these desires?

---

[8] **affliction** (ə-flĭkʹshən): a condition that causes pain and suffering.

Annotate: Mark the stage
directions in paragraphs 60–61.

Infer: How do the Pages' actions
and Tom's reaction to them create
humor in this scene? What do we
learn about Tom's character here?

59 **Tom** (*wearily, to* St. John). May it please your lordship to let me rest now?

60 **St. John.** So it please Your Highness, it is for you to command and us to obey. But it is wise that you rest, for this evening you must attend the Lord Mayor's banquet in your honor. (*He pulls bellcord, and* Three Pages *enter and kneel before* Tom.)

61 **Tom.** Banquet? (*Terrified, he sits on couch and reaches for cup of water, but* 1st Page *instantly seizes cup, drops on one knee, and serves it to him.* Tom *starts to take off his boots, but* 2nd Page *stops him and does it for him. He tries to remove his cape and gloves, and* 3rd Page *does it for him.*) I wonder that you do not try to breathe for me also! (*Lies down cautiously.* Pages *cover him with robe, then back away and exit.*)

62 **St. John** (*to* Hertford, *as he enters*). Plainly, what do you think?

63 **Hertford.** Plainly, this. The King is near death, my nephew the Prince of Wales is clearly mad and will mount the throne mad. God protect England, for she will need it!

64 **St. John.** Does it not seem strange that madness could so change his manner from what it used to be? It troubles me, his saying he is not the Prince.

65 **Hertford.** Peace, my lord! If he were an impostor and called himself Prince, that would be natural. But was there ever an impostor, who being called Prince by the King and court, denied it? Never! This is the true Prince gone mad. And tonight all London shall honor him. (Hertford *and* St. John *exit.* Tom *sits up, looks around helplessly, then gets up.*)

ANALYZE THEME

Annotate: Mark the words and
phrases that refer to Tom's use of
the "Great Seal" of England.

Analyze: The "Great Seal" is used
as a stamp of royal approval on
official documents. What does Tom
do with the seal? Do you think
he understands the importance
of this royal object? What theme
might his action suggest?

66 **Tom.** I should have thought to order something to eat. (*sees bowl of nuts on table*) Ah! Here are some nuts! (*looks around, sees* Great Seal *in armor, takes it out, looks at it curiously*) This will make a good nutcracker. (*He takes bowl of nuts, sits on couch and begins to crack nuts with* Great Seal *and eat them, as curtain falls.*)

⌇ Scene 2 ⌇

67 **Time:** *Later that night.*

68 **Setting:** *A street in London, near Offal Court. Played before the curtain.*

69 **At Curtain Rise:** Prince *limps in, dirty and tousled. He looks around wearily. Several* Villagers *pass by, pushing against him.*

70 **Prince.** I have never seen this poor section of London. I must be near Offal Court. If I can only find it before I drop! (John Canty *steps out of crowd, seizes* Prince *roughly.*)

Canty. Out at this time of night, and I warrant you haven't brought a farthing[9] home! If that is the case and I do not break all the bones in your miserable body, then I am not John Canty!

71

Prince (*eagerly*). Oh, are you his father?

72

Canty. *His* father? I am *your* father, and—

73

Prince. Take me to the palace at once, and your son will be returned to you. The King, my father, will make you rich beyond your wildest dreams. Oh, save me, for I am indeed the Prince of Wales.

74

Canty (*staring in amazement*). Gone stark mad! But mad or not, I'll soon find where the soft places lie in your bones. Come home! (*starts to drag* Prince *off*)

75

Prince (*struggling*). Let me go! I am the Prince of Wales, and the King shall have your life for this!

76

Canty (*angrily*). I'll take no more of your madness! (*raises stick to strike, but* Prince *struggles free and runs off, and* Canty *runs after him*)

77

ꙮ Scene 3 ꙮ

Setting: *Same as Scene 1, with addition of dining table, set with dishes and goblets, on raised platform. Throne-like chair is at head of table.*

78

At Curtain Rise: *A banquet is in progress.* Tom, *in royal robes, sits at head of table, with* Hertford *at his right and* St. John *at his left.* Lords *and* Ladies *sit around table eating and talking softly.*

79

Tom (*to* Hertford). What is this, my Lord? (*holds up a plate*)

80

Hertford. Lettuce and turnips, Your Highness.

81

Tom. Lettuce and turnips? I have never seen them before. Am I to eat them?

82

Hertford (*discreetly*). Yes, Your Highness, if you so desire. (*Tom begins to eat food with his fingers. Fanfare of trumpets is heard, and* Herald *enters, carrying scroll. All turn to look.*)

83

Herald (*reading from scroll*). His Majesty, King Henry VIII, is dead! The King is dead! (*All rise and turn to* Tom, *who sits, stunned.*)

84

All (*together*). The King is dead. Long live the King! Long live Edward, King of England! (*All bow to* Tom. Herald *bows and exits.*)

85

ANALYZE ELEMENTS OF DRAMA

Annotate: Reread Scene 2. Mark the words and phrases in paragraphs 74–76 that show the Prince's offer and Canty's response.

Infer: Describe the exchange between the Prince and Canty. What is the purpose of this scene?

discreetly
(dĭ-skrēt´-lē) *adv.* To act *discreetly* means to act with self-restraint; attracting little notice.

---

[9] **farthing** (fär´thĭng): a former British coin worth one-fourth of a British penny.

86 **Hertford** (*to* Tom). Your Majesty, we must call the council. Come, St. John. (*Hertford and St. John lead Tom off at rear. Lords and Ladies follow, talking among themselves. At gates, down right, Villagers enter and mill about. Prince enters right, pounds on gates and shouts.*)

87 **Prince.** Open the gates! I am the Prince of Wales! Open, I say! And though I am friendless with no one to help me, I will not be driven from my ground.

88 **Miles Hendon** (*entering through crowd*). Though you be Prince or not, you are indeed a gallant lad and not friendless. Here I stand to prove it, and you might have a worse friend than Miles Hendon.

89 **1st Villager.** 'Tis another prince in disguise. Take the lad and dunk him in the pond! (*He seizes Prince, but Miles strikes him with flat of his sword. Crowd, now angry, presses forward threateningly, when fanfare of trumpets is heard offstage. Herald, carrying scroll, enters up left at gates.*)

90 **Herald.** Make way for the King's messenger! (*reading from scroll*) His Majesty, King Henry VIII, is dead! The King is dead! (*He exits right, repeating message, and Villagers stand in stunned silence.*)

91 **Prince** (*stunned*). The King is dead!

92 **1st Villager** (*shouting*). Long live Edward, King of England!

93 **Villagers** (*together*). Long live the King! (*shouting, ad lib*) Long live King Edward! Heaven protect Edward, King of England! (*etc.*)

ANALYZE THEME

Annotate: In paragraphs 88–89, mark words and phrases that help you understand the character of Miles Hendon.

Analyze: Describe what kind of person Miles Hendon is. What possible themes are introduced by this character?

94 **Miles** (*taking* Prince *by the arm*). Come, lad, before the crowd remembers us. I have a room at the inn, and you can stay there. (*He hurries off with stunned* Prince. Tom, *led by* Hertford, *enters courtyard up rear.* Villagers *see them.*)

95 **Villagers** (*together*). Long live the King! (*They fall to their knees as curtains close.*)

꩜ Scene 4 ꩜

96 **Setting:** Miles' *room at the inn. At right is table set with dishes and bowls of food, a chair at each side. At left is bed, with table and chair next to it, and a window. Candle is on table.*

97 **At Curtain Rise:** Miles *and* Prince *approach table.*

98 **Miles.** I have had a hot supper prepared. I'll bet you're hungry, lad.

99 **Prince.** Yes, I am. It's kind of you to let me stay with you, Miles. I am truly Edward, King of England, and you shall not go unrewarded. (*sits at table*)

100 **Miles** (*to himself*). First he called himself Prince, and now he is King. Well, I will humor him. (*starts to sit*)

101 **Prince** (*angrily*). Stop! Would you sit in the presence of the King?

102 **Miles** (*surprised, standing up quickly*). I beg your pardon, Your Majesty. I was not thinking. (*Stares uncertainly at* Prince, *who sits at table, expectantly.* Miles *starts to uncover dishes of food, serves* Prince *and fills glasses.*)

103 **Prince.** Miles, you have a gallant way about you. Are you nobly born?

104 **Miles.** My father is a baronet,[10] Your Majesty.

105 **Prince.** Then you must also be a baronet.

106 **Miles** (*shaking his head*). My father banished me from home seven years ago, so I fought in the wars. I was taken prisoner, and I have spent the past seven years in prison. Now I am free, and I am returning home.

107 **Prince.** You have been shamefully wronged! But I will make things right for you. You have saved me from injury and possible death. Name your reward and if it be within the compass of my royal power, it is yours.

108 **Miles** (*pausing briefly, then dropping to his knee*). Since Your Majesty is pleased to hold my simple duty worthy of reward, I

Don't forget to **Notice & Note** as you read the text.

ANALYZE THEME

Annotate: What is Miles's opinion of the Prince? Reread paragraphs 94–102. Then, in paragraphs 100–102, mark Miles's thoughts.

Infer: Describe how Miles treats the Prince. Have his feelings changed? If so, how?

---

[10] **baronet** (băr´ə-nĭt): a rank of honor in Britain, below a baron and above a knight.

ask that I and my successors[11] may hold the privilege of sitting in the presence of the King.

109 **Prince** (*taking* Miles' *sword, tapping him lightly on each shoulder*). Rise and seat yourself. (*returns sword to* Miles, *then rises and goes over to bed*)

110 **Miles** (*rising*). He should have been born a king. He plays the part to a marvel! If I had not thought of this favor, I might have had to stand for weeks. (*sits down and begins to eat*)

111 **Prince.** Sir Miles, you will stand guard while I sleep? (*lies down and instantly falls asleep*)

112 **Miles.** Yes, Your Majesty. (*With a **rueful** look at his uneaten supper, he stands up.*) Poor little chap. I suppose his mind has been disordered with ill usage. (*covers* Prince *with his cape*) Well, I will be his friend and watch over him. (*Blows out candle, then yawns, sits on chair next to bed, and falls asleep.* John Canty *and* Hugo *appear at window, peer around room, then enter cautiously through window. They lift the sleeping* Prince, *staring nervously at* Miles.)

113 **Canty** (*in loud whisper*). I swore the day he was born he would be a thief and a beggar, and I won't lose him now. Lead the way to the camp Hugo! (Canty *and* Hugo *carry* Prince *off right, as* Miles *sleeps on and curtain falls.*)

✌ Scene 5 ✌

114 **Time:** *Two weeks later.*

115 **Setting:** *Country village street.*

116 **Before Curtain Rise:** Villagers *walk about.* Canty, Hugo, *and* Prince *enter.*

117 **Canty.** I will go in this direction. Hugo, keep my mad son with you, and see that he doesn't escape again! (*exits*)

118 **Hugo** (*seizing* Prince *by the arm*). He won't escape! I'll see that he earns his bread today, or else!

119 **Prince** (*pulling away*). I will not beg with you, and I will not steal! I have suffered enough in this miserable company of thieves!

120 **Hugo.** You shall suffer more if you do not do as I tell you! (*raises clenched fist at* Prince) Refuse if you dare! (*Woman enters, carrying wrapped bundle in a basket on her arm.*) Wait here until I come back. (Hugo *sneaks along after* Woman, *then*

© Houghton Mifflin Harcourt Publishing Company

---

[11] **successors** (sək-sĕsʹərz): those, in sequence or line of succession, who have a right to property, to hold title or rank, or to hold the throne one after the other.

---

rueful
(rōōʹfəl) *adj.* To be *rueful* is to show sorrow or regret.

ANALYZE ELEMENTS OF DRAMA

Annotate: Mark the words and phrases in paragraph 113 that reveal Canty's motivations.

Analyze: Describe Canty's behavior and motivations. What elements of drama help develop the plot in this paragraph? How?

☺**Ed**

Close Read Screencast

Listen to a modeled close read of this text.

snatches her bundle, runs back to Prince, *and thrusts it into his arms.)* Run after me and call, "Stop, thief!" But be sure you lead her astray! *(Runs off.* Prince *throws down bundle in disgust.)*

121 **Woman.** Help! Thief! Stop, thief! *(rushes at* Prince *and seizes him, just as several* Villagers *enter)* You little thief! What do you mean by robbing a poor woman? Somebody bring the constable! *(Miles* enters and watches.)

122 **1st Villager** *(grabbing Prince).* I'll teach him a lesson, the little villain!

123 **Prince** *(struggling).* Take your hands off me! I did not rob this woman!

124 **Miles** *(stepping out of crowd and pushing man back with the flat of his sword).* Let us proceed gently, my friends. This is a matter for the law.

125 **Prince** *(springing to* Miles' *side).* You have come just in time, Sir Miles. Carve this rabble to rags!

126 **Miles.** Speak softly. Trust in me and all shall go well.

127 **Constable** *(entering and reaching for* Prince). Come along, young rascal!

128 **Miles.** Gently, good friend. He shall go peaceably to the Justice.

129 **Prince.** I will not go before a Justice! I did not do this thing!

130 **Miles** *(taking him aside).* Sire, will you reject the laws of the realm, yet demand that your subjects respect them?

131 **Prince** *(calmer).* You are right, Sir Miles. Whatever the King requires a subject to suffer under the law, he will suffer himself while he holds the station of a subject. *(Constable* leads them off right. Villagers *follow. Curtain.)*

Don't forget to **Notice & Note** as you read the text.

ANALYZE ELEMENTS OF DRAMA

Annotate: Mark words and phrases in paragraphs 124–131 that show the behavior of both Miles and the Prince.

Evaluate: How is the relationship between Miles and the Prince changing?

ꙮ Scene 6 ꙮ

132 **Setting:** *Office of the Justice. A high bench is at center.*

133 **At Curtain Rise:** Justice *sits behind bench.* Constable *enters with* Miles *and* Prince, *followed by* Villagers. Woman *carries wrapped bundle.*

134 **Constable** *(to* Justice). A young thief, your worship, is accused of stealing a dressed pig from this poor woman.

135 **Justice** *(looking down at* Prince, *then* Woman). My good woman, are you absolutely certain this lad stole your pig?

136 **Woman.** It was none other than he, your worship.

137 **Justice.** Are there no witnesses to the contrary? *(All shake their heads.)* Then the lad stands convicted. *(to* Woman) What do you hold this property to be worth?

Woman. Three shillings and eight pence, your worship.

139 **Justice** (*leaning down to* Woman). Good woman, do you know that when one steals a thing above the value of thirteen pence, the law says he shall hang for it?

140 **Woman** (*upset*). Oh, what have I done? I would not hang the poor boy for the whole world! Save me from this, your worship. What can I do?

141 **Justice** (*gravely*). You may revise the value, since it is not yet written in the record.

142 **Woman.** Then call the pig eight pence, your worship.

143 **Justice.** So be it. You may take your property and go. (Woman *starts off, and is followed by* Constable. Miles *follows them cautiously down right.*)

144 **Constable** (*stopping* Woman). Good woman, I will buy your pig from you. (*takes coins from pocket*) Here is eight pence.

145 **Woman.** Eight pence! It cost me three shillings and eight pence!

146 **Constable.** Indeed! Then come back before his worship and answer for this. The lad must hang!

147 **Woman.** No! No! Say no more. Give me the eight pence and hold your peace. (Constable *hands her coins and takes pig.* Woman *exits, angrily.* Miles *returns to bench.*)

148 **Justice.** The boy is sentenced to a fortnight[12] in the common jail. Take him away, Constable! (Justice *exits.* Prince *gives* Miles *a nervous glance.*)

149 **Miles** (*following* Constable). Good sir, turn your back a moment and let the poor lad escape. He is innocent.

150 **Constable** (*outraged*). What? You say this to me? Sir, I arrest you in—

151 **Miles.** Do not be so hasty! (*slyly*) The pig you have purchased for eight pence may cost you your neck, man.

152 **Constable** (*laughing nervously*). Ah, but I was merely **jesting** with the woman, sir.

153 **Miles.** Would the Justice think it a jest?

154 **Constable.** Good sir! The Justice has no more sympathy with a jest than a dead corpse! (***perplexed***) Very well, I will turn my back and see nothing! But go quickly! (*exits*)

© Houghton Mifflin Harcourt Publishing Company

ANALYZE THEME

Annotate: Mark words and phrases in paragraphs 134–147 that reveal the character of the Woman and the Constable.

Analyze: What important ideas about human nature do these characters introduce?

jest
(jĕst) *v.* To *jest* means to make playful remarks.

perplexed
(pər-plĕkst´) *adj.* When you are *perplexed*, you are puzzled.

---

[12] **fortnight:** fourteen days; two weeks.

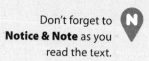

155   **Miles** (*to* Prince). Come, my liege.[13] We are free to go. And that band of thieves shall not set hands on you again, I swear it!

156   **Prince** (*wearily*). Can you believe, Sir Miles, that in the last fortnight, I, the King of England, have escaped from thieves and begged for food on the road? I have slept in a barn with a calf! I have washed dishes in a peasant's kitchen, and narrowly escaped death. And not once in all my wanderings did I see a courier[14] searching for me! Is it no matter for commotion and distress that the head of state is gone?

157   **Miles** (*sadly, aside*). Still busy with his pathetic dream. (*to* Prince) It is strange indeed, my liege. But come, I will take you to my father's home in Kent. We are not far away. There you may rest in a house with seventy rooms! Come, I am all impatience to be home again! (*They exit*, Miles *in cheerful spirits*, Prince *looking puzzled, as curtains close*.)

 Scene 7

158   **Setting:** *Village jail. Bare stage, with barred window on one wall.*

159   **At Curtain Rise:** Two Prisoners, *in chains, are onstage.* Jailer *shoves* Miles *and* Prince, *in chains, onstage. They struggle and protest.*

160   **Miles.** But I tell you, I am Miles Hendon! My brother, Sir Hugh, has stolen my bride and my estate!

161   **Jailer.** Be silent! Impostor! Sir Hugh will see that you pay well for claiming to be his dead brother and for assaulting him in his own house! (*exits*)

162   **Miles** (*sitting, with head in hands*). Oh, my dear Edith . . . now wife to my brother Hugh, against her will, and my poor father . . . dead!

163   **1st Prisoner.** At least you have your life, sir. I am sentenced to be hanged for killing a deer in the King's park.

164   **2nd Prisoner.** And I must hang for stealing a yard of cloth to dress my children.

165   **Prince** (*moved; to* Prisoners). When I mount my throne, you shall all be free. And the laws that have dishonored you shall be swept from the books. (*turning away*) Kings should go to school to learn their own laws and be merciful.

166   **1st Prisoner.** What does the lad mean? I have heard that the King is mad, but merciful.

ANALYZE ELEMENTS OF DRAMA

Annotate: Mark the stage directions in paragraph 157 that indicate to whom Miles is speaking.

Analyze: What is the purpose of each stage direction in this paragraph? What is each direction's effect on the actors and the audience?

 **NOTICE & NOTE**
AHA MOMENT

When you notice a sudden realization that shifts a character's actions or understandings, you've found an **Aha Moment** signpost.

Notice & Note: Reread paragraphs 163–165. Mark the Prince's response to the prisoners' stories.

Analyze: How might this change things?

---

[13] **my liege** (lēj): my lord.
[14] **courier** (ko͝or´ē-ər): messenger.

167 **2nd Prisoner.** He is to be crowned at Westminster tomorrow.

168 **Prince** (*violently*). King? What King, good sir?

169 **1st Prisoner.** Why, we have only one, his most sacred majesty, King Edward the Sixth.

170 **2nd Prisoner.** And whether he be mad or not, his praises are on all men's lips. He has saved many innocent lives, and now he means to destroy the cruelest laws that oppress the people.

171 **Prince** (*turning away, shaking his head*). How can this be? Surely it is not that little beggar boy! (Sir Hugh *enters with* Jailer.)

172 **Sir Hugh.** Seize the impostor!

173 **Miles** (*as* Jailer *pulls him to his feet*). Hugh, this has gone far enough!

174 **Sir Hugh.** You will sit in the public stocks for two hours, and the boy would join you if he were not so young. See to it, jailer, and after two hours, you may release them. Meanwhile, I ride to London for the coronation![15] (Sir Hugh *exits and* Miles *is hustled out by* Jailer.)

175 **Prince.** Coronation! What does he mean? There can be no coronation without me! (*curtain falls*)

© Houghton Mifflin Harcourt Publishing Company

ANALYZE THEME

Annotate: Mark the words and phrases in paragraphs 172–174 that suggest trickery on the part of Sir Hugh.

Analyze: What can you infer about Sir Hugh's character? What ideas about human nature does the dialogue suggest?

---

[15] **coronation** (kôr´ə-nā´shən): the act of crowning someone king or queen. In England, coronations usually take place at a large church in London called Westminster Abbey.

Scene 8

176 **Time:** *Coronation Day.*

177 **Setting:** *Outside gates of Westminster Abbey, played before curtain. Painted screen or flat at rear represents Abbey. Throne is in center. Bench is near it.*

178 **At Curtain Rise:** Lords *and* Ladies *crowd Abbey. Outside gates,* Guards *drive back cheering* Villagers, *among them* Miles.

179 **Miles** *(distraught).* I've lost him! Poor little chap! He has been swallowed up in the crowd! *(Fanfare of trumpets is heard, then silence.* Hertford, St. John, Lords *and* Ladies *enter slowly, in a procession, followed by* Pages, *one of whom carries crown on a small cushion.* Tom *follows procession, looking about nervously. Suddenly,* Prince, *in rags, steps out from crowd, his hand raised.)*

180 **Prince.** I forbid you to set the crown of England upon that head. I am the King!

181 **Hertford.** Seize the little vagabond!

182 **Tom.** I forbid it! He is the King! *(kneels before* Prince) Oh, my lord the King, let poor Tom Canty be the first to say, "Put on your crown and enter into your own right again." (Hertford *and several* Lords *look closely at both boys.)*

183 **Hertford.** This is strange indeed. *(to* Tom) By your favor, sir, I wish to ask certain questions of this lad.

184 **Prince.** I will answer truly whatever you may ask, my lord.

185 **Hertford.** But if you have been well trained, you may answer my questions as well as our lord the King. I need a definite proof. *(thinks a moment)* Ah! Where lies the Great Seal of England? It has been missing for weeks, and only the true Prince of Wales can say where it lies.

186 **Tom.** Wait! Was the seal round and thick, with letters engraved on it? (Hertford *nods.)* I know where it is, but it was not I who put it there. The rightful King shall tell you. *(to* Prince) Think, my King, it was the very last thing you did that day before you rushed out of the palace wearing my rags.

187 **Prince** *(pausing).* I recall how we exchanged clothes, but have no recollection[16] of hiding the Great Seal.

188 **Tom** *(eagerly).* Remember when you saw the bruise on my hand, you ran to the door, but first you hid this thing you call the Seal.

NOTICE & NOTE
AHA MOMENT

When you notice a sudden realization that shifts a character's actions or understandings, you've found an **Aha Moment** signpost.

Notice & Note: What do Tom and the Prince remember about the royal seal? In paragraphs 186–189, mark their memories.

Analyze: How might this change things?

---

[16] **recollection** (rĕk´ə-lĕk´shən): a memory or recalling to mind of something that happened before.

© Houghton Mifflin Harcourt Publishing Company

189 **Prince** *(suddenly)*. Ah! I remember! *(to* St. John*)* Go, my good St. John, and you shall find the Great Seal in the armor that hangs on the wall in my chamber. *(St. John hesitates, but at a nod from* Tom, *hurries off.)*

190 **Tom** *(pleased)*. Right, my King! Now the scepter[17] of England is yours again. *(St. John returns in a moment with Great Seal.)*

191 **All** *(shouting)*. Long live Edward, King of England! *(Tom takes off his cape and throws it over* Prince's *rags. Trumpet fanfare is heard.* St. John *takes crown and places it on* Prince. *All kneel.)*

192 **Hertford.** Let the small impostor be flung into the Tower!

ANALYZE ELEMENTS OF DRAMA

Annotate: Mark words and phrases in paragraphs 193–197 that show the feelings of Tom, Miles, and the Prince.

Analyze: What does this dialogue reveal about the characters?

193 **Prince** *(firmly)*. I will not have it so. But for him, I would not have my crown. *(to* Tom*)* My poor boy, how was it that you could remember where I hid the Seal, when I could not?

194 **Tom** *(embarrassed)*. I did not know what it was, my King, and I used it to . . . to crack nuts. *(All laugh, and* Tom *steps back.* Miles *steps forward, staring in amazement.)*

195 **Miles.** Is he really the King? Is he indeed the sovereign of England, and not the poor and friendless Tom o' Bedlam[18] I thought he was? *(He sinks down on bench.)* I wish I had a bag to hide my head in!

196 **1st Guard** *(rushing up to him)*. Stand up, you mannerless clown! How dare you sit in the presence of the King!

197 **Prince.** Do not touch him! He is my trusty servant, Miles Hendon, who saved me from shame and possible death. For his service, he owns the right to sit in my presence.

198 **Miles** *(bowing, then kneeling)*. Your Majesty!

ANALYZE THEME

Annotate: Mark words and phrases in paragraph 199 that convey the Prince's commands and the promise he makes.

Infer: What lessons about life or human nature can you infer from the Prince's speech?

199 **Prince.** Rise, Sir Miles. I command that Sir Hugh Hendon, who sits within this hall, be seized and put under lock and key until I have need of him. *(beckons to* Tom*)* From what I have heard, Tom Canty, you have governed the realm with royal gentleness and mercy in my absence. Henceforth, you shall hold the honorable title of King's Ward! *(Tom kneels and kisses* Prince's *hand.)* And because I have suffered with the poorest of my subjects and felt the cruel force of unjust laws, I pledge myself to a reign of mercy for all! *(All bow low, then rise.)*

200 **All** *(shouting)*. Long live the King! Long live Edward, King of England! *(curtain)*

---

[17] **scepter** (sĕp′tər): a staff held by a king or queen as an emblem of authority.
[18] **Tom o' Bedlam:** a mentally ill person, such as someone hospitalized at St. Mary of Bethlehem Hospital, or Bedlam Hospital, in London.

With a partner, discuss the drama you just read. Do you think the experiences of the Prince will actually change the way he will rule England? Why or why not?

ESSENTIAL QUESTION:

What hidden truths about people and the world are revealed in stories?

Review your notes and add your thoughts to your Response Log.

Assessment Practice

Answer these questions before moving on to the **Analyze the Text** section.

1. What thought is the Prince expressing when he says, "If I could wear your clothes and play in the mud just once, with no one to forbid me, I think I could give up the crown!" (paragraph 24)?

    (A) He does not enjoy wearing the heavy crown.

    (B) He understands why Tom is so jealous of royalty.

    (C) He feels that Tom should be embarrassed by the clothes he wears.

    (D) He would give up being a prince for the chance to have fun and live without rules.

2. This question has two parts. First answer **Part A**. Then, answer **Part B**.

    Part A

    Which sentence states a theme of the play?

    (A) Paupers and runaway children would make the best kings.

    (B) How well people are dressed shows what they are really like.

    (C) It is unfortunate that kings and princes must live unhappy lives.

    (D) It is important for leaders to understand the experiences of others.

    Part B

    Which sentence supports the answer to Part A?

    (A) Tom achieves his lifelong dream of becoming Prince.

    (B) The King doubts that his son will make a great leader.

    (C) After being disguised as the Prince, Tom becomes mean and willful.

    (D) After being disguised as Tom, the Prince decides that he will care for others.

Test-Taking Strategies

Analyze the Text

Support your responses with evidence from the text.

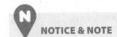

(1) **SUMMARIZE** Review paragraphs 24–34. Summarize the events leading up to the Prince being thrown out of his own palace.

(2) **CITE EVIDENCE** Do you think Tom Canty is comfortable in his new role as the Prince? Cite evidence in the dialogue and stage directions that explains why or why not.

(3) **EVALUATE** Review Scene 6. Explain how the action and dialogue affect the Prince. What important ideas and themes are developed in the scene?

(4) **INTERPRET** Give some examples of stage directions from the play that reveal information about characters. How do your examples help you understand how the characters respond or change?

TYPES	EXAMPLES FROM THE PLAY
Directions About Delivering Lines	
Directions Describing Gestures	
Directions Describing Movements	
Directions Noting How Characters Respond	

(5) **ANALYZE** In your own words, describe two **Aha Moments,** one for the Prince, the other for Tom Canty. How does the Prince's character change as a result of what he realizes while he's outside the palace? What is revealed about Tom Canty in his role as the Prince?

Choices

Here are some other ways to demonstrate your understanding of the ideas in this lesson.

Writing
↳ Character Study

Write a brief character analysis of Prince Edward, Tom Canty, Miles Hendon, or John Canty.

- Think about how the character's personality and motivations are revealed.

- Analyze how the character responds to others and to events.

- Use evidence from dialogue and stage directions to support your analysis.

- Revise and edit your analysis, using prepositions and prepositional phrases correctly.

Speaking & Listening
↳ Stage vs. Script

With a small group, rehearse and perform a portion of the play.

- Decide who will play each character, and discuss how each character's lines should be delivered.

- Rehearse together, adjusting your delivery according to stage directions and what you know about your character.

- When you perform, make eye contact, speak clearly and loudly, and pronounce words correctly.

As you watch others perform, take notes contrasting their performance with what you imagined when you read the text on your own.

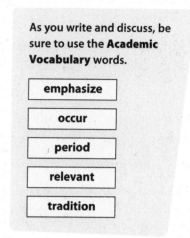

As you write and discuss, be sure to use the **Academic Vocabulary** words.

| emphasize |
| occur |
| period |
| relevant |
| tradition |

Research
↳ Will the Real Prince Edward Please Stand Up?

After the death of his father King Henry VIII, Prince Edward became king in 1547. Find out what's known about King Edward VI's childhood. Record what you discover.

KING EDWARD VI: IMPORTANT CHILDHOOD EVENTS AND PEOPLE

Expand Your Vocabulary

PRACTICE AND APPLY

Answer the questions to show your understanding of the vocabulary words.

1. If you gaze **wistfully** at a picture of a beach, do you
    want to be there or are you glad you are not? Why?

    _____

2. If someone looks **anxiously** at his watch, is he feeling
    pressed for time or relieved by the time? Why?

    _____

3. When a doctor asks to speak to you **discreetly,** is she
    trying to respect your privacy or to speak openly? Why?

    _____

4. If your friend is feeling **rueful,** should you congratulate
    or comfort your friend? Why?

    _____

5. If you and your sibling **jest** at the dinner table, are you
    making a joke or having an argument? Why?

    _____

6. If you are **perplexed** by an algebra problem, are you finding it
    hard to solve or does the solution come easily to you? Why?

    _____

Vocabulary Strategy

 ## Resources

You can use a print or online dictionary and a thesaurus to identify
synonyms and antonyms of vocabulary words. Using these
resources can help you better understand the meaning and usage
of unfamiliar words.

**Interactive Vocabulary
Lesson: Using Reference
Sources**

PRACTICE AND APPLY

Write sentences using each of these vocabulary words: *wistfully,
anxiously, discreetly, rueful, jest,* and *perplexed.* Then, use a dictionary
or thesaurus to find a synonym for each vocabulary word. Finally,
rewrite your sentences, replacing each vocabulary word with its
synonym. Has the meaning of your sentences changed? How?

Watch Your Language!

Prepositions and Prepositional Phrases

Interactive Grammar Lesson: The Prepositional Phrase

A **preposition** is a word that relates one word to another word. Some common prepositions are *at, by, for, from, in, of, on, to,* and *with.*

A **prepositional phrase** includes a preposition and a noun or pronoun—the object of the preposition. A prepositional phrase modifies or relates to another word in a sentence, telling *which one, where, why,* or *to what extent*. Prepositional phrases add detail and create imagery.

Notice the importance of these prepositions and prepositional phrases in the stage directions at the opening of Scene 4 of *The Prince and the Pauper.*

> *Miles' room at the inn. At right is table set with dishes and bowls of food, a chair at each side. At left is bed, with table and chair next to it, and a window. Candle is on table.*

The prepositional phrases add details that help readers visualize the scene.

PRACTICE AND APPLY

Think of a scene from your everyday life; for example, walking your dog, going to school, or eating dinner with your family.

Then, write stage directions for your scene using prepositions and prepositional phrases.

_____

_____

_____

_____

_____

_____

_____

Collaborate & Compare

Compare Poems

You're about to read two poems that offer interesting views of fairy tales. As you read, look for details that will help you infer themes—messages about life and the human experience.

A

Archetype

Poem by **Margarita Engle**
pages 506–509

B

Fairy-tale Logic

Poem by **A. E. Stallings**
pages 510–511

After you have read the poems, you'll get a chance to discuss and present your ideas about similarities and differences in their themes. You'll follow these steps:

- Review Ideas and Evidence
- Write Theme Statements
- Compare and Contrast Themes
- Express Your Opinions
- Present Your Group's Ideas

Archetype

Poem by **Margarita Engle**

Fairy-tale Logic

Poem by **A. E. Stallings**

Engage Your Brain

Choose one or both activities to start connecting with the poems you're about to read.

They're Just a Lot of Nonsense, Aren't They?

With a small group, identify a fairy tale with which you're familiar. It can be something old, something modern, or even something you've seen on screen. Then, talk about the purposes of that fairy tale. What is its point? Why was it told to children? Explain your group's ideas below.

A Favorite Scene

Think about fairy tales you heard or read when you were young. Which one was your favorite? Perhaps you thought it was funny. Perhaps it frightened you. Perhaps it made very little sense. What scene in that tale do you remember best? Describe or sketch that scene below.

Analyze Poetic Forms

A poem's **form,** or structure, is the way its words and lines are arranged on a page. A poem's meaning is closely tied to its form, so examining its structure will help you discover its meaning.

"Archetype" is in **free verse.** It has no regular patterns of line length, rhyme, or rhythm. To analyze free verse, pay attention to how line lengths and line breaks affect meaning, and note how ideas are arranged in **stanzas,** or groups of lines.

"Fairy-tale Logic" is a **sonnet.** Sonnets usually include 14 lines with **end rhymes,** or rhyming words at the ends of lines. Sonnet structure is also established by **meter**—usually a pattern of unstressed and stressed syllables. "Fairy-tale Logic," however, does not follow this pattern.

Many poetic forms, including free verse and sonnets, use devices such as **internal rhyme** (rhymes within lines) and **alliteration** (repetition of consonant sounds at the beginnings of words) to establish rhythm and draw attention to words and ideas.

Focus on Genre

↳ **Poetry**

- may include rhyme, rhythm, and meter
- includes line breaks and white space for effects and meaning
- may use repetition and rhyme to create a melodic quality
- often includes figurative language and a variety of poetic devices

TEXT	EXAMPLE	IMPORTANCE
I never understood all the fuss / about princesses poisoned / or rescued from dragons. ("Archetype" lines 5–7)	• princesses / poisoned / dragons = repeated *s* and *z* sounds	The repeated z sounds hiss angrily.

The p sounds make it sound as if the speaker is spitting the words out in disdain. |
| | • princesses poisoned = repeated initial consonant sounds | |

Analyze Allusions

"Fairy-tale Logic" and "Archetype" include allusions to myths, fairy tales, popular works, and biblical stories. An **allusion** is a reference to a famous person, place, event, or work of literature. Allusions connect a work's ideas to ideas in these references. Use a chart to analyze allusions.

POEM	ALLUSION	CONNECTION	POSSIBLE MEANING
"Fairy-tale Logic"	The language of snakes, perhaps, an invisible cloak. . . .	Harry Potter, can speak to snakes and has a cloak of invisibility.	We need special talents to overcome certain challenges.

Annotation in Action

The model shows one reader's notes about allusions in "Archetype." As you read, note other allusions, pausing to consider each one.

I never understood all the fuss
about princesses poisoned
or rescued from dragons.
Hansel and Gretel seemed like a recitation
of the sorrowful evening news

I know "Snow White" and "Hansel and Gretel." Those fairy tales really do talk about some pretty terrible things.

Background

Margarita Engle (b. 1951) is an award-winning Cuban American writer. She was named the Poetry Foundation's Young People's Poet Laureate for the 2017–2019 term. Among her many award-winning books are *The Surrender Tree: Poems of Cuba's Struggle for Freedom* (2008) and her verse memoir, *Enchanted Air*.

A. E. Stallings (b. 1968) is an award-winning poet, whose book *Archaic Smile* (1999) won the Richard Wilbur Award. She has studied Greek and Latin, and Greek mythology has influenced her writing, which includes sonnets, as well as other poetic forms.

Zanon/Getty Images

Archetype[1]

Poem by **Margarita Engle**

Almost every one of us loves a fairy tale or two. What might a favorite fairy tale reveal about who we are?

NOTICE & NOTE
As you read, use the side margins to make notes about the text.

ANALYZE ALLUSIONS

Annotate: In stanza 1, mark the phrase that refers to something hidden.

Connect: What is the author asking readers to consider about fairy tales?

1   Is it true that nothing reveals
    more about a person's secret heart
    than the adult memory of a favorite
    childhood fairy tale?

5   I never understood all the fuss
    about princesses poisoned
    or rescued from dragons.
    Hansel and Gretel seemed like a recitation[2]
    of the sorrowful evening news

10   a serial killer, the ovens, absent parents
    a famine, crumbs . . .

---

[1] **archetype** (är´kĭ-tīp´): model after which things are patterned; ideal type.
[2] **recitation** (rĕs´ĭ-tā´shən): a public presentation of memorized material.

Instead of magic beanstalks and man-eating giants
or wolves disguised as gentle grandmas
I chose the tale of a bird with a voice that could soothe
15 the melancholic[3] spirit of an emperor
helpless despite his wealth and power.

Of all tales, only The Nightingale[4] felt
like a story I knew before I was born
about Orpheus[5] calming wild beasts with his lyre[6]
20 King David's harp easing Saul's despair[7]
Saint Francis with his curious flocks of birds[8]
singing back and forth in a language of wishing
that even the wolf understood.

ANALYZE POETIC FORMS

Annotate: Mark alliteration and repeated sounds in lines 12–16.

Infer: How do these elements contribute to rhythm and meaning?

ANALYZE ALLUSIONS

Annotate: Mark references to music and song in the poem.

Infer: What can you infer about the meaning of music and song, especially in "The Nightingale," to the speaker?

[3] **melancholic** (mĕl´ən-kŏl´ĭk): affected with sadness or depression.
[4] **The Nightingale:** in this fairy tale by Hans Christian Andersen, the Chinese emperor prefers a mechanical nightingale until the real nightingale saves him with her song.
[5] **Orpheus** (ôr´-fē-əs): a hero from Greek mythology who played the lyre and soothed animals and trees, causing them to sway or dance.
[6] **lyre** (līr): a stringed instrument of the harp family, used to accompany a singer or speaker of poetry, especially in ancient Greece.
[7] **King David's harp easing Saul's despair:** tale from the Bible in which David played the harp to soothe Saul from the evil spirit that bothered him.
[8] **Saint Francis with his curious flocks of birds:** Saint Francis is the patron saint of animals and nature in the Catholic Church; the allusion refers to the legend of how Francis preached to birds and other animals about divine love.

ESSENTIAL QUESTION:

What hidden truths about people and the world are revealed in stories?

Review your notes and add your thoughts to your Response Log.

TURN AND TALK

With a partner, discuss the poem you just read. What point is the speaker making about what our favorite stories reveal about us? Do you agree? Why or why not?

Assessment Practice

Answer these questions before moving on to the next poem.

1. This question has two parts. First answer **Part A**. Then, answer **Part B**.

    Part A

    Which story is the most meaningful to the speaker of the poem?

    A "The Nightingale"

    B the myth of Orpheus

    C "Hansel and Gretel"

    D the tale of Saint Francis

    Part B

    Select the quotation that supports the answer in Part A.

    A "I never understood all the fuss / about princesses poisoned" (lines 5–6)

    B "Instead of magic beanstalks and man-eating giants" (line 12)

    C "I chose the tale of a bird with a voice that could soothe" (line 14)

    D "Saint Francis with his curious flocks of birds" (line 21)

2. Read the excerpt from the poem. Then, answer the question.

    > Hansel and Gretel seemed like a recitation
    > of the sorrowful evening news (lines 8–9)

    Why does the speaker compare the story of Hansel and Gretel to the news?

    A to add humor to the poem

    B to create a sad and serious mood

    C to show that the poem is about current events

    D to explain her negative feelings about the fairy tale

Test-Taking Strategies

Fairy-tale Logic

Poem by **A. E. Stallings**

NOTICE & NOTE
As you read, use the side margins to make notes about the text.

ANALYZE ALLUSIONS

Annotate: This poem alludes to some "impossible tasks." Mark lines that comment on, rather than merely list, these tasks.

Interpret: How does the author use these comments to share ideas with readers?

ANALYZE POETIC FORMS

Annotate: Mark alliteration or other repetition of sounds or words in lines 9–11.

Analyze: How do these elements affect your understanding of the poem?

Every fairy tale tells its own story, yet there's something terribly similar about what every one of them has to say. What might that message be?

Fairy tales are full of impossible tasks:
Gather the chin hairs of a man-eating goat,
Or cross a sulphuric lake[1] in a leaky boat,
Select the prince from a row of identical masks,
5 Tiptoe up to a dragon where it basks[2]
And snatch its bone; count dust specks, mote by mote,[3]
Or learn the phone directory by rote.
Always it's impossible what someone asks—

You have to fight magic with magic. You have to believe
10 That you have something impossible up your sleeve,
The language of snakes, perhaps, an invisible cloak,
An army of ants at your beck, or a lethal joke,
The will to do whatever must be done:
Marry a monster. Hand over your firstborn son.[4]

---

[1] **sulphuric lake** (sŭl-fyŏor´ĭk): a lake of sulfur, which is a pale-yellow, nonmetallic element occurring widely in nature and used to make gunpowder, rubber, medicines, etc.

[2] **basks** (băsks): relaxes, enjoying pleasant warmth.

[3] **mote** (mōt): a very small particle; a speck.

[4] **Hand over your firstborn son:** in the popular fairy tale "Rumpelstiltskin," a queen promises her firstborn son in exchange for straw spun into gold.

Get with a partner, and discuss the sonnet you just finished reading. What, according to the speaker, is the message all fairy tales share? Do you agree? Why or why not?

?

ESSENTIAL QUESTION:

What hidden truths about people and the world are revealed in stories?

Review your notes and add your thoughts to your Response Log.

Assessment Practice

Answer these questions before moving on to the **Analyze the Texts** section.

1. Which of the following sentences states an important idea that is conveyed in "Fairy-tale Logic"?

    (A) The impossible is actually possible.

    (B) Using magic is easier than you think.

    (C) Fairy tales have nothing to do with reality.

    (D) People should be brave when faced with danger.

2. Read the excerpt from "Fairy-tale Logic." Then, answer the question.

    > The will to do whatever must be done:
    > Marry a monster. Hand over your firstborn son. (lines 13–14)

    What does the phrase "hand over" mean in this context?

    (A) to hug

    (B) to punish

    (C) to protect

    (D) to give away

3. Which statement reflects an idea shared by both poems, "Archetype" and "Fairy-tale Logic"?

    (A) The best fairy tales are the ones with the happiest endings.

    (B) Fairy tales are more meaningful than children might realize.

    (C) All fairy tales have a negative message about human nature.

    (D) The most important thing about fairy tales is that we never forget them.

☺**Ed**

Test-Taking Strategies

Analyze the Texts

Support your responses with evidence from the texts.

NOTICE & NOTE

Review what you **noticed and noted** as you read the text. Your annotations can help you answer these questions.

(1) **EVALUATE** Reread lines 9–10 of the poem "Fairy-tale Logic." How would you describe the tone? Which words or phrases contribute to the tone?

(2) **SYNTHESIZE** Review stanza 1 of "Archetype." Why do you think the author begins with this particular question? What does the question reveal about the poem's speaker?

(3) **CONNECT** Reread lines 13–14 of "Fairy-tale Logic," along with the footnotes. What idea or theme do the allusions help reveal? Explain.

Allusions in Lines 13–14	Ideas Revealed by Allusions

(4) **INTERPRET** Read line 9 of "Fairy-tale Logic" aloud. Which words and syllables are stressed? What meaning does this emphasis convey?

(5) **ANALYZE** Reread stanza 2 of "Archetype." Which thoughts and ideas surprise you? What do these contrasts with your expectations reveal about the poem's speaker and theme?

Choices

Here are some other ways to demonstrate your understanding of the ideas in this lesson.

Writing
↳ Paraphrase Those Difficult Lines

Choose a set of lines in either "Archetype" or "Fairy-tale Logic" that you found especially difficult.

- Carefully reread the lines, and then write a paraphrase capturing the meaning of the lines in your own words.

- Remember that a paraphrase is similar to a summary; do not include personal opinions or judgments.

- Share and discuss your paraphrase with a partner to see if your partner can improve it.

Social & Emotional Learning
↳ Mix and Match

Work with a small group to write a messy new fairy tale. Without discussing what you will write, have each member of your group complete one of the following parts on an index card:

- Card 1: Description of a setting (time and place)
- Card 2: Description and name of a main character
- Card 3: Description of Event 1
- Card 4: Description of Event 2
- Card 5: Description of Event 3
- Card 6: Conclusion

Once you've finished, display the cards one at a time, in order. Discuss the perspectives offered by each member of your group, and then work together to create a sensible story based on what each of you has written.

Speaking & Listening
↳ Was the Story *Really* That Bad?

Each poem's speaker has *really* negative views of certain stories and fairy tales. In a small group, identify one of those stories or fairy tales. Then, discuss whether you agree with the speaker's opinion.

- Discuss the story as you remember it, as well as the speaker's opinion.

- Then, offer your own opinion, explaining why you agree or disagree with the speaker.

- Pause often to paraphrase ideas raised by group members, and make sure that you understand all perspectives, especially those that differ from your own.

Compare Poems

Poems may have similar topics but express different themes. A **topic** is the subject. The **theme** is the poem's message about life or human nature. Some themes are universal; they apply to anyone, anywhere, at any time.

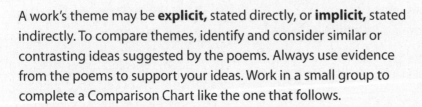

Statement of topic: **The poem is about two friends who fight a lot.**

Statement of theme: **Friendships can be difficult when personalities clash.**

A work's theme may be **explicit,** stated directly, or **implicit,** stated indirectly. To compare themes, identify and consider similar or contrasting ideas suggested by the poems. Always use evidence from the poems to support your ideas. Work in a small group to complete a Comparison Chart like the one that follows.

	ARCHETYPE	FAIRY-TALE LOGIC
Text Evidence		
Inferences About Theme		

Analyze the Texts

Discuss these questions in your group.

1. **COMPARE** Compare the approach each poet takes to draw readers into the poem. Which approach do you find more effective?

2. **INTERPRET** Each poem alludes to dragons. How do the allusions differ? How are they similar? What purpose do the allusions serve?

3. **CONNECT** Consider the kinds of fairy tales that engage the poet of "Archetype." Do you think they would inspire the poet of "Fairy-tale Logic"? Why or why not?

4. **EVALUATE** Both poems mention fairy tales and other stories. How does each poem use these references to reveal ideas and theme?

Collaborate and Present

Ideas About Theme

Your group will continue to explore the themes in these poems, using evidence to support your inferences. Follow these steps:

(1) REVIEW IDEAS AND EVIDENCE In your group, review the comparison chart you created for the poems.

(2) WRITE THEME STATEMENTS Use information from the chart to write a theme statement for each poem. Be sure to state each theme in a complete sentence.

Theme Statements:

"Archetype"

_____

_____

"Fairy-tale Logic"

_____

_____

(3) COMPARE AND CONTRAST THEMES Discuss similarities and differences in the themes you've identified.

(4) EXPRESS YOUR OPINIONS Share your personal opinions about these themes based on your knowledge and experience. Take notes on what others say. Do you agree or disagree? Identify points of agreement and disagreement and discuss them. Make sure that you understand the perspectives of all members of your group, especially perspectives that differ from your own.

(5) PRESENT YOUR GROUP'S IDEAS Share your ideas with the larger group.

Collaborate & Compare

ESSENTIAL QUESTION:
? *What hidden truths about people and the world are revealed in stories?*

Compare Themes

You're about to read two folktales from two very different cultures. As you read, notice how each tale's plot, characters, and point of view contribute to its theme.

MENTOR TEXT

A

The Boatman's Flute

Folktale retold by **Sherry Garland**
pages 520–527

B

The Mouse Bride

Folktale retold by **Heather Forest**
pages 535–543

After you have read the folktales, you'll get a chance to discuss and present your ideas about their themes. You'll follow these steps:

- Review the Lessons Learned
- Identify a Central Theme for Each Folktale
- Record Details and Evidence
- Present Your Ideas

The Boatman's Flute

Folktale retold by **Sherry Garland**

Engage Your Brain

Choose one or more of these activities to start connecting with the story you're about to read.

The Power of Music

Music can move us to tears or laughter, make us fall madly in love or encourage us to action. What's the most moving piece of music you've ever heard? What made it so powerful? Write or sketch your response below.

"Puppy" Love?

Has anyone you know ever fallen "in love" with someone they hadn't actually met? Describe what attracted them. Then, describe what happened when the two finally did—or did not—meet.

We Just Couldn't Get Along

Sometimes, when two people finally meet and learn more about each other, one of them wants nothing to do with the other one. Why does this happen? What kinds of things prevent people from building relationships once they've gotten to know each other? Discuss your answers with a small group.

Analyze Plot

A **plot** is a series of events or episodes in a story that unfold around a **conflict**—a struggle of opposing forces faced by the main character. Characters' **external** and **internal responses** to conflict, including their actions, interactions, decisions, and thoughts and feelings, help develop the plot.

PLOT STAGE	DESCRIPTION
Exposition	setting and characters established; background information provided
Rising Action	events and complications increase the conflict
Climax	conflict results in an important decision or action
Falling Action	events happen as a result of the climax
Resolution	presents how the central conflict is solved

Focus on Genre
↳ Folktale

- originates in the oral tradition of a culture
- is often set in the culture of origin
- takes place in the distant past
- includes simple but powerful themes
- focuses on human strengths and weaknesses

Explain Narrator and Point of View

The **narrator** is the voice that tells the story. A writer's choice of narrator establishes **point of view.** Use the chart to help identify and explain a story's narrator and point of view. Remember that point of view is about the story's narrator, while "perspective" concerns its characters.

FIRST-PERSON POINT OF VIEW	THIRD-PERSON POINT OF VIEW
The narrator is a character in the story.	The narrator is not a character in the story.
The narrator uses the pronouns *I, me,* and *my.*	The narrator uses the pronouns *he, she,* and *they* to refer to the characters.
The narrator does not know what other characters are thinking and feeling.	A **third-person limited** narrator knows the thoughts and feelings of just one character, usually the main character. A **third-person omniscient** narrator knows what all of the characters think and feel.

Annotation in Action

Here are one reader's notes about a stage of the plot in "The Boatman's Flute." As you read, note how the story's plot unfolds.

> Once, in the Land of Small Dragon, a wealthy mandarin lived in a large mansion on top of a hill overlooking a peaceful river. The mandarin had only one daughter, and her face was as beautiful as lotus blossoms in pale moonlight that floated atop the river.

I think this is the exposition because it introduces the story, setting, and characters.

Expand Your Vocabulary

Put a check mark next to the vocabulary words that you feel comfortable using when speaking or writing.

seamstress	☐
courtyard	☐
convince	☐
commit	☐
sincere	☐
politeness	☐

Turn to a partner and talk about the words you already know. Then, use as many words as you can in a paragraph about two people meeting for the first time. As you read "The Boatman's Flute," use the definitions in the side column to learn the vocabulary words you don't already know.

Background

Sherry Garland (b. 1948) is an award-winning author of more than thirty books for children, teens, and adults. Several of her books focus on the people and country of Vietnam, where she has traveled and done research. She also has helped Vietnamese immigrants relocate. "The Boatman's Flute" is a folktale from her book *Children of the Dragon: Selected Tales from Vietnam* (2001).

The Boatman's Flute

Folktale retold by **Sherry Garland**

A beautiful young woman falls in love with the music of a boatman's flute. She's sure she'd love the boatman, too, but she's never even seen his face.

NOTICE & NOTE
As you read, use the side margins to make notes about the text.

ANALYZE PLOT

Annotate: In paragraph 2, mark what you learn about the mandarin's relationship with his daughter.

Predict: How do you think the mandarin's actions might influence the plot?

1   Once, in the Land of Small Dragon, a wealthy mandarin[1] lived in a large mansion on top of a hill overlooking a peaceful river. The mandarin had only one daughter, and her face was as beautiful as lotus blossoms[2] in pale moonlight that floated atop the river.

2   The mandarin loved his daughter dearly and feared for her safety so much that all her life he had never allowed her to leave the mansion. She spent her days and nights in her room, high above the river, watching the world below. Servants brought her

---

[1] **mandarin** (măn´də-rĭn): a member of an elite group, especially a person having influence or high status in intellectual or cultural circles.
[2] **lotus blossoms:** flowers of the lotus, symbolic of purity.

the most delicious dishes, and talented **seamstresses** sewed her the finest gowns of silk. Musicians and poets sang to her the ballads of old.

3   But never had the beautiful girl walked barefoot on the dewy green grass nor plucked ripe fruit from a tree nor run along the banks of the river, flying kites and laughing like other children. The only sunlight that ever touched her fair skin was the few pale beams that peeked through the dappled shade in the walled-in **courtyard.**

4   One day the mandarin's daughter sat beside her window looking at the small boats and sampans[3] gliding over the peaceful blue waters below. Some were loaded with fresh fruit from the mountains, others with bags of rice or baskets of fish, and some ferried passengers back and forth across the river.

5   As she watched the activity below, one small *ghe*[4] caught her eye. The boatman stood up and skillfully steered the *ghe* out into deeper water with a long bamboo pole, then he sat down. He placed a bamboo flute to his lips and soon the most haunting, beautiful melody the girl had ever heard drifted up to her window. It was the sound of rippling waters and cool breezes, of tall bamboo and the night bird's song, all woven together. She watched the boatman, and as she listened to the sweet notes rise and fall, she imagined how young, strong, and handsome he must be.

6   All that day the mandarin's daughter stayed beside the window, until the sun began to set over the western mountain and the boatman steered his *ghe* away out of sight.

7   That night she dreamed of the strange melody and imagined herself stepping into the boat beside the young man, whose strong arms lifted her aboard with grace and ease. In her dream they drifted along the peaceful river by the light of a full moon. The boatman explained to her all the strange and wonderful sights that unfolded before them. She experienced things that she had only heard about from the poets — the sweet touch of the cool river waters on her hands trailing beside the boat, the gentle kiss of the night wind against her flushed cheeks, and the tingling fragrance of wild orchids hanging from trees in the nearby jungle.

---

[3] **sampans:** flat-bottom Asian boats usually propelled by two oars.
[4] **ghe:** a small boat.

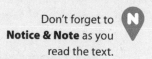
Don't forget to
Notice & Note as you
read the text.

seamstress
(sēm´strĭs) *n.* A *seamstress* is a woman who sews, especially one who earns a living sewing.

courtyard
(kôrt´yärd) *n.* A *courtyard* is an area enclosed by walls and open to the sky.

EXPLAIN NARRATOR AND POINT OF VIEW

Annotate: Review paragraphs 5–8 and mark pronouns that help you identify the folktale's point of view.

Analyze: What kind of narrator uses this point of view? How does this point of view affect your understanding? Explain.

8   A smile flickered across her lips, even as she slept. She dreamed of climbing out of the boat and running barefoot through the thick green grass and plucking wild berries that burst with a sour, tangy taste on her tongue. And when a green-eyed tiger roared deep in the jungle, the boatman held her tight.

9   The girl awakened to the sound of a brass gong. Without even stopping to taste the tray of delicacies laid out before her by her devoted handmaiden, the mandarin's daughter walked to the window and looked below. Her heart beat faster when she spotted the little boat and heard the haunting music floating up to the window once again.

10   All day she remained by the window, until she knew the tunes he played by heart. Whenever the boat came close to the foot of the hill, she dropped flower petals, hoping the wind would carry them to the boatman. If ever he looked in her direction, she waved her long silk scarf. She became **convinced** that he played the tunes just for her.

11   Every day the mandarin's daughter listened to the boatman's melodies, often making up her own words to sing along. Or she

convince

(kən-vĭns´) *v.* To *convince* is to use argument or evidence to get someone to believe or to be certain about something.

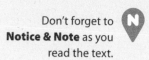

danced with her shadow, pretending it was the strong, young boatman. Every night she dreamed of riding down the peaceful river by his side. She knew that her father was planning for her to marry soon and prayed that somehow the boatman was really a lord in disguise who would be the one her father chose.

12   As for the boatman, he had seen a tiny figure at the window and had caught the petals floating down from above. He could only guess what the girl might look like or who she might be, but just knowing that she was listening made him pour his heart and soul into the melodies.

13   One day a gentleman he was ferrying across the river noticed the fine quality of the music. "Boatman, for whom do you play your little bamboo flute with such love and feeling? I see no maidens nearby."

14   The boatman smiled timidly and looked upward. "I do not know her name, but she comes to the window in that house high above the river every day and often drops flowers to show her approval."

15   The gentleman looked up toward the window, then laughed aloud. "You are a fool, young boatman. That is the mandarin's daughter—the most beautiful girl in all our land and one who is sought after by the most wealthy and powerful men, including myself. How could you be so foolish to think she would ever love a common, plain boatman like yourself?"

16   The boatman said nothing but sadly put away his flute and steered the boat down the river, for it was growing dark. *Better that I should leave now, while she is but a vision in my mind,* he told himself. *If ever I see her face, I will never have peace again.*

17   So it was that the boatman decided not to go to that part of the river anymore.

18   The next morning, when she went to the window, the mandarin's daughter did not see the small *ghe*. She thought of ten thousand excuses why the boatman might be late. As the day wore on, he still did not come. The girl's heart grew heavy and tears dropped from her dark, sad eyes. She refused to lie on her bed that night but instead knelt beside the window, staring at the dark river below.

19   Another day passed and the boatman did not come, and by nightfall the girl was weak from hunger and weeping. She soon fell ill. The servants placed her on her bed and summoned her father. The mandarin called in the best physicians, but they could find nothing wrong with her. As another day passed, the mandarin grew distraught.

ANALYZE PLOT

Annotate: Mark the words that the boatman thinks to himself in paragraph 16.

Analyze: Which part of the plot is this? How does the storyteller use this view into the boatman's thoughts—his internal response to events—to develop the plot?

EXPLAIN NARRATOR AND POINT OF VIEW

Annotate: In paragraphs 19–20, mark the sentence or sentences that focus on the handmaiden's role in this part of the story.

Analyze: How does the story's point of view affect your understanding of why the handmaiden acts as she does?

commit
(kə-mĭt´) v. To *commit* is to do or perform an action.

sincere
(sĭn-sîr´) adj. Something or someone *sincere* is genuine or heartfelt.

politeness
(pə-līt´nəs) n. *Politeness* is respectful behavior.

20   Seeing the mandarin weep over his daughter, the girl's handmaiden could not hold her tongue another moment. She told the mandarin about the boatman who played tunes on his flute that seemed to make the girl very happy. The mandarin ordered his servants to search the river for a man in a small *ghe* playing a bamboo flute.

21   Soon the men returned with the boatman and his flute. He trembled before the wealthy mandarin, wondering what crime he had **committed.**

22   "Are you the young man who has been passing under my window playing tunes upon your flute for many days past?" the mandarin demanded.

23   "Yes, but I meant no harm. If I have broken a law, it was in complete ignorance. I only played the tunes to pass the long day and because it seemed to please the girl in the window. If I disturbed your household, I beg forgiveness and promise to never bother you again."

24   "It is no bother," the mandarin replied, as he studied the **sincere** young boatman. "It seems that your simple music has charmed my daughter. Now she is deathly ill, and I pray that your tunes will restore her spirit. I have been searching the lands for the finest husband for my daughter, but if fate has something else in store, who am I to question? Play your flute again, and if my daughter chooses you above all others, then so be it."

25   The boatman stood amazed. Never in his wildest dreams had he imagined that he might become the husband of this girl so rare in beauty that no man had ever been allowed to gaze upon her face. With a surge of hope in his heart, he raised the flute to his lips with trembling fingers, and he began to play his favorite melody. Soon the tender, warm notes filled the empty halls of the grand house and reached the bed where the girl lay. In a moment she opened her eyes and a smile touched her lips.

26   "He has returned," she whispered, and she begged the handmaiden to help her to her feet. With renewed energy, the girl walked through the house to the source of the music. At first her heart pounded as she saw the strong, young man from afar. But as she came nearer and saw his face, her eyes grew cold. Though his body was young and strong, the boatman's face was ugly. Out of **politeness,** she gave a slight bow.

27 "Thank you for playing the lovely music on your flute. I feel much better now. Father, please pay the boatman for his kindness and do not worry about me. I am over my illness." Quickly she returned to her room and once again looked out the window at the boats coming and going on the river below, wondering how she could have been so foolish to dream about a simple boatman.

28 But the boatman's heart was torn apart. He had gazed on a face that men see only in their dreams. He refused to take the bag of gold the mandarin offered, and left the mansion with heavy footsteps. No longer did he have the desire to play his flute, for the music reminded him of the beautiful girl. Neither did he have the spirit to work on the peaceful river, for it, too, reminded him of the girl. Everything he saw or did caused his heart to ache with great longing for the girl that he knew could never love him. Finally, many months later, he lay down and died of a broken heart.

29 When friends and relatives prepared to send the boatman's body down the river in a farewell voyage, they saw that it was gone. But in its place, where his heart would have been, lay an exquisite piece of green jade.[5] A relative took the jade to a carver, who shaped it into a beautiful drinking goblet.

30 Sometime later the relative sold the goblet to the mandarin, who gave it to his daughter. That night the girl's handmaiden served her cool water in the new gift. As the girl lifted the jade goblet to her lips she thought she heard a melancholy tune that she had not heard for a very long time—something that was both sad and lovely. Then, as she sipped the water, she saw in the bottom of the cup the image of a small *ghe* and the young boatman steering it down the peaceful river.

31 Suddenly the girl remembered the boatman's sweet music. She thought about all the happy hours she had spent listening to his flute and the wonderful dreams she had dreamed because of him. Since he had left, no one, not even the most handsome suitors[6] in the land, had made her feel such warmth and happiness. Now, it seemed her days and nights were even longer and more empty than before.

32 Her heart ached with remorse, and tears filled her eyes.

---

[5] **green jade:** a type of jade, a precious stone, believed to promote wisdom, balance, and peace.

[6] **suitor** (sōō´tər): someone who tries to gain the love and attention of another person.

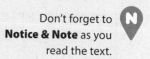

Don't forget to **Notice & Note** as you read the text.

NOTICE & NOTE
CONTRASTS AND CONTRADICTIONS

When you notice either a sharp contrast or behavior that contradicts previous behavior, you've found a **Contrasts and Contradictions** signpost.

Notice & Note: How does the girl's attitude toward the boatman change? Mark the girl's dialogue in paragraph 27.

Analyze: Why would the girl act this way?

ANALYZE PLOT

Annotate: Mark the words that the girl speaks in paragraph 33.

Analyze: Which part of the plot is this? How have the girl's interactions with the boatman affected how the plot develops?

33 "Dear boatman, your love was the truest I have ever known. You were good and kind, and I made a terrible mistake. Wherever you are, please forgive me," she whispered. A single teardrop slid down the girl's petal-smooth cheek into the goblet. When the tear touched the water, the goblet burst into pieces and a breeze suddenly rushed in through the window. The girl saw a thin wisp of fog rise from the shattered goblet and sail out into the night. The sound of a flute blended with the sound of the night bird's song, but this time the tune was full of joy. The boatman's soul was free at last to go in peace.

?

ESSENTIAL QUESTION:

What hidden truths about people and the world are revealed in stories?

Review your notes and add your thoughts to your Response Log.

TURN AND TALK

With a partner, discuss the folktale you just read. Why does the mandarin's daughter feel such sorrow at the end of the tale?

Assessment Practice

Answer these questions before moving on to the **Analyze the Text** section.

1. This question has two parts. First answer **Part A**. Then, answer **Part B**.

   Part A

   What is one reason that the boatman's music appeals to the mandarin's daughter?

   (A) The music is perfect for her wedding ceremony.

   (B) The music inspires her to write her own musical compositions.

   (C) The music reminds her of times when she floated down the river in a boat.

   (D) The music gives her dreams of experiencing the world for the first time.

   Part B

   Select the text that supports the answer in Part A.

   (A) "She experienced things that she had only heard about from the poets. . . ." (paragraph 7)

   (B) ". . . she dropped flower petals, hoping the wind would carry them to the boatman." (paragraph 10)

   (C) "She knew that her father was planning for her to marry soon and prayed that somehow the boatman was really a lord in disguise. . . ." (paragraph 11)

   (D) "The girl's heart grew heavy and tears dropped from her dark, sad eyes." (paragraph 18)

2. What happens when the mandarin's daughter drinks from the jade cup?

   (A) She drops the cup, and it shatters.

   (B) She decides to go in search of the boatman.

   (C) She realizes that she should have married the boatman.

   (D) She remembers the boatman's music and the dreams she had.

Test-Taking Strategies

Analyze the Text

Support your responses with evidence from the text.

(1) **SUMMARIZE** How does the writer build the action in paragraphs 13–18? Describe how the writer uses the narrator's point of view to create conflict in this part of the rising action.

(2) **ANALYZE** Reread paragraphs 16–17. How do the boatman's internal and external responses to conflict—his thoughts and actions—affect the development of the plot?

BOATMAN'S EXTERNAL RESPONSES TO THE CONFLICT—HIS ACTIONS	BOATMAN'S INTERNAL RESPONSES TO THE CONFLICT—HIS THOUGHTS AND FEELINGS

(3) **EVALUATE** Reread paragraphs 24–27. Consider the role of conflict at the climax of a story. In what ways can you identify this passage as the story's climax?

(4) **INTERPRET** Reread from paragraph 28 to the end of the story. Describe the falling action in the story's plot. At what point does the falling action become the story's resolution?

(5) **ANALYZE** Consider the **Contrasts and Contradictions** revealed in the daughter's behavior in paragraphs 18 and 27. Why does the character act so differently in these two parts of the story? What theme might her behavior suggest?

Choices

Here are some other ways to demonstrate your understanding of the ideas in this lesson.

Writing
↳ **Take a Different Point of View**

Retell the story from paragraph 26 through the end of paragraph 28, using the boatman as its first-person narrator. Tell what happened from the boatman's point of view.

- Be sure to include dialogue.

- Edit your work to make sure you use quotation marks correctly.

- Remember to capture the boatman's thoughts, feelings, and reactions.

When you've finished, write a brief paragraph explaining how the story differs because of this shift in point of view.

> As you write and discuss, be sure to use the **Academic Vocabulary** words.
>
> | emphasize | relevant |
> |---|---|
> | occur | tradition |
> | period | |

Social & Emotional Learning
↳ **An eCard for the Mandarin's Daughter**

When "The Boatman's Flute" ends, the mandarin's daughter is both sad and filled with regret for what has happened. Create a brief, personal eCard for the girl, explaining what she might do to overcome her feelings and how she should approach love in the future.

Research
↳ **Share What You Discover**

"The Boatman's Flute" is a Vietnamese folktale that was passed down orally from one generation to another. In a small group, find three folktales, each from a different country. Work individually to identify the topic and themes of one of your group's folktales. Once you've finished, share with the rest of the group what each of you has learned.

COUNTRY	TITLE	TOPIC / THEMES

Expand Your Vocabulary

PRACTICE AND APPLY

To show your understanding of the vocabulary words, answer each question, using a vocabulary word in a complete sentence.

seamstress	courtyard	convince
commit	sincere	politeness

1. How can you get your parents to take you and your friends out for dinner?

2. If you don't know how to sew and you tear your coat, how can you repair it?

3. Where might you find a safe place to set up a basketball hoop in a busy neighborhood with lots of street traffic?

4. What characteristic is valuable in avoiding an argument?

5. What is the opposite of being deceptive?

6. Why do drivers receive traffic violations, or tickets?

Vocabulary Strategy
↳ Word Structure

The **base** of a word is the part of the word that can stand alone. For example, the base of the word *politeness* is *polite*.

Interactive Vocabulary Lesson: Analyzing Word Structure

Many words in the English language have Greek or Latin **roots.** You can check a print or digital dictionary to learn about the roots and origins, or etymologies, of words.

An **affix** is a letter or group of letters that changes a word's meaning. Affixes can take the form of **prefixes** added to the beginning of a root or base, or **suffixes** added to the end of a root or base.

Use a dictionary to complete the chart.

WORD	BASE OF THE WORD	PREFIX OR SUFFIX	ROOT
seamstress			
commit			
sincere			

Watch Your Language!

Quotation Marks

Quotation marks set off a speaker's exact words and help distinguish narration from dialogue. For example, "The Boatman's Flute" begins with narration, and later includes dialogue between characters—set off with quotation marks—which brings variety and life to the writing.

Follow these basic rules when writing dialogue:

- Insert a period, question mark, or exclamation mark inside the end quotes, or final quotation marks.

- Insert a comma before the end quotes and name the speaker after the end quotes.

- To write a line of dialogue without naming the speaker, place the period, question mark, or exclamation point within the end quotes.

- Begin a new paragraph each time the speaker changes.

ⓔ **Ed**

Interactive Grammar Lesson: Quotation Marks

"Please stop doing that annoying quote marks thing."

PRACTICE AND APPLY

Reread the dialogue between the mandarin and the boatman in paragraphs 22–24 and study the punctuation. Then, add quotations and punctuation to the following dialogue between a mother and her two daughters. The mother is unnamed, and the two daughters are Lila and Lala.

Bring the wood in for the fire and hurry up, Lila! My arms are full already, yelled Lila. Lala, help your sister unload her basket and bring the wood in before it rains! Do I have to do it now? Lala whined to her mother. Her mother yelled impatiently, Better now than later!

The Mouse Bride

Folktale retold by **Heather Forest**

Engage Your Brain

Choose one or more of these activities to start connecting with the story you're about to read.

Quite a Test

Parents have almost always had ideas about the kinds of people their children should marry. Think of a test a "modern" parent might give to a child's "sweetheart" to prove that the person is worth marrying. Write or sketch your response.

Take a Poll

As a class, take and record a vote to see how many of your classmates agree with each of the following statements about marriage.

- Attractive looks are enough to make a marriage happy.
  Agree _____   Disagree _____

- One's sweetheart should be able to bake delicious bread.
  Agree _____   Disagree _____

- One's sweetheart should be able to weave fine cloth.
  Agree _____   Disagree _____

- Parents should meet and approve of a child's sweetheart.
  Agree _____   Disagree _____

Then and Now

Once upon a time, parents wanted their children to marry people with certain backgrounds and skills. Is that still true? Discuss your ideas with a small group. Then, summarize your group's ideas.

Analyze Theme

A text's **theme** is its message about life or human nature. Folktales often contain **multiple themes.** Some may reveal their themes directly, but readers usually must **infer,** or use evidence to make logical guesses about theme.

To make inferences about theme in folktales, ask yourself questions such as these:

- What do the characters want and how do they get what they want?

- How well do they succeed and why?

- How do the characters in the story compare to one another?

As you consider the answers, think about what they reveal about possible themes.

Focus on Genre
↳**Folktale**

- includes universal themes

- often features the "rule of three"—characters or events happen in groups of three

- may include supernatural events

- may feature animals or beings with magical powers

Analyze Purpose and Text Structure

Author's purpose is the main reason an author or storyteller relates a tale. The purpose may be to inform, entertain, persuade, or express thoughts and feelings.

Often the purpose of a folktale is to teach some sort of lesson about an aspect of life. Analyze purpose by examining what happens at key points in the plot; then, ask yourself this:

- Why is the storyteller or author telling me this?

Create a chart like the one below to explore what each part of the plot's structure—exposition, rising action, climax, falling action, and resolution—reveals about purpose.

PLOT ELEMENT	WHAT HAPPENS	HINT ABOUT PURPOSE
Exposition	*I am introduced to one kind brother and two mean brothers.*	*The contrast between brothers may teach me something.*

Annotation in Action

Here are one reader's notes about a possible theme in "The Mouse Bride." As you read, note the thoughts, words, and actions of the characters, and make inferences about the lessons they might help convey.

> Long ago, when the world was filled with wonder, there was a farmer who had three sons. The two older sons took pleasure in teasing their youngest brother, who was so kindhearted he could not even sweep a spider from the cobwebs in the corner.

Two mean brothers are picking on their little brother. The theme may be about why it's best to be kindhearted.

Expand Your Vocabulary

Put a check mark next to the vocabulary words that you feel comfortable using when speaking or writing.

amazement	☐
enchanting	☐
deceptive	☐
regal	☐
elegant	☐

Turn to a partner and talk about the vocabulary words you already know. Then, use as many words as you can in a paragraph about falling in love. As you read "The Mouse Bride," use the definitions in the side column to learn the vocabulary words you don't already know.

Background

Heather Forest (b. 1948) is an award-winning author, storyteller, and musician. In her storytelling, she incorporates many different elements, including poetry, prose, guitar, and song. "The Mouse Bride" is a folktale from Finland that she retold in her book *Wonder Tales from Around the World* (1995).

B

The Mouse Bride

Folktale retold by **Heather Forest**

A father sends his three sons off to find wives. When the sons return, he sends them back to test each of their sweethearts three times.

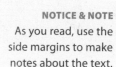

NOTICE & NOTE
As you read, use the side margins to make notes about the text.

1   Long ago, when the world was filled with wonder, there was a farmer who had three sons. The two older sons took pleasure in teasing their youngest brother, who was so kindhearted he could not even sweep a spider from the cobwebs in the corner.

2   Now one day the farmer brought his sons to a field where three trees stood. "It is time for you to be wed," he said. "Each of you must cut down a sapling.[1] When it falls, walk forward in the direction it points, and you will find your sweetheart."

3   The oldest son cut the largest sapling and it fell pointing north. "What luck!" he shouted, "I know of a fine maiden who lives in a house just north of here. I will go and ask for her hand in marriage."

[1] **sapling:** a young tree.

Shutterstock

amazement
(ə-māz′mənt) *n. Amazement* is
a state of extreme surprise or
wonder.

enchanting
(ĕn-chăn′tĭng) *adj.* Something or
someone *enchanting* is charming.

4   The next oldest son cut a sapling and it fell pointing south.
"I too shall live in happiness," said the second son, "for there is a
delightful young woman who lives in a house just south of here.
I will go and ask her to be my bride!"

5   But when the youngest son cut his sapling, it pointed
towards the forest where there were no houses at all.

6   "You'll find a pointy-eared sweetheart with sharp teeth in
that forest," laughed his two brothers.

7   "I will trust fate and my chances," said the youngest son. He
carved a beautiful walking stick from the tree and set off in the
direction of the woods.

8   The young man had not gone far into the forest when he
came upon a cottage made of gray logs. He knocked on the
door. A pleasant voice said, "Enter, please."

9   When he walked inside, he looked everywhere but saw
no one.

10   "Here I am!" said the voice, "I am so glad to have company.
I have been very lonely."

11   The young man stared in **amazement.** There on the table
was a dainty blue-eyed mouse with its gray fur as sleek as velvet.

12   "You can speak!" the young man said.

13   "Certainly I can speak, but I prefer to sing," she said gaily,
and she began a lively tune. The young man applauded her
song, amazed. Then she curtsied[2] and asked, "What brings
you here?"

14   "I am searching for a sweetheart," he replied.

15   "Well then, how about me?" said the mouse.

16   "You are not exactly the type of sweetheart I was seeking,"
said the young man politely as he turned to leave.

17   "Oh," she sighed, "I am sad to hear that, for I have longed
to meet someone just like you." She began such an **enchanting**
love song, the young man stood motionless at the door.

18   "Please don't stop," he pleaded when she finished her
song. "I want that song to go on and on … Strange as it seems,
perhaps you could be my sweetheart."

19   "Then come to visit me at this time tomorrow," she said
with a smile and a twitch of her silken whiskers.

20   "I promise I will return," said the young man as he left. And
all the way home, his heart quickened as he thought about the
mouse and her beautiful song.

21   When he arrived at the farm that evening his two brothers
were bragging to their father.

---

² **curtsied:** from *curtsy,* a gesture of respect made by bending
knees with one foot forward and lowering the body.

© Houghton Mifflin Harcourt Publishing Company

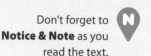

22   "The woman I met has beautiful rosy cheeks," said the oldest son.

23   "The lovely maiden I met," bragged the next oldest son, "is the fairest in the countryside. Her hair is as black as a raven's wing."[3]

24   But they teased the youngest brother before he could speak a word, saying, "Who could you find in the woods but a pointy-eared, sharp-toothed beast!"

25   "I met the most enchanting singer," said the lad hesitantly, "and I cannot stop thinking about her. She has a captivating voice, sky-blue eyes, a beautiful smile, and she dresses in the very finest gray velvet. She even invited me to return tomorrow!"

26   "A princess no doubt!" the brothers shouted sarcastically. "He is making this up! Who could love him?"

27   "Congratulations to each of you on meeting sweethearts," said their father. "But attractive looks alone do not make for a happy hearth.[4] Tomorrow, I should like to see the kind of bread your sweethearts bake."

---

[3] **as black as a raven's wing:** a raven is a large bird with glossy black feathers.

[4] **a happy hearth:** a hearth is a fireplace, which at one time represented the center of family life.

Shutterstock

The Mouse Bride   **537**

28　The next morning, the youngest son set out at dawn. When he arrived at the cottage the mouse greeted him eagerly, saying, "I am delighted that you have kept your promise to return!"

29　The lad blushed with embarrassment and said, "I told my father and brothers that ever since we met, I have not been able to stop thinking about you. But I did not tell them that you are a mouse! Now my father would like to see the kind of bread you bake! Oh," he moaned, "my cruel brothers will certainly ridicule me when I arrive home tonight empty-handed!"

30　"I cannot bear to think of them mocking you! You will not go home empty-handed!" said the mouse. "Of course I can bake bread!" She clapped her paws and one hundred gray mice appeared as she commanded, "Bring me the finest grains of wheat from the field!"

31　Fascinated, the young man stayed all day watching the marvelous effort as the little mouse directed the baking of a fine loaf of wheaten bread. She sang as she worked and enraptured the young man's ears with her music. The afternoon passed so quickly with their cheerful conversation and laughter, the young man hardly noticed that the sun was setting.

32　"I must hurry and leave," he said.

33　"Please take this loaf as a gift to your father," said the mouse, waving him goodbye. "I hope that you will come again tomorrow."

34　"Of course I'll return," assured the young man, "I would rather be here than anywhere else." He traveled back home with the loaf under his arm.

35　That night around the dinner table, the oldest brother proudly handed the farmer a loaf of rye bread made by his sweetheart and boasted, "See how hearty and well-baked it is!"

36　The second oldest brother handed the farmer some barley bread made by his sweetheart and bragged, "My sweetheart's bread is crusty and healthy to eat!"

37　But when the youngest brother handed his father the fine loaf of wheaten bread the farmer exclaimed, "Wheat bread! Only the richest among us eat wheat bread!"

38　The two older brothers bickered over who was to get the biggest piece of wheat bread and said, as they stuffed their mouths, "But there's no house in that woods for miles! What kind of sweetheart could you have found?"

39　"One whose conversation can make me forget the time of day," replied the lad.

© Houghton Mifflin Harcourt Publishing Company • Image Credits: ©Nadiya/Shutterstock

Don't forget to
Notice & Note as you
read the text.

40   "I am pleased that your sweethearts bake such fine bread!" said the farmer. "Skillful hands add comfort to a home. Tomorrow, I should like to see the kind of cloth they can weave."

41   The next morning the lad set out again to visit the mouse in the woods.

42   "Come in!" said the little mouse when she heard him knock. She sang him a tune and a smile spread across his face.

43   "I wish you could weave as well as you bake and sing. But how could that be possible?" said the lad with a sigh. "My father would like to see the kind of cloth you make."

44   "Love makes everything possible," said the mouse, clapping her paws. Once again, one hundred mice appeared as she said, "Fetch me strands of the finest flax."[5]

45   Each mouse quickly returned with one strand of flax. The little mouse spun the flax into thread on a tiny spinning wheel.[6] The young man stared in amazement as she wove a fine piece of linen on a miniature loom.[7] They kept company all afternoon, talking and laughing while she worked. The time sped by so quickly, the sun was setting before the young man realized it.

NOTICE & NOTE
AGAIN AND AGAIN

When you notice certain events, images, or words being repeated in a portion of a story or poem, you've found an **Again and Again** signpost.

Notice & Note: Why is the youngest brother's experience of time in paragraphs 31, 39, and 45 important? Mark each reference to time.

Connect: Why might the author keep repeating references to time?

5 flax: a plant whose fiber is used for making linen cloth.
6 spinning wheel: a device with a foot- or hand-driven wheel and single spindle, or rod, used to make thread and yarn.
7 wove a fine piece of linen on a miniature loom: fine linen fabric was woven using a loom, an apparatus for weaving strands of yarn together at right angles.

© Houghton Mifflin Harcourt Publishing Company

46   "It's done!" she finally said, folding the small patch of delicate cloth in a walnut shell. "Take it to your father as a gift and I do hope your heart brings you here tomorrow."

47   The lad left for home with the walnut shell tucked carefully in his pocket.

48   That night around the hearth fire, each brother brought forward the cloth made by their sweethearts.

49   "Here is some coarse but sturdy cotton made by my love," boasted the first brother proudly.

50   "Here is some cotton and linen weave made by my love, and it is fancier than yours!" bragged the second brother.

51   "Here is a walnut," said the youngest brother as his older brothers howled.

52   "He has no sweetheart! He's brought a forest nut instead of some cloth!" they squealed.

53   "Appearances can be **deceptive,**" said the lad. "Open the nut, Father."

54   The two older brothers stopped laughing and gawked in silence as the farmer opened the shell and held up the fine web of linen. "I have never seen such delicate work," said the farmer, admiring the cloth. "Sons, I must meet your sweethearts! Bring them home tomorrow so that I may see your brides-to-be," he said.

55   The lad's face flushed red as he imagined himself presenting the little mouse to his father and brothers as his bride. "This is ridiculous!" he thought. "I cannot marry a mouse! I must seek deeper in the forest for a proper human sweetheart."

56   But in the morning, as the young man approached the cottage he could not resist stopping for a moment. He thought, "I will tell her politely that I won't be visiting anymore. I need to find one of my own kind. But then, surely I will hurt her feelings! She is the most delightful companion I've ever met. Oh, I have never been more confused!"

57   As he nervously stood at the cottage door wondering what to do, the little mouse called out, "Welcome! Come in! I have composed a love song for you!"

58   The moment he entered the room she began to sing her beautiful song. His heart swelled with joy and every doubt he had about presenting her to his family disappeared with the first tones of her sweet voice.

59   "My Father wishes to meet you," he simply said. "Please come with me to visit him."

60   "Very well, I shall travel in the finest style!" replied the mouse.

deceptive

(dĭ-sĕp′tĭv) *adj.* Something *deceptive* is giving a false impression.

ANALYZE THEME

Annotate: Reread paragraphs 47–53. Mark the lad's response to his brothers in paragraph 53.

Infer: What is the meaning of this response, and how might you use the response to infer a theme?

Don't forget to
Notice & Note as you
read the text.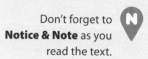

61 She clapped her paws and six black mice appeared, pulling a tiny coach made of a chestnut burr with a toadstool for a canopy.[8]

62 The mouse, **regal** as a queen, climbed into the coach. With the youngest son walking alongside, they set out for his home.

63 When they arrived at the river, a hunter passed them on the bridge. He looked down at the mouse, coach, and six and exclaimed, "Ho! What is this! A pack of vile rodents! I hate rats."

64 "If you please, sir," said the lad, "these are not vile rodents. I'll not allow you to call them so!"

65 "I've killed every rodent that has crossed my path!" said the bully, looming dangerously over the lad.

66 "Open your eyes and look more carefully," said the young man bravely. "Here before you rides the most delightful creature one could chance to meet."

67 "Disgusting rats!" glowered the man and with his heavy boot he kicked the coach and six into the swift water below the bridge!

68 "Heartless cruel man!" screamed the lad as he jumped into the river to save the mouse.

69 "I've rid the world of some useless pests!" the hunter shouted and continued on his way.

70 The lad desperately tried to reach the sinking coach. But as the raging water swirled around the little mouse, she vanished in the rushing river.

71 Exhausted and almost drowned, the lad made his way to the riverbank. He climbed out of the water and wept. "Now that you are gone," he wailed, "I regret even one moment's doubt that you were indeed my true love."

72 Suddenly, with a great splash and spray of mist, out of the water came six black horses pulling a fine golden carriage. In the carriage was a beautiful woman with sparkling blue eyes, wearing a gray velvet gown.

73 "Who are you?" the lad asked, rubbing his eyes to be sure he was seeing clearly.

74 "Don't you recognize me?" she asked. Her lovely musical voice cheered his heart.

regal
(rē´gəl) *adj.* Something *regal* appears to be royal, magnificent, or splendid.

ANALYZE PURPOSE AND TEXT STRUCTURE

Annotate: Mark the character's response to events in paragraph 71 and the resulting action in paragraph 72.

Analyze: Explain what the plot element is here and how this plot element might help reveal the folktale's purpose.

[8] **a chestnut burr with a toadstool for a canopy:** a burr is the fruit of the chestnut; a toadstool is an inedible or poisonous mushroom; and a canopy is an umbrella-like shelter.

ANALYZE THEME

Annotate: Read paragraphs 75–76. Mark the youngest son's response to the mouse.

Analyze: How does this statement connect with the theme or themes you've already identified?

elegant

(ĕl ´ ĭ-gənt) *adj.* Someone *elegant* is refined and tasteful, having a beautiful manner, form, or style.

75   She explained, "I am a royal princess. A Lapland witch,[9] jealous of my beauty, enchanted me to be a mouse until such time as a kindhearted man could truly love me for myself. You broke the spell when you risked your life and declared your love. I am your mouse bride if you will have me," she said with a shy smile.

76   "I loved you before when we were of different worlds," he said. "How could I love you less now?"

77   He climbed into the coach and together they rode to his father's house. His brothers tumbled over one another to greet the **elegant** guest at their gate. "But it's our brother!" they gawked as he stepped out of the coach holding the princess's hand.

78   After a day of celebration, the young man and the princess traveled back to the forest. Instead of finding the small cottage made of gray logs, they found a great gray stone castle filled with one hundred servants. And it was there that they dwelt in happiness for the rest of their lives.

[9] **Lapland witch:** witch characters and references appear in many traditional stories from Lapland, which is a region of extreme northern Europe within the Arctic circle that includes Finland (where this story originates), Norway, Sweden, and the Kola peninsula of Northwest Russia.

?

ESSENTIAL QUESTION:

What hidden truths about people and the world are revealed in stories?

Review your notes and add your thoughts to your Response Log.

TURN AND TALK

Get with a partner, and discuss the folktale you just read. What is the folktale's message about true love? Why do you say so?

Assessment Practice

Answer these questions before moving on to the **Analyze the Text** section.

1. What do the youngest son in "The Mouse Bride" and the mandarin's daughter in "The Boatman's Flute" have in common?

    (A) Both characters marry their sweethearts and live happily ever after.

    (B) Both characters fall in love with people who are royalty in disguise.

    (C) Both characters have overprotective fathers who punish them harshly.

    (D) Both characters fall in love through the most beautiful music they have ever heard.

2. This question has two parts. First answer **Part A**. Then, answer **Part B**.

    Part A

    What is one theme in the folktale "The Mouse Bride"?

    (A) Beauty is only skin deep.

    (B) Danger lurks in dark places.

    (C) Appearances can be deceiving.

    (D) He who laughs last, laughs best.

    Part B

    Select the text that provides relevant support for the answer in Part A.

    (A) "'Who could you find in the woods but a pointy-eared, sharp-toothed beast!'" (paragraph 24)

    (B) "But attractive looks alone do not make for a happy hearth." (paragraph 27)

    (C) "The afternoon passed so quickly with their cheerful conversation and laughter. . . ." (paragraph 31)

    (D) "'Love makes everything possible,' said the mouse, clapping her paws." (paragraph 44)

    ☺**Ed**

    Test-Taking Strategies

Analyze the Text

Support your responses with evidence from the text.

1. **SUMMARIZE** Describe in your own words the two older brothers' attitudes toward their younger brother in paragraphs 24–26.

2. **INFER** Reread paragraph 27. What can you infer about the story's theme from the father's comments to his sons?

3. **ANALYZE** Contrast the characters of the hunter and the youngest son in paragraphs 65–70. Explain what these contrasts might reveal about theme and author's purpose for this folktale.

CHARACTER OF THE HUNTER AND EVIDENCE	CHARACTER OF THE YOUNGEST SON AND EVIDENCE	DIFFERENCES BETWEEN THE TWO

4. **EVALUATE** Reread paragraphs 70–76. How does the author use a transition in the plot to help characterize the young man? Explain how this moment in the plot contributes to the folktale's purpose.

5. **ANALYZE** Reread paragraph 2, and then review paragraphs 27, 40, and 54. Consider why the author might bring up similar events **Again and Again.** Why do you think the father assigns the three tasks? What insights about the brothers do you gain with each task accomplished?

Choices

Here are some other ways to demonstrate your understanding of the ideas in this lesson.

Writing
↳ Analyze a Theme

Write a three- to four-paragraph explanation of a **theme** in "The Mouse Bride."

- Identify at least one theme in your analysis. Remember that folktales and other stories may have multiple themes.

- Provide text evidence to support your ideas.

- Revise your work. Look for ways to enhance your writing with modifiers, including adverbs, adjectives, and modifying phrases.

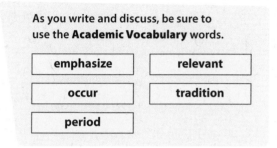

As you write and discuss, be sure to use the **Academic Vocabulary** words.

emphasize	relevant
occur	tradition
period	

Social & Emotional Learning
↳ What's Not to Love?

In a small group, discuss why the youngest son and the mouse like each other.

- First, list and describe character traits of both the son and the mouse.

- Next, discuss the folktale's view of relationships. Why does the son keep returning to the mouse? Why does the mouse want him to keep returning?

- Finally, discuss your own opinions. Which traits on your list are desirable? Which traits are not?

Media
↳ Illustrate Key Scenes

In a small group, identify key scenes in "The Mouse Bride." Then, work together to find or create illustrations that capture each one of those scenes. Include captions to explain each illustration, and present your work to the class. When you present, be sure to—

- Invite questions about why you selected the scenes you've illustrated, and answer respectfully.

- Ask for ideas about how other members of the class might have illustrated the same scene. Prompt your classmates to explain how they imagine the scene, and why.

CHARACTER OF THE SON	CHARACTER OF THE MOUSE

Expand Your Vocabulary

PRACTICE AND APPLY

To show your understanding of the vocabulary words, identify the vocabulary word that has a meaning similar to one of these words: *stylish, wonder, royal, false,* and *captivating*. Write each word pair.

amazement	enchanting	deceptive	regal	elegant

Vocabulary Strategy

↳Context Clues

Context clues are the words and phrases surrounding a word that provide hints about its meaning. The following are three types of context clues to look for when you come across an unfamiliar word.

 Ed

Interactive Vocabulary Lesson: Using Context Clues

- **Example clue:** The writer uses words that are examples of the unknown word.

- **Definition clue:** The writer defines the unknown word directly in the sentence or in surrounding sentences.

- **Analogy clue:** The writer pairs items that are related in some way.

PRACTICE AND APPLY

Find the following words in the selection, and identify clues to each word's meaning. Use those clues to guess each word's definition. Then, use the definitions in the selection's margins to check your guesses.

WORD	CONTEXT CLUES	GUESSED DEFINITION	ACTUAL DEFINITION
amazement			
enchanting			
deceptive			
regal			
elegant			

Watch Your Language!

Adjectives and Adverbs

An **adjective** is a part of speech that modifies a noun or a pronoun. It describes *what kind, which,* or *how many.*

An **adverb** is a part of speech that modifies or describes verbs, adjectives, or other adverbs. Adverbs provide details about *time, place, manner,* and *cause.*

A **clause** is a group of words with a subject and a predicate—the two main parts of a complete sentence. An **adjective clause** acts like an adjective to modify a noun or pronoun elsewhere in the sentence. Similarly, an **adverb clause** acts like an adverb to modify a verb, adjective, or other adverb in the sentence.

Ed

Interactive Grammar Lesson: Using Modifiers Correctly

PRACTICE AND APPLY

Mark and identify the adjective and adverb clauses in these sentences, along with the words they modify.

When you have finished, compare your work with a partner's, and explain how you decided which were adjective clauses and which were adverb clauses.

1. When he arrived at the farm that evening his two brothers were bragging to their father.

2. But they teased the youngest brother before he could speak a word.

3. I know of a fine maiden who lives just north of here.

4. The young man had not gone far into the forest when he came upon a cottage.

Compare Themes

"The Boatman's Flute" from Vietnam and "The Mouse Bride" from Finland are both folktales that address a similar topic. You can infer the stories' themes by noting how each character makes decisions, interacts with others, and responds to events. Recall that character responses may be internal (thoughts and feelings) or external (statements and actions).

With your group, complete the chart by citing text evidence. As you work, remember that a folktale may have multiple themes.

	THE BOATMAN'S FLUTE	THE MOUSE BRIDE
Key statements		
Key decisions		
Lessons learned		

Analyze the Texts

Discuss these questions in your group.

1. **SUMMARIZE** Describe three significant events in the "The Boatman's Flute" and "The Mouse Bride" that help develop each tale's plot.

2. **ANALYZE** Reread paragraphs 31–33 in "The Boatman's Flute" and paragraphs 56 and 75–76 in "The Mouse Bride." How did the mandarin's daughter and the farmer's youngest son learn important lessons, and how do these lessons differ?

3. **INFER** Both folktales feature a character who is freed. What do you infer about what actually sets the boatman and the princess free?

4. **SYNTHESIZE** What have your comparisons revealed about possible themes in each folktale? Which key sections of each text suggest theme?

Collaborate and Present

In your group, review the ideas about themes from your discussion, and determine a central theme for each story. Follow these steps:

(1) REVIEW THE LESSONS LEARNED Think about lessons learned by the main characters. This can help you to identify a central theme.

(2) IDENTIFY A CENTRAL THEME FOR EACH FOLKTALE Discuss which of the themes in each story is most important and why. Record the themes for each story in the chart below.

(3) RECORD DETAILS AND EVIDENCE Locate specific evidence in the stories to support the themes you identify. Be sure to include specific statements made by the characters, noting who said each one, paragraph numbers, and how each statement supports the theme.

FOLKTALE THEMES	
"The Boatman's Flute"—Central Theme: Evidence:	"The Mouse Bride"—Central Theme: Evidence:

(4) PRESENT YOUR IDEAS Present the themes you've identified to the class. Explain similarities you found in the two folktales, and present any significant differences in meaning that you found. Make sure to support all of your ideas with specific evidence from the texts.

Reader's Choice

Continue your exploration of the Essential Question by doing some independent reading about stories and their hidden truths. Read the titles and descriptions shown. Then mark the texts that interest you.

ESSENTIAL QUESTION:
? What hidden truths about people and the world are revealed in stories?

Short Reads   Available on ⓔEd

These texts are available in your ebook. Choose one to read and rate. Then defend your rating to the class.

The Golden Serpent

Fable retold by **Walter Dean Myers**

A quest to find the golden serpent uncovers truths about a kingdom and the king.

Rate It ☆☆☆☆☆

Echo and Narcissus

Myth retold by **Lancelyn Green**

Goddesses prevent a beautiful nymph and her true love from ever meeting face to face.

Rate It ☆☆☆☆☆

The Fisherman and the Chamberlain

Folktale retold by **Jane Yolen**

A fisherman outwits a greedy bully and is royally rewarded.

Rate It ☆☆☆☆☆

Urban Legends, Suburban Myths

Informational Text by **Robert T. Carroll**

Beware! Which reveal truths and which spread hoaxes: urban legends or suburban myths?

Rate It ☆☆☆☆☆

Long Reads

Here are three recommended books that connect to this unit topic. For additional options, ask your teacher, school librarian, or peers. Which titles spark your interest?

Holes

Novel by **Louis Sachar**

Stanley Yelnats, whose first name is his last name spelled backwards, has nothing but bad luck. That's how he winds up digging holes at a camp in the middle of the desert. While he's there, he unearths an old secret and learns that his own fate is connected to that of a friend.

The Lightning Thief

Novel by **Rick Riordan**

Weird things keep happening to poor Percy Jackson. Then he discovers the truth about who he happens to be, and things get even weirder. Sent off to a camp with other kids like him, he's soon involved in a quest that he never could have foreseen.

The Jungle Book

Story Collection by **Rudyard Kipling**

Rudyard Kipling's famous collection of stories relates the adventures of a young boy living among some of the wildest jungle animals. Their experiences reveal hidden truths about bravery, loyalty, family, and the order of things.

Extension
↳ Connect & Create

A HIDDEN TRUTH Select one of your favorite characters from a Reader's Choice text. What images would that character post on social media to communicate a theme revealed in that character's story? Describe, sketch, or find images that your character would post. Then, explain the significance of each image.

DON'T JUDGE A BOOK BY ITS MOVIE If you chose a book with a movie version, work with a partner to compare and contrast the book with its film version. Be sure to answer questions such as—

● Which parts of the film are similar to the book?

● Which parts of the film differ from the book?

● What are the strengths and weakness of each version?

When you've finished your comparison, write a brief essay detailing your conclusions.

 NOTICE & NOTE

● Pick one of the texts and annotate the Notice & Note signposts you find.

● Then, use the **Notice & Note Writing Frames** to help you write about the significance of the signposts.

● Compare your findings with those of other students who read the same text.

Notice & Note Writing Frames

Write a Short Story

Writing Prompt

A literary journal for teens has put out a call for short stories that reveal hidden truths about growing up. Incorporating ideas and literary elements from texts in this unit, write a short story expressing a clear **theme,** or message about life or human nature.

Manage your time carefully so that you can

- review the texts in the unit;
- plan your story;
- write your story; and
- revise and edit your story.

Be sure to

- create a plot that unfolds with an exposition, rising action, a climax, falling action, and a resolution;
- logically sequence plot events;
- use transitions to indicate shifts in time and place;
- use precise words and phrases as well as figurative language to create vivid descriptions of characters, settings, and events;
- clearly express a theme; and
- end with a satisfying conclusion that follows from the story's events.

Review the Mentor Text

For an example of a well-written story that you can use as a mentor text, review:

- **"The Mouse Bride"** (pages 535–543)

Review your notes and annotations about this story and other stories in the unit. Think about techniques the authors use to engage readers and communicate theme.

Consider Your Sources

Review the list of texts in the unit and choose at least three that you may want to use as sources for ideas or inspiration for your short story.

As you review potential sources, consult the notes you made on your **Response Log** and make additional notes about ideas that might be useful as you write your story. Note source titles and page numbers so that you can find information again later.

UNIT 6 SOURCES

- [ ] *from* **Storytelling**
- [ ] **The Prince and the Pauper**
- [ ] **Archetype**
- [ ] **Fairy-tale Logic**
- [ ] **The Boatman's Flute**
- [ ] **The Mouse Bride**

Analyze the Prompt

Analyze the prompt to make sure you understand what you are required to do.

Mark the sentence in the prompt that suggests the topic of your story. Rephrase this sentence in your own words.

Next, look for words that indicate the purpose and audience for your story, and write a sentence describing each. If the prompt only gives a general idea of the purpose and audience, make them more specific.

What is my topic? What is my writing task?

What is my purpose?

Who is my audience?

Review the Rubric

Your short story will be scored using a rubric. As you write, focus on the characteristics described in the chart. You will learn more about these characteristics as you work through the lesson.

PURPOSE, FOCUS, AND ORGANIZATION	NARRATIVE TECHNIQUES	CONVENTIONS OF STANDARD ENGLISH
The response includes: • An engaging introduction that establishes setting, point of view, and a narrator and/or character(s) • A well-developed plot • Effective transitions • A logical sequence of events • A satisfying conclusion that follows from events	The response includes: • Precise words and phrases, descriptive details, and sensory and figurative language • Effective narrative techniques, such as dialogue, pacing, description, and reflection • A variety of sentence structures	The response may include the following: • Some minor errors in usage but no patterns of errors • Effective use of punctuation, capitalization, sentence formation, and spelling • Command of basic conventions

1 PLAN YOUR SHORT STORY

Choose a Theme and a Main Conflict

☺Ed

Help with Planning

Consult **Interactive Writing Lesson: Writing Narratives.**

Begin by thinking about your story's **theme,** or its message about life and human nature. Then, invent a **conflict,** or a problem, that will unfold in an interesting way. In good stories, the theme arises from the conflict and its resolution. Write your theme and conflict below.

MY THEME	MY MAIN CONFLICT

Plan for Characters, Setting, and a Narrator

Planning story elements will help you create a cohesive story. Consider these questions:

- Who will tell your story? A **first-person narrator** or a **third-person narrator?**

- What **characters** do you need? How do they act? Talk? Think?

- What is the **setting?** When and where does the story take place? In the chart below, draft ideas about the narrator, characters, and setting.

Choose Your Narrator

Keep in mind:

- A **first-person narrator** is a character in the story and takes part in its action, relating events from the narrator's point of view. Readers experience the story's action through the perspective and awareness of this character alone.

- A **third-person narrator** is "outside" the story, relating events without participating in them. A third-person narrator may reveal the thoughts and feelings of only the main character or of some or all of the characters.

Narrator	
Main Character or Characters	
Minor Characters	
Setting	

Sequence Plot Events

The series of events in a story is called the **plot.** The plot usually centers on a conflict that the main character faces. List the key events of your story in chronological order, or time order.

PLOT EVENTS IN CHRONOLOGICAL ORDER	
1.	
2.	
3.	
4.	
5.	
6.	

Place a star next to the point of highest tension, or the point at which a key action or decision determines the outcome of events. This point is called the **climax.** Shortly after this point, the problem in a story is usually resolved.

Organize Ideas

Organize your ideas in a way that will help you draft your story.

Use Transitions

Use transitions to alert readers when a shift occurs—

- from one scene or location to another
- from one point in time to another

EXPOSITION/ RISING ACTION	• Provide vital background information about the main characters and setting. • Clearly establish the point of view and narrator. • Introduce the conflict and begin to develop it.
CLIMAX	• Create a meaningful or exciting turning point at the "peak" of the action. • Resolve the conflict. • Hint at the story's outcome.
FALLING ACTION	• Begin to draw the story to a close. • Reveal the results of the resolution to the conflict. • Reveal characters' responses to the resolution. • Begin tying up any "loose ends."
CONCLUSION	• Close the story in a way that follows logically from the progression of events.

2 DEVELOP A DRAFT

Drafting can be challenging. But you can develop your own skills by examining how professional authors craft compelling short stories.

Use Vivid Descriptions

EXAMINE THE MENTOR TEXT

Notice how the author of "The Mouse Bride" uses vivid descriptive language to help develop characters.

The Mouse Bride
retold by Heather Forest

> The young man reacts strongly. **Vivid descriptions** explain his reaction.

"Here I am!" said the voice, "I am so glad to have company. I have been very lonely."

The young man stared in amazement. There on the table was a dainty blue-eyed mouse with its gray fur as sleek as velvet.

> Details about the mouse, including use of **sensory language,** help readers form a mental picture.

APPLY TO YOUR DRAFT

In your story, bring characters and events to life with vivid descriptions and sensory language. Details that appeal to the senses—sight, hearing, smell, touch, and taste—will help readers visualize and better understand characters, setting, and plot.

Use this frame to try out some words, phrases, or sentences that vividly describe your main character. Then apply the technique to other characters as well as to your setting and events.

Try These Suggestions

Use actions to reveal a character's thoughts and feelings.

- Instead of calling your character "angry," create a vivid image by saying that he "stomped his foot in the dust," for example.

- Consider the connotations of words. Does your character do something "quickly" or "hastily"? What is the difference?

What my main character looks like	
How my main character moves	
What my main character says / sounds like	
What my main character's attitudes are	

Use Transitions

EXAMINE THE MENTOR TEXT

The author of "The Mouse Bride" uses transitional words, phrases, and clauses to signal shifts in time and setting.

Drafting Online

Check your assignment list for a writing task from your teacher.

With the phrase "long ago," the author provides hints about the time at which the story is set.

The story shifts to a particular day in which action will take place. The phrase "Now one day" signals the shift.

> Long ago, when the world was filled with wonder, there was a farmer who had three sons. The two older sons took pleasure in teasing their youngest brother, who was so kindhearted he could not even sweep a spider from the cobwebs in the corner.
>
> Now one day the farmer brought his sons to a field where three trees stood.

APPLY TO YOUR DRAFT

Transitions help guide readers through a story. When the action of your story shifts from one time or place to another, use a transition to alert your readers to the shift. In the graphic below, try out some different types of transitions.

My action begins at this **time:**
_____

And then my action happens at this **time:**
_____

Possible transitions I could use:
_____
_____
_____

My action begins at this **location:**
_____

And then my action happens at this **location:**
_____

Possible transitions I could use:
_____
_____
_____

Try These Suggestions

There are countless ways to word transitions. Be creative and use a variety.

Time transitions:
- After several weeks, . . .
- . . . not ten minutes later . . .

Place transitions:
- Once we arrived at . . .
- . . . wandered out to the shady backyard . . .

3 REVISE YOUR SHORT STORY

Even professional writers rework their drafts to improve ideas and language. Use the guide to help you revise your story.

☺ Ed

Help with Revision

Find a **Peer Review Guide** and **Student Models** online.

ASK YOURSELF	PROVE IT	REVISE IT
Introduction Do I provide necessary background information to help orient readers?	**Highlight** the exposition. **Underline** words or phrases that provide background information about the characters, setting, or conflict.	**Add** details to help establish background.
Point of View Is the narrator consistent throughout the story?	**Underline** point-of-view words such as *I*, *she*, or *them*.	**Replace** words that express an inconsistent point of view.
Organization Do plot events unfold naturally and logically?	**Highlight** the introduction of each main event.	**Reorganize** events to build suspense and clarify the plot.
Transitions Do transition words and phrases signal shifts in time and place?	**Make a check mark (✔)** by transitions.	**Add** or **revise** transitions to clarify shifts in time and place.
Narrative Techniques Are my characters and descriptions developed with sensory details and figurative language?	**Circle** words that describe the setting and characters, including their traits.	**Add** interesting details and precise descriptions that help build a reader's understanding of characters, setting, and events.
Conclusion Does my conclusion follow logically from the plot events?	**Make brackets ({ })** around the conclusion.	**Rewrite** sentences to smooth out the conclusion and draw a clear connection to plot events.

APPLY TO YOUR DRAFT

Consider the following as you look for opportunities to improve your writing.

- Make sure the point of view is clear and consistent.

- Include background information to help orient readers, but don't include unnecessary details that distract from the plot.

- Add sensory and figurative language to help readers visualize and understand your descriptions.

- Create suspense to keep readers engaged.

Peer Review in Action

Once you have finished revising your short story, you will exchange papers with a partner in a **peer review.** During a peer review, you will give suggestions to improve your partner's draft.

Read the opening paragraphs from a student's draft, and examine the comments made by his peer reviewer.

First Draft

Tough Choices
by Carlo Sanchez, Pine Middle School

I knock on the door. It has been three long months since my best friend and I have seen each other.

The November wind makes him shiver, and he shoves his hands deeper into his pockets. How long will he wait?

> You're using a first-person narrator, but I'm not sure where the narrator is. Include more background information.

> This is still the person knocking on the door, right? If so, you switched to a third-person narrator. You'll need to make your narrator consistent.

Now read the revised paragraphs below. Notice how the writer has improved the draft by making revisions based on his peer reviewer's comments.

Revision

I take a deep breath and knock on Liam's door. It has been three long months since my best friend and I have seen each other, and I have no idea if he's going to answer. Four months ago, I lied to Liam, a decision that I've regretted ever since.

The November wind makes me shiver, and I shove my hands deeper into my pockets. Suddenly, I hear footsteps from inside the house. Someone is coming to the door.

> Nice job. The context is now clear, and you're building suspense.

> Good job fixing point of view! It's consistent now—a first-person narrator creates suspense; your first-person narrator can't know what will happen when someone opens the door.

APPLY TO YOUR DRAFT

During your peer review, give each other specific suggestions for how you could make your short stories more effective. Use the revision guide to help you.

When receiving feedback from your partner, listen attentively and ask questions to make sure you fully understand the revision suggestions.

4 EDIT YOUR SHORT STORY

Edit your final draft to check for proper use of standard English conventions and to correct any misspellings or grammatical errors.

☺Ed

Interactive Grammar Lesson: Simple Sentences and Compound Sentences

Watch Your Language!

PAY ATTENTION TO STYLE

Good writing has a particular **style,** which creates cohesion and helps keep readers engaged. Style involves *how* something is said, rather than *what* is said, and can be shown through **word choice.** In the following example from "The Mouse Bride," word choice reveals the author's descriptive style.

> Suddenly, with a **great splash** and **spray of mist,** out of the water came **six black horses** pulling **a fine golden carriage.**

Style is also revealed in **sentence variety,** which helps hold readers' interest and creates clear and suspenseful descriptions.

APPLY TO YOUR DRAFT

Now apply what you've learned to your work.

1. Read your story and note where you might improve descriptions by making different, more interesting word choices.

2. Discuss sentence patterns. Work with a peer to analyze your sentences. Have you included a variety of sentence types?

3. Revise your style. Develop your style by revising word choices and incorporating a variety of sentence patterns.

Types of Style

Words used to describe an author's style include:

- **formal**
- **conversational**
- **flowery**
- **direct**
- **eloquent**
- **restrained**
- **humorous**

Ways to Share

- **Illustrate** your story and share it with others. How will your illustrations add to a reader's experience?

- **Make an audio recording** of your story. Practice with a partner to perfect your delivery before recording.

- Imagine that your story gets published. In an interview, a magazine editor asks, "What was your motivation behind this story?" **Write a response.**

5 PUBLISH YOUR SHORT STORY

Share It!

The prompt asks you to write a short story that reveals hidden truths about growing up for a teen literary journal. You may also use your story as inspiration for other projects.

Reflect & Extend

Here are some other ways to show your understanding of the ideas in Unit 6.

Reflect on the Essential Question

What hidden truths about people and the world are revealed in stories?

Has your answer to the question changed after reading the texts in the unit? Discuss your ideas.

You can use these sentence starters to help you reflect on your learning.

- **I think differently because . . .**
- **I want to learn more about . . .**
- **I still don't understand . . .**

Writing
Write a Literary Analysis

Think about your favorite story or poem from this unit. Then, write a literary analysis identifying one of its themes, or lessons about life or human nature. Use the chart to develop details you might include in your literary analysis.

Project-Based Learning
Create a Movie Trailer

You've read stories that express hidden truths about life and human nature. Now, create a trailer for a movie adaptation of one of those stories.

Here are some ways to guide development as you storyboard and script your trailer:

- Establish your story idea in the first thirty seconds of the trailer you'll create.

- Introduce the story's conflict so that viewers will want to know what happens.

- End with a sense of suspense; don't give away any plot twists, surprises, or the turning point of the story.

⌣Ed

Media Projects

To find help with this task online, access **Create a Movie Trailer.**

ASK YOURSELF	MY NOTES
What themes have I inferred from the story or poem?	
What evidence from events in the plot supports an inference about theme?	
What evidence from how a character develops supports an inference about theme?	
What evidence from imagery and any other use of language supports an inference about theme?	

Resources

HMH *Into Literature* Resources ⌣Ed

For more instruction and practice, access the *Into Literature* Resources and Interactive Lessons.

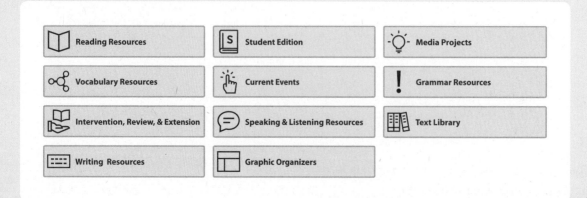

Reading Resources

Vocabulary Resources

Intervention, Review, & Extension

Writing Resources

Student Edition

Current Events

Speaking & Listening Resources

Graphic Organizers

Media Projects

Grammar Resources

Text Library

? ESSENTIAL QUESTION:
What are the ways you can make yourself heard?

Use this Response Log to record your ideas about how each of the texts in Unit 1 relates to or comments on the **Essential Question.**

from Brown Girl Dreaming	
from Selfie: The Changing Face of Self-Portraits	
What's So Funny, Mr. Scieszka?	
A Voice	
Words Like Freedom	
Better Than Words: Say It with a Selfie	
OMG, Not *Another* Selfie!	

Response Log

Use this Response Log to record your ideas about how each of the texts in Unit 2 relates to or comments on the **Essential Question.**

A Schoolgirl's Diary *from* I Am Malala	
Speech to the Young: Speech to the Progress-Toward	
The First Day of School	
from New Kid	

Response Log

ESSENTIAL QUESTION:
How do you find courage in the face of fear?

?

Use this Response Log to record your ideas about how each of the texts in Unit 3 relates to or comments on the **Essential Question.**

from The Breadwinner	
Life Doesn't Frighten Me	
Fears and Phobias	
Wired for Fear	
Embarrassed? Blame Your Brain	
The Ravine	
from Into the Air	
from The Wright Brothers: How They Invented the Airplane	

Response Log

Use this Response Log to record your ideas about how each of the texts in Unit 4 relates to or comments on the **Essential Question.**

from Pax	
Zoo	
from Animal Snoops: The Wondrous World of Wildlife Spies	
Animal Wisdom	
The Last Wolf	
Wild Animals Aren't Pets	
Let People Own Exotic Animals	

Response Log

Use this Response Log to record your ideas about how each of the texts in Unit 5 relates to or comments on the **Essential Question.**

from A Long Walk to Water	
Salva's Story	
Into the Lifeboat *from* Titanic Survivor	
from After the Hurricane	
from Ninth Ward	

Response Log

Use this Response Log to record your ideas about how each of the texts in Unit 6 relates to or comments on the **Essential Question.**

from Storytelling	
The Prince and the Pauper	
Archetype	
Fairy-tale Logic	
The Boatman's Flute	
The Mouse Bride	

NOTICE & NOTE
Handbook

Get More Out of What You Read

Two educators spent years working with students and reading and rereading the books that students read most. They identified a handful of common things authors include in literary and informational texts that signal the reader to pay attention. They call them **signposts.** When you notice a signpost and think about it, you can take control of your own reading.

Learn more about the signposts below.

Answer your own questions!

SIGNPOSTS FOR LITERARY TEXTS
(such as poetry, plays, and fiction)

CONTRASTS AND CONTRADICTIONS
p. **R8**

AHA MOMENT
p. **R9**

TOUGH QUESTIONS
p. **R10**

WORDS OF THE WISER
p. **R11**

AGAIN AND AGAIN
p. **R12**

MEMORY MOMENT
p. **R13**

SIGNPOSTS FOR INFORMATIONAL TEXTS
(such as articles and arguments)

BIG QUESTIONS
p. **R14**

CONTRASTS AND CONTRADICTIONS
p. **R15**

EXTREME OR ABSOLUTE LANGUAGE
p. **R16**

NUMBERS AND STATS
p. **R17**

QUOTED WORDS
p. **R18**

WORD GAPS
p. **R19**

Contrasts and Contradictions

LITERARY ANALYSIS CONNECTION

Paying attention to Contrasts and Contradictions can help you analyze

- character development
- internal conflict
- theme
- relationship between setting and plot
- mood

Contrasts and Contradictions occur either when there is a sharp contrast between what we would expect and what we observe happening, or when the character behaves in a way that contradicts previous behavior or well-established patterns. Contrasts and Contradictions can occur with setting, too.

Read carefully and be alert for moments when a character begins acting or thinking in a new way, or in a way that surprises you because it's not how most people would react. Words like *but* or *despite* can provide clues to these differences.

When you notice Contrasts and Contradictions, pause. Think about what this unexpected or unusual behavior tells you about the character or setting.

A good question to ask is . . .

> Why would the character act (feel) this way?

"Do you want to watch?" Mother asked, nodding toward the mirror.

Parvana shook her head, then changed her mind. If this was the last she would see of her hair, then she wanted to see it for as long as she could.

Mother worked quickly. First she cut off a huge chunk in a straight line at her neck. She held it up for Parvana to see.

"I have a lovely piece of ribbon packed away," she said. "We'll tie this up with it, and you can keep it."

Parvana looked at the hair in her mother's hand. While it was on her head, it had seemed important. It didn't seem important any more.

—from *The Breadwinner*, p. 184

© Houghton Mifflin Harcourt Publishing Company • Image Credits: (tl) ©Luria/Shutterstock; (t) ©Maximova Evgeniya/

Aha Moment

Ed

Notice & Note Peer Coach Videos

An **Aha Moment** occurs when characters realize something that shifts the way they act or what they understand about themselves, others, or the world.

Be alert for these realizations, because they often mark important turning points.

Some phrases that can signal an Aha Moment are:

That's when he knew that . . .

For the first time . . .

She finally understood . . .

It was then that he realized . . .

When you notice an Aha Moment, pause. Think about what effect the character's new knowledge might have on the story.

A good question to ask is . . .

LITERARY ANALYSIS CONNECTION

Paying attention to Aha Moments can help you analyze

- character development
- internal conflict
- plot

How might this change things?

It was then that the fox realized his boy was crying. He twisted around to study his face to be sure. Yes, crying— although without a sound, something the fox had never known him to do. The boy hadn't shed tears for a very long time, but the fox remembered: always before he had cried out, as if to demand that attention be paid to the curious occurrence of salty water streaming from his eyes.

—from *Pax*, p. 310

T? Tough Questions

LITERARY ANALYSIS CONNECTION

Paying attention to Tough Questions can help you analyze

- *internal conflict*
- *theme*
- *character development*

Tough Questions are questions characters raise that reveal their inner struggles.

Be alert to the times when characters ask themselves difficult questions, or when others ask questions that make a character think hard or feel deeply. At these moments, you can learn about characters' internal conflicts and gain insight into the theme of the story.

Tough Questions are sometimes expressed as statements, but ones that reveal difficult trade-offs or hard truths. Some phrases that can signal Tough Questions are:

> What could I possibly do . . .
>
> How could I . . .
>
> If she tells the truth, then . . .
>
> Would he ever understand why . . .

When you notice Tough Questions, pause. Think about what the questions suggest about the character or the theme and how these struggles might affect the rest of the story.

A good question to ask is . . .

"There's water trucks held up on the highway.
Gallons, girl! Water by the gallons.
Fresh drinking water.
Clean shower water.
See that, Freddie. The water company loves us.
Somebody thought to send us water."
Even with our trumpets drowned, King's chest swells.
He booms, "Brass Crew, are you with me?
Let's get outta here, bring back some water."
How can I leave TK and Grandmama?
How can I leave, and be happy to leave?
—from "After the Hurricane" p. 428

What does this question make me wonder about?

Words of the Wiser

⊙**Ed**
Notice & Note Peer Coach Videos

Words of the Wiser are pieces of advice or insights a wiser character, who is usually older, offers about life to the main character.

Look for moments when a character is receiving advice or wisdom about how to deal with a difficult problem or decision. These moments often occur when a character is wrestling with an inner conflict, and the advice can offer clues to the theme of the story.

When you notice Words of the Wiser, pause. Think about what the advice or insight suggests about the story's theme and how it is likely to affect the way the character deals with a problem or decision.

A good question to ask is . . .

LITERARY ANALYSIS CONNECTION

Paying attention to Words of the Wiser can help you analyze

- theme
- internal conflict
- relationship between character and plot

What's the life lesson and how might it affect the character?

Vinny turned away and swam back over to the other side of the pond, where he'd first gotten in. His mother would kill him if she ever heard about where he'd come. After the boy drowned, or was taken by the goddess, or whatever happened to him, she said never to come to this pond again. Ever. It was off-limits. Permanently.

But not his dad. He said, "You fall off a horse, you get back on, right? Or else you going to be scared of it all your life."

—from "The Ravine," p. 240

Again and Again

LITERARY ANALYSIS CONNECTION

Paying attention to Again and Again can help you analyze

- plot
- setting
- symbolism
- theme
- character development
- conflict
- mood

Again and Again is when events, images, or particular words recur over a portion of the story or novel.

Authors include these words, images, or events Again and Again to

- reveal things about character motivation
- offer insight into the story's theme
- make connections between elements of the plot
- help create the story's mood

When you notice the Again and Again signpost, pause. Think about the meaning the repeated words, images, or events might have and how it relates to the setting, plot, theme, or character development.

A good question to ask is . . .

Why might the author bring this up again and again?

As Salva walked, the same thoughts kept going through his head in rhythm with his steps. *Where are we going? Where is my family? When will I see them again? . . .*

. . . Some of the rebels then joined the back of the line; now the villagers were surrounded.

What are they going to do to us? Where is my family?

—from *A Long Walk to Water*, pp. 394–396

Memory Moment

Notice & Note Peer Coach Videos

A **Memory Moment** occurs when a character has a recollection that interrupts the forward progress of the story.

Be alert for places where the character is thinking about something that occurred at an earlier time. These moments can

- provide insight into the current situation
- explain character motivation
- offer insight into the theme of the story

Some phrases that can signal a Memory Moment are:

When she was in elementary school . . .

I remember when . . .

Twelve years ago . . .

The last time he . . .

When you notice a Memory Moment, pause. Think about why the author included this detail from the past.

A good question to ask is . . .

LITERARY ANALYSIS CONNECTION

Paying attention to Memory Moments can help you analyze

- character development
- theme
- plot
- relationship between character and plot

Why might this memory be important?

Suddenly the girl remembered the boatman's sweet music. She thought about all the happy hours she had spent listening to his flute and the wonderful dreams she had dreamed because of him. Since he had left, no one, not even the most handsome suitors in the land, had made her feel such warmth and happiness. Now, it seemed her days and nights were even longer and more empty than before.

—from "The Boatman's Flute," p. 525

Q? Big Questions

When you read any informational text or argument, it's important to remember that the author is presenting only one version of the truth. This version may be factual and mostly free of bias, or it may include slanted, overstated, or even untrue claims or descriptions. Either way, you have to think critically about the author's relationship to the topic. That's why it's important to approach these texts from a **Questioning Stance,** or position. To do that, keep these three **Big Questions** in mind as you read:

- What surprised me?
- What did the author think I already knew?
- What changed, challenged, or confirmed what I already knew?

These questions will not only help you evaluate what you read and avoid falling for things that aren't entirely true, they will also help make the things you read more interesting. In addition, they can help you get to the root of things that might confuse you. The chart below gives more detail about each of the Big Questions.

What surprised me?	Look for parts of the text that make you think "really!?" and put an exclamation point there. **You might think:** • *"I didn't know that!"* • *"Really? Is that true?"* • *"Oh! Now I get it."* • *"How could anyone think that way?"* or *"I hadn't thought of it that way."*	!
What did the author think I already knew?	Look for places where the language is tough or where the author is writing about things you don't know much about, and put a question mark there. **You might think:** • *"The author thought I'd know what this word means."* • *"The author thought I could picture this."* • *"The author thought I'd know something about this."* • *"The author thought I'd get how this happens."*	?
What changed, challenged, or confirmed what I already knew?	Look for ideas that change your thinking. Put a C by those places. **You might think:** • *"I realize now . . ."* • *"This makes me rethink my opinion about . . ."* • *"That supports what I already thought."*	C

Contrasts and Contradictions

Notice & Note Peer Coach Videos

Contrasts and Contradictions occur either when the author shows you how ideas, things, events, or people differ from one another, or when you come across something that goes against what you would have expected.

To help you find Contrasts and Contradictions <u>within the text,</u> look for signal words and phrases such as

- yet
- but
- unlike
- instead of
- however
- as opposed to
- on the other hand

For Contrasts and Contradictions <u>between the text and your own expectations,</u> be on the lookout for things that surprise you as you read.

When you notice Contrasts and Contradictions, pause. Think about why the author may have chosen to focus on these differences or how your knowledge contrasts with what's described in the text.

A good question to ask is . . .

> What is the difference, and why does it matter?

RELATED READING SKILLS

- *Compare and contrast*
- *Generalize*
- *Identify main idea*
- *Infer*
- *Identify cause and effect*
- *Identify details*
- *Understand author's purpose or bias*

Trade in these beautiful creatures thrives in the USA, where thousands are bred and sold through classified ads or at auctions centered in Indiana, Missouri and Tennessee. There's too little to stop it.

A 2003 federal law, which forbids the interstate transport of certain big cats, has stopped much of the trade on the Internet, according to the Humane Society of the U.S. But monkeys, baboons and other primates were left out, and measures to plug that hole have twice stalled in Congress.

—from "Wild Animals Aren't Pets," p. 361

Shutterstock; (b) illustration adapted from ©Daniel Ernst/Adobe Stock

Extreme or Absolute Language

RELATED READING SKILLS

- Draw conclusions
- Generalize
- Identify author's point of view
- Identify main idea
- Infer
- Recognize hyperbole
- Identify cause and effect
- Understand author's purpose or bias

Extreme or Absolute Language occurs when the author uses language that leaves no room for doubt, allows for no questions, and may seem to exaggerate or overstate a claim.

This language includes words such as

- all
- never
- everyone
- always
- totally
- unarguably
- no one
- perfectly

It can also include dramatic phrases intended to cause a strong reaction, such as "blood-sucking monster," "absolutely destroy," or "it is imperative."

When you notice Extreme or Absolute Language, pause and think. An author might be expressing strong feelings, overstating things, or even trying to mislead the reader. This language can reveal things about the author's purpose or bias.

A good question to ask is . . .

Why did the author use this language?

In our digital age, the selfie is the best way to express oneself, empower oneself, and even surround oneself with friends. Everyone everywhere owns and uses a smart phone, and, with at least a million different social media platforms available, you'd have to live in a cave not to take part in and appreciate this form of communication. . . .

—from "Better Than Words: Say It with a Selfie," p. 62

Numbers and Stats

⌾ **Ed**
Notice & Note Peer Coach Videos

Numbers and Stats occur either when authors use specific figures to show amounts, size, or scale, or when they are vague when you would have expected more details.

Some key words that may show when an author is being vague include

- many
- most
- some
- longer
- bigger
- farther
- oldest

When you notice Numbers and Stats, pause. Think about why the author may have chosen to use or leave out specific figures in describing something.

A good question to ask is . . .

> Why did the author use these numbers or amounts?

RELATED READING SKILLS

- Draw conclusions
- Find facts
- Generalize
- Identify details
- Infer
- Make comparisons
- Recognize evidence
- Understand author's purpose or bias

Dangers from exotic animals are low. On average in the United States, only 3.25 people per year are killed by captive big cats, snakes, elephants and bears. Most of these fatalities are owners, family members, friends and trainers voluntarily on the property where the animals were kept. Meanwhile, traffic accidents kill about 125 people per day.

—from "Let People Own Exotic Animals," p. 364

" " Quoted Words

RELATED READING SKILLS

- Compare and contrast
- Draw conclusions
- Identify author's point of view
- Infer
- Identify cause and effect
- Separate fact from opinion
- Understand author's purpose or bias

Quoted Words occur when the author cites or quotes a person or group to provide support for a point. Authors often include opinions or conclusions from people who are experts on a topic or from people who were participants in or witnesses to events.

When you notice Quoted Words, pause. Think about why the author may have chosen to quote this particular person or group.

A good question to ask is . . .

> Why was this person quoted or cited and what did this add?

Dr. Allison Chase, a psychologist and behavior specialist in Austin, Texas, also has weighed in. "This is particularly challenging for kids and teens, as they are trying to figure out who they are and what their identity is." In that 2016 *ParentCo* article, Dr. Chase warns about getting caught in the trap of worrying too much about appearances and approval.

She warns against believing that posting and sharing and liking creates actual friendship and intimacy. As Dr. Chase says, we "create the illusion of feeling more connected and more 'liked' in a way that is controllable and oftentimes, staged. The end result is a competitive environment with increased self-focus, less true connection and, more often than not, increased self-criticism."

—from "OMG, Not *Another* Selfie!" p. 71

 # Word Gaps

⊙Ed

Notice & Note Peer Coach Videos

Word Gaps occur either when authors use vocabulary that is unfamiliar or when they use familiar words in ways that are new to you. Authors of informational texts often use words with multiple meanings, technical or scientific words, or words that are unique to specific subjects.

Sometimes authors provide clues to these words, such as putting them in boldfaced or italic font or highlighting them. Other times, authors follow a less-known word with the phrase *is like* to help explain it. Many times, however, the way you identify a Word Gap is simply by noticing that you've come across a word that you don't understand.

When you notice Word Gaps, pause. Ask yourself the following questions. The answers will help you decide if you need to look the word up or keep reading for more information.

Do I know this word from someplace else?

Does this seem like technical talk for experts on this topic?

RELATED READING SKILLS

- *Generalize*
- *Identify details*
- *Infer*
- *Make comparisons*
- *Understand author's purpose or bias*
- *Use context clues*

> Can I find clues in the sentence to help me understand the word?

Photinus fireflies, for instance, broadcast their mating messages with a light show. These plant-eating beetles flash luminescent abdomens to wow potential mates on warm North American summer nights.

A bigger relative is named *Photuris.* They also blink biological tail lights during courtship, but are not always looking for a mate. These fireflies are predators that eat their smaller *Photinus* cousins. They spy on their blinking prey and follow the flashing beacon to a nighttime meal.

—from "Animal Snoops: The Wondrous World of Wildlife Spies," p. 334

Using a Glossary

A glossary is an alphabetical list of vocabulary words. Use a glossary just as you would a dictionary—to determine the meanings, parts of speech, pronunciation, and syllabification of words. (Some technical, foreign, and more obscure words in this book are defined for you in the footnotes that accompany many of the selections.)

Many words in the English language have more than one meaning. This glossary gives the meanings that apply to the words as they are used in the selections in this book.

The following abbreviations are used to identify parts of speech of words:

adj. adjective   *adv.* adverb   *n.* noun   *v.* verb

Each word's pronunciation is given in parentheses. A guide to the pronunciation symbols appears in the Pronunciation Key below. The stress marks in the Pronunciation Key are used to indicate the force given to each syllable in a word. They can also help you determine where words are divided into syllables.

For more information about the words in this glossary or for information about words not listed here, consult a dictionary.

Pronunciation Key

Symbol	Examples	Symbol	Examples	Symbol	Examples
ă	pat	m	mum	ûr	urge, term, firm, word, heard
ā	pay	n	no, sudden* (sŭd´n)	v	valve
ä	father	ng	thing	w	with
âr	care	ŏ	pot	y	yes
b	bib	ō	toe	z	zebra, xylem
ch	church	ô	caught, paw	zh	vision, pleasure, garage
d	deed, milled	oi	noise	ə	about, item, edible, gallop, circus
ĕ	pet	ŏŏ	took	ər	butter
ē	bee	ōō	boot		
f	fife, phase, rough	ŏŏr	lure		
g	gag	ôr	core		
h	hat	ou	out		
hw	which	p	pop		
ĭ	pit	r	roar		
ī	pie, by	s	sauce		
îr	pier	sh	ship, dish		
j	judge	t	tight, stopped		
k	kick, cat, pique	th	thin		
l	lid, needle* (nēd´l)	*th*	this		
		ŭ	cut		

Sounds in Foreign Words

Symbol	Examples
KH	*German* ich, ach; *Scottish* loch
N	*French*, bon (bôN)
œ	*French* feu, œuf; *German* schön
ü	*French* tu; *German* über

*In English the consonants *l* and *n* often constitute complete syllables by themselves.

Stress Marks

The relevant emphasis with which the syllables of a word or phrase are spoken, called stress, is indicated in three different ways. The strongest, or primary, stress is marked with a bold mark (´). An intermediate, or secondary, level of stress is marked with a similar but lighter mark (´). The weakest stress is unmarked. Words of one syllable show no stress mark.

Glossary of Academic Vocabulary

achieve (ə-chēv´) *v.* to succeed in accomplishing something; to bring about by effort

appropriate (ə-prō´prē-ĭt) *adj.* suitable for a particular person, occasion, or place

authority (ə-thôr´ĭ-tē) *n.* an accepted source, such as a person or text, of expert information or advice

benefit (bĕn´ə-fĭt) *n.* something that provides help or improves something else

circumstance (sûr´kəm-stăns´) *n.* a condition, or set of conditions, that affects an event

consequence (kôn´sĭ-kwĕns´) *n.* something that logically follows from an action or condition

constraint (kən-strānt´) *n.* something or someone that limits or restricts another's actions

distinct (dĭ-stĭngkt´) *adj.* easy to tell apart from others; not alike

element (ĕl´ə-mənt) *n.* an essential part of something

emphasize (ĕm´fə-sīz´) *v.* to give prominence or emphasis to

environment (ĕn-vī´rən-mənt) *n.* the natural world surrounding someone or something; surroundings

evident (ĕv´ĭ-dənt) *adj.* easily seen or understood; obvious

factor (făk´tər) *n.* someone or something that contributes to an accomplishment, result, or process

illustrate (ĭl´ə-strāt´) *v.* to show, or clarify, by examples or comparison

impact (ĭm´păkt´) *n.* something striking against another; also, the effect or impression of one thing on another

indicate (ĭn´dĭ-kāt´) *v.* to point out; also, to serve as a sign or symbol of something

individual (ĭn´də-vĭj´oo-əl) *n.* a single human being apart from a society or community

injure (ĭn´jər) *v.* to hurt or cause damage

instance (ĭn´stəns) *n.* an example that is cited to prove or disprove a claim or illustrate a point

justify (jŭs´tə-fī´) *v.* to demonstrate or prove to be just, right, reasonable, or valid

occur (ə-kûr´) *v.* to take place; happen

outcome (out´kŭm´) *n.* a natural result or consequence

period (pîr´ē-əd) *n.* a particular length of time, often referring to a specific time in history or culture

principle (prĭn´sə-pəl) *n.* a rule or standard, especially of good behavior

relevant (rĕl´ə-vənt) *adj.* important to, connected to, or significant to an issue, event, or person in some way

respond (rĭ-spŏnd´) *v.* to make a reply; answer

significant (sĭg-nĭf´ĭ-kənt) *adj.* meaningful; important

similar (sĭm´ə-lər) *adj.* alike in appearance or nature, though not identical

specific (spĭ-sĭf´ĭk) *adj.* concerned with a particular thing; also, precise or exact

tradition (trə-dĭsh´ən) *n.* the passing down of various elements of culture from generation to generation; a custom

Glossary of Critical Vocabulary

accurate (ăk´yər-ĭt) *adj.* Something *accurate* is correct.

activate (ăk´tə-vāt´) *v.* To *activate* something means to cause it to start working.

adversity (ăd-vûr´sĭ-tē) *n.* *Adversity* is misfortune or hardship.

agonizing (ăg´ə-nīz´ĭng) *adj.* To be in an *agonizing* state means to feel great mental suffering and worry.

amazement (ə-māz´mənt) *n.* *Amazement* is a state of extreme surprise or wonder.

amplify (ăm´plə-fī´) *v.* To *amplify* something is to make it stronger or more intense.

angular (ăng´gyə-lər) *adj.* Something that is *angular,* such as a peaked roof, has two sides that form an angle.

anonymous (ə-nŏn´ə-məs) *adj.* Someone who is *anonymous* has an undisclosed or unknown name.

anxiety (ăng-zī´ĭ-tē) *n.* *Anxiety* is a feeling of uneasiness, fear, or worry.

anxiously (ăngk´shəs-lē) *adv.* To think of something *anxiously* means that you dread it.

apology (ə-pŏl´ə-jē) *n.* An *apology* is an expression of regret or a request for forgiveness.

apparatus (ăp´ə-răt´əs) *n.* An *apparatus* is a piece of equipment.

calculate (kăl´kyə-lāt´) *v.* To *calculate* is to figure out an answer by using math.

cascade (kăs-kād´) *v.* Something that can *cascade* will fall, pour, or rush in stages, like a waterfall over steep rocks.

celebrity (sə-lĕb´rĭ-tē) *n.* A *celebrity* is a famous person.

chastise (chăs-tīz´) *v.* To *chastise* is to punish or criticize.

collapse (kə-lăps´) *v.* When something is said to *collapse,* it falls down.

commit (kə-mĭt´) *v.* To *commit* is to do or perform an action.

constantly (kŏn´stənt-lē) *adv.* *Constantly* describes something that is regularly occurring.

convince (kən-vĭns´) *v.* To *convince* is to use argument or evidence to get someone to believe or be certain about something.

courtyard (kôrt´yärd´) *n.* A *courtyard* is an area enclosed by walls and open to the sky.

debate (dĭ-bāt´) *v.* To *debate* is to discuss opposing points or ideas.

deceptive (dĭ-sĕp´tĭv) *adj.* Something *deceptive* is giving a false impression.

defeat (dĭ-fēt´) *v.* To *defeat* a person or his or her efforts is to prevent his or her success.

defy (dĭ-fī´) *v.* To *defy* someone is to oppose him or her or refuse to cooperate with that person.

demonstration (dĕm´ən-strā´shən) *n.* A *demonstration* is a presentation meant to show how something works.

dictate (dĭk´tāt´) *v.* To *dictate* something is to require it to be done or decided.

discourage (dĭ-skûr´ĭj) *v.* To *discourage* is to take away hope or confidence.

discreetly (dĭ-skrēt´lē) *adv.* To act *discreetly* means to act with self-restraint; attracting little notice.

displease (dĭs-plēz´) *v.* To *displease* someone is to cause annoyance or irritation.

eavesdrop (ēvz´drŏp´) *v.* To *eavesdrop* is to listen secretly to others' private conversations.

edict (ē´dĭkt´) *n.* An *edict* is a command or pronouncement enforced as law.

elegant (ĕl´ĭ-gənt) *adj.* Someone *elegant* appears to be refined and tasteful, having a beautiful manner, form, or style.

embrace (ĕm-brās´) *v.* To *embrace* someone is to hug or hold the person close.

enchanting (ĕn-chăn´tĭng) *adj.* Something or someone *enchanting* is charming.

endure (ĕn-dŏŏr´) *v.* To *endure* is to carry on despite difficulty or suffering.

essential (ĭ-sĕn´shəl) *adj.* Something *essential* is so important that you can't do without it.

etch (ĕch) *v.* To *etch* is to cut or carve a drawing into a surface such as wood or metal.

eternity (ĭ-tûr´nĭ-tē) *n. Eternity* refers to infinite time, without beginning or end.

exempt (ĭg-zĕmpt´) *adj.* A person who is *exempt* is freed or excused from following a law or duty that others must obey.

exotic (ĭg-zŏt´ĭk) *adj.* Something that is *exotic* is from another part of the world.

experiment (ĭk-spĕr´ə-mənt) *n.* An *experiment* is a test to determine if an idea is true or to see if a device works.

fascinate (făs´ə-nāt´) *v.* To *fascinate* someone means to capture the interest or attention of that person.

focus (fō´kəs) *v.* When you *focus* on something, you keep attention fixed on it.

foil (foil) *v.* If you *foil* someone, you stop that person from being successful at something.

fortitude (fôr´tĭ-tōōd) *n.* To have *fortitude* is to show strength of mind and face difficulty with courage.

fume (fyōōm) *v.* To *fume* about something is to feel or show displeasure or resentment.

generate (jĕn´ə-rāt´) *v.* To *generate* is to create and develop something.

hesitate (hĕz´ĭ-tāt´) *v.* To *hesitate* is to pause or wait in uncertainty.

history (hĭs´tə-rē) *n. History* is a chronological record of events of a person or institution.

horizon (hə-rī´zən) *n.* The *horizon* is the intersection of the earth and sky.

humiliation (hyōō-mĭl´ē-ā´shən) *n.* A feeling of *humiliation* is even more intense than a feeling of embarrassment.

immaturity (ĭm´ə-tyŏŏr´ĭ-tē) *n. Immaturity* is the state of not being fully developed or grown.

incorrect (ĭn´kə-rĕkt´) *adj.* Something *incorrect* is faulty or wrong.

indulgent (ĭn-dŭl´jənt) *adj. Indulgent* means excessively permissive. *Self-indulgent* is when one is overly permissive with oneself.

injury (ĭn´jə-rē) *n.* An *injury* is damage or harm done to a person or thing.

integral (ĭn´tĭ-grəl) *adj.* Something that is *integral* is necessary or essential for completeness.

intercept (ĭn´tər-sĕpt´) *v.* To *intercept* is to stop or interrupt something.

interplanetary (ĭn´tər-plăn´ĭ-tĕr´ē) *adj. Interplanetary* means existing or occurring between planets.

intimacy (ĭn´tə-mə-sē) *n. Intimacy* means close friendship and familiarity.

invariably (ĭn-vâr´ē-ə-blē) *adv.* Something that happens *invariably* occurs again and again or constantly.

jest (jĕst) *v.* To *jest* means to make playful remarks.

lament (lə-mĕnt´) *v.* If you *lament,* you are wailing or crying as a way of expressing grief.

linger (lĭng´gər) *v.* To *linger* means to leave slowly and reluctantly, not wanting to go.

microphone (mī´krə-fōn´) *n.* A *microphone* is an instrument that is often used to amplify the voice.

murky (mûr´kē) *adj.* Something *murky* is dark, obscure, and gloomy.

narcissist (när´sĭ-sĭst´) *n.* A person who is preoccupied with his or her looks is a *narcissist.*

nurture (nûr´chər) *v.* To *nurture* is to provide love, affection, nourishment, or something else necessary for development.

passion (păsh´ən) *n. Passion* means boundless enthusiasm.

pause (pôz) *v.* To *pause* is to hesitate or suspend action.

perplexed (pər-plĕkst´) *adj.* When you are *perplexed,* you are puzzled.

poised (poizd) *adj.* To be *poised* means to be calm and assured, showing balanced feeling and action.

politeness (pə-līt´nəs) *n. Politeness* is respectful behavior.

portrait (pôr´trĭt) *n.* A *portrait* is a person's likeness, especially one showing the face, which may be painted, photographed, or otherwise represented.

precipice (prĕs´ə-pĭs) *n.* A *precipice* is an overhanging or extremely steep area of rock.

predator (prĕd´ə-tər) *n.* A *predator* is an animal that survives by eating other animals.

prediction (prĭ-dĭk´shən) *n.* When someone makes a *prediction,* they make a guess about something that has not yet happened.

prepare (prĭ-pâr´) *v.* To *prepare* is to get ready for an event or occasion.

preserve (prĭ-zûrv´) *v.* To *preserve* something is to keep it or save it.

pseudonym (sōōd´n-ĭm´) *n.* A *pseudonym* is a fictitious name, particularly a pen name.

reassure (rē´ə-shŏŏr´) *v.* To *reassure* someone is to give comfort or confidence to that person.

reflection (rĭ-flĕk´shən) *n.* A *reflection* is an image shown back, as from a mirror.

regal (rē´gəl) *adj.* Something *regal* appears to be royal, magnificent, or splendid.

regulate (rĕg´yə-lāt´) *v.* If you *regulate* something, you control or direct it according to a rule, principle, or law.

reluctance (rĭ-lŭk´təns) *n.* Showing *reluctance* to do something means you are unwilling.

resentment (rĭ-zĕnt´mənt) *n.* If you feel *resentment,* you feel anger or irritation.

responsibility (rĭ-spŏn´sə-bĭl´ĭ-tē) *n.* A *responsibility* is a duty, obligation, or burden.

rivulet (rĭv´yə-lĭt) *n.* A *rivulet* is a small brook or stream.

rueful (rōō´fəl) *adj.* To be *rueful* is to show sorrow or regret.

saturated (săch´ə-rāt´ĭd) *adj.* Something that is *saturated* is filled until it is unable to hold or contain more.

scurry (skûr´ē) *v.* Something that can *scurry* will run with quick, light steps.

seamstress (sēm´strĭs) *n.* A *seamstress* is a woman who sews, especially one who earns a living sewing.

sensitive (sĕn´sĭ-tĭv) *adj.* Something *sensitive* is able to perceive small differences or changes in the environment.

serene (sə-rēn´) *adj.* If you are *serene,* you are calm and unflustered.

shoulder (shōl´dər) *v.* To *shoulder* something is to carry it on one's shoulders.

sincere (sĭn-sîr´) *adj.* Something or someone *sincere* is genuine or heartfelt.

solution (sə-lōō´shən) *n.* A *solution* is a way of handling a problem.

span (spăn) *v.* To *span* is to extend over a period of time.

stake (stāk) *n.* A *stake* is something that can be gained or lost in a situation, such as money, food, or life.

stammer (stăm´ər) *v.* To *stammer* is to speak with involuntary pauses or repetitions.

stealthily (stĕl´thə-lē) *adv.* To do something *stealthily* means doing it quietly and secretly so no one notices.

terror (tĕr´ər) *n. Terror* is extreme fear of something.

trance (trăns) *n.* When someone is in a *trance,* that person is in a daze or is daydreaming.

trigger (trĭg´ər) *v.* To *trigger* something means to cause it to begin.

turbulence (tûr´byə-ləns) *n.* In flying, *turbulence* is an interruption in the flow of wind that causes planes to rise, fall, or sway in a rough way.

universal (yōō´nə-vûr´səl) *adj.* Something that is *universal* affects every member of a group.

unrestrainedly (ŭn´rĭ-strā´nĭd-lē) *adv.* Doing something *unrestrainedly* means doing it without control.

veer (vîr) *v.* Something that can *veer* will swerve, or suddenly change course or direction.

wistfully (wĭst´fəl-ē) *adv.* When you think of something *wistfully,* you do so with sadness and longing.

Index of Skills

Turn and Talk, 12, 26, 38, 50, 52, 66, 72, 108, 118, 132, 154, 188, 198, 211, 228, 246, 266, 280, 312, 323, 336, 347, 350, 361, 364, 398, 417, 432, 442, 472, 497, 508, 511, 526, 543

U

universal themes, 116, 139, 319

V

Venn diagrams, 158, 252
verb phrases, 327
verb-subject agreement, 403
verb tense, 327
video blogs. *See* vlogs
videos
　digital texts, 217
　documentaries, 405–407
　interpretations, 121
　presentations, 419
　public service announcements, 75, 367
　summaries of, 218
visual elements, 17, 217
vivid descriptions, 556
vlogs, 157
vocabulary. *See* Academic Vocabulary; Expand Your Vocabulary; Vocabulary Strategy
Vocabulary Strategy. *See also* Academic Vocabulary; Expand Your Vocabulary
　antonyms, 136, 232
　connotations, 30, 222
　context clues, 76, 222, 250, 270, 415, 418, 420, 446, 476, 546
　denotations, 30
　multiple-meaning words, 192, 270
　parts of speech, 192
　prefixes, 112, 208, 214, 316, 530
　reference resources, 105, 136, 222, 279, 284, 500
　roots, 42, 112, 316, 326, 332, 340, 530
　suffixes, 112, 316, 530
　synonyms, 136, 232
　thesaurus, 136, 500
　word origins, 42, 368, 402
　word structure, 530
voice. *See also* narrator; speaker
　dashes and, 215
　evaluation of, 56

language in creation of, 33
　word choice and, 307, 311, 314
volume of speaking, 191

W

Watch Your Language! *See* language conventions
web diagrams, 6
Word Gaps (Notice & Note), 66, 74, 209, 212, 230
words. *See also* meaning of words
　base, 530
　choice of, 307, 311, 314, 424, 560
　commonly confused, 77, 369
　connotations of, 30, 222
　denotations of, 30
　descriptive, 33, 409
　families of, 340
　origins of, 42, 368, 402
　prefixes, 112, 208, 214, 316, 530
　pronunciation of, 402
　relationships among, 232
　roots, 42, 112, 316, 326, 332, 340, 530
　structure of, 530
　suffixes, 112, 316, 530
　syllabication of, 402
　technical terms, 217, 222, 224
　transitional, 170, 213, 285, 382, 557
Words of the Wiser (Notice & Note), 120, 148, 156, 183, 190
write
　advertisement, 231
　analysis, 41, 325, 401, 545, 561
　analytical essay, 135, 157
　argument, 75, 82–90, 374–382
　characterizing speakers, 55
　character study, 191, 499
　compare and contrast essay, 159, 213, 249, 461
　email, 111
　explanatory essay, 452–460
　fictional story, 315
　field research, 339
　freewriting, 111
　informative essay, 290–298
　letter, 15, 111, 367
　nonfiction narrative, 162–170
　poetry, 121, 201, 435
　research report, 231

short story, 552–560
social media post, 81, 419
speech, 475
storyteller guide, 475
summary, 29, 269, 283, 407
text messages, 445
writing prompts
　argument, 82, 374
　explanatory essay, 452
　informative essay, 290
　nonfiction narrative, 162
　short story, 552

Index of Titles and Authors

Acknowledgments

Excerpt from "After the Hurricane" by Rita Williams-Garcia from *Free? Stories About Human Rights* by Amnesty International. Text copyright © 2009 by Rita Williams-Garcia. Reprinted by permission of Rita Williams-Garcia.

Excerpts from *The American Heritage Dictionary of The English Language, Fifth Edition.* Text copyright © 2016 by Houghton Mifflin Harcourt Publishing Company. Reprinted by permission of Houghton Mifflin Harcourt Publishing Company.

Excerpt from *Animal Snoops: The Wondrous World of Wildlife Spies.* Text copyright © 2010 by Peter Christie, published by Annick Press Ltd. Reprinted by permission of Annick Press Ltd. All rights reserved.

"Animal Wisdom" from *Sacred Fire* by Nancy Wood. Text copyright © 1998 by Nancy Wood. Reprinted by permission of the Nancy Wood Literary Trust.

"Archetype" by Margarita Engle. Text copyright © 2005 by Margarita Engle. Reprinted by permission of Margarita Engle.

"The Boatman's Flute" from *Children of the Dragon: Selected Tales from Vietnam* by Sherry Garland. Text copyright © 2001 by Sherry Garland. Reprinted by permission of Sherry Garland.

Excerpts from *The Breadwinner*, "Glossary," "About the Author," and "Chapter Six" by Deborah Ellis. Text copyright © 2000, 2015 by Deborah Ellis. First published in Canada by Groundwood Books Ltd. Reprinted by permission of Groundwood Books Ltd., Oxford University Press, Allen & Unwin Pty. Ltd., and Penguin Random House Audio Publishing Group, a division of Penguin Random House LLC. All rights reserved. Any third-party use of this material, outside of this publication, is prohibited. Interested parties must apply directly to Penguin Random House LLC for permission.

"Embarrassed?" by Jennifer Connor-Smith from *Odyssey,* March 2015. Copyright © 2015 by Carus Publishing Company. Reprinted by permission of Carus Publishing Company. All Cricket Media material is copyrighted by Carus Publishing Company d/b/a Cricket Media, and/or various authors and illustrators. Any commercial use or distribution of material without permission is strictly prohibited. Please visit http://cricketmedia.com/licensing for licensing and http://www.cricketmedia.com for subscriptions.

"Fairy-tale Logic" from *Olives* by A. E. Stallings. Text copyright © 2006 by A. E. Stallings. Reprinted by permission of Northwestern University Press.

"Fears and Phobias" from *kidshealth.org.* Text copyright © 1995-2018 by The Nemours Foundation/KidsHealth®. Reprinted by permission of The Nemours Foundation.

"The First Day of School" from *The Happy Marriage and Other Stories* by R. V. Cassill. Text copyright © 1966 by R. V. Cassill. Reprinted by permission of the Estate of R. V. Cassill.

Excerpt from *I Am Malala: How One Girl Stood Up for Education and Changed the World, Young Reader's Edition* by Malala Yousafzai with Patricia McCormick. Map by John Gilkes. Text copyright © 2014 by Salarzai Limited. Reprinted by permission of Little, Brown Books for Young Readers, New York, NY USA. All rights reserved.

Excerpt from *Into the Air* by Robert Burleigh. Illustrated by Bill Wylie. Text copyright © 2002 by Robert Burleigh. Illustration copyright © 2002 by Bill Wylie. Reprinted by permission of Rubin Pfeffer Content, LLC on behalf of Robert Burleigh and Bill Wylie.

"The Last Wolf" by Mary TallMountain. Text copyright © 1994 by the TallMountain Estate. Reprinted by permission of the TallMountain Estate. All rights reserved.

"Let People Own Exotic Animals" by Zuzana Kukol from *USA Today,* October 20, 2011. Text copyright © 2011 Gannett-USA Today. Reprinted by permission of PARS International on behalf of Gannett-USA Today. All rights reserved. Protected by the Copyright Laws of the United States. The printing, copying, redistribution, or retransmission of this Content without express written permission is prohibited. www.usatoday.com

"Life Doesn't Frighten Me" from *And Still I Rise: A Book of Poems* by Maya Angelou. Text copyright © 1978 by Maya Angelou. Reprinted by permission of Random House, an imprint and division of Penguin Random House LLC, Penguin Random House Audio Publishing Group, a division of Penguin Random House LLC, and Little, Brown Book Group, Ltd. All rights reserved. Any third-party use of this material, outside of this publication, is prohibited. Interested parties must apply directly to Penguin Random House LLC for permission.

Excerpt from *A Long Walk to Water* by Linda Sue Park. Text copyright © 2010 by Linda Sue Park. Reprinted by permission of Houghton Mifflin Harcourt.

"The Mouse Bride: A Folktale from Finland" from *Wonder Tales from Around the World* retold by Heather Forest. Text copyright © 1995 by Heather Forest. Reprinted by permission of Marian Reiner on behalf of the publisher August House, Inc.

Excerpt from *New Kid* by Jerry Craft. Copyright © 2019 by Jerry Craft. Color by Jim Callahan. Reprinted by permission of HarperCollins Publishers.

Excerpt from *Ninth Ward* by Jewell Parker Rhodes. Text copyright © 2010 by Jewell Parker Rhodes. Reprinted by permission of Little, Brown Books for Young Readers.

Excerpt from *Pax* by Sara Pennypacker. Text copyright © 2016 by Sara Pennypacker. Reprinted by permission of HarperCollins Publishers.

The Prince and the Pauper by Mark Twain, as adapted by Joellen Bland from *Plays: The Drama Magazine for Young People* and from *Stage Plays from the Classics* by Joellen Bland. Text copyright © 1987, 2012 by Joellen Bland. Reprinted by permission of the publisher Plays. This play is for reading purposes only; for permission to produce or perform, write to Plays, 897 Washington Street #600160, Newton, MA 02460. On first page of reprint: *The Prince and the Pauper* by Mark Twain, as adapted by Joellen Bland.

"The Ravine" by Graham Salisbury from *On the Edge: Stories at the Brink* edited by Lois Duncan. Text copyright © 2000 by Graham Salisbury. Reprinted by permission of Jennifer Flannery Literary Agency.

Excerpts from *Selfie: The Changing Face of Self-Portraits* by Susie Brooks. Text copyright © 2016 by Wayland Publishers. First published in the UK by Wayland, an imprint of Hachette Children's Books, Carmelite House, 50 Victoria Embankment, London, EC4Y 0DZ. Reprinted by permission of Wayland Publishers.

"Speech to the Young, Speech to the Progress-Toward" from *Blacks* by Gwendolyn Brooks. Text copyright © 1945, 1949, 1953, 1960, 1963, 1968, 1969, 1970, 1971, 1975, 1981, 1987 by Gwendolyn Brooks. Reprinted by permission of Brooks Permissions.

Excerpt from *Storytelling: An Encyclopedia of Mythology and Folklore* by Josepha Sherman. Text copyright © 2008 by M.E. Sharpe, Inc. Reprinted by permission of Taylor & Francis Group.

Excerpt from *Titanic Survivor* by Violet Jessop. Text copyright © 1997 by Sheridan House. Reprinted by permission of Rowman & Littlefield Publishers, Inc.

"A Voice" from *Communion* by Pat Mora. Text copyright © 1991 by Pat Mora. Reprinted by permission of the publisher Arte Público Press – University of Houston.

"What's So Funny, Mr. Scieszka?" from *Knucklehead: Tall Tales and Almost True Stories of Growing Up Scieszka* by Jon Scieszka. Copyright © 2005, 2008 by Jon Scieszka. Illustrations, photographs, and text reprinted by permission of Viking Children's Books, an imprint of Penguin Young Readers Group, a division of Penguin Random House LLC. All rights reserved. Any third-party use of this material, outside of this publication, is prohibited. Interested parties must apply directly to Penguin Random House LLC for permission.

"Wild Animals Aren't Pets" from *USA Today*, October 23, 2011. Text copyright © 2011 Gannett-USA Today. Reprinted by permission of PARS International on behalf of Gannett-USA Today. All rights reserved. Protected by the Copyright Laws of the United States. The printing, copying, redistribution, or retransmission of this Content without express written permission is prohibited. www.usatoday.com

"Words Like Freedom" from *The Collected Poems of Langston Hughes* by Langston Hughes, edited by Arnold Rampersad with David Roessel, Associate Editor. Text copyright © 1994 by the Estate of Langston Hughes. Reprinted by permission of Alfred A. Knopf, an imprint of the Knopf Doubleday Publishing Group, a division of Penguin Random House LLC and Harold Ober Associates Incorporated. All rights reserved. Any third-party use of this material, outside of this publication, is prohibited. Interested parties must apply directly to Penguin Random House LLC for permission.

Excerpt from *The Wright Brothers: How They Invented the Airplane* by Russell Freedman. Text copyright © 1991 by Russell Freedman. Reprinted by permission of Holiday House, Inc.

"writing #1," "late autumn," "the other woodson," "reading," "stevie and me," and "when i tell my family" from *Brown Girl Dreaming* by Jacqueline Woodson. Text copyright © 2014 by Jacqueline Woodson. Reprinted by permission of Nancy Paulsen Books, an imprint of Penguin Young Readers Group, a division of Penguin Random House LLC and William Morris Endeavor Entertainment. All rights reserved. Any third-party use of this material, outside of this publication, is prohibited. Interested parties must apply directly to Penguin Random House LLC for permission.

"Zoo" by Edward D. Hoch. Text copyright © 1958 by King-Size Publications, Inc., copyright renewed © 1986 by Edward D. Hoch. Reprinted by permission of Sternig & Byrne Literary Agency.